To Terry and Jennifer,

fondly and
gratefully,

Joseph S Leary

RELIGIOUS PLURALISM
AND
CHRISTIAN TRUTH

RELIGIOUS PLURALISM
AND
CHRISTIAN TRUTH

Joseph Stephen O'Leary

EDINBURGH UNIVERSITY PRESS

© Joseph Stephen O'Leary 1996

A revised version of *La vérité chrétienne à l'âge du pluralisme religieux*, Paris: Éditions du Cerf, 1994.

Edinburgh University Press
22 George Square, Edinburgh

Typeset in Garamond
by Pioneer Associates Ltd, Aberfeldy
Printed and bound in Great Britain

A CIP record for this book is available
from the British Library

ISBN 0 7486 0727 7

CONTENTS

CONTENTS

I dedicate this book, with affection and gratitude,
to David and Gillian Nicholls in whose home
at Littlemore its first lines were written, and to
Philippe and Kathleen Bernard who helped so
generously with the earlier French version.

The thoughts that find quiescence here have been
with me for some dozen years. To all who have
helped them on their way I should like to express
my heartfelt thanks: to hospitable academies,
especially Sophia University, Nanzan Institute for
Religion and Culture, and Trinity College,
Dublin; to alert readers and communicative
friends, such as Stanislas Breton, Claude Geffré
and John Keenan; to Dr Ian Clark, for valuable
suggestions at the copy-editing stage; to Derek
Massarella and Masaaki Morishita, who kindly
helped with the proofs.
A work such as this is inevitably fraught with
error. May it nonetheless offer its readers hints
towards an intellectual and spiritual freedom
based on openness to truth.

'The hint half guessed, the gift half understood,
is Incarnation . . .'
T. S. Eliot

PREFACE

The present work, like *Questioning Back* (1985; revised French version forthcoming), is an attempt to clarify the conditions under which theological thinking can be fruitfully pursued today. It is to be followed by a third volume which will focus specifically on the role of reason in faith and theology. This critical trilogy, a quasi-Kantian 'prolegomenon to any future theology', differs from its tremendous prototype in that theology, as an empirical, historical science, has no place for the exercise of the pure theoretical or practical reason which provides the infrastructural plumbing of philosophy. It is not a science which constitutes basic principles, but one which reflects on concrete traditions. Hence our three critiques belong rather to the mixed realm explored in the *Critique of Judgement*. They deal with human ratiocinations about realities that exceed the conceptual perspectives brought to bear on them, and with the attempt at a critical sifting and demystified retrieval of the religious languages to which the long history of these attempts has given birth.

The three critical approaches respond to three fundamental demands affecting theology as a whole, none of which can be flouted today without a lapse from responsibility and rationality. These imperatives of theological judgement may be stated as follows:

1. *It must be 'phenomenological'*: Theology must constantly question back to the primary level of faith, the original concrete contours of the revelation-event, the 'matter itself' that is apprehended by a contemplative thinking. This requires an 'overcoming of metaphysics': the theological tradition is deconstructed by querying the tensions between its metaphysical

elucidation of the biblical events and the quite different cast of these events as apprehended in faith.

Heidegger found a lack of fit between the space projected by metaphysical concept-formation and the space within which the phenomena give themselves to be apprehended by meditative thinking. Similarly, there is a complex topology of the world of faith that can never be fitted into the horizons of metaphysical theology, which rather act as a screen against it. A creative retrieval of the tradition today works toward a clearing of the fundamental horizons of faith, and subordinates the quest for metaphysical intelligibility to this prior openness.

Of course, just as there is not an original revelation-event that can be recovered in a pure form, so there is no monolithic metaphysics that can be overcome once for all. Nonetheless, an ongoing labour of critical clarification, in a constant stepping back from rationalisations to the vision of faith that they obstruct has to become an inbuilt self-critical moment in theology. One might date the emergence of this imperative in its modern form to Luther.

2. *It must be pluralistic*: Christian thought has to be fully open to the plurality of religious and secular voices that situate and relativise it as a contingent cultural history, which can be responsibly continued only in attentive response to these other voices. This imperative has begun to make itself strongly felt only in the recent past, and it has given rise to the most interesting religious thinking of today. Dialogue, as the present work wants to show, saves Christianity from turning in on itself in an incestuous rehash of its traditions, lets in some fresh air, and restores a human, natural complexion to religious language.

My hypothesis is that pluralism is an irreducible aspect of religious life and thought that can never be ironed out in the final triumph of a single viewpoint. The reasons for this lie in the grain of religious language itself, its reliance on ideas and images that are always culture-bound. The vitality of religion, like that of art, depends intrinsically on the maintenance of a variety of divergent styles.

At a time when science has made mighty strides toward a grand unified theory of the physical universe, this celebration of pluralism might seem regressive. But the religious equivalent of scientific unity would be a general theory of religious pluralism, which justifies it and shows its inherent necessity. Accepting pluralism as a basic fact of religious life, rather than a surd or a regrettable contingency, we can pose the question: if religion is intrinsically pluralistic, then what does this tell us about religion? I seek the answer here in a picture of religions as products of finite, historical, situation-bound struggles, each of which projects images and a rhetoric of the transcendent, and develops these in a constant ferment of self-deconstruction.

The possibility that these open-ended, incomplete, dialogical quests can actually be vehicles of the mystery with which they grapple is the crucial nexus by which they stand or fall. In this field subjective projection and objective revelation are intertwined even more enigmatically than observer and observed in quantum physics. That is another reason why we cannot step outside the pluralistic milieu of the religious enterprise in order to reduce it to a more 'objective' pursuit. Theological reflection has, then, to remain an art of attunement and discernment. Of course it must cultivate logical rigour in the texture of its discourse, but it cannot hope to constitute a system of context-independent principles, that would then be the logical foundation of the merely empirical flow of culture-bound religious ideas and practices. Even when theology has seemed to attain such objectivity, as in Aquinas, a critical historical retrieval may reveal that the apparent monolith is in reality a path of pluralistic open-ended questioning.

3. *It must be rational*: This is an old, and very prosaic dictate; but we miss the scope of what it currently prescribes when we take the word 'rational' in one of its older senses rather than as denoting contemporary conditions of rationality. All three critical approaches have to do with reason in a wide sense, notably in its aspects of openness to the phenomena and critical questioning of traditions. But here the focus is on reason in the most mundane sense of argument and proof. The concern is not with further enlarging the horizons of religious meaning, but rather with showing that such meaning is in harmony with criteria of rational intelligibility. Having clarified the particular phenomenological modalities of Christian truth and the pluralistic contexts of its enunciation, we can now take stock anew of the rational justification of the entire discourse. Despite the long tradition of apologetics and the rich panoply of rational argumentation in scholastic theologians, this stocktaking remains necessary, for those who have sought to defend and exemplify the reasonableness of Christianity have usually been remiss in fulfilling the phenomenological and pluralistic imperatives of theological judgement, so that their justification of belief does not quite match the conditions of contemporary rationality.

All three approaches are concerned with truth. The first is concerned with the 'truth of revelation' in a phenomenological sense, remotely analogous to Heidegger's 'truth of being', and it sees this as the essential foundation of all subsequent Christian truth-claims. The second attempts to show that within the always limited and contingent horizons of a pluralistic religious universe it is possible for a discourse to refer objectively to an absolute truth or truths, though this truth can never be sighted or formulated independently of the interplay between the divergent discourses. The third will focus more sharply on the ultimate rational justification for maintaining religious claims, concerned less now with the modalities whereby religious truth is apprehended than with the rational justification and upshot of our adherence to this truth. Heidegger and Derrida, our guides in the first and second critiques, are no longer of direct service here; instead we turn to those most intently concerned with rationality as such, Kant and his heirs down to Frege and Quine.

It might be imagined that the phenomenological and pluralistic emphases put old-fashioned rational argument out of play. Some have worried that the approach in *Questioning Back* lay open to a 'fideism' that would be dismissive of Christian rational achievements; others feared that the present work, in its French incarnation (*La Vérité chrétienne à l'âge du pluralisme religieux*, 1994) could not escape a 'relativism' that would be unable to do justice to the objective ontological bearing of Christian doctrinal claims. Friendly readers of sceptical disposition have objected that both works remain comfortably ensconced within the religious language-game, offering no justification for adopting it in the first place. In the third volume, even at the risk of 'rationalism', a danger against which the first two provide ample preservation, I shall attempt to allay these misgivings by offering a positive account of the rationality of belief and sketching a clear definition of what reason can (and therefore must) do in the realm of religious thinking.

If the real is the rational, and the rational the real, then religion is unreal to the degree that it is irrational. It may have a powerful phenomenological basis in encounter with the living God, and it may unfold radiantly in a pluralistic, dialogical horizon, but if the suspicion of its being mere projection is not explicitly faced and dislodged, then we have not left the doomed enclosure mapped by Freud in *The Future of an Illusion*. Religion draws its strength ultimately from the phenomenological level, not from reason, but reason has an indispensable role not only in defending authentic revelation against the suspicion of unreality, but also in curbing and channelling the religious energy that gives rise to lethal delusions when it shrugs off rational accountability.

This entire critical enterprise is being conducted at a happy distance from matters of immediate ecclesiastical concern. Crises of faith and morality, authority and structure, liturgy and social practice can induce a panic and precipitation which is inimical to thought. Fundamental theology can only be pursued in a quiet place, where one may take the measure of such crisis and analyse its underlying cause: the failure to present Christian claims in a manner that is thoroughly intelligible and convincing in a contemporary horizon. Then one must work out patiently and in the most general style the first methodological steps towards a demystified account of doctrine. Every generation in which Christianity has successfully confronted a non-Christian world has had its labourers at this task. Today the labourers are few; we shall be meeting some of them in the following pages. Moreover, the necessity of the task, and its 'pastoral relevance', is not as keenly appreciated as it was in healthier periods of Christian history. Instead there is an over-reliance on the rhetoric of Scripture, or on encyclicals and catechisms, whereby one loudly tells people what to believe while dismissing as impertinent the question why.

Serene open dialogue, respect for the phenomena of biblical and traditional faith, in their variety and irreducibility, alert rational argument, such are the secrets of wholesome, truthful theological judgement. They are not secrets at all, but plainest common sense. However, the unmastered irrationalities of the past still hold us in their sinister clasp, so that the struggle for freedom – the freedom to think, the freedom to explore the rich texture of biblical revelation and of contemporary experience, and the freedom to affirm the Christian faith in dialogue with all faiths – remains as taxing and as challenging as it has ever been.

I

INTERRELIGIOUS SPACE

Unhomely guests have sat at theology's banquet before, and a place has been found for them. Plato, Aristotle and the retinue of philosophers have honoured status, and even the troublesome proponents of secular or nihilist suspicion have proved impossible to expel. But how accord a welcome to the *religious* others, whose claims to supreme and saving truth rival ours on the same terrain? They are too near us to be turned away, nor can we confidently make their acceptance of subordinate status a condition of welcoming them. There they sit, subversive presences, as anchored in their truth as we in ours. Nothing for it, then, but to embark on a dialogue of life and of thought, a theological and philosophical negotiation, which is sure to be as long-drawn-out and as full of thrilling twists and turns as those we have conducted with our earlier Western guests.

To clear the air we need to make the terms of the debate as wide as possible, asking again, in this new key, what the meaning and purpose of religions is, and whether and how they can claim to be true. In this book I explore one avenue to dealing with this question, drawing on Nāgārjuna and Derrida – a tandem that has become an inevitable reference for many scholars aiming at a deconstructive retrieval of Eastern and Western tradition in the present pluralistic situation.

PROSPECTUS OF THE ARGUMENT

I proceed from two premises: that everything in the religions is a cultural, historical construction, and that nonetheless some ultimate reality is objectively manifested in them. Neither those who deny the historical relativity of religious conceptions, nor those who think that this relativity proves religion to be an illusion, are likely to be gripped by the basic question of this book, namely: how can one reconcile the subjective (historical, cultural, metaphorical) texture of religious traditions with the recognition of an objective reality grounding them?

Transcendent or transcendental realities – God, grace, truth, the moral ought, salvation – elude direct expression. They emerge obliquely through a play of finite, historical and contingent forms produced by religious or philosophical consciousness as it works within traditions of discourse. Theological truth is never grasped in a style that is completely independent of this play. It is involved in constant negotiations with the undecidable, correcting one doubtful approximation by another, with some help from logic but more from the kind of flair with which a painter applies successive brushstrokes.

In attending to this mobile, contingent, plural and relative aspect of religious discourse, we face the peril of an enveloping Heracliteanism, in which neither faith nor reason can any longer claim a secure grasp of truth. The post-modern nightmare looms, sealed by the disappearance of the very notion of truth. But it is only at the heart of this Heraclitean peril that there can emerge convincingly the contemporary face of Parmenides. Such emergence of stable truth from the midst of universal relativisation is a possibility sighted in each chapter of this book. It appears that religious truth – which generally presents itself as absolute truth – is such that one can stay in touch with it only by cultivating a sense of the relative. When one believes one can grasp it or state it in a definitive way, it disappears.

I attempt in the present chapter to reimagine the relations between religious worlds by deepening the awareness of historical relativity which affects believers when they realise that they are not alone in interreligious space and that their identity must be rethought in relation to the other traditions. The antidote to the disorientation of pluralism is sought in these relations themselves. A religion that has become dialogical is better able to distinguish between the deep and shallow levels of its own heritage, or between its tribal conditioning and its universal spiritual reach, and thus acquires a critical relation to its own truth. Retrospectively, and contrary to what was traditionally thought, it turns out that the meaning of a religion is never given once for all, but takes the form of a mobile history, marked at each epoch by exchanges with the surrounding culture. The powerful identity of a religious tradition has no need to be protected against the contamination of the other by being conceived in an essentialist way. Religious identity, like individual identity, is made to be reborn, modified but recognisable, in diverse situations and relationships in which it has to construct itself. In all of this my focus is chiefly on Western Christian identity, and the displacement it undergoes particularly in reaction to the questions of Buddhism, which resonate ever more persuasively with its own internal qualms.

To give these ideas more systematic coherence, I shall go on in the next chapter to examine Derrida's theory of dissemination, which draws the ultimate consequences of the contextual character of meaning. I shall offer some suggestions as to how theological hermeneutics might be refashioned along these lines. In the reading of the Bible throughout history, and in the development of Christian tradition, effects of indetermination appear each time the message is translated into a new language or transmitted from one epoch or culture to another. Taking these effects into account, one can rethink tradition according to its intrinsic dynamics and grasp in a more realistic way what has been going on in this history. The recognition of a babelesque pluralism does not sound the knell of all meaning, for amid the Babel the powerful and flexible machine of a living tradition may be throbbing away, weaving and reweaving inherited meanings in ever-changing contexts. Such tradition, however, is less the accumulation of a capital of acquired meanings, than a process of adaptation, the resourceful invention of a sustainable Christian (or Buddhist) discourse in each epoch.

Chapters 3 and 4 take up the philosophical issue which has imposed itself more and more as central to the issues of religious pluralism, namely the nature of truth. Though truth is an obstacle to dialogue when each of the partners believe themselves to be its sole possessor, nonetheless religions which forfeit their truth-claims hardly deserve to survive. Interreligious theology thus requires a concept of truth which is both firm and flexible, compatible both with a historical relativisation of all religious discourse and an affirmation of the referential objectivity of dogmatic language. Against the reduction of faith-statements to expressions of a religious experience or to the symbolisation of a revelation ultimately inaccessible to language, I defend the cognitive bearing of these statements, while stressing the fragility of the historical modalities according to which this cognition is communicated.

To focus more sharply this notion of truth as context-bound but objective I turn again to Derrida, contesting his reduction of truth to an effect inscribed within an enveloping textuality from which it can never be extracted. To be sure, religious truths are inscribed in historical texts of such complexity as to make them seem ambiguous and problematic. The solemn affirmations in such texts – 'Amen, Amen, I say unto you' – could seem effects of rhetoric produced by a textual machine which surpasses and relativises them. If truth itself is never more than a secondary effect of the operations of textuality, such grandiose declarations betray the futile pretention of escaping from the laws of finitude and 'inscription', and the hollowness of this rhetoric is denounced by its very construction. Yet it can be argued that rather than spelling the disappearance of truth, the effects brought to light by Derrida render truth, even religious truth, more accessible, by clarifying the concrete modalities of its inscription in our historical languages.

Having thus argued for both the mobility and the stability of meaning and truth in the Christian tradition, I take up more explicitly the interreligious theme in chapter 5, turning to Buddhist thought with the question: 'What do you say about the problems just discussed?' I approach texts of Mahāyāna Buddhism in the perspective of Western scholars who are intrigued by its philosophical aspects and who have read Nāgārjuna in the light of Wittgenstein and Derrida. I focus particularly on the distinction between world-ensconced truth and ultimate truth (the two-truth theory) and on the notion of religious language as a 'skilful means' (upāya). These probing Buddhist accounts of the status of religious language seem to offer an indispensable key for solving the antinomies of the interreligious situation.

The notion of emptiness (śūnyatā) allows us to rethink our language about God and Christ, the two Christian topics that raise the highest barrier to recognition of a parity among religions. Taking the word 'God' (chapter 6) as the cipher of the entire history of the construction and deconstruction of monotheism, and the word 'emptiness' as similarly resuming a great swathe of Buddhist history, we retrieve the mobility of the monotheistic tradition by setting it in tense interaction with its non-theistic Eastern counterpart. God communicates himself only in the Babelian war set off by the name of 'God', and the dialogue with the silence of Buddha has today become an essential dimension of this ongoing process of revelation.

As to the riddle presented by the claims made for Christ, unique Son of God and Saviour (chapter 7), I argue that a Christology compatible with Nicaea and Chalcedon can be worked out in the pluralist and relativist terms expounded so far, if we attend to the fact that Jesus Christ himself is plural, that he has no identity except in relation to others, that he is disseminated across history, and that our construction of his identity is a contingent historical upāya, subject to profound alterations in the light of new encounters. Thus the mode of Christ's historical existence accords with the texture of divine revelation as we have gradually come to see it. I seek to characterise his status as Saviour as a specific historical role, insofar as he is the one who orients history toward its eschatological goal. Setting the Christology thus limned in the interreligious horizon, I note the universal resonances of the Christ-event, which elicit echoes from other religious traditions, while its eschatological singularity emerges amid these convergences. The confrontation with Buddhism is particularly illuminating: it is because Christ is 'dependently co-arisen' and empty of all 'self-nature', as Buddhists put it, that he can be universal, pointing beyond himself in his eschatological role, and be seen as God's Word spoken into human history.

Our argument views the play of religious traditions from a variety of angles, sometimes focusing on its critical and dialectical aspect, sometimes using Derrida's vocabulary of 'dissemination' and '*différance*', sometimes invoking the Buddhist notion of 'skilful means' – conventional language which can indicate ultimate reality from afar as it registers its own provisional, context-dependent status. Though attentive to the interplay between these different categorisations, I shall try to avoid forcing them into an artificial synthesis. The correction or purification undergone by theological discourse when it is made to bend to the laws of dissemination and *différance,* or to the Buddhist dissolution of substantial self-identity, is not a merely negative process. Negation is indeed given full play, for God, as mystics tell us, is known in subtraction (Plotinian *aphairesis*) far more than in addition. But the negation carves out new lineaments of Christian identity, which only specifically theological categories can descry. Thus in addition to the deconstructive and Buddhist terms, I shall evoke a quasi-Trinitarian interplay between eschatological provisionality, incarnational dialectic, and pneumatic immediacy in the functioning of Christian language. The mobility of this language is not only that of temporality, spacing, dialectic, dissemination, which deconstruction finds inscribed in all language. It is also a spiritual mobility, a trace of the movement of the Spirit.

ARE RELIGIONS MEANINGFUL?
ARE THEY TRUE?

Christian thinkers who delight in the cornucopia of religious traditions now so easy of access – both in scholarly sources and in daily life – find themselves launched on an open path of inquiry in which their own identity is exposed to constant redefinition. For them, there is no going back to the top-heavy dispensation in which Christianity, while perceiving in other religions 'a ray of that Truth which enlightens all human beings' (Vatican II, *Nostra Aetate* 2), presumes itself to be the sole possessor of truth in its fulness. The open-ended pluralistic context brings their faith into fresh perspective, as one voice in a wider polyphony, wherein other voices, that once were despised, now fall gratefully on the awakened ear. Its rough edges smoothed away, Christian discourse, in yielding to the give and take of dialogue, finds healing, enrichment, and relief from sectarian doggedness.

Yet this seachange in religious awareness poses difficult problems which demand our scrupulous reflection. At the existential level, there is a nagging suspicion that this embrace of pluralism diminishes the gravity of the act of faith, making one's religious complexion as insignificant and arbitrary a matter as one's style of dress. Even if in practice individuals and communities can negotiate a happy blend of diverse sources, passing over and back between traditions, this performance has implications that need to be clarified. Whether they compose their own religion, as from a menu, or labour to retrieve ancient indigenous traditions which the mainstream has repressed, or to integrate into their native affiliation the perspectives of an alien tradition, in each case their faith undergoes a displacement which unsettles established doctrinal stances and implicitly inaugurates a new religious order, or disorder. Theology can no longer censor these explorations or dictate their outcome; its function now becomes that of a secondary reflection, underpinning this eclectic religious culture, and preserving it from superficiality or irrationalism, by providing discernment and synthesis and by negotiating between the claims of tradition and the critical impact of the new situation.

Religious pluralism poses a *problem of meaning*. How does one manage the abundance of data dealt with in religious studies? In the absence of a strong theory, one falls into encyclopaedism, setting religious worldviews alongside one another like so many mounted butterflies. The absorbing study of beliefs comes to have less and less to do with reality, and the myths and doctrines that shaped people's lives are reduced to evanescent simulacra in a kaleidoscope. Sociological or structuralist approaches may confer order on the data, but not a significance commensurable with what they claim for themselves – the husk is grasped, the essence evaporates. Philosophers of religion may isolate an 'essence', but in a form too lacking in profile to inspire an investment of faith. It seems that to make sense of religious diversity, what is required is a theory that is itself specifically religious or theological.

When we meet religious others not in books but as flesh-and-blood neighbours, we ourselves are as much their others as they are ours, and the problem of meaning takes a more human twist. We ourselves are inside the kaleidoscope, and if its diversity becomes phantasmagoric, it is our own reality that suffers. A principle of symmetry operates here. If we see the religious views of others as quaint relics or external customs, the suspicion immediately arises that our own are nothing more. If we are ready to find as much truth and life in their religion as in our own, then we open to the stranger in a way that makes us strangers to ourselves, for the language of our tradition no longer quite fits what we are becoming, and the elements of a viable self-definition can no longer be sought within the Christian sphere in isolation from other religious cultures.

A defeatist fixation on the notion of 'crisis' can distort our perspective on what is afoot in the field of the religious. To bemoan a crisis is to concentrate attention on the anxiety of threatened identity, failing to see in the threatening other an agent of the Spirit inviting us to a revision of our basic perspectives. To welcome alternative religious worlds brings not only theological headaches but a spectacular enlargement of the space in which faith articulates and seeks to understand itself. The other 'solicits' us, seduces, shakes, urgently demands something from us, draws us out of our habitual orbit. Recall Derrida's use of this word:

> Structure is perceived through the incidence of menace, at the moment when imminent danger concentrates our vision on the keystone of an institution, the stone which encapsulates both the possibility and the fragility of its existence. Structure then can be *methodically* threatened in order to be comprehended more clearly and to reveal not only its supports but also that secret place in which it is neither construction nor ruin but lability. This operation is called (from the Latin) *soliciting*. In other words, *shaking* in a way related to the whole (from *sollus*, in archaic Latin 'the whole', and from *citare*, 'to put in motion'). (*WD*, 6)

Communication with the other on equal terms intensifies awareness of the lability of Christian self-definition, pushes its crisis to breaking-point. Christians are thrown into a process in which their identity is redefined in function of newly arising questions and needs. Much of our religious rhetoric can be interpreted precisely as a defensive shield against this unwelcome fate. The Buddhist ontology of non-self in particular methodically solicits the keystone of Western religion, the primacy accorded to substantial being, whether our own or that of God. On the corresponding epistemological front, it liberates the mind from clinging to views, thus undoing the roots of dogmatist and fanatical fixation. Many find in Buddhism a relief from entanglement in the codes of belief and morals which have had such importance in Christianity. In Buddhism, doctrinal claims are all subordinate to the growth of insight as one follows the path. It is a religion that is much more insistent on the necessity to doubt than on the claims of belief. If the Buddhist solicitation of Western dogmas reinforces the Nietzschean one, it also heals it, resolving the struggle with nihilism into a liberating embrace of emptiness.

Pluralistic-minded Christians are learning to move around in the element of pluralism and cultural relativism with ever greater agility.

They may feel like astronauts walking in space, disoriented by a milieu where the laws of perspective no longer apply, and which seems to be a chaos until laws not yet discovered allow them to find their bearings. In interreligious space the received perspectives of theology come to seem askew or confining, and one gropes about for rules of thought and lines of research fit to deal with the new situation. At first one feels there is an irritating indeterminacy in which no thought seems able to stand up – for one hesitates even to proffer the name of 'God' in face of so many religions that represent the absolute in a different way (or that do not have any absolute at all). Even terms such as 'the absolute' or 'ultimate reality' may ring hollow. But little by little one does come to grips with the unaccustomed element, and the words of faith take form according to new lines of force that one discerns intuitively before being able to trace them in an adequate conceptuality.

In a secularised society, people no longer live within a religion as if the world were tailored to its measure; they begin to see their religion from the outside as one among others. The sociological levelling that forces us to admit a parity of religions is the surface manifestation of the finite status all religions share, their contingent and incomplete character as historically developing identities. Religions – whatever else they may be – are finite historical formations, constructions of the human spirit in its struggle with the problems of existence. All religions, in a post-religious climate, are summoned to give a credible account of themselves in a critical retrieval of their historical performance. Each has to take responsibility for its constructions, rethinking them in a manner more adequate to the texture of history. This revisionist stocktaking is best carried out against the widest possible background in the history of religions. In this process, each religion presents to the others an image of the historical contingency and proneness to illusion from which none can claim to be exempt. They become cruel but liberating mirrors for each other, in mutual confirmation and critique. On the confirmatory side, two traditions

> may shine on each other to bring out the hidden qualities of each ever more brightly... For the sake of one's peace, one may come to a point where one sees fit to follow one path rather than the other, even with the latter shining on the chosen path to give an added hue. (Lee, 9)

Such interreligious critique and illumination can take effect 'without disturbing one in walking on the chosen path safely and steadily'. Theological reflection now becomes a critical, mobile interrogation of what is afoot on the religious terrain, exposing the discourse of faith as a

8

contingent, provisional melange or bricolage of representations engendered by history, and undoing the mystique of pure origins or absolute status, which has outlived its usefulness. This permits a demystified use of religious languages so that they can once again transmit the shock of an encounter with the real, rather than cushioning against such a shock by lending themselves an illusory stability and permanence.

However, it may be doubted whether any of the great traditions is yet ready to face fully the consequences of its historicity. Since Kant, a basic task of thinking has been to face our finitude, to put ourselves back in our skin, to return to where we already are. If the religions refuse to see the real conditions of their historical existence, the reason is that they transfer to their language, representations and history the ultimacy that properly appertains only to that supreme reality to which these have served to witness, thus falling into self-idolatry. 'What is basically wrong with humanity', according to Simone Weil, is 'the substitution of means for ends. It is this reversal of the relation between the means and ends, this basic madness, which accounts for everything absurd and bloody throughout history'. Only by taking stock of their extreme fragility can those 'means' which are the religions testify to their 'end' – to that mystery which can be felicitously named in certain conditions, but which eludes any definitive grasp.

Did the great searchers for the absolute unmask the fallacy of absolutism, the confusion of means and ends? Even those who felt most keenly the insufficiency of words – Augustine, Eckhart, Luther – were still far from realising their own historical and cultural relativity. Even in Buddhism, despite the provisional and pragmatic character it claims for its teaching, the conviction of this or that school (T'ien-t'ai, Hua-yen, or Shingon, for example) of having attained the correct view, in light of which all other schools were classified hierarchically, dampened curiosity about others and prematurely stilled the spirit of questioning. The contemporary awareness of cultural relativity prescribes a less sweeping approach to the quest of the absolute; it must now go by the way of a meditation on the relative, referring all religions to their historical roots.

Despite their finitude and relativity, religious traditions contain treasures of perennial wisdom. Essentialist theories of a Perennial Philosophy cannot do justice to the particularity and heterogeneity of the religions; yet one would not wish to deny that these contingent, finite, in part obsolete formations are vehicles of perennial wisdom. One might image them as antennae picking up signals from the unknown, signals difficult to decipher but so powerul that they put a strain on the makeshift apparatus prepared for their reception. The work of decipherment, and the elaboration of a more adequate matrix for receiving the signals, today demands interreligious consultation. Both the wealth of their fundamental content and the poverty of their historical means of expression make it wasteful and irrational for religious traditions to despise or ignore one another.

What lends urgency to the problem of meaning created by religious pluralism is the pressure of an ulterior problem, that of *truth*. To appreciate all religions seems to imply that real assent is refused to any. The great world religions lose their appearance of permanence when one treats them as human institutions born in function of the needs of an epoch, deploying the range of their possibilities over time, and now, to a sceptical observer, nearing the exhaustion of their resources. Yet as they broach a millennial threshold the religions seem in better shape than had been foretold, their mighty engines purring, their rich traditions relucent, despite – or rather because of – critical contestation and pluralist dispersion. Perhaps the greatest challenge they face is that of assessing, rationally and responsibly, their status and function, so that in addition to arousing faith and devotion they will also continue to illuminate human minds questing for what is not only meaningful but true.

They can fail to meet this challenge either through dogmatic reinforcement of traditional identities or through yielding to a pluralist liberalism which undermines faith. The antidote to both failures lies in sustained attention to the issue of truth. The question, 'how true is religion?', weighs on all our traditions, inducing sobriety if it does not push us over into scepticism. It should not cast a pall on the life of faith, yet neither can it be wished away. Its nagging persistence reminds us how much remains to be clarified in our religious ideas, how many adjustments are required to bring these ideas into satisfying accord with the contemporary sense of the real. The ideas may indeed light up of their own accord, and show themselves vessels of spirit, dispelling doubts and difficulties in a trice. Such inward confirmation does not however dispense from the public task of apologetics, or from dealing with the riddles of religious pluralism.

The question, 'how true is religion?', may best be met by asking another question: 'how is religion true?' According to what modalities can religious propositions legitimately be expected to make sense? What sort of reference should we expect them to have? Under what conditions are they statements of truth? How does this truth differ from other kinds of truth? To what procedures of verification or falsification should religious propositions be subject? Since religion is not a unitary entity, the answer to these questions is likely to vary from tradition to tradition.

Many people think of religions as 'supreme fictions', poetic interpretations of the world with no objective cognitive content. They plausibly suggest that the reality underlying the fabrications of religious discourse is nothing more than 'the foul rag and bone shop of the heart'. Yet within the constructions of the religious imagination, so easily dismissed as wishful projection, there are found at key points words which rupture the predictable fabrications and allow a glimmer of the ultimate reality to penetrate.

A vital religion harbours a capacity for stepping outside the circle of inherited concepts to mime their breakdown before what they attempt to designate. This can be done by an act that speaks at a pre-conceptual level, as when Zen Buddhism names some homely object as the locus of ultimate truth, or when Christianity points to some despised neighbour as the presence of Christ. It can be done in a secondary way by inventing new words or words with new meanings ('emptiness', 'charity', 'grace') which spell an overhaul for the entire discourse in which they are inserted. Such creative acts and words are experienced as a step in the direction of lived truth, rather than as defensive moves to prop up a crumbling belief-system. Assessment of the basic revelation-events (as we may call them), and of the detailed historical claims and doctrinal underpinnings that attend them, seems to demand that we exit from religion as convention-ally understood to retrieve its heritage in a more discerning, critical mode, making explicit the subversive potential lodged in it.

Beyond the proliferation of *imaginary* representations and of contra-dictions in the *symbolic* order, the conviction of being in touch with something supremely *real* (to use Lacan's terms) gives religious traditions their catching face, so that the resonances or dissonances between them continue to engage the contemporary mind at the level where basic ques-tions are posed. If the real were nothing more than a puncturing of imaginary ideals and symbolic authority, then religion would be shown up as illusion. But if we are persuaded by love, by beauty, by the deliver-ies of ethical conscience and intellectual insight, that reality is ultimately gracious, then we have a fundamental validation of religion over nihilism, and the question of the truth of religions becomes one of ongoing critical assessment of the different traditions.

Today, the shock of the real, the shock of truth, comes to Christian faith not only from the deflating critique of secularism or atheism, but above all from the alternative languages of spiritual reality which it con-fronts in interreligious encounter. The inclusivist attempt to place those languages in relation to the Christian one is unpersuasive, for it rides roughshod over history and its sectarian character is apparent. The apologetic ambition to validate Christian truth-claims against the other traditions by logical argument runs aground on the awareness that these truth-claims function only within the total context which carries them, and that the prior task is to clarify their meaning and truth by reference to the ways of perceiving and living in the world which lie at their base. To respect the reality of the other languages is to respect their claim to truth, beyond all the necessary demythologisations. These languages grip and unsettle us only when we recognise that they are basically true, just as we believe our own language to be true. The question then is, *how* are they true?, and the answer we give for other languages must be applied also to our own.

If one admits such symmetry in judging the truth of religious traditions, then the objective referentiality of Christian faith-statements acquires another status. It corresponds to the validity of a perspective or an angle of vision which coexists with other perspectives, without the possibility of embracing the relation between them from a viewpoint outside all perspectives. The puzzling coexistence of religious worlds, incommensurable with one another, irreducible to one another's terms, and yet each the bearer of objective truths, seems to call for a logic of relativity which is not at present available. Seen from within, the space constituted by a particular religious world is perfectly inhabitable and worthy of credence, but seen from another religious space it seems deformed and uninhabitable, somewhat as in the relations between different 'inertial frames of reference' in the theory of relativity. Should we look for 'transformation formulas' to correlate these contradictory spaces? Could we resist uniform conceptions of the ultimate horizon governing the quest for interreligious understanding by imagining something like a curvature of hermeneutical space? Each religion maps its path according to principles which are radically different, or according to fundamentally diverse senses of what it means to be-in-the-world. 'The relativity of meaning to a religious world implies radical and systematic ambiguity in the sense of terms between different religious languages' (A. K. Gangadean, in Dean, 225f). Homologies between religious worlds or anthropological constants that hold across all worlds are serviceable only at a flat surface level. We cannot step outside perspectivism, and each of the perspectives is itself a world.

The Christian perspective has its distinctive themes which no other religion offers, but there is in the other religions no pressing need to tune in to these themes. The Buddhist perspective has perhaps a more universal pertinence today, and all other religions may need to be tempered by Buddhist wisdom. Biblical faith, so often a destructive principle, may have lost its way, and the Gospel may need to be tempered by Buddhist wisdom so as to become good-tempered, recovering from a sorry history of theological acrimony; even-tempered, freed from the extremes of dogmatic 'eternalism' and sceptical 'nihilism' denounced by the Buddha; and well-tempered, in Bach's sense – each of its notes freshly defined and given lucid, penetrating resonance.

Faith without wisdom is blind. But one could equally argue in the opposite direction, as Christian apologists have not been slow to do, to the effect that wisdom without faith in a personal saving God is vacuous. I take it for granted that the critical impact of historical relativisation on Buddhism is analogous to what the Western ontological and monotheistic traditions are undergoing, but this topic will not be central in the present work, which aims rather to open up to the full impact of Buddhist questions in contemporary Western consciousness. If in doing so I lend a privileged position to Buddhism to a degree that even seems doctrinaire, this can be justified by the sense that it is in this direction that our most pressing task for thought lies.

THE FINITUDE AND COMPLEMENTARITY OF RELIGIOUS TRADITIONS

When one observes how recent Christianity rejoins the sequence of epochal structurations of Christian history, and how this history itself is assigned its place in the religious evolution of humanity, one feels oneself becoming historical. Perhaps Buddhism, as its American and European proponents interpret it in independence of its prior inculturations in Asia, is undergoing a similar discovery of historicity. The family of religions claims Christianity as one of its members, and as Christians yield to this claim they find themselves reinserted in history, as pursuers of one quest beside others no less valuable, and as one historical tradition having to negotiate its place anew in a confrontation with the others. As this historicist awareness deepens it precipitates more concrete insights into our place in the history of religions. Christianity, we begin to see, subsists only in reference to other religious identities, all equally plural and fragile. Daughter of the religion of Israel and essentially subject to the interrogation of Judaism, disturbed by the simpler and purer identity of Islamic monotheism, and needing now the refinements of Buddhist contemplation and analysis to grasp itself properly, the Christian tradition can less than ever be understood as an invariable message; its voice can make itself heard only in the form of a concrete call addressed to a particular partner in dialogue, a call accompanied by a listening. Universal in principle, its message nonetheless becomes flesh only in contingent encounters, and it is on the successful continuation of these encounters that the actualisation of its universality depends.

The series of forms in which faith has been embodied in the course of history, each born of a contingent encounter, does not fit into the neat categories of 'development of dogma', 'inculturation', *'aggiornamento'*, or even that of ecumenical and interreligious dialogue – for each of these terms evokes a perspective on history in function of the specific concerns of a given moment in Christian self-definition. Every major encounter discredits the received schemas of comprehension and engenders some fresh formula for the way faith exists in history. When the encounter of Christianity and Buddhism has attained more substantial dimensions, the corridors of communication it will open may entail an upheaval in our ideas of the historical unfolding of the Gospel. Nothing is more unpredictable than two histories which cross.

Christian identity can never assemble itself in a self-sufficient unity, for it is born only in dependence on the other, 'in the lack of the other'. Following Lacan, one could say the same thing of human identity in general. In order to bring our image of Christianity and of its history into accord with the image of humanity and its history traced by contemporary thinkers such as Lacan, Heidegger, Wittgenstein, Foucault and Derrida, one must descend to the humble and prosaic infrastructures of Christian discourse. Such a katabasis toward the repressed genealogy of Christian discourse is not an effort to humiliate the pretentions of religion, as Kafka or Beckett humiliate those of humanism, but rather a 'step back', analogous to that by which Heidegger recalls metaphysics to its nourishing soil in the thinking of being. It takes its cue from the dynamics of the Incarnation – the way God makes himself known in history in a play of relative perspectives rather than by an irruption of the naked absolute.

A reading of its history starting from the current pluralist awareness reveals the surprising fact that Christianity has existed as a series of strategic constructions born of always unforeseeable cultural circumstances, to such an extent that all attempts to formulate its essential and invariable form find themselves contaminated by references proper to a certain period, which contradict this claim to permanence. Even its origins betray this contamination. The new religion was not a self-sufficient monad or a flawless crystallisation of the whole previous tradition. Its dependence, for its initial formulation, on the Greek language and the Hellenised culture of Palestine, its links with an Iranian heritage from which it drew the concepts of Heaven and Hell, angels and devils, and even the temporal framework of Christ (protological past, historical manifestation, eschatological return), the transfusion of the institutions and ideologies of the Empire carried out by Constantine: everything in this genealogy invites us to dream of what the Christian movement might have been (if it could have been) within another culture.

Radically to separate the religions is impossible. Their roots intertwine.

Their lights are always ready to blend, even across thick veils of language. One can repress the memory of the Canaanite sanctuaries which were the places of cult of the Patriarchs, or of all that links nascent Christianity to the religious movements within Judaism or the Graeco-roman world, but still this impurity of origins forbids any later closure. Thus any attempt to judge, or reject, the other religions in the light of a single one elevated to normative status comes undone. A religious tradition is not a cathedral which contains everything, but a crossroads open to everything. Every religion, but especially Christianity, has a police which guards its frontiers; this theological vigilance is a necessary precaution, but of uncertain effect, for spiritual movements are characterised by great permeability, so that Christianity is incessantly transforming itself in response to the pressure of all the currents of the surrounding culture and of newly encountered foreign cultures.

INADEQUATE MODELS OF THE INTERRELIGIOUS SITUATION

Religious pluralism is a playground for hermeneuticians, who hope to enter empathetically into the various religious cultures, identify their true depths, and overcome, by the pure desire to understand, the self-imprisonment of the religions within archaic dogmatic horizons. A comprehensive hermeneutics can avoid on the one hand the scholarly positivism that leads to a fragmentation of beliefs in a pluralism bereft of meaning, and on the other the pitfalls of a 'phenomenology' that attempts itself to be 'religious' (Eliade), installing a unitary theology of the sacred that overrides the diversity of the historical phenomena. But in the end does the critical patience of the hermeneut suffice to establish a perspective at the heart of the interreligious kaleidoscope? The critical interpretation of different religious worlds cannot do justice to their basic significance to the degree that it loses its anchorage in believing engagement, the very thing that makes those worlds real for those who live in them. To confine the study of religions to the level of a disinterested hermeneutical assessment is to stave off the claims of any particular religion to engage human beings in the quick of their existence. In contrast, a theological point of view, based in believing engagement, can bring dialectical sinew to the study of religions by addressing them in function of an interest commensurate with their basic concern. (Of course the bracketing of this theological concern in the scientific hermeneutic of religions may have a methodological justification, ensuring a critical autonomy over against theology.)

The concrete texture of the relations between Christianity and its interreligious interlocutors is of a complexity which defeats convenient schematisation. Yet there is a temptation for philosophers and theologians to impose a hierarchical or democratic order on the family of religions. Such schemas are constructed from an external point of view and again prevent us from entering fully into the 'loving strife' about human existence and ultimate reality which goes on between the religions.

Take for example Ernst Troeltsch. 'It is only at lower cultural levels that one finds an infinite multiplicity, which remains however of a formal and external kind and conceals a great monotony' (Troeltsch, 49). A penetrating look at religious history reduces this diversity to 'the struggle between two worlds of ideas: the prophetic-Christian-Platonist-Stoic world and the Buddhist-oriental world' (51). This position is still Hegelian, aiming to gather all the religions in some higher-order formations. The desire to reduce the interreligious situation to a privileged colloquy between biblical monotheism and Indian contemplation does not take seriously enough the constant emergence of differences within each of the great traditions, the way that the two 'worlds of ideas' are themselves endlessly diverse and riven by inner tensions, such as that between 'prophetic' and 'Platonist'. Meanwhile, the religions of 'lower cultural levels' powerfully solicit the great traditions, insofar as they can be grasped as religions of the earth and of life, correcting the forgetfulness of nature and the hostility to life of which the great traditions have been accused. James Mackey has suggested that even the religions which most aim at universality, and most persuasively embody that aim, notably Buddhism and Christianity, nonetheless remain close to primitive local religions in that they exist empirically as a congeries of local traditions; and the higher their vitality, the more is this the case (*Studies in World Christianity*, 1:1, 1995).

Troeltsch refuses to accept that the variety of religions could be as normal and as desirable as that of poetry, language or works of art. Such variety seems to compromise the truth and certitude expected from religion. Yet that ideal of certitude may itself be a rather primitive absolutism, reinforced by the rationalism of Western metaphysics. Better to accept diversity as the element in which religion thrives, a basic law of religious life, than to try to impose the yoke of a single ideal which would in the end deny any legitimacy to religious plurality. Despite so many contradictory claims, neither the biblical tradition nor that of philosophy have succeeded in defining such a universal ideal.

However, a certain Darwinianism presides over the growth of religious knowledge as it does over scientific knowledge. A system of belief in which numerous gods impose arbitrary penalties (as appears to be the case in the indigenous religion of Okinawa) is no doubt less advanced than ethical monotheism. Again, in the clash between Gnosticism and orthodoxy in the early Church, the latter emerged as the clear winner not only because of its institutional prowess, but on intellectual and spiritual grounds. But when theories of natural selection are applied to the relation between Christianity and Judaism, or between Mahāyāna Buddhism and early Buddhism, or between the world religions and local cults, they have at best a partial validity.

Troeltsch saw history as a constant accumulation of meaning, tending toward an ideal unity. 'The rare great breakthroughs of the religious idea do not culminate in a futile play of variations, but much rather in the victory of the purest and deepest conception of God' (61). As a regulative idea, such a conception may have some value for the critical evaluation of traditions. 'The concept of a common goal which always hovers before the historical movements in which it cuts a passage for itself with greater or less force and clarity', 'the idea of a goal of which the general direction and outline are glimpsed though in its full content it always remains transcendent, and which lets itself be grasped in history only as conditioned in an individual way' (57) is so intangible that it hardly threatens the integral experience of pluralism, though it may serve to protect this experience from a nihilistic relativism. But the more the relation of the religions is pluralised, relativising every determinate concept by which one claims to master it, the more this ideal goal withdraws into the clouds of the indeterminable.

Troeltsch was right to insist that Christian thought has to come to terms with the realities of historical existence, just as it must adjust to the discoveries of physics and biology. Restorationist ventures such as neoscholasticism or Barthian biblicism can be severely faulted as an attempt to evade historical and scientific reality. Yet Barth was right too: the history of religions cannot dictate the status of revelation. Troeltsch's attempt to appraise the relatively superior status of Christianity on the basis of historical comparisons offers theology a foundation of sand. Revelation, sealed by the biblical names of God and of Jesus Christ, is an irreducible self-sufficient reality which cannot be explained from some higher perspective. However, Barth's strictures against *religionsgeschichtliche Theologie* may not apply to a more strictly theological dialogue with the religious other, one in which the specificity of biblical revelation is vigilantly upheld even as one recognises effects of 'grace' and 'revelation' elsewhere as well.

Barth draws two crucial distinctions, which can be used to wedge his thought open to pluralistic horizons. The first is the classical reformation distinction between the Word of God and the Bible. Scripture is a means, not an end; it attests to revelation; 'to attest means to point in a certain direction, beyond oneself, towards another' (*KD* I/1, 114). Dogmatics tests the Church's proclamation against the biblical word (306). But it could be argued that dogmatics has a more radical task, that of assessing Scripture itself against the revelation to which it attests.

How could this be done? First of all by reference to the internal tensions of Scripture, which as Harnack urged against Barth is by no means a unified document. These tensions open onto the struggle between the spirit and the letter which is an unavoidable aspect of biblical hermeneutics. Secondly, the limits of the historical vision of Scripture are shown up by subsequent history and by the discovery of alternative religious horizons. To expose Scripture fully to the critique these prompt is not to undermine its role as attesting to revelation, but rather to clarify it. Barth insists that, when God wills, the word of Scripture, heard in faith, becomes identical with the Word of God; the same is true of the Church's proclamation; yet he opposes a 'finding of the Word of God in the Bible' to a 'question after the Word of God in the proclamation' (307). But the Bible itself is full of questioning after the Word of God, as becomes apparent if we read it historically, with an eye on its inner tensions and self-corrections. We best appropriate the sacred text when we continue that questioning, rather than seeing it as foreclosed by the biblical answer.

Barth's second distinction is the one between revelation and religion. He sees religions as constructions of human unbelief, excluding obedience to the Word: 'religion is never and nowhere as such and in itself true' (I/2, 356). This is over-stated, and dismissive in its concrete application to Islam and Buddhism (330, 375), but we may agree that all religions, including Christianity, are judged to fall short of the truth of which they attempt to speak. The distinction between the truth of revelation and the deceptiveness of religion can be extended to them all. In each of them is a happening of truth, mixed up with the doubtful chiaroscuro of mere religion.

Barth admits that religion, like the justified sinner, can be sanctified by the grace of revelation: 'Revelation can accept religion and distinguish it as true religion' (357). For Barth this act of grace applies only to Christianity. But it can be argued that this grace can befall any religion, so that there are not one but many true religions, all true by grace, and not in reason of the cleverness of their founders. The Bible shares with all 'religious' texts a falling short of the event of revelation which is at its heart, its letter betraying its spirit; and conversely, these texts, despite their human origins, can become vehicles of transcendent revelation.

To be sure, the biblical revelation is quite different from the truth-events at the heart of other religions, and at least from some angle we must claim for its a certain centrality or primacy within the spectrum of religious revelations. Even if we reserve the word 'revelation' to mark the specificity of the biblical event of truth, the truth-core of other religions nonetheless makes its powerful claim felt, deep calling to deep, and it cannot be turned away as an unfit dialogue partner for biblical revelation.

In a later text (IV/3, 122–53), Barth opens a chink towards a positive appreciation of the glimmers of truth in other religions, seen inclusivistically as deriving from the prophetic mission of Christ. After Vatican II and Karl Rahner, not many Roman Catholic theologians will have any problem with recognising divine grace at work in other religious traditions. The Spirit at work in all hearts is Christ's Spirit; yet one hesitates to link that work directly to the prophetic mission of Christ. Though here we flounder among metaphors, the need is felt to distinguish between a universal revelation of the Logos and the particular mission of the Logos incarnate, a universal motion of the Spirit and the particular action of the Spirit within the Christian covenant. Barth unduly telescopes the pre-existent Logos with the concrete figure of Jesus Christ who is also thought of as somehow pre-existing. His Christocentrism, or Christomonism, cannot do justice to the autonomy of the other religions as sources of truth. To ascribe such truth more vaguely to God's Logos and Spirit allows those religions to speak for themselves. Christians will receive the truth of other religions as a new manifestation of Logos, reading it in the light of their own partial grasp of Logos as glimpsed across the historical Christ-event.

Thus the truth of Hinduism or Buddhism is not necessarily pre-contained in Scripture, and it can supplement the scriptural perspectives. It can even correct Scripture, or at least serve as a catalyst to Scripture's own self-correction, the correction of the letter by the spirit. For Barth, 'no true word can replace the biblical testimony in any point', and there is 'no need to squeeze, to shorten or to broaden the biblical word in order to bring it into accord with the word received from outside' (142). This is clearly untrue even on such elementary matters as the biblical attitudes towards torture (Mt. 18:34), slavery (Eph. 6:5), women (1 Cor. 11:3–9), homosexuality (Rom. 1:26f), capital punishment (Rom. 13:4), or the Jews (Mt. 27:25). One may say that no true word can diminish or add to the revelation-event to which Scripture attests, for God's covenantal self-revelation is a transcendent reality, which it would be absurd to speak of shortening or widening. But this does not exclude a dialectical, developmental movement at the level of the actual empirical manifestation of this covenantal event in the words of Scripture and the contingencies of Christ's human historicity, which are our access to that event. The grace and truth found in other religions are 'uncovenanted'. That is not a slighting expression, but can mark their otherness, the possiblity that they offer further avenues into the mystery of the divine other than those opened up in the covenant with Israel and in the Christian covenant.

Barth applied his dialectical finesse only to the relation between the

Word of God and human misunderstandings of it, but we can import such critical dialectic into the Christ-event itself, seen not as a clothing of the Word with a fixed set of historical forms, but as a critical ferment of the Word within our history. The unfolding of the Christ-event constantly sheds old and creates new historical forms, and it does so in the wider context of the universal Logos which is expressed in all forms whatever. The Johannine Prologue sets the unique enfleshment of the Word in the Christ-event against the background of this universal communication of divine light and life. To say that all revelation happens henceforth in and through Jesus Christ is a simplification which misses the dialogical mode of Christ's presence to the world. Christ is brought into new perspective in these encounters, or rather comes into new perspective by the working of his own Spirit, which lights up the affinities with other religions at the level of Spirit even when at the level of Logos they seem poles apart.

These true words that come for outside have only a temporary, not a permanent significance for the Christian community, Barth claims, and then only for a special group within it, not for the community as a whole; and they can do their work without any need to dogmatise or canonise them (IV/3, 150–1). This undermines the reality of the Gospel's dialogal encounter with other cultures and religions. It could happen that an insight coming from outside – the values of democracy or social liberation for example – could become so much part of the interpretation of Scripture that any regression to a time when one was ignorant of that insight would be a betrayal of Scripture itself. Or it could happen that Christianity and Buddhism are destined for a long cohabitation which will deeply affect Christian self-understanding and understanding of Scripture. Scripture does not entitle us to set limits to what it may mean. The price one pays when one sets such limits is the degeneration of scriptural language into biblicist fustian.

The liberalism denounced by Barth is most influentially represented today by John Hick's quasi-Kantian conception of religious pluralism, in which different religious languages refer to the Real as experienced humanly, presenting different phenomenal aspects of the underlying noumenal reality, whether they image this as a personal God or an impersonal Absolute. Each religion distinguishes between the real in itself and the real as humanly experienced; this allows us to see Yahweh and Śiva not as rival gods or rival pretenders to the status of the one and only God, but as two concrete forms in which ultimate reality is made known to different communities (Hick, 42).

But once the phenomenal status of these personal gods is recognised, will the believer not henceforth give all his attention to the noumenal level, however inaccessible it may be? This noumenal God will become a rival of the phenomenal God known through the Bible. However, this alleged noumenal God shows itself in its turn to be phenomenal, a new addition to the list of impersonal forms of the divine, such as Brahman or the Tao, experienced in the concrete traditions. The idea of God is thus consigned to a to-and-fro between these two registers, personal and impersonal, each marked by a great pluralism, a pluralism reproduced even within each of these traditions of personal or impersonal naming of the ultimate.

The reduction of God to a more universal instance, the real, can scarcely do justice to the phenomenality of the biblical God. Nor does the leap from the biblical God to the noumenal real capture the precise contours of the mutation the idea of God is undergoing in our culture. It imposes an abstract solution instead of awaiting the concrete transformation of biblical discourse demanded and made possible by the interreligious horizon. To put Christianity side by side with Buddhism or Islam under the rubric of theocentrism, or of the absolute, denatures these religions; these phenomena cannot be observed from such a theoretical altitude. It is at the historical level that their relation takes shape. Against the distinction between a surface pluralism, at the level of phenomena, and a basic noumenal unity, glimpsed in mystical experience, the analogy of aesthetic experience suggests that pluralism is no less a feature of this deep level. There are striking convergences between the religions at this depth, but they do not point to any uniformity.

There is no 'essence of religion': the category of 'religion' – like those of 'art' and 'literature' – is a pragmatic formation for bringing together historical phenomena having 'family resemblances' in Wittgenstein's sense, scattered traits which cannot be accounted for in a single essential definition. Whether we consider their doctrinal formations or the less easily definable dimension of their ethical investments and contemplative attunements, it is their rough similarity as existential projects, rather than any definable concept of religion, which unites the varied spiritual trajectories of humanity. Even the simple question of identifying the religious element in a given culture can give rise to many uncertainties, for the frontier between the religious and the other modalities of spiritual experience – including the arts and the sciences – is by no means firm.

The unity that Hick postulates a priori can be represented only vaguely, and to give it any precise contours makes it a rival to established religions. This regulative idea of unity adds nothing to the clarity of exchanges between religions. Better to study in detail the process of mutual confrontation to which the invocation of the different names leads. The contradiction between the claims of superiority proper to each of the great religions can be resolved neither by the triumph of one of them over all the others nor by a leap to the ultimate real, but only by a long process of negotiation based on the full acceptance of pluralism.

Kenneth Surin has denounced Hick's pluralism as yet another edict of the imperialist West, obscuring the radical historical particularity constitutive of true otherness (D'Costa, 200). But a pluralism lodged in the flesh and sinew of actual religious worlds can speak to, rather than of, the other, inviting not a sacrifice to abstraction but participation in an exchange which may itself become part of the vital activity of the other religion. Just as what animates the dialogue of two people is not an abstract theory of human nature, but rather the excitement of discovering their mutual strangeness, and by that very token the wonder of their shared humanity, so what animates interreligious dialogue is not a philosophical theory of ultimate reality, but the thrill of empathy that both suggests how very strange must be whatever it is that takes flesh and blood in such diverse forms and at the same time gives a sense, even as one's provincial preconceptions are wedged open, that one has somehow been brought a step nearer to this ultimate reality.

It may be felt that any attempt to theorise religious relativity is still caught in a universalising European mental framework.

> It is the idea itself of the grand explanatory theory – and not any version of it, liberal or conservative, theological or secular – that is a real contemporary stumbling block, because the information on religions now available to us is far too complex and far too concretely situated to be accounted for justly by one or another of these theories and because, by extension, there is, in fact, no universal position from which one could adequately articulate such a theory. (Clooney, 403)

Certainly, any such theory remains only a provisional hypothesis, and one must formulate it in so open-ended a way that it is constantly modifiable by dialectical interplay with empirical observations. Its categories retain the particularity of the tradition from which they spring, and remain only theological perspectives of that tradition on the others. I shall try to keep in mind this situatedness of the universalising categories (history, dialogue, relativity, etc.) which inform my discussion, leaving them as open as possible to adaptation in light of the contingencies of concrete encounter.

Perhaps in reaction to the arbitrariness of both liberal and Barthian assessment of the religions, some recent writers have felt that the objectivity of religious truth requires insistence on the logical contradictions between the doctrinal theses of different religions, and have called for a revival of apologetical debate from which the true religion will emerge victorious. However, it seems to me that this no-nonsense logical approach is likely to be premature.

If one opposes such imponderables as Christian theism and Buddhist a-theism, can one give to this opposition a form sufficiently precise to reveal in it a logical contradiction? In what space of thought is the opposition set forth? One cannot define such theses independently of the contexts that they carry with them. Pluralism reveals the historical, thus contingent, character of any formulation, undoing the process whereby religions have repressed awareness of the genealogy of dogma. Even if one succeeds in organising a confrontation of theses – contrasting, for example, the theism of Rāmānuja and that of Aquinas (Griffiths, 28) – this debate is likely to be marginal to the encounter of the two traditions in all the density of their culture. We assuredly understand something of the thought of Rämänuja, contrary to claims that there is a radical incommensurability between distinct cultural or historical horizons. However, there may be no secure conventions of communication between the disparate horizons, so that a clearcut face-to-face argument between an Indian and a European thinker, or between a modern and a medieval thinker, is impeded by the sense that they live in differently-shaped worlds. To say with Donald Davidson that 'there is at most one world' (Davidson, 187) so that we cannot live in different conceptual worlds is to confuse two different senses of 'world'. Of course there is a general space within which all cross-cultural dialogue takes place, and there is a fund of shared understanding that can be drawn on by both parties in such a dialogue. Nonetheless, the two ways of mapping the world, or of being in the world, may be such that they cannot be thought together in a single comprehensive world view.

We have more reason to mistrust hasty accords between different conceptual worlds than to fear that they will split asunder in radical mutual unintelligibility. A commensurability of terms on the logical plane can mask an incommensurability on the plane of the lived, the kind of incommensurability one may note between the systems of images or the styles of two poets: if one were to set up a debate between the God of Victor Hugo and that of Baudelaire, it would miss the atmosphere, the vibrations which constitute the very stuff of their poetic universes, and would be a mere play of shadows. There is no extra-poetic space in which one could co-ordinate the worlds of these two poets. Different religious worlds confront one another in a similar irreducibility. I shall discuss this topic more fully in chapter three.

If one gives up looking for the universal logical form underlying the religions – whether conceived as the biblical Logos under which all other religions are subsumed, or as a philosophical logos which provides a fully rational grasp of what untutored Christianity apprehends only at the level of representational thought (Hegel) – and instead allows the debate between religions to proceed freely and largely, using logical analysis and argument only when appropriate in particular contexts, is there not a risk that the encounter will lack all urgency and become an idle comparativism? The risk is not countered, however, by insistence on the laws of logic, for these laws do not seem capable of placing the rival traditions in an illuminating perspective, and one is never certain whether one has applied them in a really pertinent way. Their contribution to tracing the complex topology of religious space is a secondary one. They become positive obstructions to vision if made the governing framework of inter-religious thought. It is as if the space-walker sought to situate the relative movements of celestial bodies in a Euclidean spatial frame; nothing of the sort offers itself, and the more one attempted to impose it, the less would one accede to the intrinsic intelligibility of these movements.

The formulation of propositional truths and logical contradictions in the religious domain seems to introduce a violent tear in the texture of religious life, which hardly recognises itself in these constructions. Even if one succeeds in setting up a conflict of theses on the logical plane, nothing guarantees the possibility of resolving the contradictions in a speculative vision, which would require a superior mastery of all religious discourses, reduced to their transparent essence. This Hegelian temptation is no longer actual, one might think, but it still underlies many constructions of the truth of the religious, both 'inclusivist' and 'pluralist'. It is forgotten that any perspective on the religions, like any perspective on poetries, will fail to bring into view their living contours, for such surveys are retrospective constructions, schematisms destined to break down on any nearer approach to phenomena too complex to be understood otherwise than from within. Renouncing, then, all englobing frameworks, we explore religious space through the interferences of religious traditions in their perpetual alterations.

The pluralism I am advocating is not a pluralism erected into a system, wherein a conceptual relativism on the empirical level would issue in a flattening out of differences at the transcendental level. Rather it is a contextual pluralism emphasising the finite and historical character of every religious discourse. It admits that no historical tradition is able to exclude a priori, or to include, the truth of others, but seeks in the collision of their heterogeneous styles the occurrence, on both sides, of a rediscovery of truth, truth which on each occasion destroys venerable mythic or dogmatic illusions, but at the same time reveals unsuspected riches within each tradition which permit their mutual understanding.

FAITHS AND BELIEFS

For a more satisfactory account of how the religions relate to one another we should attend closely to the felt impact, often painful, that they have on one another. When faced with Buddhism, for example, Christians are likely to feel both a threat and a promise. The threat is to their own identity, now shown up as limited and contingent. The promise is that Buddhism can meet a sense of lack, of unfulfilled desire, offering resources that seem to be missing in the Christian tradition as historically constituted. If these are the ineluctable existential implications of the Christian-Buddhist encounter, and perhaps of all interreligious encounter, then it is best to start from there rather than from disengaged theories about how the religions must relate.

The confrontation with another great tradition brings intense awareness of the historical particularity of Christianity. Christian identity, which has become opaque and enigmatic, is now grasped as the identity of a singular historical trajectory. The enigma is not dissolved by being put in this perspective, but it can be accepted serenely, as Christianity along with the other traditions come to see themselves as starting-points of an ongoing quest rather than as final possession of the true. Identity in each case turns out to consist in an open and relative project. In contrast to past versions of the Gospel, each of which took itself for the definitive enunciation of Christian truth, those emerging in a pluralist culture carry an inbuilt awareness of their local and historically situated character, not only as regards practical application, but at the level of the basic terms of their presentation of the Gospel.

The Gospel appears as an open, plural project, from the rupture with Judaism that set it going, through its various exemplary classical expressions, none of which has been able to impose itself as a definitive exhibition of the Christian essence. Every attempt to recover the pure essence of Christianity succeeds only in producing new, original versions, incommensurable with the preceding ones. Christianity has never existed and never can exist in a 'pure' state. It is a set of movements within the complex world of the religions and it has advanced by hybridisation – especially in its first bold refashioning of the Graeco-Roman world in the light of Scripture and of Scripture in the light of that world. A genealogy of Christian identity that recognises the contingency, almost the opportunism, of these epoch-forming amalgams, and that works out a discerning critique of their sinister or occluding aspects, will free us to express the Gospel in equally daring forms of cultural thinking, but now with an awareness of their historical provisionality which should make it easier to dissolve them when they have served their purpose. The Pietist theologian Gottfried Arnold saw Christian history as a diabolical labyrinth, a maze of illusion, and took refuge from its tragic particularity by turning to the infinite within (Osculati, 289). Yet the Incarnation encourages us to take a more trusting view. We need not seek to step back from the hybrids of tradition to a pure language of Logos, for at their base, in the Christ-event, lies an inseparable conjunction of Logos and flesh, of ultimate reality and human contingency.

The leap of evangelical faith takes place within history and is not a leap outside of history. Faith cannot lean on a naked Gospel, abstracted from any context, but is rather nourished from the dialogical situation which roots Christianity in the religious quest of humankind. Its essential kernel, the revelation of the living God in the figure of Christ crucified, can be actualised only as caught in the texture of history. Christianity, like every other religion, is a path to follow, and offers no complete grasp of the truth of the world and of life. Each religion is in contact with an absolute reality; but none is itself absolute, or rather each religion claims a different type of absoluteness. The fragmentary character of sacred texts, the deep marks of historical contingency on the culture which produced them and on their very composition, betray the impossibility of giving an absolute status to the traditions they found.

In the case of Christianity, the claim to witness to the absolute takes an eschatological form: the unsurpassability of Christ as full accomplishment of the promises of God. But this fulfilment remains proleptic. The dispute between Christians and Jews marks not only the fact that the eschatological revelation has not been fully accepted, but more radically that this revelation has not yet found its definitive form; the Church without Israel is not yet itself. Rather than seeing this as a tragic failure, one can look at it as an aspect a general situation, namely that no religion possesses an identity without flaw, and that each is attached to the others by complex bonds. Rather than a communication of the perfect form of the Gospel, Christian mission could be interpreted as part of the Gospel's quest for its own full meaning, through contact with the other; and it is this quest itself, this lack of the other, which is the truth of Christianity's existence, that no discovery of its essence can fill in.

If the encounter of religions is to be an experience of mutual critique, supplementation and transformation, then it must not become bogged down in quarrels about the details of belief, but must focus on what divides and unites them at a deeper level, which Wilfred Cantwell Smith would call the level of faith. This is a treacherously simple distinction, for one can hardly siphon out 'faith' from the entirety of the religious world which embodies that faith, a world which will contain in itself a great variety of contrasting, even conflicting styles of thought and action.

Nonetheless, some such distinction has imposed itself since the very beginnings of inter-religious ecumenism, and we need to retrieve it critically in order to map lucidly the present possibilities of dialogue.

Even though all the religions seem to annul one another on the level of beliefs, it could be claimed that they produce at a deeper level, in their very difference, a reciprocal confirmation: Śaṅkara and Augustine, Nāgārjuna and al-Ḥallāj, Dōgen and Luther have a comparable existential radicality, despite the always unique and irreducible profile of their distinctive religious vision. This shared depth can be named only in poor abstractions, as one names 'beauty' that which is manifested in the diversity of works of art, or 'conscience' that which different ethical styles witness to. Though at this level too pluralism reigns, in contrast to what happens at the level of doctrinal pluralism the foundational contemplative visions draw close in mutual appreciation. 'All the truths which concern God are, in a higher region, in immediate contact with one another' (F. Schlegel, in Schwab, 179).

The identity threatened by the challenge of the other belongs less to this basic level of faith than to the level of habitual beliefs that have become confused with faith. Beliefs remain necessary landmarks. If, with the Savoyard Priest, one rejects positive beliefs to save natural religion – 'when everything is shaken, one should preserve the trunk at the expense of the branches' (Rousseau, 406) – what survives such a critique of every revelation is too weakly determined to influence human life and society for long.

Though Schleiermacher, unlike Rousseau, insists that religion exists only in the form of the positive religions, and that religious intuition is always particular ('only the individual is true and necessary'), he nevertheless maintains an essence of religion as 'a feeling and a taste for the infinite', 'an intuition of the universe', so that 'the divinity can be nothing other than a particular mode of religious intuition' and the fact that someone gives a theistic interpretation of the fundamental sentiment 'depends on the orientation of the imagination' (Schleiermacher, 41, 36, 83, 86). This primacy of intuition does not correspond to the texture of religions in their historical development, which does not advance only by intuitive leaps but also in doctrinal debates. To say that the only function of these debates is to liberate the founding intuition from distorting encumbrances misses the degree to which they actually create new intuitions.

None of the attempts to differentiate the level of faith from the level of beliefs allows one to distil the pure essence of a religion. For there is a perpetual interference between the two planes; the contemplative apprehension of faith is expressed only in particular beliefs and these have religious valency only as they remain at the service of the core-vision.

According to the diversity of historical contexts, different distributions of these two levels appear. For a faith which distinguishes itself from its representations, questioning is a constitutive part of its essence. It is defined less in terms of a concrete content (*fides quae*) than by its confidence (*fides qua*) in the truth with which it remains in contact across concrete teachings. There is a basic 'yes' which is a blind trust in the ultimate referent of the language one assumes, a referent which withdraws from a precise grasp, but is focused by definitions of a negative and provisional order. This inner certitude or basic affirmation permits the questioning of all that is secondary in relation to it; it is a deconstructive 'yes, yes' which leaves one free to say 'no' even to the most hallowed formulae when they no longer match its conviction. The restraining role of the formulae holds in contexts similar to that of their original creation. If in another context they no longer serve to focus the intention of faith, that intention gets to work on them in a critical way, displacing and undermining them.

Raimundo Panikkar enlarges the notion of the *fides qua* by introducing the term 'Christianness' (*Christlichkeit*). Christianness surpasses not only historical Christendom, but Christianity itself as presently constituted: 'Christianness differentiates itself from Christianity as Christianity extricated itself from Christendom' (Hick and Kitter, 105). This is no longer an individual and pietist attitude, as in the mysticism of the past, for it can inspire political and contestatory movements. The Christic principle, understood in all its generality, is implicitly present in the heart of every human being; this is true equally of the Buddhist principle or the Islamic principle. At this level there is no obstacle to mutual comprehension between the great spiritual traditions of humanity. The present situation obliges us to put the accent on Christianness rather than on the beliefs and claims of Christianity, thus rejoining the most radical dimension of the Gospel: 'Seek first the kingdom of God' (Mt. 6.33), as well as its most radical openings to universality: 'I have other sheep, that are not of this fold' (Jn 10.16).

The mysteries of the Creed prompt the community confessing them to inquire of their religious others as to their true meaning. A tradition become an enigma to itself will find only partial clarity in attempts to explicate itself rationally; it must attempt the step back to the radical level of faith. This faith itself is stripped of every sectarian character, and can listen for what in another tradition, below the complexity of beliefs, reveals an affinity with it. The encounter at the level of beliefs brings only an enlargement of knowledge; an encounter 'from faith to faith', below all the mediations of critical historical reason, can support a 'loving strife' at the level of the question 'what is to be believed?' and prevent this from degenerating into sterile controversy.

Much of the Christian resistance to the relativisation effected in interreligious encounter stems from a confusion between the basic teachings of the faith and metaphysical interpretations of them. Thus Joseph DiNoia makes much of

> significant disagreements between Muslim and Christian communities about whether the unity of God excludes or permits relations in him, and between Buddhist and Christian communities about whether the ultimate state entails or negates personal identity and interrelationships. (Hick and Knitter, 130)

The stability attributed to the signifiers in play here comes from their metaphysical definition. When religious visions allow themselves to be understood in terms of a metaphysical method of thought whose normative authority has not been put in question, all dialogue between these visions is doomed to flounder in false problems. But DiNoia is right to contest a pluralist dogmatism which refuses to see any points of contention between the religions. These differences make themselves powerfully felt, even if they are never simple logical contradictions. If Christians blandly take Buddhist non-theism or Islamic monotheism in their stride, registering no unease, that shows a theological insensibility that poorly fits them for the interreligious debate. The pluralist co-existence of religious forms of life does not mean that each hunkers down in a self-sufficient fideism, ignoring all the others, contrary to the defeatism of Jürgen Moltmann who recommends the friendly coexistence of religious communities without disputation or dialogue (150f). This would entail a suspension of the question of truth, a paralysis of theological thought.

If, as Hans Küng insists, the true Church is the ecumenical family of churches, might one equally say the true religion is that which is constituted in interreligious dialogue? Or would this again be the projection of a modern Western construction onto traditions to which it is alien? Yet if one measures religion in terms of their truth, and if one presupposes that truth is ultimately one, then it is almost a truism to say that the truth of religion belongs fully to no one religion, but lies in the ecumenical relation of the great traditions. It is not only the urgency of world peace which forces the religions to come together; all of them equally face together the question of truth, given sharp contours in a secularised culture, and a reply to it demands discussion between them. As the distinctive force of biblical faith is established in an empirical way in various encounters and confrontations, mutual influences and exclusions, the other great traditions also discover in the same process their distinctive roles. The site of the absolute truth is not one religion but the debate between all, a debate aroused and governed by the desire for this truth. This desire remains unsated, for its fulfilment would be the end of the conditions of historical human existence.

PNEUMATIC IMMEDIACY

There is a popular style of dialogue which aims to seek out the contemplative or mystical depth-dimension in the other religion, taking this to be the essential core of faith, and treating all else as mere belief. This, again, is a dangerous simplification. For a start, it connects with an age-old distortion within Christianity itself, whereby a striving after mystical contact with God replaces the hearing of the Word in faith as the central concern of the Christian life. Ever since Luther's denunciation of Pseudo-Dionysius as more a Platonist than a Christian (*magis Platonizans quam Christianizans*), this has been a topic of subtle tensions between the Catholic and Protestant branches of Christianity, and a certain imperviousness on the Catholic side has begun to be remedied only with Vatican II and the Catholic reception of Karl Barth.

Faith in the promises of God already unites the Christian with God and with Christ. The enhancement of this unity in a contemplative experience is a supplementary gift produced by the Word as it dwells richly in our hearts. To focus on that experience as if it were the origin or essence of faith is misguided. Karl Rahner's oft-quoted remark to the effect that the Christianity of the future must be mystical if it is to survive at all has had the effect of distracting people from the essential structure of biblical faith, as the reception of God's covenantal *agapē* rather than the climax of a Platonic ascent of *eros*. The focus on spiritual experience can also bring a distorting perspective to bear on the other religion, as when Zen is boiled down to disincarnate 'enlightenment-experiences'. Such experiences never enjoyed this prominence in classical Zen tradition, where they remained a side-effect of a general cultivation of wisdom.

Still very influential is the thesis of a perennial core of spiritual experience which is more or less identical in all religions at their mystical peaks. This is strongly resisted today by the counter-claim that even in its richest forms, where it is characterised by visionary immediacy, religious experience is elaborately structured, bearing the marks of the culture, tradition and historical circumstances which form its environment. We should beware of subscribing too unreservedly to this counter-thesis. Its assurance of modern sophistication may be delusive. I propose to examine here how it may be reconciled with recognition of the powerful immediacy of contemplative experience and its role as a magnet in inter-religious encounter.

Even experiences of physical pain in different cultures of perception and sensation do not seem to allow of a context-free description. This is likely to be much more the case for higher-order experiences such as those to which the religions point. Is the Kantian duality of concept and intuition of service here? Are the religions ways of cutting a pre-given experiential cake according to culturally conditioned conceptual schemes? Donald Davidson is sceptical about such a division. All efforts to construe or imagine the experiential level fall into mythology. William James's 'big blooming buzzing confusion' – the 'perceptual flux' which *means* nothing and is but what it immediately is' (Levine, 215) – is as much a myth as the postulates of positivist sense-datum theory. We experience the world as always already intelligibly shaped. When James says that 'out of this aboriginal sensible muchness attention carves out objects, which conception then names and identifies', he is extrapolating a fictional situation from the real one in which we are always already dealing with objects, but with the capacity to discover or invent new objects by critical attention to the texture of our experience. The step back from the conceptual order to the perceptual order stumbles not on chaos but on a more or less luminous array of phenomena. C. I. Lewis's distinction between 'the thick experience of the world of things' and 'the thin given of immediacy' (211) is one between actual experience and an abstract ideal that can only be approximated by such rarefied exercises as Husserlian bracketing.

John Keenan objects that

> In everyday living one often has experiences that obviously have no mediating image or conceptual structure. Take, for example, the unpleasant occasion when one touches a hot stove. The interpretation that mediates that experience and identifies the stove as hot follows almost immediately but not soon enough to avoid having a finger burned. No interpretation is given prior to or during the initial duration of the experience itself . . . We seem to live in a world of immediacy, which only gradually, over the course of one's life, and only in part is ever mediated. (Keenan, 193)

But as the fortunes of empirical positivism show, the search for pure immediacy ends up clutching the wraith of an ephemeral sensation, which is allowed to last only a single instant; for if its duration can be divided into two instants, the second instant already functions as an interpretation, a narrative continuation, of the first. The idea of a purely instantaneous experience seems a contradiction in terms. Pointing out that the retention of the past in the present cannot itself be something fully present to consciousness (as Husserl thought), Derrida finds a constitutive absence at the heart of every presence as its very condition of possibility – and thus of impossibility, in the sense that there never is a full, immediate, undivided presence:

> the deconstruction of phenomenology proceeds by treating retention as a non-fullness that infects perception. Thus, because there is no perception without retention, the 'trace' of nonpresence emerges as essential to constitution of perceptual presence. The originarity of the Now is seen as dependent upon the repetition of the not-now. (Staten, 52)

The presence of the perceived present entails continuous reference to a before and after which cannot be presented or perceived. (In a forthcoming work on apologetics, Keenan argues against the rationalist approach of Paul Griffiths, who assumes a homogeneity of human experience, overlooking different patterns of attentiveness and concentrating on the end-product truth claims; in this context, Keenan now agrees that there are no pure experiences, since even the most basic levels are already the product of a limited attentiveness.)

It is important to distinguish two senses of immediacy. There is the abstract notion of 'pure immediacy' – akin to the 'pure intuition' of Kant's *Critique of Pure Reason*, which never exists in abstraction from some categorical framework in which it is embedded. But there is a richer sense of immediacy in which experience is enhanced, and becomes prodigal of concrete intuitions that are in excess of any conceptual or interpretative frameworks brought to bear on them. The work of art as analysed in Kant's third *Critique* is a 'saturated phenomenon' (J.-L. Marion) apprehended in an experience of rich immediacy of this kind. The highest religious experience is marked by a luminous immediacy and is felt as absolute and universal. But even for the Zen master such experience is not to be thought of as a clinically pure immediacy, but rather as a cleansing of the gates of perception, which allows us to see things as they are. It is doubtless true, however, that cultural determinations are far more apparent in the realm of everyday deluded thinking than in those breakthroughs to living vision in which the very structure or perception or cognition seems to be altered.

However, the many objections to pure immediacy do not affect the reality of what one may call pneumatic immediacy, a presencing of spiritual reality that lies before or beyond all conceptual and linguistic constructions. Anne Klein, discussing the direct perception of emptiness in Tibetan Mādhyamika Buddhism, suggests that such immediate experience has a universality that common experience lacks:

All three of these – the absence of a mental image (necessarily the product of one's own unique experience), the mind's not being produced through response to a specific object, and the mind's non-replication of characteristics associated with cognitions that precede and lead up to direct cognition of emptiness – suggest that the usual ways in which experience is particularized no longer operate. Each of these attributes of 'immediate' cognition tends towards a univer-salization of the cognitive experience, even if it does not do away with objections to claims for complete universality. (Klein, 276)

In the immediacy of a cognition of emptiness which is no longer a matter of analytical discriminations, 'cultural and personal conditioning becomes so ephemeral as to be virtually nonexistent' and 'there is no sense that the observing mind is here and the observed emptiness is there' (280). Emptiness 'exists as it appears, and thus no analytical corrective is required' (283). The mind has rejoined its goal and is released from mediations:

Virtually no contemporary Western thinker would take seriously, much less agree with, the notion that conditioned persons can have an experience outside of historical, cultural, psycho-social, and other sets of conditionings... From the Buddhist perspective such a viewpoint is limited and reductionistic in its fascination with condi-tionality. The Buddhist position also emphasizes conditionality but does not subsume all other perspectives to it. For Buddhists, the unconditioned is epistemologically meta to the conditioned – not the other way around. (298)

The experience of emptiness lights up the Buddhist sūtras as the *testi-monium internum Spiritus sancti* lights up the New Testament for the Christian. Such pneumatic immediacy does not succumb to Derrida's critique of the illusion of a pure present from which *différance* would be excluded. A phobic attitude to the *différance* that splits open the self-containment of the present would betray a false notion of contemplative immediacy. Emptiness is not a substance to be contemplated but a dynamic movement of liberation. Similarly, in Christian experience, the presence of the Spirit is lived as repetition of Christ, as actualisation of his kenosis and resurrection, and in prophetic thirst for the eschatological future. It is not posed as the unshakeable foundation of a metaphysics of presence, but rather arises as unpredictable spontaneity making all closure impossible.

A homely analogy can be found in the experience of self-awareness. The self, when it represents itself reflexively, is always already other than itself. It situates itself objectively in the symbolic order, and never succeeds in reconstituting a unitary, primordial self-presence; indeed that ideal is disqualified as a narcissistic lure. Yet consciousness in its intimate immediacy remains a luminous reality, though it be the consciousness of a decentred subject, who is non-self (*anātman*), a being-in-the-world whose selfhood cannot be abstracted from the opening up of world realised in its existential project. This first upsurge of subjectivity, this ineffable element which precedes all objectification, is sometimes invoked as a fortress of individuality against all suggestions that the self is a secondary or derived effect, inscribed in a code. But in clutching at the categories of 'self' and 'individual', one misses the immediacy of consciousness as opening up of world. In its most intimate consciousness the self is already a 'between', 'caught among things' (Merleau-Ponty), stretched out in time, living space as a bodily existence. The self is caught in the maze of *différance*, which is 'older' that any self-constitution of an ego. Yet far from abolishing immediacy, such contextualisation rids subjective consciousness of the metaphysical illusions which have attached to it, and so makes it in a sense more purely immediate.

Similarly, the contextuality of the meaning of religious discourses does not prevent them from being vehicles of a pneumatic immediacy. The Spirit is a 'between': it opens us to a world as real and indubitable as that of sensible perception, and which like the latter can never congeal in pure objectivity, but always bears the hues of the subjectivity that apprehends it. Neither this world nor this subjectivity have a substantial self-nature; their interdependence is the mark of their emptiness. This pneumatic subjectivity remains ours, but elevated and enlarged, freed from the illusion of a fixed identity. The world it opens is equally freed of the illusory substantiality we projected on it and the routines of perception that hid its radiance.

The dimension of Logos depends for its continuing clarity and vitality on an underlying pneumatic consciousness, on 'the spirit of sonship' by which we cry 'Abba! Father!' (Rom. 8:15). When this pneumatic immediacy is replaced by some less appropriate disposition our religious language becomes routine and sounds hollow. Its versatility and flexibility are then degraded into gesticulations which are no longer guided by an instinct of the Spirit. Authentic emptiness (*śūnyatā*) controls by tactful wisdom (*prajñā*) the movements of conventional language. The void of uprootedness, in contrast, makes this control the sole responsibility of critical reason. This predominance of Logos over Spirit, a professional hazard of theologians, causes a forgetfulness against which contemplative theology wages a constant battle, as do Zen and Heidegger. Yet contemplation cannot upstage the essential common theme of all Christian lives, which is faith.

The Spirit is the freedom of Christianity which surpasses all its forms, itself without form or essence: 'Freedom has no essence' (Sartre). The Spirit draws us into a performative hermeneutics, in which we cannot interpret inherited discourses and representations without at the same time reconstructing them and putting ourself in a transferential relation with them. Like Zen kōans, these discourses, if they are to produce pneumatic awakening, require us to play the game they set up. They put us in a double bind: to repeat them lacks meaning, we must alter them without betraying them, actualise them without falling for simulacra. The happy touch this demands is acquired through intimacy with the vital power of the tradition, as accorded by the Spirit.

If the Spirit is seen as the subjectivity of religion, its interiority, it prompts us to seek in the other religions the equivalent dimension, as a human subject is fascinated by the enigma of the other's subjectivity. The dialectical movement of all religious traditions, in their opening to the always greater future, would be a chaotic process if it did not translate a current of life. To ignore this dimension, which gives meaning to the religions, is to treat their adherents as less than fully human. To judge a religion from the outside, without exploring it on the level of intersubjective empathy, is a hermeneutical injustice which no dogmatic certitude can sanction.

We do not really grasp another religious tradition as long as it has not allowed us to enter its intimate dimension. But if the interiority of our own tradition is closed to us most of the time, how much rarer it is to penetrate the secret life of a foreign tradition. If it is at this level of inwardness that religious traditions draw nearest to each other, then 'interreligious dialogue' leads necessarily to the well of contemplation. The perspectivist pluralism which fascinates on the secondary level of ideas and representations yields to the reality of a spiritual world in which the play of perspectives is no longer an affair of shadows and suppositions but the very movement of the real. This 'quiescence of fabrications' (Nāgārjuna) is the final goal of theological reflection, its self-dissolution.

Yet this is a rarefied dimension of encounter, and can be a treacherous short-cut. When two worlds of faith meet, the encounter sets off a critical ferment within each of them. This will lead each to a more radical apprehension of its own most essential inspiration, not only in a contemplative sense, but in terms of basic convictions of faith or of wisdom. At the same time it will force these convictions to be rethought in new terms. In the case of the Christian-Buddhist encounter, the issue is joined at the level of philosophy, for Buddhism puts in question not so much any specific tenet of Christian faith as the dominant philosophical preconceptions with which Christianity has worked. At first sight, indeed, it seems to blast as illusion all our common sense notions about the reality of the world, history and persons and about the stability of logic and language. But I shall argue that in reality Buddhism lights up the authentic texture of these things in a way that can cleanse and clarify Christian discourse. In order to show this we must first take a long detour through some modern Western philosophical sources which anticipate in part what Buddhism has to teach us. Our discussion will be much more a matter of logos than of Spirit, but it may be that in the stretching and breaking to which logos will find itself subjected we may discern a trace of the working of Spirit.

2

DISSEMINATION

As Christian identity is relativised in the pluralistic situation, tensions within the Christian tradition itself are reactivated. A new strategic significance accrues to old fault-lines, especially that friction between Jewish and Greek origins which has been seen as the dialectical driving-force not only of Christianity but of Western civilisation. Metaphysical theology has sought to erase that tension; a subtle strategy of recuperation underlies even the generous, irenic and comprehensive style in which Origen took the Old Testament aboard and established the place of the Jews in the total economy of salvation. As the hold of the classical synthesis loosens, the relation of Christianity to Judaism as well as to its Greek metaphysical components is again becoming an open question.

In a pluralistic culture, the internal pluralism – denominational, cultural, historical and ideological – of Christianity itself can be reappraised in more positive terms. Aware that older styles of Christian vision are each tied to a contingent context, and that none of them can be taken over in its entirety, we can clarify our relationship to them by a hermeneutics that traces their genealogy and by the same token produces their death certificate, thus preventing their ghostly return to confuse the bearings of present debates. This negative clarification goes hand in hand with positive strategies of reappropriation aiming to retrieve the dynamic of faith at work in the formation and dissolution of successive versions of the Christian vision.

HERMENEUTICS AFTER DERRIDA

Derrida counters the metaphysical illusion that sees the meaning of statements as founded on a transcendental logos by turning attention to the

37

dependence of meaning on certain 'quasi-transcendental infrastructures' which are themselves quite foreign to the register of meaning. He attempts to show that every statement finds itself enframed, staged, exceeded by the complex web of language which, far from guaranteeing a stable foundation, undermines the apparent stability of meanings by inscribing them in a general context of non-originarity, of irreducible secondariness. Thus meaning is from the start alienated from itself, referred to otherness, by this law of its inscription. It can never be recollected in the purity of an origin or *telos*. An effect of meaning on the first, immediate level takes place in every act of thinking or writing. But this effect remains provisional, conventional, vulnerable. It is when one speaks of meaning reflexively, on a second level, convinced of its inevitability, that the logocentric mystification slips in, for now one is reifying or absolutising something that has only a relative or functional validity. The idea of dissemination is not opposed to meaning, reference or truth in their first and ordinary reality, but only to the metaphysical myths which attach themselves to this in a parasitical way and which seek to confer on it an illegitimate stability.

Every use of signs and every attempt to interpret them has the status of a strategic intervention within the linguistic network, a throw of the dice whose results elude the control of the user of the signs, and which is exposed not only to ulterior revisions but to the possibility of finding itself bereft of all meaning. Writing is no longer a transparent presentation of ideas, for inscription subjects every concept to the murk and indeterminacy attached to the usage of signifying marks. Nor is reading simply the apprehension of meaning; the reader participates in the play of the marks, a play which cannot be recalled without residue to the register of meaning. 'Writing is read, and does not give rise "in the last analysis" to a hermeneutic deciphering, to the decoding of a meaning or truth' (*M*, 329). The reader cannot grasp the meaning of the text as a totality or recover its original purity, for this meaning was never set up as a united whole to begin with. In its initial formulation it was already pluralised, since every element designed to convey it was already caught up in the play of signifiers, each jostling and contaminating the others in constant semantic slippage.

This infrastructural system of differences, or *différance* – which both enables the constitution of meaning and keeps it from being complete or definitive – cannot itself be made transparent in terms of meaning. It does not give itself to be thought, for then it would fall back into the regime of the concept, which it intrinsically exceeds. Even if any particular naming of the infrastructures is recoverable by philosophy, there is always a residue which escapes this naming, an irreducible margin which is the ghost of otherness at the heart of the same. Derrida is always inventing new strategies of writing that can allow this margin to make itself felt and to come fully into play.

Dissemination forces thought to renounce ideals of ultimate unity, and to accept gaps and (quasi-typographical) blanks that can never be made to disappear. This heterogeneity lies beyond polysemy:

> Polysemy always puts out its multiplicities and variations within the *horizon*, at least, of some integral reading which contains no absolute rift, no senseless deviation – the horizon of the final parousia of a meaning at last deciphered, revealed, made present in the rich collection of its determinations. (*D*, 350)

Meaning is irremediably knit together with non-meaning. 'All the moments of polysemy are, as the word implies, moments of meaning'; the difference between this and dissemination, in which the spacing of the marks bears no assignable meaning, is 'implacable' although 'very slight' (350f).

It is not only for his overcoming of metaphysics but above all as a thinker of 'otherness' that Derrida is attractive to theologians, who themselves are concerned with the otherness of the biblical God. His constant effort to resist the totalising thinking he calls logocentrism makes his thought a structure of openness to an other over which it relinquishes mastery. If deconstruction unmoors fixed meanings, it is in order to allow this unsettling otherness to emerge. Yet, against Levinas, he insists that there is no pure otherness, no face of God uncontaminated by being. The various deconstructive openings to otherness are sorties towards an originary 'space', the 'place' of the entirely other, or 'the non-place or *non-lieu* which would be the "other" of philosophy' (Derrida, in Kearney, 112) and from which Western identity can be put in question. There are three main avenues to this non-place in Derrida's work. 1. By commentary on thinkers of otherness such as Freud, Heidegger and Levinas, he seeks to espouse the dynamics of their thought, freeing it from the metaphysical obstacles that impede the desired opening to the other. 2. By a style of writing which is increasingly porous to otherness, he cultivates vulnerability to a kind of circumcision by which the other inscribes itself in the discourse of the same. 3. By a formal reflection on the origin of all language and concept-construction, Derrida uncovers a difference older than being, an originary structure of supplementarity which is the condition of all presence but which contaminates the purity of that presence, making it dependent on the non-present.

This last is the most ambitious aspect of his thought, where it rivals

Hegel, Heidegger and Levinas in constructing the equivalent of a *philosophia prima*. Disciples with a penchant for formalisation, such as Rodolphe Gasché and Geoffrey Bennington, give a systematic cast to this reflection on general laws of otherness inscribed in the very texture of language. But the 'invention of the other' is less well secured by such logical laws than by writerly practice which in specific instances unravels philosophical monoliths to allow the emergence of the otherness they repress. Archi-writing and *différance* have a deadening effect when grasped as supreme grammatological principles; better to take them as heuristic strategies for lighting up concrete semantic effects. In each case the instability of a meaning is the particular story of that particular construction of meaning. It is not that all constructions of meaning invariably run up against the same disqualifying barrier.

In comparison with the otherness of Heidegger's Being, Levinas's Infinity, a Pseudo-Dionysian God beyond being, or the Freudian unconscious, the otherness that guides the writing of Derrida is rather indeterminate, and risks vacuity, when presented as a general principle. When he suggests that *différance* embraces all previous glimpses of otherness and reduces them to a single principle – the process which makes possible all the differences there are – this speculative claim may work against a true experience of pluralism. The law of *différance* is indeed claimed to be itself thoroughly heterogeneous, and thus irreducible to any notion of principle or origin. But this only makes it all the easier to show *différance* at work in every text studied, thus creating parallels between the most diverse sources at the expense of their singular identity. However, the present work is not the place to study or to emulate the detailed texture of Derridian readings. Instead, we attempt to move from a template of general deconstructive notions to the invention of reading strategies suited to the targets of theological hermeneutics.

Though Derrida speaks of it as abyssal and monstrous, dissemination, viewed from another angle, appears as a regulated process, close to the 'continuous series of transitions' between Wittgensteinian family resemblances (*Philosophical Investigations* 161). Reading and writing may no longer be reducible to conceptual transparency, but they have not thereby become absolutely random activities. Their play is more complex, demanding constant alertness, something of the tight-rope sensitivity that Mallarmé and Joyce found necessary in their dealing with words. In 1966 'Derrida was already defining "play" not as unlimited polysemy, but as a kind of "looseness" in the relations between the elements of a given structure' (C. Johnson, 203). His distinction between 'two interpretations of interpretation' – a recuperative one which 'dreams of deciphering a truth

or an origin which escapes play and the order of the sign' and a disseminative one which 'affirms play' and tries to pass beyond man and humanism
('the name of man being the name of that being who, throughout the
history of metaphysics or of ontotheology – in other words, throughout
his entire history – has dreamed of full presence, the reassuring foundation, the origin and the end of play' [WD, 292]) – does not imply a one-sided
option for the Nietzschean pole, but stresses the play of *différance*
between the two poles.

True, dissemination thrives on a Joycean sense of the sheer conventionality of language: when we agree to write standard English or French,
we are subscribing provisionally to a useful convention, but nothing
prevents us from altering the rules of the game at any time. Dissemination
is another name for this precariousness of linguistic arrangements. But a
sheerly meaningless babble would not be an interesting illustration of it.
It shows up in precisely inflected departures from what seemed a settled
norm, symptomatic stumblings, which prompt thought by their subversive relation to the expectations they transgress. In theology, too, when
statements or terms are experienced as labile or indeterminate, this does
not mean that randomness has taken over. Analysis may illuminate the
particular infrastructural determinations of this slippage, perhaps even
seeing it as part of an epochal shift in the functioning of theological signs.

To make a sudden leap from determinate meaning to general indetermination is to lose contact with the pluralist texture of meaning, courting
instead mythic notions of chaos, flux, abyss, drift, delirium. Those who
use deconstruction as an ideology, rather than a method for clarifying the
processes by which meaning emerges, reduce dissemination to a pattern
mechanically imposed on the data, which in turn are reduced to indifferent flux. Finding *différance* everywhere, their Midas touch reduces all
meaning-effects to mere epiphenomena, accidents thrown up by the production of traces. They may work with a quasi-Kantian hylemorphism,
in which the mind projects its forms on the chaos of pure intuition:

> To put it brutally, there *is* no ready-ordered objective reality any
> more: there is only the flux of becoming, and the continuing ever-
> changing human attempt to imagine and impose order. We have to
> *make* sense; *we* have to turn chaos into cosmos ... There is not any
> Reality or Truth in the old sense; there are only the endlessly varied
> visions and values that human beings project upon the flux in order
> to give their lives a kind of meaning. (Don Cupitt, in Banner, 3)

This cult of flux falls into a sameness and self-enclosure which are themselves impervious to further deconstruction.

Dissemination, as I understand it, is not simply another name for the flux of becoming. It is rather a method for making sense of pluralism, by discerning its conditions of possibility and its inherent order. It does not celebrate 'freeplay' but articulates the play (*jeu*) of meaning. If we trace the precise contours of the dissemination-effect in individual instances, then in each case it lights up the event-quality of the idea or text analysed. A deconstructed poem should be more luminously itself, whereas in most deconstructive readings the poem dissolves into colourless scribbling. In addition to its negative impact as undermining the illusory stability of meanings, archi-writing also has a positive role as the condition of possibility of meaning, a meaning freed from unnecessary ontological ties and which, like the rose of Angelus Silesius, is no longer self-regarding. Thus deconstructive readings can allow the meaning of a text to breathe freely, to blossom in its instability, no longer constrained by an overarching metaphysical design.

If every enunciation of meaning is in dependence on a play of traces that no effort of justificatory reflection can master, then meaning is bereft of any proper substantiality: its texture is marked by a certain emptiness. To accept this emptiness comes as a release – of the sort Wittgenstein was aiming at – a reconciliation with the authentic, finite, fragile texture of our signifying activities. 'It is within the general field of writing thus defined that the effects of semantic communication can be determined as effects that are particular, secondary, inscribed, supplementary' (*M*, 311). This secondarisation, far from destroying all meaning, spells a liberation of meaning, in that it allows our statements to be content with making sense, here and now, within the limits of their eminently provisional contexts, without seeking to assure for themselves a foundation in some autonomous logos. Such acceptance of the brokenness of meaning puts us back into contact with the real, for the drift or slippage which insinuates itself into every formulation of meaning is related to an exteriority, to an anterior otherness, a real which causes all concepts and formulations to tremble but from which they also derive whatever validity they have.

The import of dissemination can be clarified by reflection on the notion of context or contextuality, which has played a great role in theological hermeneutics (*Sitz im Leben*, etc.). Every significant expression supposes a context which makes its meaning clear. A signifier does not refer immediately to a thing-in-itself but is produced in dependence on an illimitable number of other signifiers. This dependency, which exposes the signifier to indetermination and corrodes from within its claim to univocity, is the necessary condition of its capacity to signify anything at all. Thus every articulation of meaning is a fragile performance, always attended by the possibility of subversion. All of this is close to the Wittgensteinian insight that 'the meaning of a sign is always dispersed across the sequence of elements that constitute the sign situation' (Staten, 80).

Context is never simply accessory or exterior to meaning, for meaning depends on context for its determination and disambiguation at every moment. This determination is never furnished in a fully satisfying way. What is more, the very notion of context remains vague. 'No meaning can be determined out of context, but no context permits saturation' ('Living On', 81). 'A context is never absolutely determinable . . . its determination is never certain or saturated' (*M*, 310). Thus context stabilises meaning only in destabilising it, for in seeking to determine meaning from context we refer it to a range of new sources of indetermination.

Meaning depends on context, and context is caught in a process of *différance* which keeps it from closing on itself. But with this dependence of meaning is associated an autonomy of the signifier. 'A written sign carries with it a force of breaking with its context . . . No context can enclose it' (*M*, 317). 'It can break with every given context, and engender infinitely new contexts in an absolutely nonsaturable fashion' (*M*, 320). It is this effect above all which makes possible 'the subtraction of all writing from the semantic horizon or the hermeneutic horizon which, at least as a horizon of meaning, lets itself be punctured by writing' (*M*, 316). Every sign, in principle, denies and surpasses the context in which it is inserted. This 'work of the negative' is no longer Hegelian, for it is no longer 'in the service of meaning' (*M*, 317). If I say 'the sky is blue', this expression has the capability of 'functioning as an empty reference, or cut off from its referent' (*M*, 318f). It communicates an intelligible message in a particular context, but outside of this context it signifies only a possibility of meaning. Moreover, in its brute materiality as a collection of letters it signifies nothing at all, it is no more than a mark. This materiality of the iterable mark is the condition of every use of a signifier, which prevents it from being purely transparent to the signification that it carries. It is by this relation with the materiality of the mark that every statement is caught in the play of textuality, which offers no ideal extra-contextual place where meaning can be articulated irreducibly, but rather exposes every formulation to the risks of iterability and *différance*.

Theology often works with a reassuring notion of context as a well-rounded horizon, an island of stability in the flux of history. It seeks to link these horizons in an encyclopaedic panorama or in dialogal exchanges. But the indetermination of every context means that such hermeneutic horizons cannot be defined in a stable way. The projection of a stable horizon is but the provisional arrest of an incessant drift, though the illusion of stability inevitably continues to reinstate itself both in everyday life and in historical study. One might object that contexts are often clear enough to render otiose continued puzzling about the meaning of an expression and that historical horizons are often so well-defined that the historian can identify clearly their major preoccupations and possibilities of thought. Derrida does not directly attack the stability of meaning at this level; he questions its borders, the protocols of its definition, in order to make felt its intimate dependence on certain conditions repressed from memory. The production of meaning proceeds as before, but a step back now becomes practicable, which makes more precise and vivid what had been only a vague consciousness of the fragility of this performance.

Take the expression, 'God created the world'. What does 'world' mean? The answer seems obvious: it is that which I have before my eyes. The context is empirical, and immediately accessible at any time. This is sufficient anchorage to give a stable meaning to the expression 'world', but not to protect it against all destabilisation. If we seek to define the extent of this 'world' we find ourselves obliged to have recourse to other expressions: 'the universe', 'all that is, except the supreme being'. These expressions, which are no longer empirical, show themselves in turn to be more difficult to clarify and render unambiguous. To define 'world' one can consult the various ways of constructing the world developed in different religions and philosophies. What this reveals is that the notion of 'world' implied in 'God created the world' is idiosyncratic, an invention of biblical discourse and sharing the pluralism that marks that discourse in its historical variations and its intertextual relations. It appears that 'the word "world" would have no literal meaning at all, but would be metaphorical, all the way down' (M. Gaipa and R. Scholes, in Davenstock, 178). The plasticity of metaphor is noted by Emerson:

> There is no word in our language that cannot become typical to us of Nature by giving it emphasis. The world is a Dancer; it is a Rosary; it is a Torrent; it is a Boat; a Mist; a Spider's Snare; it is what you will; and the metaphor will hold, and it will give the imagination keen pleasure. Swifter than light the world converts itself into that thing you name, and all things find their right place under this new and capricious classification. (in Bloom, 119)

Religions are such metaphorical constructs, which are unaware of the repressed fluidity of the imaginings they have canonised. They are ways of naming the world by an imaginative leap and then ordering all perception in light of the metaphor constructed. Religious renewal comes with the re-naming of world, humanity and divinity in some more spacious and liberating style, instead of continuing to choke on dead metaphors.

We are still seeking a religious naming of world that would be commensurate with the enlarged cosmos of our astronomy and biology and the subtle apprehensions of being-in-the-world in phenomenology and modernist literature. Such a naming requires that religious thought recognise the obsolescence of inherited frameworks and immerse itself in these contemporary experiences of world – a process of acculturation that may take centuries to complete.

If so unproblematic an expression as 'world' turns out to be so vulnerable to destabilisation, the situation is worse for an expression as mysterious as 'God'. Even more than other signifiers, 'God' lends itself to the endless slippage of meaning in successive contexts. This is not to say that God is dissolved in an indeterminacy which would amount to a soft form of his 'death'. The slidings of the meaning of 'God' give rise to a series of precise determinations, a significant history. In the case of common things: 'Comprehensive knowledge of the reference would require us to be able to say immediately whether any given sense belongs to it. To such knowledge we never attain' (Frege, in Moore, 24f). In the case of God the ascription of sense becomes much more controversial, and the senses themselves are much less easy to define. 'The first mover' and 'my Creator' have different senses, but the same referent, God. But the two modes of presentation seem to conflict, situating God in qualitatively different horizons. Should one drop the philosophical senses in favour or the religious ones, or vice versa? If the two are retained, must one be given a lower status than the other, as referring to God less properly or directly?

Is there any sense of 'God' that lies beyond this tension between philosophical and religious modes of presentation? If there is not, then every sense one attributes to 'God' involves a decision, a partisan choice. The referentiality of 'God' can never be automatic, but depends on prior options at the level of sense. Many of the senses supposed to pick out the referent God may be so at odds with the reality of God as not to succeed in referring to God at all. Of course this failure in sense can be patched up by treating the expressions used as metaphorical, and ascribing to the user an intention to refer to God. Following this generous hermeneutics, even a statement such as 'God is three ounces of pepper' could be taken as an expression of Zen enlightenment, or construed as a blasphemous reference.

Serious, canonical ways of speaking about God are distinguished from such untamed use of the word 'God' not by any foolproof distinction between proper and improper, but by a decision which remains to some degree arbitrary. Approved speech about God is that fashioned by a long tradition, and even within both branches of that tradition – the biblical and the philosophical – there is ample room for unfitting or irreverent uses of the word; the philosophical side is always suspicious of theological diction, and vice versa. The constant labour to fashion suitable ways of speaking of God binds itself to the best rules it can devise (fidelity to reason on the one hand, and to the integrity of the biblical witness on the other), but the entire project remains a flimsy arrangement, a clumsy courtship of the inscrutable.

Statements about 'God' need to be interrogated on the levels of meaning, sense and reference before we can pose the question 'true or false'. To what do we effectively refer when we use the word 'God'? That depends on the sense or senses whereby the word is defined; and the sense cannot be cleanly abstracted from the mobile play of meaning that surrounds our everyday use of the word. The effort to separate meaning and sense cleanly has little success in this context. Fregean 'sense' is abstracted from the wider, vaguer 'meaning' of a term; this penumbra of meaning is only an 'associated idea' or 'internal image' which cannot be an essential part of the sense. Meaning is subjective and differs for each individual, but sense is objective and universal. The sense of an expression is 'that ingredient of its meaning which is relevant to the determination as true or false of a sentence in which it occurs' (M. Dummett, in Moore, 233).

The variability of sense and meaning of the term 'God' is the surface manifestation of the infrastructural adventures of this mark. In its iterations in the current epoch, whether in a conservative or subversive style, the mark often functions as an unmeaning x, so that sentences such as 'God made the world' are grasped only as a recycling of past concatenations of marks, as citations bereft of immediate present sense. Iteration implies that there are no pure statements about God; such statements have a shifting margin of significance, depending on which other terms resonate with the term 'God'. It follows that there are no statements about God that are true once and for all. The dissemination of God-language implies an inbuilt undecidability in its reference, which can be allayed only through critical cultivation of the traditions of usage which keep religious language oriented to that which it cannot definitively name or conceive.

DECONSTRUCTION AND ANALYTICAL PHILOSOPHY

The heirs of Frege may say that our reflections on dissemination are valid only for the vague, ill-defined meanings which circulate in everyday speech, or for the subjective apprehension of a sense rather than its objective content. But can the border between objective sense (*Sinn*) and subjective representation (*Vorstellung*) be made as foolproof as Frege prescribes? There is a wider context to these differentiations which limits their bearing. The Fregean distinctions offer an elegant grammar of thought, but one that does not perfectly coincide with thought's actual processes, so that it needs to be supplemented by a Wittgensteinian and Derridian mapping of margins; margins which threaten to subvert the Fregean quest for order. Against Frege's insistence on clearly defined concepts, Wittgenstein (*Philosophical Investigations 71*) advances the claims of the fluid concepts which are the stuff of ordinary language (and therefore of religious language). Such concepts are picked up in practical use. For instance, we know what a 'game' is without being able to define it. There is a necessary core of blindness to our use of any concept, which no amount of clarification can completely reduce; yet our language games work quite adequately despite the contingency of their arrangements and the shifting denotation of the counters we employ. Conceptual clarification remains an imperative of the logical and scientific mind; yet the institution of the cleanly defined concept has an irreducible element of arbitrariness at its base. It is only as the quest for clarity is relentlessly pursued that this foundational instability is more lucidly grasped.

Raising a secondary demand for clarity to the supreme criterion of rationality, Fregean analysis risks cutting itself off from the wider reality within which clear and distinct ideas can cut only the most provisional of clearings.

> If the 'undecidedness' of the frontier between the philosophical and the poetical is what most prompts philosophy to think, as Derrida asserts in *Schibboleth*, then one must say that the philosophy which draws its inspiration more or less directly from Frege is the one which tries most firmly to refuse thinking. (G. Bennington, in Mallet, 72)

Analytical philosophers also admit that utterances occur only in a context which they cannot master, so that 'in the traditional Fregean sense according to which a concept is a kind of pure crystalline entity that allows for no marginal cases, there simply cannot be any such concepts' (Searle, 642).

Derrida's contextualism is at the antipodes from the thesis of the context-independence of sense propounded by Michael Dummett:

> The sense of a word cannot vary from context to context, but is a property of the word itself, apart from any context: for it is by knowing the sense of the constituent words, independently of their occurrence in *this* sentence, that we understand the sentence. If the sense of a word varied from context to context, this would have to

be according to some general rule, if we were to understand the sentences in which it occurs: and then this general rule would in reality constitute the *one* common sense which the word possessed. (Dummett 1981a, 268)

Derrida would say there is a constant slippage of sense from context to context, and that it is impossible to isolate one sense as 'the' intrinsic sense of the word: dictionary definitions are imprecise descriptive résumés of usage or arbitrary prescriptive attempts to arrest the slippage. The variation in sense slips at times over into outright ambiguity. But at what point this occurs cannot be decided in a foolproof way. If 'God' for one person refers to a primordial world-breath and for another to the transcendent biblical God, are we dealing with a slippage in sense (both senses having perhaps the same reference, God) or with a radical ambiguity (two quite different things being referred to by the same word)?

Derrida tends to argue from the shifting character of meaning to the undecidability of the reference of a given expression. Frege would counter that pluralism at the level of sense does not necessarily entail undecidability at the level of reference: 'morning star' and 'evening star' have different senses but the same referent, different connotations but the same denotation; they designate different modes of presentation of the same referent (Frege, in Moore, 24). There is no problem about referring to the planet in question, though each of the alternative descriptions under which we refer to it cuts out a slightly different concept. We cannot define the planet independently of the various alternative descriptions. Nonetheless, we can be sure that they all refer to the same thing, making communication between them very easy.

But, Derrida might reply, even when identity of reference seems obvious, as in the case of morning star and evening star, there is room for undecidability to seep in with a change of viewpoint. If a poet in some astronomically uninformed age wrote two poems, one on the morning star, and another on the evening star, would it be correct to say that the two poems had the same referent? Perhaps it is only by confining attention to one aspect of the meaning of morning star – i.e. its aspect as a physical substance – that one can truly identify it with the evening star. If one picked out as the essential thing another aspect – e.g. its role as an emblem of Venus – its physical identity with the evening star might appear as a tasteless irrelevance.

Reference is always a blind leap, for we do not have the reference independently of the terms denoting it. Derrida reveals that these terms themselves (the 'sense') imply a blind leap, for we never know what the full implications of any expression may be, even at the level of its sense and independently of the obscurity of its referential *fundamentum in re*. Sense is no longer a pure eidos - a clear view. To signify is as risky as to denote. The analogical nature of religious language makes its reference even more a blind leap; it is sustained by the intention of prayer reaching out in the darkness. To speak of the objective reference of the term 'God' does not imply that one is 'objectifying' God, but that the term, however inadequate, can work in given contexts to effect an objective reference to transcendent reality.

Some analytical philosophers stress the inseparability of meaning from use. A word or even a proposition has no pure literal meaning on itself, but receives its precise meaning from the use to which it is put or the question (in the case of a proposition) which it serves to answer. 'If what Davidson calls "use" is, as we claim, already present in the determination of what he calls "literal" meaning, then we must entertain the possibility that use goes all the way down' (Gaipa and Scholes, in Davenstock, 168). Dissemination can be grasped as consisting in part in 'the constant pressure of use upon meaning' (178), or of the metaphorical upon the literal, or of the context upon individual utterance. None of these pressures are purely random; they are grounded in the interplay between the web of our linguistic constructions and the reality which these attempt to explore and grasp.

The basic principle of dissemination is close to Wittgenstein's and Peirce's view that understanding signs consists in translating them into other signs, a process that never comes to an end:

> To interpret a sign, in Wittgenstein's sense, is simply to *translate* it into another sign; and translation cannot by itself determine meaning or understanding, since the sign into which the translation is made must itself be understood or meant in a particular way. At some point understanding must break out of the circle of signs.

Wittgenstein does not break out of the circle by establishing 'privileged signs which *terminate* questions of meaning – special signs which are such that if translation is made into *them* then meaning is determined' (McGinn, 117f). He warns against the hypostasisation of 'meaning':

> When the scene of language is unfolded the word *meaning* appears there as one word among others, and there is nothing left over besides this appearance ... The term meaning is just another member of the set 'language', although it does play a special role because it is language about language. This 'reflexive' character of the term is what gives rise to the illusion that it has a different or higher character than other terms ... Citation is the means by which language

becomes the object of language, without thereby acquiring depth distinct from a surface but only a new articulation of the surface. (Staten, 87f)

The term 'meaning' is always cashed in local clarifications and cannot be given a universal, transcendental sweep. However, is the question of 'meaning' so easily tidied up? Is there not an element of reductive naturalism in this account?

Wittgenstein is tempted to repose in everyday unreflective linguistic use as a means of bringing the play of dissemination to a halt. He might well regard Derrida's constant puzzling about the slippages of meaning as typically misguided philosophical intellectualism. Yet naturalistic appeals to ordinary language can only be an arbitrary and provisional arrest of the play of signifiers, if only because ordinary language itself is constantly changing. It might be claimed that in mathematics or science a process of translation is possible whereby imprecise signifiers are reduced to the terms of the canonical scientific terminology. But is that terminology ever definitely established? Be that as it may, in the field of religion there is much plausibility in the notion that understanding consists in a process of constant translation which never comes to a halt in the finally correct language. Whether we try to translate the imprecise language of faith into an abstruse and scientific theological terminology, or whether, reversing this process, we try to recall theological terminology to its roots in the primary language of faith, the end-point in both cases lacks the desired stability.

THE DISSEMINATION OF SCRIPTURE

To ideals of semantic coherence, Derrida opposes the 'seminal', which 'disseminates itself without ever having *been* itself and without coming back to itself' (D, 351). We might view the words of Scripture, too, as disseminated from their origin. Their seminal density is in proportion to the impossibility of fixing their single proper meaning.

A theology seeking to found itself on a pure Word-event is undermined when one becomes aware that every attempt to formulate the alleged original meaning has the character of a supplement, which obeys 'the general law of textual supplementarity through which all proper meanings are dislocated' (D, 254). One could regard the Word-event as a transcendental happening, to which the biblical writings bear broken, imperfect witness, but which itself remains uncompromised by this brokenness. That is a somewhat abstract consideration, operative only as a regulative idea. For in practice theology cannot remedy the brokenness of Scripture, thinking back to the Word-event in its purity. Its only recourse is to espouse the disseminated condition of Scripture, dwelling in it reflexively and taking its cues from it.

Classically, the drift and slippage in the interpretation of Scripture was controlled by a hierarchical ordering of its senses, which prevented the endlessness of interpretation from becoming a Hegelian 'bad infinite' and made it instead a reflection of the infinity of God. This fruitful myth needs to be rethought. Medieval exegesis was a step forward in the history of hermeneutics only within a narrow metaphysical sphere; it brushed aside a range of sharper hermeneutical problems that surface when the materiality of the text, its muddy opacity and ambiguity as a set of marks notched at different historical moments, is fully faced.

If the biblical text grows with its readers, *aliquo modo cum legentibus crescit* (Gregory the Great, *Moralia in Job* 20:1), that growth is not only in the direction of metaphysical and spiritual depth. As study of Scripture stumbles on the opacity of the text, the biblical world rears itself to its full stature, as another world, culturally and historically remote, a world that is past, and the readers understand that their world in turn is exiled from the biblical horizons, that it is an independent project to be lived out with only oblique guidance from the biblical constructions of worldhood. Such historical and textual alertness no longer builds higher stages on the literal sense, but allows this sense to show itself in its disturbing alienness and indeterminacy. To make sense of the text is no longer to subject its plurality of meanings to a grand metaphysical design, but rather to grasp a history, to see the formation and reception of the Bible as a tangled, errant human adventure. It is only through immersion in this history, in a critical struggle to retrieve its legacy, that one begins to glimpse its spiritual sense: the fact that the Spirit has used and still uses this vessel of clay. If the Spirit is inseparable from the Word, this means that it is tied to the endless Talmudic play of linguistic interpretation. Yet within this history, every so often, one may turn a corner, stumble on a new perspective, which suddenly lights up the pneumatic sense of the entire enterprise.

The imposition of a metaphysical pattern is not the only strategy for controlling the drift and slippage of biblical textuality. The effort to fix the precise literal sense of the texts is an equally defensive manoeuvre. Indeed the very idea of the literal sense is a metaphysical construction, forcing sense into a logocentric unity, totality and originariness. The quest for the literal sense always takes place within a horizon that prescribes its function. The *sensus litteralis* of medieval exegesis was shaped by its relation to the spiritual sense. If one seeks to overcome such stylisation of the Letter by a dogged quest for the *hebraica veritas*, this strategy in turn is dictated by a specific situation, and changes with the perspective of the interpreter. One never closes in on the literal sense, for each sentence of the text carries fragmentary allusions to a wider context. If we fill out the picture these allusions suggest, we inevitably draw on our own horizons to do so. If we try to lop away the allusions, we create a positivist reading of the text which is again our own construct. The quest for the factual, historical sense is integral to the critical reception of Scripture, but it is itself so varying and mobile that it confirms the disseminative character of both text and reception.

Because of the authority ascribed to it, the biblical text has been a site of intensive interpretative activity during its long gestation and in the subsequent controversies between three religions and between innumerable schools of thought within these religions. Its claim of immediate practical and existential bearing has made it a 'hot' text, one that is not merely read, but that reads its readers, sounding the secrets of their hearts. Divorced from this existential function it would no longer be the same text, but just a piece of ancient literature posing desultory puzzles. In practice, the existential weight of the text is uneven, and at a given time only some parts have live import, while others are esteemed merely as background lore. The breakdown of the allegorical machinery has consigned many parts of Scripture to this relative insignificance. Many perspectives which opened up luminously in the past have lost their relevance or become an embarrassment, while new hermeneutic approaches have brought neglected aspects to the fore. In a liturgical setting, even the remotest parts of Scripture may acquire a semblance of religious relevance; but this is a matter of metaphorical association rather than of sustained reading.

Many other great texts which have formed humanity have a grip on us that prevents us from wandering about in them indifferently, for they seem to light up the intimate pathways of our own minds, formed by the tradition of these texts. The Bible however demonstrates its power by its resistance to such identifications.

> To read is to be *in* the text, but it is not a matter of establishing one's domicile there. For Derrida, the reader's 'belonging' to the text is inseparable from the idea of a textual labyrinth. To belong to a text means to wander in it endlessly. In this errance, irreducible to the paths of *Erinnerung*, we learn that we are surrounded by 'a text extending far out of sight' (D, 203)... The textuality of the text acquires a dimension of *unhomeliness* which no appeal to hermeneutic intimacy can suppress. (Greisch, 188f)

The Bible unsettles us not by the imposition of an univocal meaning on our life, but by unforeseen solicitations which make of our belonging to it a dangerous adventure. Instead of giving us a meaning it disseminates us, situates us in unexpected ways in its discourse, now as sinners, now as righteous. A book claiming divine authority has so strategically inserted itself in our life, at the level of the deepest anxieties and hopes, that even centuries of tenacious unbelief cannot dislodge it from its key position and make it again an ordinary book. The interpretation of great literature is interminable to the same extent as is the interpretation of human life. The interpretation of Scripture implies articulating a divine judgement on human life; far from spelling a termination of the process of interpretation, this judgemental impact lends it deeper urgency and increased capacity for surprising turns and shifts.

This hermeneutical situation is further enhanced by the phenomenon of intertextuality. 'One text reads another... Each "text" is a machine with multiple reading heads for other texts' ('Living On', 107). Far from preserving an impossible purity, the Word of God makes itself known only in the infinite intertextual relations in which the biblical text is entirely caught. For what Harold Bloom remarks of texts in general applies with special force to Scripture:

> A single text has only part of a meaning; it is itself a synecdoche for a larger whole including other texts. A text is a relational event, and not a substance to be analyzed ... There are no right readings, because reading a text is necessarily the reading of a whole system of texts, and meaning is always wandering around between texts. (Bloom, 106ff)

The biblical text, in making its authority respected, is set up as a commentary on all other literature. But in return that literature can be seen as harbouring an implicit reading of the Bible, an unending reading, which no fixed frontier separates from the biblical text. The intertextual condition of its founding document thus prevents Christian theology from being a one-way discourse, a *Glaubenslehre* subordinating non-Christian and secular categories to the unfolding of biblical vision. This vision is inflected from the start by those extraneous categories, and their role in every subsequent reinterpretation of the biblical text cannot be suppressed. Thus a theology true to the Bible is obliged to be a relational event, a dialogue. If the Bible retains a certain authoritative primacy in regard to all other texts, it does to, paradoxically, only by exposing itself fully to the critique these other texts direct at it. The more its finite, fragmented status is shown up, the more the specificity of its witness can emerge.

A one-sided application of the notion of intertextuality can lead to a kind of biblical imperialism:

> If we remember that the Bible defines the world in which these other texts are written, heard, and read, then we must read these

religions in the context of the Bible, and reread the Bible with these religions and their texts as part of its context. Indeed, this biblical starting point dismisses the idea that there is anything 'outside' Christianity. If the Bible constitutes the world, this is a world which has no outside, no place beyond it. From the start, the non-Christian is already *within* the Christian, biblical world. (F. X. Clooney, in D'Costa, 68)

If the Bible is caught in the world, and cannot be isolated from a world that would be outside-the-text, then this must mean that it has no truth independent of its insertion in the worldly context and intertextual play which it cannot master. The fact that every text reads the whole world and every other text – with a force of reading which varies from one text to another – in itself confers no special status on the biblical texts. The Bible's authority as a vehicle of Spirit emerges, obscurely enough, in the actual dialogal interplay with other texts. These texts are not 'within' the biblical text, or if they are it is in a sense that does not prevent them from being equally 'outside' it, and it is this exteriority that cracks open the biblical world and opens up new lines of vital intertextual play. The Bible guides a Christian reading of the world, but one so mobile and complex that it cannot congeal into fixed dogmatic judgement, for it is itself constantly changing in response to that which it reads.

The Bible is also subject, in an exemplary way, to the condition of citationality. For Derrida, 'citationality' is a transcendental condition of all language; it is not reducible to literal quotation, or the 'mention' as opposed to the 'use' of a text or expression. It contaminates discourse at its root, undermining clear distinctions between the authentic and parasitical, direct and citational, use and mention. Derrida rejects the commonsense view that the latter member of each of these pairs is logically dependent on the former, pointing out that the former depends on the possibility of the latter. The parasitical is never simply external but affects the proper, and gives it a differential character from the start. This interdependence, or structure of mutual enveloping, is a recurrent feature of Derrida's logic.

The use of the Bible is pervaded by a palpable citationality. It is used by being mentioned, and has its power from the quotation marks with which it comes invisibly attired. Outside the performative function in which it is cited as a canonical text and as a word of saving power it is no longer the same text. True, it was as inspired texts that the biblical books were received in the canon (Vatican I, *Dei Filius*), but one can suppose that this inspired character emerged simultaneously with their performative use, even on the level of individual psalms or parables, before their insertion into a book of the Bible. Canonicity is the citation of the whole

Bible by the Church, a citation which transforms its meaning. The Bible is between quotation marks, and 'once quotation marks demand to appear, they don't know where to stop' ('Living On', 76). If I cite a biblical text – 'Love one another' or 'The just lives by faith' – what I am putting forward is already a citation of a citation: I cite this text only because it is always already cited, not only in virtue of the long history in which it has always figured as a hallowed quotation, but in virtue of its status as a canonical text. Even if one went out of one's way to quote a biblical passage that no one had ever quoted before, the very fact of citing it as biblical entails a doubling which disjoins the text from itself. One could cite it as just a piece of Hebrew literature, but the strain involved in such an exercise, which seems a violent twisting, indicates the degree in which the Bible's citational condition, its existence within quotation marks, has become its natural element. Even theologians who contest the sacred status of some biblical text, or exegetes who examine it in a drily empirical way, find themselves at every step overshadowed by the awareness that what they are dealing with is a quoted text, and that it is only by a fiction that they pretend to ignore the quotation marks which have seized on the object of their study. Canonisation has placed the text between quotation marks and positivist exegesis seeks to put these quotation marks between parentheses, under the pretext of an (impossible) return to a virgin text.

The canonised text is thus rich in echoes. But the sounding-box which is the believing community preserves these echoes from unlimited dispersion. Perhaps every classic text forms about it a circle of readers and users who somehow arrest its dissemination. Literary criticism is the art of reaping the resonances of such texts, so that they are not drowned out by the white noise created by endless intertextual drifting. To preserve the eventhood of reading and preaching, one must resist the tendency of deconstruction to reduce the event to an insignificant play of traces and to suspect:

> the eventhood of an event which supposes in its allegedly present and singular emergence the intervention of a statement which in itself can be only of a repetitive and citational structure, or rather, since those two words may lead to confusion: iterable. (M, 326)

There is a short-circuiting here: one should distinguish citation in the strict sense; the citationality implicit in performative utterances that draw on a code; and the vague sense in which any word at all is a citation, since its meaning supposes prior usage or at least the possibility of future usage. While giving their full transcendental sweep to iteration and citationality, we must somehow retain the capacity to think the immediacy and singularity of the event.

TRADITION AS DISSEMINATION

If we seek out effects of dissemination in Christian tradition, we can break the tyranny of homonyms which has concealed the immense diversity of the Christian project. At the same time we can make sense of this diversity, understanding dissemination not as a random process but as a productivity of language which is always in excess of authorial control but which can nonetheless be espoused in a creative and venturesome fashion. Our religious statements are opaque in their ultimate reference, but even in their semantic content they are subject to a constant slippage. To speak at all we must cast out these nets into the deep, but we cannot predetermine either their reach or their catch.

In a totalising view, all the books of Bible represent the Word of God; all doctrines converge in an organic whole; all rituals serve to effect the single reality of salvation or sanctification; all ecumenical councils possess a common essence, an identical authority. Theology is full of expressions aiming to impose unitary meaning on the dissemination of language. Thus 'inspired text', 'sin', 'sacrament', 'God', 'creation', 'providence', 'grace' function as if they stood for stable referents controlling the activity of these signifiers. But historical scholarship can reveal a latent heterogeneity and discontinuity inscribed in every item of the theological vocabulary.

The regime of essence has permitted the transmission of faith, but to the detriment of the free unfolding of meaning. In Buddhism, or in the more relaxed periods of Islamic and Jewish philosophy, religious thought knew a peaceful abundance, whereas in Christianity pluralism has flourished chiefly in the guise of bitter polemics among rival claimants to orthodoxy. Yet even within orthodoxy, the tradition has its ruptures and interstices which no organic model of the development of dogma can integrate. The appearance of organicity is maintained only by retouchings which revise history in function of current preoccupations and idealise present events in light of this rewritten history.

For a speculative dogmatic theology the historical and linguistic conditions of the emergence of dogma tend to be seen as inessential swaddling cloths of eternal truth. But even the hermeneutic phronesis which replaces this dogmatic horizon tends to project a unitary instance such as faith, religious experience, tradition, the Word of God, or the essence of Christianity as the central theme of the Christian quest. In making liberation, or creation-centeredness, or faith itself as with Luther, the principle of a revisionist hermeneutics, one should beware of the homonymic illusion that liberation, faith, creation had formerly the same meaning as they now have. Faith after Kant and Nietzsche corresponds only faintly to what Paul or Luther would have understood by faith; liberation after Marx and Freud has only distant resonances in Scripture. As to the metamorphoses of 'creation', the more science brings definition and closure to our picture of the universe, the more its mystery demands new religious and poetic interpretations.

Gradually the residual essentialism of hermeneutics is succumbing to a keener sense of historical differences. When Paul or Luther speak of faith, or Aristotle or Hegel of reason, the question that occurs to us is, 'What, precisely, was the meaning of "faith" or "reason" in that vanished culture?' – and the answer will be a long time coming. Both faith and reason are now being pluralised and contextualised, and defined in terms of their history as traditions, narrations, practices, to be continued and renewed. The debate on incommensurability (of conceptual schemes or of forms of life) conducted by Kuhn and Feyerabend for the natural sciences, Winch and Geertz for the social sciences, can be continued on a still richer terrain in theology, as historical study establishes an incommensurability between the conceptions of God or grace or faith formed in different Jewish and Christian cultures. The Gospels themselves present little that can be directly appropriated; their message is transmitted through the filter of memory; as the product of a historical past it has a remote and oblique relation to our present, leaving a free space for us to invent a contemporary evangelical practice and wisdom. Its inbuilt obsolescence keeps Gospel language from becoming an all-enveloping monopoly – with consequent loss of its summoning-power, for it would have no space in which to echo. Obsolescence can also be a protective bark under which the sap of a tradition is conserved, the patina that seals its authenticity.

In a strict regime of ecclesiastical semantics, the conceptuality of metaphysics was employed to impose limits on the use of theological terms, and was applied retrospectively even to the diction of Scripture. This metaphysical topology of faith and its content is no longer practicable, for a change in the texture of the rational has put out of play the principal figures of the metaphysical ordering of reality. The Heideggerian strategy vis-à-vis metaphysics – to overcome it by reappropriating it as a historical project, in its finitude – can be pursued in a more full-blooded way in dealing with the historical trajectory of Christianity. Heidegger cultivated a mode of thought so exclusively meditative that he had to reject three things: the demands of the linguistic turn, the illumination of the human sciences, and an empirical historicity which cannot simply be scanned as a succession of epochs. But the critique of Christian tradition in its living diversity cannot forgo these resources. Wittgenstein provides a supplementary antidote, as he counters the fascination of unitary explanations by finding under each category a multitude of forms of life irreducible to one another, so that the unitary language fragments into a plurality of contextualised discourses which make sense in another way.

Take the word 'grace': there is no one essential sense of this word, but a whole series of uses linked by family resemblance. What we thought was a debate about an identical reality turns out to be a sequence of textual strategies related to one another intertextually, not according to a one-way logic of progressive clarification, but in a history of misreadings, which are inevitable given the impossibility of anchoring a signifier such as 'grace' in some signified immunised against the movement of dissemination. If what Augustine derived from Paul, or Luther from both, rests on hermeneutical shortcircuits that can no longer be corrected, and if current reconstructions of the meaning of their texts turn out to be at best 'strong readings', new strategies for giving resonance to the old signifiers, what becomes of the identity of tradition? In theology today, 'grace' is no longer thought of as an absolute quantity; this master-word now functions as the résumé of a varied history of discourse. We continue to appreciate the great moments in that history: the Pauline kerygma, and its retrievals and displacements in later preachers of grace such as Augustine, Luther, Pascal, Newman or Barth. In the case of the more scholastic mappings of grace in systematic theology, what we are most likely to value is the degree in which the theologians' *esprit de finesse* was able to resist convenient metaphysical and dogmatic shorthand so as to keep in touch with a story irreducible to such terms.

A deconstructive theology retrieves this family of texts not in the key of speculative or hermeneutic synthesis, but as an exercise of writing motivated by 'hints and guesses'. Where their authors intended unequivocal doctrinal affirmations, the inner tensions of the writing tell another story. The antinomies and confusions that shadow the theology of grace do not invite speculative resolution, but mark the points at which the attempt at system comes under strain as a plural, vital reality makes itself felt in the slippage and sliding of the unitary concepts brought to bear on it. 'Grace' does not have the same reference from one use of the term to the next; in each new context it evokes a different set of phenomena. It functions only as a pointer to the general situation of human relations to the divine as focused in the Christ-event, as the word 'love' might function as a pointer to the relations within a family.

The traditional use of situational scriptural utterances as proof-texts in demonstrations of doctrine about 'love' or 'grace' or 'God' implies a distorting rationalism. Responsible rationality attends first to the character of the terminology from which it takes its departure. If the terms 'love', 'grace' and even 'God' function as pointers somewhat as the words in a poem might do, then they cannot be reduced to a single univocal meaning.

Each effective use of them starts a new story and rewrites the previous ones. The analysis of their significance cannot be a merely conceptual exercise, but has to use methods comparable to those of literary criticism. The rational retrieval of theological tradition works not through systematic definition of its terms but through a discerning clarification of how they have functioned in a series of particular life-situations. To make sense of classical theology, in which these terms are given a deceptive stability, one must trace the process of dissemination underlying the iteration of the homonyms.

Dissemination brings a new perspective on the enigmas stemming from the historical heterogeneity of inherited theological statements and their present opacity, for it shows that such heterogeneity and opacity are built into all meaningful statements, by reason of their inscribed condition, their subjection to the play of iterable marks. Theological clarification does not reorder an array of pure concepts, but is more an attempt to rewrite the text of Christian knowledge. As such, it is caught within this text and cannot step outside it; nor is it possible to confront this constantly rewritten text with some extra-textual thing itself. If one tries to rectify, by appeal to a supposed original meaning, the semantic slippages which every Christian word, idea and text has undergone, all one succeeds in doing is to complicate further the texture of rewriting. The immense writing exercise of Christian tradition leaves us with only a handful of findings, embedded in a network of interpretative possibilities. The exercise is continued by adroit interventions in the linguistic network of today, and these do not enjoy entire lucidity, for every manipulation of signifiers is a negotiation with the machinery of textuality, which largely eludes authorial intention. When it represses awareness of the risks and blind spots its textual inscription entails, religious language loses even the grip on truth it thinks it has, and is blinded by its delusion of full vision. Acceptance of dissemination frees us to construct intelligible messages in precise contexts, free from the crippling ambition to grasp the totality of what Christian intelligibility has been and can be.

According to the laws of contingency and errance, it is inevitable that some counterfeit coins circulate among the innumerable 'truths' that tradition offers. Some ring hollow – too much of the imaginary has entered their alloy. Others are no longer legal tender. Others have been devalued. As the value of coins depends on conventions which provisionally guarantee it, so received truths are re-evaluated as successive ages sift them according to principles that cannot be foreseen. Centuries of consolidation can lose their weight when a change of perspective poses the questions differently. New contexts prescribe a torsion and reinscription of received terms. This cannot fully respect their original intent, any more than Nicaea respected that of the New Testament Christologies. We use the words 'God', 'grace' or 'salvation' intelligibly today only by altering their meaning, as a poet alters a worn-out image.

It might be objected that theological writing has fixed the meaning of these terms, putting a limit to this perpetual alteration. But this stabilising role of writing has in fact made visible the process of alteration which on the oral level had been going on unnoticed. The transition from oral preaching to writing (confessional formulas, the Canon of Scripture, liturgical books) imposed on local communities a dogmatic *koinē*, which itself was originally only one of the local dialects. By such procedures, as in the case of language in general, religion is kept from being 'abandoned to its natural evolution' (Saussure, 268).

In religion as in language, a minute innovation, like a move in chess, can have 'reverberations on the whole system' (126). Yet language is less subject to mutation than other social institutions: 'for each of them there is a different balance between imposed tradition and the free action of society' (105); 'the very arbitrariness of the sign shelters language from every attempt to modify it ... For in order that something be put in question, it must rest on a reasonable norm' (106). A literary language is less prone to change than the spoken one (193, 207), and has a stabilising influence comparable to that of theological orthodoxy within a religion. The intelligence of the users of a language surely also contributes to its evolution, as the initiative of believers affects in the long run the texture of Christian language.

The destiny opened by the preeminence accorded to writing embraces all of ecclesiastical life: every relation between Christians, and even their relation with God, will be regulated in writing. The apparent permanence and continuity which result are largely illusory, for the meaning of what is fixed in writing is also subject to a subtle process of alteration. The flaws in this stability became manifest in the sixteenth-century war of interpretations. Every branch of divided Christianity in turn produced formulas and documents claiming to fix the identity of faith; these contingent decisions acquired the status of destinies, permitting distinctive versions of the Christian adventure while barring openness to a more basic questioning. Three centuries sufficed to show the narrowness of these texts and the impossibility of imposing them as permanent and universal definitions. Revised versions, ecumenical agreements, synodal pronouncements produced a flood of texts whose claims to universal authority became ever less convincing. The durable institution of a written faith is ruined by the perpetual variations of writing itself. Thus opens

O Dieu!. vous seul me suffisez...
en vous seul je trouve tout ce qui est
nécessaire à mon âme!. (St Fcl de S)

Mon Ch. LETAILLE, BOUMARD FILS édit. pontif. PARIS

I

Personne ne connaissait mieux que lui la plus haute perfection, mais il se rapetissait pour les petits et ne dédaignait jamais personne.

II

Il se faisait tout à tous, non pour plaire à tous, mais pour les gagner tous, et les gagner à Jésus-Christ sans songer à soi.

III

Il avait une parfaite condescendance aux humeurs des autres, et supportait avec douceur les manières rudes et fâcheuses.

IV

Il surmontait courageusement ses passions, et disait qu'en toute sa vie il ne s'était fâché qu'une fois, de laquelle il s'était toujours repenti.

V

Il renonçait à ses plus petites inclinations et affections imparfaites, et combattait avec effort ses aversions et ses répugnances.

VI

Il se réjouissait quand il se présentait une occasion de faire connaître quelqu'une de ses imperfections, afin d'avoir sujet de s'en humilier.

VII

Il s'appliquait singulièrement le matin, à midi et le soir, à posséder la douceur et la suavité de cœur, et à tenir son âme dans une égalité parfaite.

VIII

Il aimait à accueillir ceux qui médisaient de lui ou censuraient ses actions, et à leur faire du bien.

IX

Enfin, il était parvenu à un si haut degré de pur amour, qu'*il n'aimait, ne voulait, et ne voyait plus* QUE Dieu *en toutes choses.*

Pl. 157. Boumard et Fils, Édit., 15, rue Garancière. Paris.

a new epoch for Christian identity, which now sees itself as irremediably plural.

In a recent lecture (Tokyo, November 1994), Regis Debray underlined the material aspect of these processes, the way that new techniques of transmission (the codex, the printing press) shape not merely the channels of communication but the direction of the flow. Christianity is a religion of intermediaries, of incarnations, and cannot escape the limiting and distorting effects thereof. Despite appeals to some originary naked truth, it exists only as a conflict among its transmitters. For transmission is always a combat against other transmitters. The angels that announce the birth of Christ or sustain his ascension are not peaceful, transparent messengers; they are a militia, declaring authoritatively the sense of events and inevitably shaping this sense in the process. Paul, Christ's terrestrial angel, and the ecclesiastical hierarchy which mirrors the celestial one, place themselves totally at the service of their message, only all the more effectively to redraft it. There is no spiritual transmission from mind to mind which is not skewed by material mediations (as Bernard Faure and others have shown in the case of Zen); but conversely the mediations are traversed by a spiritual vitality. Sad, tragic, impure is the fate of consignment to the mediatic; yet the Christian message espouses this fate in incarnational self-emptying, undergoing every sort of hybridisation while constantly projecting fictional images of its original purity and unity.

The appeal to the continuity of tradition can be a logocentric mask, obscuring the most creative events in the history it covers – interstitial ruptures, nomadic heterologies. Yet such discontinuities cannot make up a tradition either. There must be a deeper life that survives despite them or through them, an irrepressible inventiveness to which the reshapings and rechannellings of transmission lend new opportunities. Within the play of tradition there is ample space for the function of a Heideggerian mechanism of retrieval, the revival at key moments of what is lodged in the foundational texts. Novel departures turn out to chime with a deeper fidelity, uncovering what habit has obscured. Ruptures and reinventions are the necessary means by which the quite non-objectifiable 'spirit' or 'life' of Christianity is sustained.

To read the classics of theology as one reads literature, emphasising the irreducibility of every original vision, the impossibility of translating it into the terms of another epoch, is to see that the tradition never accumulates into a Summa, but remains a series of incomplete sketches of the meaning that the Gospel has acquired in the most diverse situations. This freedom toward tradition is not authentic unless it corresponds to a constraint coming from tradition, in a relation of mutual indebtedness which allows neither gratuitous manipulation of the received text nor literal translation without reference to the pressure of present needs. When Christianity is placed in the interreligious context or in the psychoanalytical perspective, the notions of sin, grace, salvation, eternal life undergo a thorough overhaul. Underlying this metamorphosis, certain transcendental instances – meaning, truth, reason, ethics, faith – undoubtedly make themselves felt, but every attempt to define them has only a provisional validity.

Explicit recognition of these effects of contextuality threatens to consume the last vestiges of Christian identity, leaving only a selective exploiting of the tradition, unconstrained by any supra-contextual instance:

> The principle of stability has long disappeared even from the Bible; as changeable as is human opinion, so changeable is the divine revelation... But just this is the advantage of the Christian religion, that one can rip the heart from its body and nonetheless still be a good Christian. (Feuerbach, 438)

But even as it undergoes the violence of a new perspective of reading, the tradition can make the irreducibility of its identity felt. As archaic segments collapse, the voice of the past makes itself heard in a different way, emitting new imperatives. This vital subsistence of tradition is not the static permanence of a *depositum fidei* – the only form of authentic continuity Feuerbach seems able to imagine – but the force of a history with multiple possibilities, of which some wither away only to leave others free to unfold. The objective truth of tradition is not that signalled by the formulas and is not contained in them, for it remains true only as living thought:

> The dogmas of religion have arisen at certain times, from particular needs, under particular relations and representations; and for that reason they are to people of a later time, in which these relations, needs, representations have vanished, something incomprehensible, inconceivable, merely transmitted, i.e. revealed. The contrariety between revelation and reason reduces to that between history and reason, to the mere fact that humanity at a given time is no longer *able* to do what at *another* time it could accomplish with ease. (444f)

It is true that dogmatic headaches are a feature of old religions, burdened with a complex past; one finds them in the later, not the earlier, books of the Old Testament (Job); in later, not earlier, Buddhism; in Christianity from Augustine (earlier doctrinal controversy did not give the sense that the Trinity was an inscrutable conundrum). Today we are less likely to take an inaccessible past for a transcendent mystery; nor is what we are 'able' to believe necessarily any less worthy the name of faith than the more direct and unproblematic utterances of earlier times.

To the eyes of faith, the pneumatic presence of Christ is the most fundamental warrant of continuity between the Christian past and present. But this presence exists only as the contemporary vitality of tradition, that is, not as a heritage which is conserved, or a dream in which all times are fused, but as a constantly surprising event. For instance, if a certain hierarchical and clerical Church is vanishing, to be replaced by a Church of the people, this would be a surprise comparable to the dramatic turning-points in biblical history. From such a *krisis* at the heart of our historical actuality the testimonies of the past and the Bible itself would acquire their present meaning. Again, if the everyday practice of love of neighbour is still a possible lifestyle, and has a salvific efficacy, or if the grace of Christ sustains lives of self-forgetting generosity, or if the sufferer is enabled to embrace the divine will and to come near to God, or if an oppressed group is inspirited and united by the Gospel, each such event testifies to the discreet potency of Christ's teaching and his Spirit which more than any credal formula is the unifying thread of Christian history.

Even at this fundamental level, continuity is not the simple repetition of a pattern but its imaginative reinvention. The Incarnation deploys itself as play, a sequence of unpredictable breakthroughs of the transcendent in the everyday. Affirming the play, we can retrieve the tradition as a mobile history of which the departures and halts, the wanderings and catastrophes, the inspired advance and the fatigued ebb, come under no common denominator. The Logos circulates in this history, losing and scattering itself, and this errance, rather than any *recapitulatio omnium* reveals the nature of the Incarnation.

BABELISING THEOLOGICAL REASON

Theological reason has been too ashamed of its flaws and wounds. For faith to give a truly rational account of itself, it should take full cognisance of the vulnerable condition of all reason; not to declare itself superior to or independent of reason, but to bring its reflections into accord with the conditions of a sane and modest rationality. The humble, contextual reason of our time is a better ally of faith than speculative metaphysics, and could spare theologians the Sisyphean toil of justifying faith before a tribunal of reason presided over by Hegel, Schelling or Whitehead. The ambition of integrating religious statements in a system which would confirm and unify them causes theology to lose touch with the functional sense of the statements, which it has unwittingly reduced to pawns in an abstract game. If, however, there is no majestic synthesis behind first-level religious statements, but only the irreducible and irrecoverable web of archi-writing, then theology is free to put itself entirely at the service of the first-level language, seeking to assure its authentic impact, here and now, with no temptation to leap beyond it to its transcendental foundations. The scope of theological reason is not however merely that of phenomenological clarification or grammatical therapy, as Heideggerian or Wittgensteinian theologians respectively suppose. The labour of the concept must be pursued to the end, for to arrest it by fiat is irrational. But theological reflection, carried far enough, itself discovers the limits of conceptuality – not the historical limits of Western metaphysics, but the limits of conceptual knowledge as such; and learns to situate itself discreetly in regard to a more basic language and enactment of faith.

Religions commonly claim access to realities that elude 'mere reason', and they situate rationality within an existential or contemplative wisdom that exceeds it. By reason here I understand not an invariant structure but a set of practices varying from one culture to another and showing a family resemblance. According to Heidegger:

> *The dominance of theoretical knowing* as the true criterion of all knowledge is so strong in the development of our cultural history that even the phenomenon of faith is viewed in regard to the phenomenon 'knowledge'. A look at the history of theology shows what basic distortions this gives rise to. (*Gesamtausgabe* XVII, 121)

The theoretical and speculative drive of Western theology has fallen short of the novel sense of truth which was emerging in the New Testament (125f). Yet it also brought a luminous articulation which ensured the worldwide reach of the Gospel. A critique of theological reason, which would identify the scope and responsibility of logical reason within religion, is not merely a theoretical desideratum but a practical one in a world where religious irrationalism has been so productive of bloodshed and crime. To legislate on the proper function of concept, argument, logic and proof in theology, one must first accept the classic Buddhist and Christian critiques of rationalism as well as the contextualisation of reason effected by Heidegger, Wittgenstein and the poststructuralists. Then one can clear the present space of rationality and free the intellect for its indispensable role, disburdening it of theoretical obsessions at odds with the phenomenality of religious truth. Buddhism offers the best guidance here, for it has been able to exploit to the full the resources of reason while showing that in the end reason is subordinate, not supreme, since the ultimate reality that reason can negatively vindicate against all counterfeits is positively apprehended only in a stilling of conceptual activity.

The concern of contemporary philosophers with marking limits of reason – Heidegger's insistence that 'the question of Being is not from the start determined on the ground of rationality' or Derrida's sense that rationality 'is suspended over a *nihil*, a groundless abyss which cannot be thought by reason' – is itself a rational concern, an effort to do full justice to reason:

> This does not mean that thinking becomes irrational, but rather that it is caught in a double bind or double gesture, between rationality and its 'nihilation', clinging to the ground while looking down into the abyss... A deconstructive reading operates by employing the resources of logocentric or rational conceptuality... in order to engage that conceptuality in a dislocation where it is drawn outside itself and where the rational is led beyond its own reasonable limits. (Critchley, 151ff)

Derrida, like Heidegger, thinks in the wake of German Idealism, understood as the coming of reason into its own, in free systematic self-deployment. If he recalls reason to its finitude, it is not by a restoration of the Kantian and Fichtean limits dissolved by Hegel, but by fully embracing Hegel's achievement, and then uncovering a further context whereby Hegelian reason opens onto an otherness to which it is answerable and over which it relinquishes mastery. It is by being re-marked in writing that Hegelian reason is made thus vulnerable to another.

The identities and master-themes of a totalising metaphysics tirelessly reconstitute themselves, but every reconstruction is at the same time a deconstruction, the tower as it is erected betrays ever recurrent cracks that threaten its ruin. If reason does not take cognisance of this situation, it slumbers, even amid its most intense systematic activity: 'The slumber of reason is not, perhaps, reason put to sleep, but slumber in the form of reason, the vigilance of the Hegelian logos. Reason keeps watch over a deep slumber in which it has an interest' (*WD*, 252). Georges Bataille would break this slumber with festival, laughter, sacrifice, the absolute risk of death (as opposed to the calculated risk of the Hegelian slave), eroticism, excess, absolute spending, practices which cannot be brought back under the economy of the logos. But faith and hope might be invoked for the same ends: the pagan extreme rejoins the biblical one insofar as both oppose the grip of a totalising logos. If both stress laying down one's life, it is so that life can be lived as a death to self at every moment, whereas the cult of a full, immutable, unified, originary life, in its denial of mortality, turns out by its abstraction to represent a grip of death on life.

The rational demand for grounds and for totalisation is not simply a transcendental illusion, that could eventually be undone once and for all. Its ruses are not simply those of a paranoiac who clings to a fixed idea. If textuality exceeds reason, it is reason which grasps this situation and accommodates itself to it by ever more adventurous strategies of writing. To become aware of the finitude and fragility of our signifying activities, stripping away logocentric simplifications, is to advance in insight, in a triumph of logos. His awareness of this antinomy obliges Derrida to develop a series of apophatic techniques worthy of negative theology. The double bind underlying all the antinomies of deconstruction concerns its relation to reason. Far from denying the force and necessity of reason, Derrida leans on it to pit reason against itself, so as to enlarge and open its dialectic onto the irreducible complexity of *différance*. One could say that he plays the texture of Kant's and Hegel's writing against its structure, for in their reflexive styles, with their innumerable capillaries and subtle resonances, reason deploys a differential force which no structure can any longer enclose. This force depends essentially on the resources of writing, of the textual element in which it is deployed and to which it sacrifices a great part of its autonomy.

Reason, in Derrida, renounces the aspiration of recalling to a synthesis the margins of indetermination and the contradictory strata in which all writing (every articulation of meaning) becomes entangled. It cultivates, on the contrary, the art of becoming always more irremediably caught in:

> that strange strategy without finality, the debility or failure that organizes the *telos* or the *eschaton* which reinscribes restricted economy [that which reason can control] within general economy [that of textuality as what exceeds reason which is inscribed in it] (*D*, 7)

– a movement 'that no speculative dialectic of the same and the other can master, for the simple reason that such a dialectic always remains an operation of mastery' (5). In assuming thus the materiality of its inscribed condition, reason no longer masters the play of the signifiers; if it can create within that play a hermeneutic clearing or systematic ordering, this is no more than a limited strategy, always surpassed by the play. The author loses himself in his text 'as a spider who finds he is unequal to the web he has spun' (*Spurs*, 101). Thought turns out to be only a moment in the play of textuality (the play of the world itself).

Though it is impossible to find descriptions of the rational which do not turn out to be contingent, contextual, self-dissolving constructions, this does not entail a total dissolution of the rational in the textual.

Reason enjoys a universal, transcendental sweep, and will always be able to give a conceptual account of that which may intrinsically elude the grasp of the concept, be it from below (writing as *différance*) or from above (ultimate reality as given in non-conceptual intuition). As long as we speak at all we are within reason's domain:

> The unsurpassable, irreplacable, and imperial greatness of the order of reason, that which makes it not just another actual order or structure (a determined historical structure, one structure among other possible ones), is that one cannot speak out against it except by appealing to it, that one can protest against it only from within it; and within its domain, reason leaves us only the recourse to stratagems and strategies. Which amounts to summoning a historical determination of reason to appear before the tribunal of reason in general ... Since the revolution against reason, from the moment it is articulated, can operate only *within* reason, it always has the limited scope of what is called, precisely in the language of a department of *internal* affairs, an agitation. (*WD*, 36)

Reason has embodied itself in the categories of metaphysics, and Derrida is prepared to admit that one cannot surpass these categories without drawing on them:

> There is no sense in doing without the concepts of metaphysics in order to shake metaphysics. We have no language – no syntax and no lexicon – which is foreign to this history; we can pronounce not a single destructive proposition which has not already had to slip into the form, the logic, and the implicit postulations of precisely what it seeks to contest. (*WD*, 280f)

Even if one consigns all the figures of Western metaphysics to an era now closed, the transcendental realities at work in metaphysics – meaning, truth, reason – are not subject to epochal closure or confinement to some grammatical or phenomenological regime reducing them to finite quantities. Reason is always limited, contextual, historical, inscribed; but what is at work in every rational statement is not only a blind materialist textuality; the laws of textuality cannot fully account for it. To retrieve the transcendental power, perhaps ineffable, of an enlarged reason (which is perhaps also Derrida's aim), one can begin from the phenomenon of their perpetual rebirth despite their inscribed condition. Reason, including theological reason, can content itself with this modest survival, which dispenses it from worry about securing its foundations in a definitive, extra-textual form.

Language is falling in its very erection; no statement can be formed without being simultaneously deformed. A signifying mark is such only by its iterability, which implies an irreducible polysemy and equivocity, and by its difference from every other mark, in an infinite network of interferences wherein each mark is altering the meaning of all the others. The best guide to this Babel is *Finnegans Wake*:

> One cannot pardon him for this Babelian act of war, unless it always occurs, from all time, in every event of writing, thus suspending the responsability of each person. One can pardon him only if one recalls that Joyce himself must have suffered this situation. (*Ulysse gramophone*, 22)

The extreme of Babelisation as pure heterogeneity is courted by Paul de Man:

> His is a world of unrelated singulars, each so idiosyncratic that in it everything universal becomes extinguished; it is a world of heterogeneous fragments forming a whole only insofar as, by their mutual indifference and lack of generative power, they are all the same, endlessly repeating the punctuality of their lone meaninglessness. (Gasché 1989, 287)

Derrida avoids this extreme by deciphering a law at the heart of Babel. Babel is the name of the father, the name of God, ultimate guarantor of the symbolic order, 'for *Ba* signifies father in the oriental languages and *Bel* signifies God' (Voltaire, quoted in *Psyché*, 204). That the last instance of meaning should be a source of confusion reveals the constitution of all signification: an ineluctable double bind, which permits neither total utter ruin and dispersion nor the completion of a solid edifice. 'It delivers a universal reason (one no longer subject to the rule of a particular nation) but it simultaneously limits its very universality: prohibited transparency, impossible univocity' (210).

Religious language, too, is in a collapsing state, unable to attain the full clarification it aims at by abolishing the last residues of opacity. Strategies of retrenchment are a futile reaction; it is not by shoring up the crumbling masonry but by allowing oneself to topple into new contexts and encounters that one finds material for the constant task of rebuilding. Reason aspires to a transcultural condition, yet it can generate knowledge only according to the particular style of a given culture; every knowledge is local, whatever its eventual migrations. Faith likewise aspires to continuity across time, yet it best maintains a living continuity only by accepting the epistemological breaks marking its migration from a collapsing paradigm to a more promising site of construction.

It might be objected that just as Western science is a concrete knowledge that has been accepted in all cultures, so Christian knowledge can have a global reach. But this image of science can be queried. The concept of 'science' is not a scientific concept; it is undefinable, and names a set of practices which undergo constant alteration throughout history. The logical formalisation of these operations and their results is never fully achieved, for the concrete practice always outstrips it. Thus the received scientific teachings of a given period and their systematic form are provisional or transitional states of affairs.

A religion, unlike a science, carries its past with it. If one tries to snatch from history some pure sample of the essence of Christianity or any other religion, one catches up 'at the same time, a yet quite unformed mass of roots, soil, and sediments of all sorts' (G, 161). The path of a religious tradition toward greater universality takes the form of an extension of this history, as the tradition acquires new local manifestations. Whereas a scientific concept can be the same always and everywhere (at least until replaced by another), a religious idea, like a literary or musical one, comes alive only when it has the colour of a particular time and place. It communicates across cultures in a dialogical reception in which it is transformed.

Theological reason, then, far from being abolished by the pluralistic texture of religion as currently grasped, must acquire a new flexibility in its work of discernment, reflection, synthesis and argument. Method in theology is no longer a matter of building a dogmatic edifice on the data of Scripture or of providing systematic transcendental foundations for the life of faith; rather it means clarifying the functioning of both scriptural and dogmatic language within the concrete historical situations in which they emerge and tracing the routes for a viable continuation of the tradition they form. At no time can theological reason step outside history and language, in all their enigmatic opacity; it is a systematic stocktaking of the limited attainments, the limited clearing of insight within this milieu, and a marking of these limits (cf. Kant, *Critique of Pure Reason*, A xx), limits which can however never be purely and definitively marked since reason can never recollect itself out of its inscribed condition into an ideal unity or autonomy. Does this leave reason intrinsically frustrated? No, rather it frees reason, in its very incompleteness, to become a dialogal reason, opening onto the other which it can never master, and an incarnate reason, reflecting in its procedures the tension and the drama of human finitude.

3

RELATIVE TRUTH

'*Spiritus sanctus non est scepticus*' (Luther); 'the Holy Spirit is not a sceptic'. Yet theology, as a reflexive double-checking or taking stock of religious traditions, is led by a skepsis of the Spirit working in tense alliance with the lowlier hunches of secular reason. No part of a religious tradition - its texts, factual claims, mythic representations, ideological investments, metaphysical conceptuality – can be above suspicion. We have to bring to our reading of Christian tradition both the complete freedom of critical reason, which never shirks the question 'true or false?', and a basic confidence in that tradition as the Spirit's field of action and the vital milieu of theological thought. Having seen how limited, relative, and questionable all religious statements are, by reason of their inscription in historical contexts, and having begun to see that the progress, or survival, of religious reason and knowledge is even bumpier and more broken than in the case of the sciences, how can we continue to affirm that religious discourse retains a cognitive grip on objective truth?

FOUCAULT'S REGIMES OF TRUTH

To find a telling answer to this question we need to cash in our common-sense notions for sharper empirical insight into how truth is enunciated in historical contexts. Faced with the diversity of the truths that history has produced and the impossibility of bringing them back within a single regime, whether a religious dogmatics or a rational synthesis, we are tempted to project a mythical or Platonic image of the unity of the true: imagining it perhaps as a constellation formed by the fragments we have grasped, to be completed by the addition of still latent truths, unsighted stars in the night of the unknown, sleeping beauties that await their discoverer. Michel Foucault disqualifies such imaginings by clarifying the punctuation – discursive constraints, epistemological breaks, social inscription – which differentiates effects of truth from one another and makes them as irreducible to unity as are great poems.

The heterogeneity of truth lies deeper than the variability of what societies accept as true or the frameworks within which significance, identity, causal interactions, and relationships are established. Foucault's critique of truth is not limited to a sociological register, but sights the violent breaks and the radical incommensurabilities between the successive regimes reason constructs in the course of history. The rationality of history is no longer the unfolding of a single homogeneous force, for in each epoch the notions of truth and knowledge have a quite different bearing and are enabled and constrained by quite different conditions, nor can these successive acceptations of truth and knowledge be reduced to a dialectical sequence wherein the later forms subsume the earlier ones:

> Reason, *recovered* in its underlying coherence, remains *lost*, for it is always caught in a lure ... 'The order in terms of which we think has not the same mode of being as that of the classics'. ... The ground of our security is shaken by the realisation that we can no longer *think* yesterday's thoughts ... Reason is thus put in question by its history ... With the technical rigour of a historian of ideas, he formulates *philosophically* an issue that is fundamental today: the possibility of truth. (de Certeau 1987a, 18f, 25, 28)

The successive structurations of knowledge do not link up together to constitute a transepochal synthesis. They are the sites of a thinking that is always finite and local. Thus reason discovers itself to be mortal. This pluralism of historical forms of the rational could be seen as testifying to the wealth of reason as a transcendental reality, unrepresentable as such, and taking form only as a history of roughly comparable practices. It more emphatically underlines, however, the poverty of reason as always determined by the conditions of a historical conjuncture, while remaining largely unconscious of their power over it. The historicisation of reason means that faith (itself grasped as a historical series of practices) can no longer address reason in general, but only debate with local, conjunctural instances of the rational. The truth which can be stated each time, which like most or all Christian truths is an amalgam of reason and faith, is as it were doubly historicised. It is a truth for that moment in the respective histories of faith and reason, sharing the narrowness and provisionality of that particular epistemological context.

The successive epistemological orders are mutually exclusive, and none can claim the privileged status of being the truth of the others. One can confirm or deny the truth of particular statements, especially scientific ones, but it is impossible to judge the truth of an epoch as a whole. Any such judgement would be a political option rather than a pure cognitive process. Thus, in theology, it is not possible to recover the previous structurations of Christian truth within the currently viable dispensation. Theological reason cannot master its own past, for the older dispensations have become opaque. Even if we can read, say, a medieval commentary on Peter Lombard's *Sentences* with a perfect grasp of the argument at every turn, the total sense of the enterprise has become elusive for we no longer know what it meant to live in such a world. We can identify here and there some correct insights and some clear errors, but the general framework is withdrawn from our judgement as well as from our appropriation. Such incommensurability between the present topography of the true and that of past cultures transforms Gadamer's 'fusion of horizons' into a bricolage from which no satisfying totalisation emerges.

A religious truth – e.g. 'Jesus is the Saviour' – can be confidently affirmed within a cultural milieu in which it has a central place, or in which it is immediately related to current vital problems. But when this epistemological setting becomes obsolescent, this truth loses its radiance. To repeat it obstinately is merely to confess one's impotence to connect with the contemporary order of knowledge. To speak today's truth about Jesus requires that one negotiate present constraints, either bending to them or resisting them, in the hope that the resultant language will bring a dynamic equivalent of the lost truth.

A truth cannot pre-exist its historical moment or the language in which it can be stated. It is a language of a certain thickness, linked to a certain conjuncture, which constitutes the concepts of 'pleasure', 'flesh', 'sexuality' according to which the erotic is defined in the Greek, Christian, and modern periods respectively. However, this does not entail a radical constructivism which would dissolve the referent of these categories in the language-games that engender them. New fields of possible discourse do produce new forms of knowledge, though the knowledge is never absolutely objective, that is, its objective cognitive core can never be purely formulated, for its culture-bound status makes such clearly defined objectivity impossible.

Foucault would see such categories as 'God' and 'grace' as receiving their valency from a given conjuncture and as permitted by a given order of discourse. Even though a certain language of God and grace is specific to an epoch of Western culture, this does not mean that it cannot have been a vehicle of truth. It may be obsolete now, and to speak at the same depth today we may have to find equally valent religious terms permitted by the present context. As 'human rights' have a valency in current ethics which the term 'honour' has lost, so if the term 'God' is less weighty than in the past, it can be retained in the background while prominence is given to other terms serving to express for today the call of the transcendent.

Here a second consideration arises. The possibility of truth is put in question not only by the finitude of all epistemes but also by the play of power which governs their formation and dissolution, imposing constraints which have no purely rational basis. When we lay claim to the truth, our gesture is always overdetermined by the pressures of the ideological milieu. The will to know, the will to truth, is governed by a system of exclusion, a historical formation which is modifiable and institutionally constraining (Foucault 1971, 16). The true is established in function of the permitted discourses. When one sees the degree to which use of the term 'true' is socially and institutionally conditioned, one is obliged to relinquish claims to be in immediate contact with the truth as an ultimate instance, or to have a substantial or definitive vision of it. The will to know, and the primacy it ascribes to the value of truth, are not innocent; they establish relations of power. Thus one passionately committed to truth, whether dogmatic or critical, is not absolved from critical reflection on the will to power implicit in this passion. If every Christian truth is blood-stained, it is because this self-questioning was deemed unnecessary. Openness to the true does not begin at the foreground of our minds, where we face particular issues, but in the background where our prejudices lodge. It demands an economic calculation, in which one invests alternately in the stability of tradition and in critical questioning.

In Foucault's claim that every truth is the effect of pressures of power and its institutions, the word 'truth' has a limited historical sense; otherwise it would fall into the paralogisms of philosophical (as opposed to cultural) relativism, and its liberative political force would be nil. Foucault's cultural relativism aims to discern the concrete conditions of the production of truth in its historical singularity. A 'political history of truth' would show 'that truth is not free by nature, or error in bonds, but that its production is pervaded through and through by relations of power' (Foucault 1976, 81). 'Pervaded', not 'created': it really is truth which is produced, but always under the conditions of historical finitude. What is denied is an unconditional freedom of truth to manifest itself.

THE LIMITS OF RELATIVISM: RORTY

Some American academics seem to have derived from Foucault the idea that truth is intrinsically oppressive, and that it must be shaken off: 'Nothing is true, all is permitted'. They point to the indoctrination which kept the Vietnam war going as an example of how power exploits the appeal to truth. But they might more sagely point to the Gulf War, where power worked through control of mediatic images rather than through ideological dogma. Resignation to the disappearance of truth plays right into the hands of such manipulation. Whereas in the Vietnam case the cold-war ideology could be argued against by rational demonstration of its untruths, in a mediacratic environment one has first to establish the right to invoke truth at all. Relativists for whom truth is a thing of the past see themselves as liberators, but in fact they bend with utter docility to the conditions that ensure their disempowerment.

Among leading philosophers the one who seems to come closest to propagating such dogmatic relativism is Richard Rorty. Rorty's target is not some culture-bound myth such as Foucault's epistemes of 'resemblance' or 'representation', but the very idea of a truth that is not relative. Truth itself becomes nothing more than social acceptability. His superb articulation and enactment of the direst philosophical temptations of the age – within the framework of a humanist liberalism – gives him a Mephistophelian aura, or perhaps makes him a scapegoat saving us from the cliff towards which he himself precipitously charges.

Philosophy, he teaches, no longer has cognitive content and can no longer claim to grasp the principles of the intelligibility of things. Instead it is a play of critical reflection on the cognitive acquisitions of the sciences and of daily experience. Thus the philosophical debates of the past take on retrospectively a hermeneutical allure. Kant and Hegel, who mistakenly sought to discover absolute foundations or criteria, turn out to have been hermeneuticians without knowing it. Obsessed by the myth of truth as correspondence between the mind and the real it mirrors, Plato, Descartes and Kant were blind to the merely hermeneutic character of their thought. They saw truth as an object to be discovered, whereas Hegel showed it is a human historical construct. Now this allegedly Hegelian tradition is overcoming the myth of correspondence, as philosophy becomes a civilised conversation between possible interpretations of reality, which no longer claim the status of an accurate mirroring; rather they are on a par with the visions of the world projected in works of imaginative fiction. Knowledge is understood in terms of the social justification of belief, with no need to invoke accuracy of representation; epistemic authority is a matter of 'what society lets us say' (Rorty, 174). The ascendancy of the hermeneutical brings a greater social tolerance: 'Hermeneutics is an expression of hope that the cultural space left by the demise of epistemology will not be filled – that our culture should become one in which the demand for constraint and confrontation is no longer felt' (315). We can now say much more though it means much less, since its claims to any objective truth have been suspended.

Against Rorty's reduction of rationality to hermeneutics, one might see hermeneutical inquiry and rational inquiry as circumscribing one another. Rational judgements are caught in the network of interpretation, yet interpretations are subject to the judgement of reason. Phenomenology shows that neither science nor metaphysics can establish a definitive vision of the world which would abolish the pluralism of interpretative perspectives. Reason in its turn prevents us from resting in a perspectivism or relativism that would have relinquished the goal of truth. Phenomenology or hermeneutics cannot overcome relativism, either through the discovery that the relative worlds converge on some original world that embraces them all, or through laying bare the formal structure of world in general. Here reason comes autonomously into play. The 'hermeneutical age of reason' (Greisch) remains an epistemological age insofar as the question of truth/falsehood still presides over our consciousness of the contextuality of every particular truth.

But the insights of relativist hermeneutics can keep this concern for objectivity from becoming an abstract attitude unrelated to the present frameworks of the thinkable. The incommensurability of scientific horizons or religious worldviews makes doubtful any appeal to some truth-as-such against which diverse theories may be measured, and any talk of one theory as more approximately true than another. For Kuhn, '"truth" may, like "proof", be a term with only intra-theoretic applications' (Banner, 26). To ask about the objective truth of a philosophy, a religion, a culture, a language, or a form of life is to invite the accusation that one has fallen into the objectivist illusion, that is, 'the basic conviction that there is or must be some permanent, ahistorical matrix or framework to which we can ultimately appeal in determining the nature of rationality, knowledge, truth, reality, goodness, or rightness'. The relativist holds that 'all such concepts must be understood as relative to a specific conceptual scheme, theoretical framework, paradigm, form of life, society, or culture', and that 'there is (or can be) an irreducible plurality of such conceptual schemes', implying a basic plurivocity in these concepts (Bernstein, 8).

Against an account of truth as 'what you can defend against all comers' (Rorty, 308), one may object that the word 'truth' has no sense or function whatever unless it is intrinsically independent of the cognitive faculties that grasp it and the epistemic situations in which it is attained. Even if the actual content of true statements is always relative to a context, is there not about the very fact of their being true something that transcends this relative status? It is hard to see how one can undertake any scientific or philosophical inquiry without presupposing such a nonrelative conception of truth, be it only as a regulative idea, or as a myth which comes up inevitably as soon as one starts to think. Our tacit belief in truth as a transcendental instance of judgement, which bears on every statement we make, need not be equated with the questionable 'Platonic' notions which immediately offer themselves as the natural transcription of this belief. The postulate of non-relativisable truth can be demythologised, formulated more rigorously; but the same scruple that makes us question our Platonising projections of the true, forbids us to deny the reality of the true as such. To talk of it we may find ourselves forced to use these dubious projections, but henceforth we do so provisionally, as regulative ideas, and putting them between parentheses. The mirror metaphor, for example, is not a necessary accompaniment of testing how well our judgements correspond to reality. When a judgement is falsified by a fact, this does not involve a comparison between the real in itself, before language, and the real constituted by our language (which would be impossible, since 'objects' are not identifiable independently of conceptual schemas). Rorty's critique of the mirror-myth seems to gloss over the implications of the occurrence of objective judgements of fact.

SITUATED OBJECTIVITY

Can we still hold with Aquinas that statements of faith are objective apprehensions of divine truth – *Articulus est perceptio divinae veritatis tendens in ipsam* (Isidore of Seville, quoted, *Summa Theologica* II.II q.1, a.6) – even if the language of faith has become more oblique, relative, provisional, and mediated than it was for him? John Keenan sees this language as originating from a mystical contact with the divine: 'After that experience of direct contact (*sparśa*), wisdom mediates that experience and, however obliquely, objectifies it in teaching' (Keenan, 217). He argues that these objectifications are means or models that harmonise with the ineffable experience, but do not constitute objectively referring propositions. But let us recall that a proposition may objectively refer to its object without pretending actually to define it, and that to make true statements about God does not imply any claim to have grasped or comprehended God in the terms of the proposition. Thus objectively referring propositions put us in touch with the reality of God in a way that is largely a blind leap. The act of faith finds its term not in the proposition as such, but in that to which the proposition refers, just as in the case of an act of knowledge: *Actus autem credentis non terminatur ad enuntiabile sed ad rem: non enim formamus enuntiabilia nisi ut per ea de rebus cognitionem habeamus, sicut in scientia, ita et in fide* (q.1, a.2 ad 2). An analogical language, or a hodological language (a language of the path), is one that intrinsically points beyond itself; but by the very fact of pointing in the right direction it has a claim to objective referentiality.

The objectivity of a statement such as 'God is good' does not depend on a correlation between the word 'God' and the divine subject and between the word 'good' and a divine attribute. Such a logic does not fit God. Scholastic theories of analogy dwell on the gap between our *modus significandi* and the thing signified, but these theories depend on an ontology which is no longer the obligatory framework of religious thought. The statement 'God is good' is better taken as a normative rule, meant to exclude the opposing statements, or as a doxological expression, having meaning only in a context of faith. It is a linguistic gesture which can effectively point in the direction of ultimate reality, at least in a given cultural context. Its objectivity or referential force is mediated by its function and its context and remains provisional. To recognise such objectivity in religious statements goes beyond expressivist and pragmatist reductionism without relapsing into a naively objectivist account of religious language.

A perspectivist account of religious discourse, as a 'skilful means' for designating what infinitely surpasses it, does not contradict the objective referentiality of religious propositions, but it underlines the situation-bound character of this objectivity. Indeed, I would claim that perspectivism is the condition of objectivity, and that a religious proposition which claimed more than perspectival objectivity would turn out to be meaningless. When I say 'God made the world', both 'God' and 'world' are concepts or symbols hewn out in a particular perspective; if I try of strip away all the concreteness they acquire from the history that produced them, I end up with laboratory artefacts that no longer refer to the God or to the world of human experience.

Their situated and dated condition does not undo the referentiality of true statements, but on the contrary makes it possible, permitting it to remain in touch with what Bergson calls 'currents of reality':

> Every truth is a route traced across reality; but, among these routes, there are some to which we could have given a very different direction if our attention had been oriented in a different way or if we had aimed at another kind of utility; there are others, to the contrary, of which the direction is marked by reality itself, and which correspond, so to speak, to currents of reality. (Bergson, 1448)

Bergson says that it is truths of sentiment which correspond to a current, like sailing ships, while scientific truths, like steamships, depend on artificial mechanisms, and hardly serve to lead us into the real. But it is more interesting to note the degree in which scientific truth shares the condition of aesthetic or religious truth: a scientific theory, like a religious vision, is a provisional construction in function of a particular epistemic context. Both types of truth depend on artifices of style and thought born of the culture of an epoch. Just as a scientific theory is confirmed by the facts that it permits us to observe, so a religious vision is confirmed by the experiences that it makes possible. It is this latter phenomenon, more than any internal coherence of our system of thought, which guarantees that a contact with the real has taken place, despite the contingent and idiosyncratic character of our frameworks of understanding and the distortions of perspective their historical finitude necessarily entails. Every perspective is in itself a distortion, but the truth emerges only in perspective.

The propositional truth-claims of the Creed cannot be formulated outside of any context, nor can we provide for them a sheltered scientific space such as that within which we utter the proposition '2 + 2 = 4'. Their sense and reference are intimately dependent on the tradition which transmits them. They belong to a narrative before becoming theses: cut off from the narrative roots and from the renewal of the narrative in the contemporary community, they lose their meaning and by the same token their truth. Paul Griffiths would reduce this narrative element to a mere psychological auxiliary to grasping a truth of a logical order:

> That exposure to and faith in certain stories is a necessary condition for understanding (and even for properly making) religious utterances is surely an important psychological truth for most members of most religious communities; but it is equally obviously not a logical truth. (Griffiths, 43)

In fact, however, it seems that this psychological truth is not merely an empirical fact but concerns the constitutive structure of a religious statement. If 'God' signifies a concrete identity, the object of familiar acquaintance on the part of the faithful, this knowledge of God is inseparable from the narratives which have transmitted it and which keep the power of making it present whenever the old story finds a contemporary resonance. To this concrete identity of God corresponds the believer's identity which is dependent on the God that he or she names. This identity can be expressed only in a narrative grasp of the here and now. To extract from these concrete discourses an abstract, objectified notion of 'God' or of 'man' would be almost as futile as the attempt to decipher a poetic image – *'les couleurs du couchant reflétées par mes yeux'* – by an objective analysis of its referents: the various tints of pink, angles of reflection, etc.

Torn from their hodological context religious statements can lose their objective truth. Religious knowledge is less a definitive possession than something one invents anew under changed epistemological conditions, in which older forms of religious knowledge become irretrievable and non-rectifiable. There are theological truths, or ex-truths, which contradict themself in their very enunciation, discredited by the entire context they must presuppose. Statements such as 'angels are pure spirits' or 'the human soul is immortal' are so remote from present scientific and cultural structures of plausibility that they fall outside the limits of the credible, subsisting only as a residue of myth. It is across the skilful mapping out of new shapes of knowledge, in adroit stylistic interventions in the text of what is thinkable today, that the objective referential thrust of our language – its cognitive grip on truth – is maintained. To be sure, this puts our utterances in an exposed and risky situation, but there is no way of stating truth outside this enveloping pragmatic and writerly context, no automatic mechanism whereby a credal statement touches the 'thing'.

As long as theology has not clarified this problem of referentiality, it is vulnerable to such accusations as the following:

> Theology blindly presumes that it can pierce the opacity of language and make substantial truths present in broad daylight. As scientific utterances, the statements that God or the angels exist, that man exists throughout the variation of his figures, or that there exists a continuity of history, seem equally untenable. These propositions are not so much untrue as meaningless, since any such assertion remains internal to a language. (de Certeau 1987b, 198)

To set about proving that angels do or do not exist is to miss the fact that the very notion of angels is constructed within a historical language or way of life, and that this entire way of life is what has become questionable. One can no longer count on a direct link between discourse and the thing itself. The cognitive take of religious language on its object is mediated by the 'truth', in the broad sense, of the life-context of this language. The truth of a proposition such as 'God is good' depends on the entire orientation of the community in relation to its tradition and to the culture in which it is inserted, and on all sorts of discriminations as to the adequacy and authenticity of its language. Even if one could extract some skeletal but unattackable propositions, which would be independent of every reference to a 'truth' of life or of praxis, the status of these truths would suffer from this alienation, they would lack existential 'truth'.

As we bring to awareness the blind spots of each of the diverse regimes of truth in the Christian past – blind spots that have become more evident to us than the general sense of the obsolescent world-picture that gave rise to them – we become more alert and clearsighted for the construction of our own. The truth of the Great Church of the first centuries banishing the incoherence of Gnosticism; the platonising truth of Origen; the triumph of the dogmatic regime in the fourth century; the biblicist regimes of Protestantism; all the forms of questioning integrity which Christian intellectuality has adopted in modern times, these 'transformations in the essence of truth' (Heidegger) had each a shadow-side and caused a narrowing and a stiffening. When we adopt without criticism the rhetoric of an epoch of truth, we inscribe ourselves in a historical current which can empower us, in positions of domination or of resistance, but which precludes openness to truth at some crucial point. We risk the excesses of an inflation or deflation of the style of truth in which we invest.

On an interreligious level, the shade cast both on Judaism and on classical culture by the Church's claim to be the only true fulfilment of their traditions can be considered to result from a decision which was violent and in large part unjust, even if it is this decision that animates the luminous arguments of Paul and John, Justin and Irenaeus. The Church was able to bring about the mutual transformation of Hebrew truth and Greek truth: it universalised the first and rooted the second in existence and in history. But neither Judaism nor Hellenism thereby became obsolete. Their power of resistance to the Christian synthesis was shown from the outside – from Trypho and Celsus to Spinoza and the Enlightenment – and from within, preventing a stabilisation of the synthesis. This inability to reduce alternative horizons marks the finitude and situatedness of any regime of truth. To accept that our own regime of truth is bounded by such modest conditions should not paralyse us but give our praxis more scope and freedom by disburdening it of mystification.

The contemporary experience of pluralism further radicalises this sense of the situated character of all truth-claims. Facing the barriers to dialogue between people proceeding from different visions of the world, the impossibility for any thinker to survey the various religions, and the impossibility of shaking off pre-understandings to attain a completely objective outlook, we are thrown back on our finitude. Does this mean, as Harold Coward claims, that 'there is no longer any ground upon which a theologian can make absolute claims for a particular theological position' (Dean, 57), that 'all future theologizing in the sense of establishing ultimate claims to knowledge must cease' (58)? Remembering that in the Bible it is God and Christ (not bumptious theologians ignorant of their own finitude) who are represented as making ultimate claims for themselves, the Christian is likely to be unhappy with this curtailment of ultimate claims. Can we not have a pluralism which respects the religions' conviction of being vehicles of ultimate truth? Coward grants that 'in all religions there is experience of a reality that transcends human conception' and that this 'particular experience' may 'function in an absolute sense as the validating criterion for our own personal religious experience'

(59). But what is the meaning of 'absolute' in this sentence? The word is 'used simply to describe the felt nature of commitment to the transcendent through a particular personal experience' (60). If it is only a feeling it is not absolute; if a valid perception of the absolute is involved, then the finite, instrumental and perspectival status of religions is no barrier to their making absolute claims.

It is a tight-rope exercise to reconcile dogmatic objectivity with a full recognition of cultural contingency. What may bridge the gap between the two is a sense of the practically embedded character of truth, what de Certeau calls its writerly character: 'The status of truth is changing; truth is gradually ceasing to be that which manifests itself, becoming instead that which is produced, and in this way it acquires a rather "writerly" form' (Geffré, 167f). Relaxed in one sense, tightened in another, the pragmatic, historically embedded, writerly conception of Christian truth corresponds to the incarnational character of Christianity. But how can the kerygma, caught in the texture of history, depending for its authenticity on its concrete social and political correlatives at a given juncture, and identified with the plurality of its relative forms, still summon us with sovereign authority as a word of judgement and salvation? Perhaps its force becomes less immediate than before; but more persuasive, and encouraging a more reflective, and thus more durable, appropriation.

The social and historical embeddedness of truth tightens the bond between truth and practice. But the tightness of the bond, paradoxically, depends on the irreducible autonomy of the search for truth. If we see truth primarily or only as a tactical weapon in political struggles, we dissolve the very thing that gives truth its power of resistance. There remains a sense in which the objectivity of the true depends on its social and political enactment; there are truths which are manifested and proved only by means of a social change. The conceptual transformations enlightened praxis engenders are not merely an enrichment of one's logical apparatus, but constitute a new space of consciousness, incommensurable with what they replace. Moreover, they install a new relation between thought and world, and in this sense a transformation in the very nature of truth. The present ecclesiastical crisis is partly due to the co-existence of rival essences of truth: the Roman one, based on definition – definition of dogmas, duties, powers, frontiers of orthodoxy and of denominational identity – and the prophetic one, based on reading the signs of the times and grounding every discourse of faith in concrete struggles for liberation. We miss the latter kind of truth not by bad definitions, but by a deficient ethical and political consciousness. In this regime of truth, concepts once quite peripheral (such as the Kingdom of God, or the People

of God) can take a central place, as more apt to apprehend Gospel liberation, while concepts once central become marginal.

Propositions have an objective hold on the reality of God only in the
context of a religious attitude that is truthful at ground level. Perhaps the
divine otherness is less manifest in such propositions than in a vivid sense
of what even the finest religious language fails to encompass. Across the
inspired or judicious linguistic performance of kerygma or theology the
reality they aim at insists without form or figure: as that which is lacking
to the discourse, that which is witnessed to by its recurrent flaws or
cracks. This lack itself, this 'emptiness', would be the mode in which the
ineffable real makes itself present. No further meta-discourse can succeed
in identifying or defining this transcendent reality better than does a discourse which integrates awareness of its own historical finitude and
assumes it fully. In seeking to stop up the holes in our religious language,
speculative theology actually blocks out transcendence. One could see
religious discourse as formally bringing into relief the constitutive finitude
of every human discourse, thus opening all human discourse, in confiding
abandon, to the divine emptiness and distance.

Finally, how does truth take place? How is it incarnated? That is to ask
the question from above down. Better to put it from below: in what situations is the expression 'true' found to be indispensable? What is the
function and the concrete meaning of this expression in these contexts? It
will be found that there is a great plurality of contexts, functions, and
meanings for the expression 'true'. Yet questions are formulated in every
epoch which demand a yes-or-no answer; and if the reponse is true nothing in the future can annul what is thus accomplished. Scientific progress
can impose a redescription, so that the judgement 'the pen is on the table'
would have to be rewritten as follows: 'the quark-complex A342 is in a
relation of superposition to the quark-complex Z546'. The meaning of the
second sentence does not precisely overlap that of the first; this would be
impossible, for the entire epistemological context has changed. But in its
turn this sentence, as a true judgement, also possesses indelible objectivity.
Truth has emerged, yet it cannot be enunciated independently of the concrete realisations of meaning. We may no longer be able to say 'the pen is
on the table'; the epistemological epoch within which such propositions
could be formulated may have become a distant memory, inaccessible to
our efforts at reconstruction; nonetheless, within that vanished world it
was at one time true that the pen was on the table and it never will be the
case that it would have been true to say that the pen was not on the table.

The same claim can be made for a true religious proposition such as
'God is the creator of the world', even if successive redescriptions go so

far as to drop the terms 'God', 'creator' and 'world' in favour of some dynamic equivalent, so that the statement can no longer be uttered meaningfully, belonging as it does to a vanished epistemological order (indeed this may already be the case). Every truth has its place, its date, its particular form. The concrete content of a judgement is never immunised against the possibility of radical redescription. The dogmatic judgements of Christianity are doubly exposed to this possibility when transferred to interreligious space, which accelerates the process of redescription underway within the Christian world since Hegel and Schleiermacher.

We need to note as well that 'God is the creator of the world' is not a judgement of fact comparable to 'the pen is on the table'. Its truth belongs more to the vaguer realm of adequation, in contrast to the precise sense in which a proposition is true or false. Truth as adequation depends even more than truth as correctness on the conditions of its enunciation, and has much less power to transcend its context. The judgement of fact, 'Wordsworth and Hölderlin were born in 1770', will remain eternally true, despite the possible obsolescence of its terms. But when one seeks to name the truth of something, its essence or being, in an adequate way, one is plunged immediately into the element of time, relativity and incarnation. The 'truth' of Wordsworth or Hölderlin, in this sense, is conceivable only at a certain moment of the evolution of the English and German languages and the intellectual and spiritual adventure of Europe: a moment which is no longer ours. Similarly, 'true' utterances about God tend to be evocations of a total historical situation, and much of their illuminating impact is lost with a change of epoch. Perhaps there are no simply factual truths about God. Even 'God exists' is problematic, if only in view of the classic claim that God's essence is identical with God's being. Even if one did assemble a series of eternally and indubitably true propositions about God, these might lack truth in the sense of adequation; rather than illuminate God's nature they might be screens against it. A relatively adequate language about God is one that espouses time and incarnation, and is content with a provisional validity, for its own day.

THE REFERENCE OF DOGMATIC LANGUAGE

The contextuality of religious propositions, in something like the sense we have been exploring, is received wisdom in contemporary theology. The strongest resistance to it comes from philosophers of religion in the analytic tradition. Characteristic is the discourse of Richard Swinburne, in which Christian truths are decontextualised, shorn of their vital resonances, and in their dehydrated form made into pawns in a logical game:

> A God who made human beings with capacities to do actions of supererogatory goodness and to make themselves saints would

think it good that they should do so, and might well help them to do so. If they do become saints, he would think that this was such a good thing that it was worth preserving them after this life to pursue the supremely worthwhile life of Heaven, centred on the worship of God. (Swinburne, 70)

Here, the phrase 'make themselves saints' is in tension with biblical diction and savours of Pelagianism; to speak of God as finding humans 'worth preserving' is again unbiblical, and projects a dehumanising conception of God; to sum up the meaning of human life as 'to become a saint and go to Heaven' implies a threadbare phenomenology of Gospel salvation, which ignores such aspects as its social or communal scope, the vision of God's Kingdom as breaking into human history, or the Johannine sense of eternal life as a present reality – as well as flattening out the pluralism of these conceptions. Another mark of Swinburne's phenomenological insouciance is the fact that he sees no difference between the God of Christian revelation and the God of classical ontology. His own phenomenology of God cannot even be seen as a philosophical reduction or purification of biblical representations, for in retaining a literalistic version of these representations he falls far short of the philosophical apprehension of the divine as found in Plotinus, Kant or Hegel.

This thin phenomenological basis offers no resistance to the construction of ratiocinations attributed to God himself. The procedure is classical (one finds it in Athanasius, *On the Incarnation*), and may still be useful in sermons as a rhetorical device, but used for purposes of speculative explanation it is in dissonance with the present conditions of a meaningful discourse on God. We believe that we have been created by God, the source of all that we are. But to think of God as relating to his creatures and pondering on what is best for them is to reify the creatures and to anthropomorphise God by giving him a 'point of view'. Theology should reduce such representations to less anthropomorphic terms. Otherwise, removed from the intimacy of a liturgical context in which they are charged with symbolic resonance, they become bizarre suppositions in a kind of theological science fiction.

According to Swinburne, 'there is a priori reason for supposing that the revelation which God provides will be such as requires searching out with the help of others, and such as not to be completely evident even to those who have found it' (75); God chooses this pedagogic means to make us more thirsty for heaven so that our happiness on arriving there will be greater. But has not the obscurity of revelation its sufficient reason in the texture of human language and of historicity? A theology which is not familiar with this texture through long historical study is bound to lose itself in jejune speculations. Swinburne's insistence on the propositionality of revelation disregards the concrete mediations by which doctrinal propositions emerge. Claiming that God communicates revealed propositions directly to the prophets, he ignores what critical study of Scripture suggests about the concrete modalities of revelation, e.g. the possibility of seeing all revelation as a form of interpretation, born of a tradition of interpretation. If revelation is mediated by interpretation, there are no naked core-events (miracles, prophets' encounters with God) accessible independently of faith-understanding and no core-propositions independent of the entire semiotic web of religious interpretation. 'God exists' (in the sense defined by the development of monotheistic tradition) is a revealed proposition; but the fluctuation in the biblical and post-biblical representations of this God suggests that the frontier between divine revelation and human religious thought is far from clear, or that the former is mediated by the latter. 'Christ is risen' is not, as Swinburne thinks, the simple description of a visible miracle verifying Jesus's propositional claims, but one of several ways of interpreting the post-paschal experience. It summarises a cluster of interpretations in tension with one another, and it remains open itself to constant reinterpretation. The experience itself is plural – Peter's in Galilee is not Paul's on the road to Damascus – and it may be that it is not distinguished by a firm border from more everyday experiences. Philosophers who reduce such complex processes to simple propositions are spared from having to bother with the concrete texture of revealed religion; they cook up instead a skeletal religion of their own.

Though at the antipodes of Derrida, Swinburne betrays an inkling that the meaning of a statement cannot be definitively settled by reference to its context, since the context allows of indefinite enlargement or alteration. What he says of the biblical books can be extended to all texts and statements: 'Putting the books together into a whole Bible involved giving them a change of context and, in consequence, by processes similar to those involved in the formation of an individual book, a change of meaning' (175). In the same way, when Christianity is put in the interreligious context, it acquires a new meaning; and when a dogmatic proposition is put in this context, many presuppositions inscribed in that proposition have to be corrected, and the proposition may acquire an unexpected pertinence as it resonates with propositions drawn from foreign religious domains. The meaning of 'Christ is risen' changes subtly when one makes it rhyme with 'the Buddha is enlightened'.

The most influential recent statement of the practical rootedness of Christian truth is that of George Lindbeck, who says of religious statements that their correspondence to reality 'is not an attribute that they have when considered in and of themselves, but is only a function of their role in constituting a form of life, a way of being in the world, which itself corresponds to the Most Important, the Ultimately Real' (Lindbeck, 65). Religious performance which is not merely routine always carries implicit affirmations and engenders statements of truth. To say that these have no truth 'in themselves' but only in view of their relation to practice may be a simplification. Religious language is rather characterised by the impossibility of separating the practice and the enunciation of truth; the two contaminate one another in a perpetual to-and-fro.

The Wittgensteinian claim that religious propositions make sense only in the context of a religious language game, itself embedded in a religious form of life, does not entail a non-objectivist interpretation of religious language in the manner of D. Z. Phillips. As Vincent Brümmer insists, 'the constitutive propositions of a language-game refer to the *factual nature* of the world within which the language-game is to be played' (Byrne, 96). Yet there is some justice in Phillips's comment that to say the religious form of life corresponds to the ultimately real is an example of 'language idling':

> No use of capitals in talking of the 'Most Important' and the 'Ultimately Real' can hide the fact that [Lindbeck] is trying to place these concepts, whatever they are, in a logical space which transcends the language-games and forms of life in which concepts have their life. The notion of such a logical space is an illusion. (Phillips, 142)

The objective referentiality of 'God' has to be defended without any overstepping of the language in which this expression functions, towards some dimly imagined object 'out there'. Otherwise we end up using the expressions 'God' and 'what "God" refers to' as if two different referents were involved, in which case the true object of belief would no longer be God but what 'God' refers to. The reason Lindbeck tends to such an impossible doubling of religious discourse is that he immunises religious forms of life against a critical rationality external to them. The practical embeddedness of religious discourse does not necessarily imply such isolation, nor the presumption that the religious forms of life and religious discourse are always 'in order', which Lindbeck takes to warrant the 'self-evidence' of Christian faith. If the religious language-game remains answerable to the facts, and so subject to critique and alteration, then there is no need to posit a logical space which transcends it; the language-game is objectively engaged with the real, in an inadequate and endlessly revisable way.

Lindbeck underestimates the mobility of religious language, and the degree to which a diction that is liberative in one context may be oppressive in another. Pragmatically, a religion is true only if it can be lived as liberative under particular cultural and political circumstances. Of course, one may leave space for a secondary, less urgent realm of reflection on the primary language of faith, which reflects on the conditions of its authenticity. As to philosophical constructions of transcendence independent of every religious life, it may be noted that the God thus constructed also has a concrete visage, derived from the underlying existential style of the philosophical quest. Even a God who was merely the logical explanation of the universe, interchangeable with a computer of infinite capacity, would also carry an intrinsic reference to the form of life that produced him, for even the cold intellectuality which abstains from any existential abandonment is itself a concrete style of existing.

For Lindbeck, it is only in the ordinary religious language of prayer and preaching that 'human beings linguistically exhibit their truth or falsity, their correspondence or lack of correspondence to the Ultimate Mystery':

> Technical theology and official doctrine, in contrast, are second-order discourse about the first-intentional uses of religious language. Here, in contrast to the common supposition, one rarely if ever succeeds in making affirmations with ontological import, but rather engages in explaining, defending, analysing, and regulating the liturgical, kerygmatic, and ethical modes of speech and action within which such affirmations from time to time occur. (Lindbeck, 69)

Lindbeck is not denying the ontological bearing of first-order discourse, which can directly claim to be true. But dogmatic statements make the same claim, whether carrying over truths already stated in the first-order discourse or introducing a new set of statements with an ontological bearing. For dogmas to meet Lindbeck's restrictions, they would first have to be changed into statements whose critical and secondary status would be made explicit. As things stand, his analysis concerns what dogma and theology should be, not what they have actually been or claimed to be.

Can one, in any case, distinguish between first-order and second-order religious utterances? If I say 'God is good' or 'Jesus Christ is divine' this is at one and the same time a rule for the use of the term 'God' or 'Jesus Christ' and an ontological statement. Distinctions between first-order and second-order take as many forms as there are authors who propound them and within any one of these forms the frontier between the two orders remains vague and penetrable. If 'My Lord and my God' (Jn 20:28) figures in dogmatic or theological language only as a citation, the same is true of its use in the first-order language: the believer who utters it has already accomplished a theological and dogmatic labour, quoting terms drawn from the tradition. One cannot uncover beneath dogmatic language a layer of pure performatives, nor can one isolate a layer of grammatical or regulative utterances that have no ontological upshot.

Controlling the internal pluralism of Christian tradition by appeal to a rather arbitrary set of 'regulative principles', Lindbeck pays little attention to the constant solicitation of other traditions and new situations which makes the Christian quest for truth more an open-ended conversation than the intratextual or intrasystematic clarification of a settled form of life. Lindbeck would have us measure the truth and irreversibility of dogmas by underlying rules of grammar implied in the primary performances of a religion. Thus the Christological dogmas are to be understood as realising under the conditions of Hellenistic culture three basic regulative principles: the monotheistic principle, the principle of historical specificity (anti-docetist), and the principle of Christological maximalism, which ascribes to Jesus every possible importance that is not incompatible with the first two principles (94). Would Lindbeck admit that these dogmas remain open to a possible critique insofar as one could take up the accusation, in the light of a contemporary understanding of God and of the historical humanity of Jesus, that they infringe the first two principles? In any case, these principles are formed only by abstraction, in a second-order discourse, and are subject to reformulation in the light of a better understanding of the first-order discourse. Nor is the first-order discourse stable and homogeneous. Governed by dogmas and principles derived from critical analysis of its previous states, it is not confined to the field thus regulated but experiments with new styles of speech, whose authenticity is measured less by the principles or dogmas than by an instinct or tact comparable to those which preside at the creation and reception of works of art.

What is the source of Lindbeck's fundamental rules? Far from being a natural grammar of faith they are the product of a historical genesis which includes the entire biblical reflection on God, history, and the Messiah. The monotheistic principle can in turn be seen as the dogmatic precipitate of a still more fundamental principle of religious behaviour. The more one goes back the more difficult it becomes to state the rule supposed to be at work. The very notion of rule seems to be only a retrospective projection on the performativity of religious language. Thus the querying of the foundations of a religion can come to rest only in an integral grasp of this performativity in its entire historical sweep, which includes the history of the discourses inscribed in it. No tidy principles can master this history, which has the openness and freedom of a creative project, comparable to an artistic tradition.

Lindbeck opposes the conception of doctrine as normative rule to the claim that doctrinal statements have an ontological reference:

> Rule theory does not prohibit speculations on the possible corre-spondence of the Trinitarian patter of Christian language to the metaphysical structure of the Godhead, but simply says that these are not doctrinally necessary and cannot be binding. They are like discussions as to whether there is a substance-attribute structure of finite entities corresponding to the substance-attribute structure of sentences. (106)

Here Lindbeck seems to confuse two things: 1. the necessity of making certain statements on the being of God in order to preserve the integrity of the Trinitarian structure of Christian language; 2. the speculative play which seeks to map the celestial archetype of the Trinitarian functions and relations manifested in the New Testament economy. The latter sup-poses a metaphysical horizon which can bring God into its sights and then relate this God to his manifestation in the biblical economy. But one does not exchange the horizon of revelation for such a distorted perspec-tive when one contents oneself with the affirmations that Father, Logos and Spirit are divine, that there is only one God, and that nonetheless the Trinitarian distinctions are not ephemeral but correspond to reality. These affirmations may be reformulated as negative rules of language, thus reducing still more their metaphysical appearance. Dogmatic language:

> is not in tension with the apophatic. Properly speaking, it reinforces the apophatic impulse, in confronting us simultaneously with the narrative of Israel, Jesus and the Church, and with an austerely formal structure for referring to the God who gives coherence to the narrative, and of whom nothing can be said *substantively* but that this God is such as to give coherence to this narrative, that we meet this God thus and are constrained to organise what we say thus. (Rowan Williams, in Byrne, 47)

Dogma does not add an 'immanent' God to the 'economic' one, but ensures that in speaking of God as Father, Son and Spirit we are indeed speaking of God and not merely of appearances of God.

Our discussion of Swinburne and Lindbeck allows a firmer grasp of the contours of the Christian truth, with emphasis on its situated and event-ful character. In the Bible, truth emerges in opposition to rival truth-claims in a particular context. The truth of the prophets, Jesus, Paul and John is of this conjunctural kind and eludes a formulation valid for all time. Truth is always in crisis and always calls for a judgement (*krisis*) which will decide it. Once given, established, taken for granted, it begins to decline into non-truth. Items of ancient wisdom become true again when they are rediscovered or reinvented as a resource for opposition to some dominant wisdom, as when the prophets give a shocking turn to venerable traditions. Although truths abound in past and present, one cannot rest in them tranquilly, for their radiance and force appear only when they take on a new pertinence in contexts of conflict.

That is the reason why the biblical texts are literature. As such they give each statement a precise, unique context and resist the encroachment of platitudes presenting themselves as trans-contextual and trans-textual truths, such as 'God exists'. Even the quasi-dogmatic formulas in the New Testament are enframed in radiant hymns or marked by some other striking literary trait. If this is how truths emerge in the Bible, the expressions 'biblical truth' or 'Christian truth' may be distorting. One can admire the many effects of truth in Shakespeare, but if one talks of 'Shakespearian truth' one has already lost sight of them. Similarly, in the Bible, one cannot go beyond the dramatic confrontations which are the very element of revelation towards a synthesis which integrates them. Dogmas do not bring this drama to an end, but rather keep open the space for its continuation, as Christian thought goes beyond them even while trying to avoid the perils they signposted.

THE SCOPE OF INTERRELIGIOUS CONTRADICTIONS

Uneasy with the proliferation of religious traditions and the contradictions between their formal justifications, Paul Griffiths hopes to solve this confusion by giving back to apologetics its strictest form of logical refutation of error and proof of truth. Only in recognising the need of such apologetics can we understand

> why some British Muslims feel impelled to burn anti-Islamic books in Bradford, why some Buddhist monks in Sri Lanka feel called upon to foster and encourage anti-Tamil violence, and why some conservative Catholic Christians in the United States of America are willing to bomb clinics in which advice on abortion is given to pregnant women. (Griffiths, xi)

A strange claim. Liberal theologians would say that what needs to be understood and corrected here are the phenomena of fundamentalism and fanaticism, and they seek to soften the sharp edges of apologetics precisely because apologetical crusades so often reinforce such religious pathologies. Griffiths opposes a scholarly orthodoxy which suggests 'that judgement and criticism of religious beliefs or practices other than those of one's own community is always inappropriate'. But he misses the point that all questioning theology, especially of the interreligious kind, constitutes by its very existence a sustained polemic against fundamentalism.

I agree that apologetics is a part of interreligious dialogue, and moreover that the quest for orthodoxy is intrinsic to the theological clarification of one's tradition. But these enterprises are far more open-ended and delicate than Griffiths allows. They correspond to imperatives of theological reason, but this reason operates within a quest of faith which is never quite satisfied with its own self-understanding, still less with its understanding of other faiths. Apologetic precipitation is untrue to this incompleteness of the vision of faith, and leads to sterile doxography. To trust in the basic truth of the other tradition, according it parity with our own, is the only workable basis for an entente within which, at a subsequent stage, apologetic clarification of differences may proceed. Moreover, a positive apologetics, which 'takes the battle to the enemy's camp' (14), for example by proving the cognitive superiority of biblical monotheism to Buddhist non-theism, ought to move in tandem with an admission of the cognitive superiority of the non-Christian doctrine in other respects. For instance, the role of revelation in Christian thinking could be reconsidered in view of the primacy of insight in Buddhism. Whereas the light of revelation supervenes on the light of reason from outside or from above, in Buddhism reason opens to intuitive wisdom (*prajñā*) according to the intrinsic dynamic of its own self-deconstructive processes. This may be one of many features whereby a foreign tradition provides therapy for stressful aspects of the Christian dispensation. Apologetics, even against secular atheism, thus proves not to be a one-way street; if it is worth pursuing at all it becomes a give and take.

'God has spoken to us, not to them' or 'God has spoken fully to us, only partly to them' are slogans that impede the unfolding and clarification of the Gospel in new religious milieux. The clarity of the biblical word is unique, definitive, universal; but so is the clarity of the Buddha-word. In the process whereby each of these great truth-events opens to the other, the real or apparent doctrinal contradictions between them figure only as secondary problems, to be resolved in long negotiations, or to be left unresolved as belonging to the realm of the undecidable.

According to Griffiths, 'in order for any performative utterance (religious or otherwise) to function as such, what is expressed by some set of nonperformative utterances must be ontologically true' (Griffiths, 42), and this dependence of performative utterances on dogmas is not reversible. Against this, we have maintained that, while first-order faith statements are never mere performances bereft of implicit ontological affirmation, what secures their ontological bearing is the entire historical form of life within which they emerge. Any nonperformative ontological utterances one might extract from this total context would at best be pale shadows of the truth affirmed in the first-order language rooted in tradition and praxis. 'God is love' (1 Jn 4:8,16) has inexhaustible meaning within such a lived context, whereas it is a thankless task to sift out its nonperformative ontological implications. Griffiths' stark distinction of performative and nonperformative is impracticable for significant religious statements, such as those of the Creed.

The contextuality of religious statements makes Griffiths' attempt to establish clearcut contradictions between religions highly problematic. If one opposes two first-order statements, e.g. 'the soul is immortal' and 'the self is illusory', one has not necessarily pinned down a contradiction, for when the statements are replaced in the religious contexts which elicit their spontaneous utterance, then it is two forms of life, both charged with salutary impact, that one is trying to put in contradiction. A living faith eludes such summary logic. It is true that 'if doctrine-expressing statements cannot make direct claims to truth but can function only regulatively within the bounds of specific communities, then they cannot be directly incompatible' (39). It is also true that if doctrine-expressing statements can indeed make direct claims to truth, but only as they function within a specific culture of faith, then their incompatibility cannot be read off by simply juxtaposing the two statements. It emerges only in a dialogue between the traditions from which they emerge. Even when one tradition deliberately seeks to contradict a belief of another tradition – e.g. 'for us Jesus is divine, for you he is only a prophet' – the sharpness of the opposition can be softened if instead of taking it at face value one refers each position back to its historical context; even if the contradiction subsists, it may now weigh no more heavily than one between divergent theological stances within a single tradition.

Griffiths' principles cut too brusquely through the tangles of hermeneutics and ruin the enterprise of ecumenical dialogue. For instance, he declares:

> If the profoundly personal theistic mysticism of Teresa of Avila is veridical and the doctrine-expressing sentences that both formed it and express it are true, then a Zen Buddhist's *satori* cannot be veridical, and the doctrine-expressing sentences that both form it and express it cannot be true. (59)

The realities of history and of culture forbid us to say that Teresa's mysticism and Zen *satori* are one and the same experience. But neither are they necessarily poles apart: a Zen reader of Teresa might intuitively appreciate what she is talking about just as Teresa herself intuitively grasped the meaning of Augustine's language. As to the doctrine-expressing statements, they do not make it all that clear what the referent of theistic petition, praise and meditation is. They function performatively as a system of representations orienting an existence which wants to dedicate itself to an unfigurable truth. Zen meditation seeks, more radically, to suspend all representations; it traces another route through the real, orienting itself according to a different way of cutting up spiritual space. Neither of these two paths can judge the other. Each leads to a contact with the real, but neither embraces objectively all the modalities of this contact.

Griffiths contrasts the Christian defence of the substantial and immortal soul with the Buddhist doctrine of non-self (85–108). The immortal soul has little attraction for contemporary theologians, who feel that instead of resolving the surd of mortality it introduces new complications; thus they refrain from translating into ontological terms the Gospel promise of 'eternal life'. The Indian sensibility to the processual interlinkedness of things induces a thinking in terms of karmic networks in which life and death interpenetrate. On this basis the Buddhist notion of dependent co-arising (*pratītya-samutpāda*) dissolves the deluded clinging to a substantial ego, not to fall into an equally deluded nihilism but to espouse the processes of life in a demystified way. Much of the paralysis of our thinking on death is due to a rigid idea of the substantiality of the self. The interaction between Buddhism and Christianity on this point can hardly be reduced to a mere apologetic argument.

Griffiths does not pursue far enough the attempt to reinsert the differing religious experiences and doctrine-expressing statements in their human contexts. That reinsertion makes dialogue between traditions subtler and more laborious, obliging each to apprehend the other as a culture which approaches ultimate truth along paths hewn by a quite different history. Indeed, one can scarcely speak of an 'ultimate truth' which would unite them, for each can postulate this elusive X only starting from its own historical horizon and language. It is easier to compare the concrete ultimacy in one's own tradition with what one may gropingly identify as the equivalent depth in the other tradition. Beyond this encounter of concrete visions of ultimacy, the reference to ultimacy in general is a logical abstraction carrying no weight in first-order religious language. Thus we elude Griffiths' strictures against the view of rival doctrines as 'valuably representing different perspectives upon or reactions to "ultimate reality" or some such abstract periphrasis for the full-blooded religious realities about which the representative intellectuals of religious communities have typically taken themselves to be talking' (45f). A pluralism which respects the ultimacy of each religious perspective does not contradict the self-understanding of the individual religions.

Griffiths thinks it highly improbable that a single ultimate reality would manifest itself in such drastically different ways. The diversity must spring in large part from error. Here again, parity would oblige the concession that no religion is without its fringe of error, its blind spots. This fallibility, compounded with the contingency of cultural constructions and the analogical and provisional character of religious language, provides ample basis for seeking religious truth in the interplay of perspectives rather than in a showdown which proves one true and others false. Perspectivism can leave the door open to value-judgements and judgements of truth and falsehood in regard to another tradition, nor does it even exclude claims to primacy in one respect or another – a primacy of Christ as historical saviour or a primacy of the Four Noble Truths as the most probing analysis of the human condition. But these will emerge much more slowly and discreetly than in a uni-dimensional apologetic regime, and they will never so dominate the field as to annul or absorb its fundamentally perspectivist topology.

Harold Netland, rejecting John Hick's vision of a single soteriological pattern in all religions, points out that in order to evaluate the salvific schemas of the religions, one must first judge the truth of their initial diagnosis of the human condition: 'the question of truth is inescapable: What is the ultimate nature of the human predicament and how can one attain release from it?' (Netland, 164). This question seems to me to be poorly posed. First, the diagnosis made by a great religion is inseparable from its liberative impact and does not precede it. It is impossible to formulate the diagnosis coherently except in the light of the liberation which is already at work. The Buddha announced that 'all is suffering' only in the context of pointing to *nirvāṇa* and the path; Paul talks of original sin only as a presupposition of his presentation of grace.

Netland's insistence on propositional truth in religion is a wholesome corrective of the reduction of truth to an experiential event. But he mistakes the priority of event over proposition, championed by many theologians, for a radical disqualification of propositional truth, to which these theologians would not subscribe. The human condition can be understood only from within, especially in the style of discourse we call religious. The truth thus glimpsed can be expressed in propositions, but they draw their truth from this existential context. Moreover, the terms of such propositions will be analogical, metaphorical or symbolic, and dependent on a mobile historical setting, for no statement on the human condition can be formulated outside a contingent historical enchainment. To refer to 'the' human condition is to gloss over the varied figures of that condition, especially the present needs of salvation or liberation, which differ from those of the past and among themselves; indeed it may be that each individual seeks salvation in an irreducibly singular way. A static adjudication of Buddhist claims from the Christian standpoint is rendered problematic by the fact that any version of the Christian standpoint has already begun to alter when put in dialogal relation with a version of the Buddhist vision. Nor is there a neutral viewpoint from which the two might be independently assessed.

Netland proposes that 'belief in the existence of an eternal creator God' (181) is a Christian truth which can be invoked as normative in the evaluation of other religions. Given the polyvalence of the terms, 'existence', 'God', 'creator', 'eternal' and the difficulty of determining their epistemic status, such an expression is unlikely to function well outside its concrete religious contexts. To give it an extra-contextual sense, one would have to construct an onto-theology, and the God thus constructed would no longer invite religious worship. The problem is not to 'determine whether the religious ultimate is the monotheistic God of the Semitic tradition or the monistic *nirguṇa* Brahman of Hinduism' (203). The confrontation of these two theses falsifies the total situation in which the two traditions that carry these theses and give them their meaning are brought into dialogue. In the irreducible differences that emerge in this encounter, in which neither tradition can dominate or recuperate the other, the quest of ultimate reality is renewed. Certainly, cultural relativism cannot be absolute, for cultures can mutually understand and criticise one another, in implicit reference to a universal ethics and reason, even if no formulation of this universal can escape the particularity of its context. The question of truth presides over the epochal changes which take place within cultures and the upheavals caused by the encounter of cultures, even if it, too, does not admit of extracontextual formulation.

The overcoming of substantialist notions inaugurates a style of thinking which respects 'the inscrutability of reference' (Quine) characteristic of religious discourse, at the same time that it draws our attention back to the concrete historical texture of a religious world as it lies open to analysis and interrogation. A religious system is but a makeshift net trawled in the sea of spiritual reality; yet insofar as it is pervaded by the vibrations of the reality it envisages and glimpses, one can trust such a system, and dwell in it not only affectively but intellectually. We have no other access to religious reality than what these fragile and contingent systems offer. A thinking that bypasses them, on the basis of some original spiritual breakthrough, cannot claim to have an objectivity they lack; at best such thinking may in its turn found a tradition, which will be subject to the same conditions. *Am farbigen Abglanz haben wir das Leben.*

Logical argument has a role in every interreligious confrontation, but to give it primacy as an authority judging every discourse from above, immune to inscription in a context that puts it in its place, is to distort the space of interreligious dialogue. Apologetic discussion should be deferred to the time when a transparent understanding of the other has been attained. That point has not yet been reached in Catholic-Protestant dialogue, and even within a single denomination there is an incommensurability between different cultural horizons. *A fortiori* the Buddhist-Christian differences cannot be smoothed out to fit the demand of apologetics for direct confrontation. It is not enough to master the logic of Buddhist texts; one would also have to grasp the relations between the entire life-contexts of the Christian and Buddhist traditions, a task so daunting as to suggest that religious cultures are permanently incommensurable and hence not amenable to the simplifications traditional apologetics requires.

An individual can participate in the life of two distinct traditions, or create a hybrid religious lifestyle by yoking together elements from diverse quarters. Here we have a play of complementary perspectives, not the domination of a single objective perspective, just as a musician's frequentation of Mozart and Wagner does not imply a siting of the two in some objective musical space, or a denaturing interpretation of one in terms of the other, or their absorption into a superior musical synthesis. Some Western Zen enthusiasts exploit contradictions between Zen and Christianity to overcome the latter. They see Christianity as encumbered with the alienating projection of a 'God', a notion whose obscurities condemn one to perpetual qualifications, whereas Zen, proceeding on an assured phenomenal basis, has no need of such problematic hypotheses. Such a view does not do justice to the historical condition of Zen, or to possible resonances between Zen insights and the biblical experience of divine transcendence. Conversely, Christian absorption of Zen as a simple clarification of the spiritual life misses its stylistic otherness and its critical force over against Christianity. Perhaps the most fruitful interreligious use of logical argument is to sustain the sense of such differences, rather than to iron them out in the triumph of one tradition or the other.

The main reason why theologians contest the contextuality of religious truth is their fear of the relativism to which it leads. According to Ian Hacking, it is a given style of reasoning which determines the truth-or-falsity and the meaning of the propositions it serves to establish, and they have no existence independently of these paths of reasoning; we cannot reason about whether alternative systems of reasoning are better or worse than our own (see Baghramian, 22). This relativism soon slides into the nightmare evoked by Langdon Gilkey:

> There seems here no firm ground to stand on, either in a given tra-dition and its symbols, or in religious experience and its various aspects. And note, this is a *real* relativism: if they are relativized, God, Christ, grace and salvation, higher consciousness, *dharma*, nirvana and *mukti* alike begin to recede in authority, to take on the aspect of mere projections relative to the cultural and individual subjectivity of the projectors, and so in the end they vanish like bloodless ghosts. We have no grounds for speaking of salvation at all, a situation of relativity far beyond asking about the salvation of *all*. A drift toward radical relativity has come to light, and any the-ological basis we might suggest for stopping that drift also begins itself to drift. (Hick and Knitter, 43f)

The therapy of this situation cannot lie in a refusal to admit that the situation exists. The real is mediated by the great variety of creative 'pro-jections' produced by our cultures, and we have little choice but to confide ourselves to the play of these mediations, without claiming a privileged position. This relativity, far from reducing beliefs to something spectral, is the condition of their proper functioning. As Gilkey says, even the primary beliefs of Western culture – in democracy, science, or historicity – themselves turn out to be relative. Must one then suspend all judgement, condemning oneself to absurdity and silence? One cannot avoid subscribing to certain conventional truths, even while knowing they give no grip on any inconceivable thing in itself. But how can one trust oneself to the conventional? One can do so only when one sees that it is the only language at our disposal, and that we do not have a discourse for directly grasping the ultimate, which however insists across the play of our languages.

4

DERRIDA ON TRUTH

Our task of defending the objective truth of religious doctrines while clarifying the modality of their historical emergence and transmission has made some philosophical reflection on the notion of truth indispensable. A dialogue with Derrida's idiosyncratic account of truth might seem a luxury, but it will, I think, be found doubly instructive: his exploration of the textual inscription and the writerly character of truth undoes the fixation on Truth with a capital 'T', which is the foundation of religious dogmatism; meanwhile he himself exemplifies mistaken ideas about truth which are the staple of agnosticism.

If the meaning of a statement is destabilised by its contextuality, its inscription in the network of archi-writing, this instability affects in turn the judgement of truth that one makes in regard to such a statement. Thus to the wound inflicted by 'dissemination' at the level of 'meaning' is added that of undecidability at the level of truth (a distinction Derrida tends to blur). Whereas in classical philosophies the condition of possibility of judgements is some transcendental truth, whether conceived as residing in being, in the subject, in a totality of meaning, or in the correspondence of a thing with its notion (Hegel), deconstruction focuses on the inscribed, textual status of all propositions, revealing archi-writing as the quasi-transcendental condition of possibility of truth-effects. A contextual theory of truth has a quite different upshot here than in Hegel: where Hegel dissolves partial truths in the integral grasp of that which is to be thought, Derrida dissolves them in an element which is essentially non-truth. The truth of truth is realised not in an 'absolute knowledge' but in a textual performance which refuses to be defined in terms of knowing or truth.

Far from gathering themselves in the totality of the true, judgements are always threatened with being swallowed up by this *khōra*, this undecidable medium which permits their formulation.

Derrida sees himself as 'a philosopher motivated by concern with reason and truth', but 'there comes a moment at which this interrogation of truth is no longer subject to the authority of truth' (in Rötzer, 72f); that is the moment at which the structure of archi-writing comes to light as one that permits and enframes effects of truth but cannot itself be judged true or false. This entails no destruction of truth, but merely puts it in context: 'The value of truth (and all those values associated with it) is never contested or destroyed in my writings, but only reinscribed in more powerful, larger, more stratified contexts' (*Limited Inc,* 146). If Derrida does sometimes speak of destroying truth, what is meant is a deconstruction that reveals the complex conditions of the truth-effect:

> The 'rationality'... which governs a writing thus enlarged and radicalized, no longers issues from a logos. Further, it inaugurates the destruction, not the demolition but the de-sedimentation, the de-construction, of all the significations that have their source in that of the logos. Particularly the signification of *truth*. (G, 10)

Deconstruction brings to light a realm of undecidability which is 'beyond truth' and which is the condition of possibility of our true statements while also marking the provisionality of any formulation of truth:

> Far from being a sort of empiricist agnosticism or skepticism, deconstruction is, so to speak, a hyper-cognition of a truth beyond truth, 'a supplement of truthless truth' ('Living On', 139), to the extent that it also inscribes the structural limits of cognition – thus, however, radically altering the concept of cognition as such. (Gasché 1986, 267)

This hyper-cognition dissolves the classical concern with the foundations of truth and knowledge by showing how the true always withdraws, defers itself, leaving only traces of itself in the play of the signifiers. Truth is not exhausted by the set of true statements one can enunciate, but if one asks what knowledge the statements convey beyond their explicit content one is thrown back on the enigma of their textuality, as the medium in which all truths emerge and into which they recede. The cult of upper case Truth, a Lacanian master-signifier which becomes a paralysing Gorgon, obscures this abyssal textual ground of true statements and seeks to found them instead in some direct transparent encounter of the mind with the real. Archi-writing checks this dogmatism at its root and invites us to find a gentler method, more poetic and indirect, of insisting on truth, or rather of letting truth insist across the play of our speech and writing. This insistence of truth, even amid textual complexity, needs however to be meditated on more intensively. It is doubtful if textuality, as the truth of truth, entirely sublates the truth of particular judgements. Derrida's apparent claim that it does is largely based on a notion of truth that has not well differentiated the truth of rational judgement from three other matters which are quite distinct from it: truth as unconcealment or presencing, truth as conceptual adequation, and reference.

FALSE IDENTIFICATIONS OF TRUTH

Derrida shows that its inscribed condition undoes classical conceptions of truth as phenomenal presence or as conceptual adequation, obliging philosophers to develop a subtler responsiveness to the 'truth' of textuality which is always marked by traits of absence, inadequation, undecidability. But he seems to gloss over what is more central and crucial in the philosophical tradition: the truth of propositions as affirmed in the act of judgement. This is realised at a level beyond the givenness of the data and their conceptual ordering, and cannot be subsumed under the notions of unconcealment or adequation. What Derrida sees as the classical conceptions of truth in reality deserve the name 'truth' only in a secondary and derivative sense. They are metaphysical myths which obscure truth's actual mode of being. Derrida effectively dismantles these myths, but he falls victim to them himself when he takes their deconstruction for a deconstruction of truth proper.

Truth is not phenomenal. A principal target of Derrida's critique is the phenomenological understanding of truth as coming-to-presence or unconcealment. Derrida constantly identifies truth with presence, whether in Hegel's terms: 'the presence or presentation of essence' (M, 120); 'the presence of the being, here in the form of presence adequate to itself' (M, 80); in Husserl's: the givenness of the thing itself in intuition; or in Heidegger's: 'the alleged simplicity of the opening, of the aperity – the letting-be, the truth that lifts the veil-screen' (D, 314). If these thinkers really reduce truth to coming-to-presence, this prevents them from doing justice to the truth of rational judgement, for the contact with being which a true judgement achieves does not take place in the mode of presence.

Heidegger opposes truth as unconcealment to 'mere correctness' and sees unconcealment as the ultimate condition of possibility of correctness. He seeks to render his thought adequate to the being of what is, not by forming rational judgements, but by a suspension of concept and argument in favour of the fine discriminations of a contemplative attending

on the phenomena. In his view, the truth of judgement, as correspondence between propositions and states of affairs, can be the bearer of a
cognition of beings, but never of a knowledge of being. Whereas for
Aristotle, it is propositional discourse alone that shows that things are
and that they are what they are, Heidegger, more concerned with the
first openness of human existence, sees speech in general as the lighting-
up of beings in their being. Without this prior opening of being, better
attested by a poetic word than by a proposition, the sense of the 'is' in
any proposition we affirm remains fundamentally unclarified.

Though it is a simplification to present the truth of being as the foundation and origin of the mere correctness of propositions, the Heideggerian
rhetoric is not simply mystificatory. If it were, the Johannine or any other
religious vocabulary of truth would be even more so. One would have to
reduce the notion of religious truth to the sum of correct religious propositions, as some analytical philosophers of religion seem happy to do.
Heidegger has recovered for thinking a lost continent whose existence
such stunted rationalism studiously ignores.

What can be objected to Heidegger, and to Derrida insofar as he identifies truth-as-presence with truth as such, is that the truth identified in a
correct judgement is not intrinsically reducible to unconcealment; its core
or essence is something that eludes the register of phenomenality. The
difference between the propositions 'Caesar crossed the Rubicon' and
'Caesar crossed the Thames' (one true, the other false) can be identified
by empirical verification and falsification, but the fact of truth or falsehood is not reducible to empirical or phenomenological terms. The limit
of the phenomenological view of truth is seen in its inability to bring into
view the difference between true and false propositions. If I utter a true
judgement – 'Caesar crossed the Rubicon' – one could say that the truth
of this judgement presents, represents, shows itself, reveals its presence,
in the judgement. But does this way of speaking focus at all precisely the
manner in which the judgement attains truth? Phenomenological theories
of intentionality or the pre-predicative foundations of the act of judging
tell us much about how truth is known, but this phenomenality of truth
remains secondary to the fundamental concern of judgement. Judgement
is a matter of correctness, veridicity, objectivity, rather than anything
phenomenal.

For Derrida, Western philosophy has been obsessed with truth as
presence. It has repressed all memory of the impurity of its written condition and:

> watches over its margins as virgin, homogeneous, and negative
> space, leaving its outside outside, without mark, without opposition,
> without determination, and ready, like matter, the matrix, the *khōra*,

to receive and repercuss type. This interpretation will have been *true*, the very history of truth. (*M*, xxvii)

This repression of the margins proceeds from 'an active indifference to difference' (*M*, 17) by which is maintained the artifical identity of 'truth as the presentation of the thing itself in its presence' (*M*, 18). All of this seems irrelevant to the truth of propositions or the truth of judgements. Indeed, one might maintain against Derrida that truth, as the truth of judgement, has often functioned in Western philosophy as an instance that undermines the metaphysics of presence.

Truth is not conceptual. The only other sense of 'truth' that Derrida attends to is truth as adequation:

'Truth' has always meant two different things, the history of the essence of truth – the truth of truth – being only the gap and the articulation between the two interpretations or processes... The process of truth is *on the one hand* the unveiling of what lies concealed in oblivion... *On the other hand*... truth is agreement (*homoiōsis* or *adaequatio*), a relation of resemblance or equality between a re-presentation and a thing (unveiled, present), even in the eventuality of a statement of judgment. (*D*, 192f)

Do presence and adequation cover all the senses of truth? Is a true judgement merely an adequation (of predicate to subject) ultimately grounded in 'the ambiguity or duplicity of the presence of the present' (192), or is there a specific truth of judgement which cannot be satisfactorily grasped either as presencing or as adequation? If *différance* reveals the non-originarity of presence and the impossibility of an adequation of *logos* to *eidos*, has it thereby put truth as such in question?

Derrida amalgamates two distinct levels, that of sense and meaning and that of the true; the level of concept and interpretation and the level of judgement. When he speaks of truth he means that which answers the question 'what is it?', not that which answers the question 'is it?'. Truth is 'that by which the question *what is? wants* answering (ce qu'il *faut* répondre)' (*D*, 177). But if the factors that constitute meaning are not those involved in the determination of truth, if the demand for the definition of an essence is not the same thing as the demand for a judgement of truth or falsehood, then semantic complications which make meaning too mobile to be controlled by the resources of phenomenology and dialectics do not necessarily involve any disabling of judgements of truth. Ignoring the scholastics' distinction between the first and the second acts of the intellect, between concept (locus of meaning) and judgement (locus of truth), Derrida puts forwards a conceptualist account of the classical notion of judgement, seeing it as essentially a matter of *adaequatio*: 'the essence of judgement being to say the essence (S is P)' ('Préjugés', 93; though a little further on he does link judgement with the 'thesis of existence' and deconstruction with the Husserlian *épochè* of that thesis, 96).

A theory of judgement which affirms the irreductibility of the 'yes or no', whereby every judgement anchors itself in being, gives the question of truth some independence from the level of meaning and hence from the structure of *différance* in which the articulation of meaning is caught. Truth in the sense of adequation, in Hegel for example, is unfolded on the level of the relation between subject and predicate, but the truth of a judgement, which affirms or negates a proposition, has to do not with defining an essence or a thought but with deciding the relation of the proposition to what is the case.

'Why is the metaphysical concept of truth in solidarity with a concept of the sign, and with a concept of the sign determined as a lack of full truth?' (*M*, 80). Again Derrida is talking about one metaphysical concept of truth, a conceptualist one, which is not the best that Western philosophy has to offer, and which misses the existential force of judgement. Hegel did not overcome the conceptualist notion of judgement that Kant expressed in these words:

> The objective criterion of truth is the correspondence [*Uebereinstimmung*] of the representations in a judgement with one another according to general rules of understanding and reason, that is, through intuitions or concepts ... All truth consists in the accord of all thoughts with the laws of thinking, and thus with one another. (Eisler, 595)

This is meant to correct the unsatisfactory definition of truth as correspondence of knowledge with its object (*Critique of Pure Reason*, A 57–62, B 82–6). How measure our knowledge against an object that is independent of our knowledge? We can measure our knowledge only against the object as known, which means we measure our knowledge by immanent criteria: 'All truth consists in the necessary correspondence of a cognition with itself' (*Akademieausgabe* XVII, 373). The abstract criterion of truth as correspondence of cognition to object is 'cashed' in a more concrete demand for the adequation of intuition to concept. But the slippage from correspondence (of knowledge to object) to adequation (of intuition to concept) confuses the level of judgement and truth with that of concept-formation and sense. A sharper focusing of truth as the correspondence of a judgement to a state of affairs frees truth from the ideal of adequation and the logic of concept-formation, instead showing truth to reside not in the 'objective validity' of concepts and the *Grundsätze* spun out of them (A 242, B 300), but exclusively in the correctness of what a judgement asserts.

Joseph Maréchal, building on the scholastic tradition, sharply distinguishes the two aspects of the propositional judgement in Aristotle, namely, synthesis and affirmation. Judgement remains for Kant a conceptual synthesis, and he fails to differentiate the specific contribution of affirmation and negation:

> The *Critique of Pure Reason* makes existential judgement a 'synthesis', under the supreme type of the formal unity of consciousness. *Affirmation (reality)* and *negation* figure only as 'categories' – we could say: as formal a priori modes of the concretive synthesis. (Maréchal, 217)

But synthesis is as yet only a conceptual achievement:

> If we arrest any proposition at the last stage before it crosses the threshold of affirmation, what we find is an expression in which are grouped the terms of the judgement, under a form that abstracts from the true and the false. (219)

Judgement is not merely a static proposition but the dynamic act that sets the mind in relation to being.

Frege's warnings against confusing predication with assertion, the level of thought with the level of truth, might also be invoked in this context. Like the scholastic distinction between abstraction and judgement it seems the merest common sense. But it becomes a source of illumination when confronted with common confusions of philosophical discourse and with the reluctance of many contemporary thinkers to cross this *pons asinorum* of epistemological analysis. Truth is not included in the logos; it is the logos (the object of the first act of the intellect) that permits the judgement (the second act of the intellect): judgement transcends the conceptual level. What most distinguishes logos 1: 'Caesar crossed the Rubicon' from logos 2: 'Caesar crossed the Thames' is not the difference in sense (though this determines their truth-value) but the fact that one is true and the other false.

There is a secondary sense in which one may retain the usage of 'truth' in the sense of conceptual adequation, the truth of the notion (Hegel), while refusing the conceptualist temptation to see this adeqation as founding the truth of individual propositions (so that the truth of each proposition depends on the truth of the whole). 'Socrates is mortal' is truer (at least in one perspective) than 'Socrates is not a banana' – in the sense that the first predicate is more adequate to the notion of the subject. Indeed any discourse on facts has to bring in truth as adequation:

In matters of fact there is not only factual reference but also, and consequently, adequacy or inadequacy with respect to fact. Moreover such adequacy or inadequacy is rarely complete: unlike logical truth and logical falsity, factual truth and factual falsity are not polar opposites, but contraries since, though incompatible, they are not exhaustive. (Bunge, 81)

Derrida's critique of truth as adequation bears on ideals of a logos that concords ever more fully with the presence on which it is superimposed; or, conversely, à la Husserl, of a complete intuitive filling of the empty signifying intentions of language, in which the object they envisage will finally be fully given. But the quest for increasing adequacy in the statements we make does not require that we entertain these ideals, which are in fact an encumbrance to it. Surrendering all notions of a perfect adequation to the real, we say these statements are 'more or less adequate' – meaning 'more or less true' – without laying ourselves open to Derrida's critique.

The distinction between reference and truth. Derrida equates truth with reference. The famous essay in which he plays the Mallarmean economy of writing off against the Platonic one is in reality more a critique of referentiality than of truth. In Plato,

It is through recourse to the truth of that which is, of things as such, that one can always decide whether writing is or is not true, whether it is in conformity or in 'opposition' to the true ... In each case *mimēsis* has to follow the process of truth. The presence of the present is its norm, its order, its law. It is in the name of truth, its only reference – *reference* itself - that *mimēsis* is judged. (D, 185, 193)

As in the case of truth, deconstruction seeks not to undermine the referentiality of language but to bring it into perspective:

It is totally false to suggest that deconstruction is a suspension of reference. Deconstruction is always deeply concerned with the 'other' of language ... Certainly, deconstruction tries to show that the question of reference is much more complex and problematic than traditional theories supposed. (in Kearney, 123)

Our discourse engages the real, but one can never survey reflexively the relation between words and things, for the things are not accessible in their purity, uncontaminated by the words, nor can the words be cut off from the world they name. This mutual contamination is the sense of the statement that 'there is no outside-the-text' (G, 158; translation modified). Much of what Derrida says about truth thus applies better to the question of how words name things or how language reflects the world than to the quite different question of how propositions correspond to the true. In supposing that they do so somewhat as names correspond to things, he can carry over the deconstruction of the referential text-thing relationship to the veridical proposition-truth relationship. This is an illegitimate move.

Frege might be of help here if he had more consistently distinguished reference and truth; his well-known view that the truth-value of a sentence constitutes its reference is toned down when 'in a letter to Russell of 1904 he concludes (more reasonably) only that the reference of a sentence must be "most intimately connected with its truth"' (Currie, 90). In equating truth-value with reference, Frege makes the truth of a sentence a composite from the references of its parts; distinguishing truth from reference, we can maintain that truth is incomposite, consisting in nothing more than the fact that the state of affairs picked out by the sentence really is the case; truth, correlated with the assertoric force of the sentence, has to do not with any synthesis established at the levels of sense or reference, but with an affirmation of what is the case.

'Both sense and reference are prior to any assignment of truth value' (Bunge, 47). I can say that the referent of the expression 'Creator' is God, without thereby making the truth-claim that God exists. Reference can be fully determined while truth remains undecidable (as in Gödel). When Derrida speaks of the undecidability of certain expressions, what is principally in question is the indeterminacy of their reference. Yet it may be that undecidability of reference does not necessarily entail impossibility of judgement. It might be maintained that the reference of religious statements such as 'God is good' is undecidable, although we affirm them as true. Reference may always involve a blind leap, an act of faith; the formation of sense or meaning may also be an arbitrary cut in the endless movement of dissemination; but the judgement 'true or false?' though intimately connected with sense and reference is not reducible to them, and the instability descried in them is not immediately transferable to it.

Truth has no essential connection with speech. Metaphysics has always assigned the origin of truth in general to the logos:

> the history of truth, of the truth of truth, has always been ... the debasement of writing, and its repression outside 'full' speech ... All the metaphysical determinations of truth ... are more or less immediately inseparable from the instance of the logos, or of a reason thought within the lineage of the logos ... Within this logos, the original and essential link to the *phonē* has never been broken ...

This experience of the effacement of the signifier in the voice ... is the condition of the very idea of truth. (G, 3, 10f, 20)

Derrida's implausible and much-criticised thesis of phonocentrism clearly derives from his understanding of the 'metaphysical determinations of truth' as presence and adequation. Truth as presence, adequately grasped in a logos, requires the immediacy of speech and abhors the indirections of writing. In reality, however, Derrida's claims about the interweaving of thought with speech, and the impossibility of reconstituting a 'private language' of the pure self-presence of consciousness, affect only the level of meaning (so that even clearly defined mathematical meanings depend on linguistic arrangements for their formulation and cannot be conceived as existing apart from these in a realm of pure thought). They do not necessarily affect the level of truth. The true and the false have nothing to do with phonocentrism, the uncontaminated self-presence of concepts in a pure inner voice: they are unrepresentable, unconceptualisable, and as such have nothing to do with logocentrism either; indeed, their autonomy in regard to *phonē* and logos subverts the totalising project of logocentrism.

As an account of what truth has meant in the West the myth of the logocentric, phonocentric metaphysics of presence is askew, for the value of truth has not been systematically yoked to presence and linguistic transparency, and is therefore less vulnerable than these are to the demonstration that presence is originarily compounded with non-presence. The notion of originary *différance*, which is the heart of Derrida's thought, erects a barrier against a recurring temptation of Western metaphysics: the lure of pure presence, absolute origins, and a language that is simply transparent to them. But when these myths of immediacy are equated with 'truth', and when their demise is proclaimed to be the demise of truth, Derrida himself succumbs to a metaphysics of presence.

To speak of 'a truth, or a meaning already constituted by and within the element of the logos' (G, 14) is to blur the distinction between meaning and truth. The two equations, truth = presence, truth = meaning, imply the equation meaning = presence. By identifying presence, meaning and truth, Derrida can conclude that the notion of truth is only an epoch in the history of archi-writing, or rather, the dominant notion of the epoch we call history:

the value of truth in general, which always implies the *presence* of the signified (*alētheia* or *adequatio*), far from dominating this movement and allowing it to be thought, is only one of its epochs, however privileged. A European epoch within the growth of the sign. (286)

'The very concept of history has lived only upon the possibility of mean-ing, upon the past, present, or promised presence of meaning, of its truth' (*D*, 184; translation modified). In this epoch some supreme instance – paradigmatically God – ultimately assures the determination of meaning and the judgement of truth.

> The word or concept of truth has sense only within the logocentric closure and the metaphysics of presence. When it does not imply the possibility of an intuitive or judicative *adequation*, it nevertheless continues in *alētheia* to privilege the instance of a vision filled and satisfied by presence. (*G*, 337)

The alleged European epoch is far from being as homogeneous as this suggests. Many philosophical views of truth not only escape the charge of logocentrism but reveal that truth, correctly grasped, overcomes logo-centrism. If it is myths of truth that writing inscribes and punctures, one could say that the metaphysical tradition has never been entirely under the spell of such myths. If it had been, how could Kant have written: 'in itself truth has nothing to do with time and eternity, since it is nothing existing'? (Eisler, 594). Few have been more convinced of the reality of truth than Frege, yet this conviction is precisely what kept him from adopting any of the stereotypical conceptions of truth which Derrida ascribes to Western philosophy. His references to the notions of mimesis and correspondence scarcely make him an easy target here:

> An idea is not called true in itself but only with respect to an inten-tion that it should correspond to something. It might be supposed from this that truth consists in the correspondence of a picture with what it depicts. Correspondence is a relation. This is contradicted, however, by the use of the word 'true', which is not a relation-word and contains no reference to anything else to which something must correspond.

Indeed, not only is the notion of correspondence useless for the purpose of defining the true, but it turns out that no definition is possible:

> The attempt to explain truth as correspondence collapses. And every other attempt to define truth collapses too. For in a definition certain characteristics would have to be stated. And in application to any particular case the question would always arise whether it were true that the characteristics were present. So one goes round in a circle. Consequently, it is probable that the content of the word 'true' is unique and indefinable. (Frege, in Strawson, 18f)

As Dummett explains: '"True" is said by Frege to be undefinable: but the

True can be picked out from other objects by means of any true sentence' (Dummett, 1981b, 170).

Later philosophers have not accepted Frege's rather peremptory declarations of indefinability in regard to truth and other key-notions. But when Tarski, for example, sets about defining truth, the result again suggests that truth has nothing to do with presence. The sentence 'snow is white' is true if and only if snow is white: this disquotational definition 'tells us what it is for any sentence to be true, and it tells us this in terms just as clear to us as the sentence in question itself' (Quine, 82), without any reference to truth being unveiled for a cognitive subject or to truth as presence. The quoted sentence can refer to a presence, but this epistemic content doesn't affect the definition itself. Even if this account of truth is seen as a correspondence-theory, it is so in a sense remote from that attacked by Frege. To say that truth is a correspondence between statements and facts becomes merely a convenient generalisation of truisms such as '"Snow is white" is true, for snow is white'. What Kant, Frege and Tarski have to say about truth seems free, then, of the illusions denounced by Derrida. This renders inoperative any claim that deconstruction brings into view the possibility of a disappearance of truth, since deconstruction turns out to miss the most authoritative contemporary accounts of what truth is.

Redundancy theories of truth such as those propounded by F. P. Ramsey and the later Wittgenstein (according to which 'it is true that snow is white' is merely a verbose way of saying 'snow is white') have been rejected on logical grounds or because they cannot do justice to the practice of testing whether or not a given statement is true. A reductive, merely disquotational theory of truth is also contested within the analytical tradition, with a tendency to swing to the opposite extreme that sees truth as dependent on its role in human epistemic performance. It is evident in any case that such theories are at the antipodes of a mythology of truth as presence. A discourse on truth which examines the conditions of possibility and the philosophical implications of our capacity to utter correct judgements remains a plausible project. The Derridian critique can save this discourse from metaphysical illusions, but does not disqualify it.

THE TEXTUAL INSCRIPTION OF TRUTH

1. *How Writing Exceeds Truth.* Every signified is marked by secondarity from the beginning: 'The secondarity that it seemed possible to ascribe to writing alone affects all signifieds in general, affects them always already, the moment they *enter the game*' (G, 7). Since the signified is reduced to being the signifier of another signifier, the trace of a trace, it

follows that a true statement does not pin the signs to the things themselves but deploys strategically the available marks so that they accord with the insistence of the true. Even in affirming the clearest fact – 'it is raining' – I consign my assertion to language, textuality, intertextuality, iterability, non-saturable context. The truth-effect my statement achieves is already 'inscribed' in language, and cannot be abstracted from this inscribed condition as a pure proposition immune to its mobile play.

Nothing prevents one from writing a truth. But to do so one sets in motion the complicated and treacherous machine of writing, which escapes the vigilance of the writer. The true sentence, caught in this web, cannot be assured of its relation to the thing itself. If one tries to envisage this relation according to the schemas of adequation, correspondence, unveiling, coming to presence, they turn out to be defective. The judgement 'Caesar crossed the Rubicon', if true, is eternally true. But if we try to grasp the absolute essence of this truth we manage to catch only a verbal form. The actual fact as such eludes our clutches, in its 'self-dissolving absoluteness'. The verbal form, iterated each time we want to assert the truth of the fact, is caught in the play of dissemination. Despite the purity that logic and mathematics can attain, the same situation seems to prevail for truths of reason such as 'two and two are four'. Truths of faith are still more vulnerable to this textual condition: in the case of 'God exists' or 'Jesus Christ is the Son of God', one cannot appeal to the data of 'sense-certainty' (the most elementary stage in *The Phenomenology of Spirit*); the terms of such propositions draw their meaning from the most advanced forms of consciousness, and are the product of a historical labour of mind, which exposes them to all sorts of contingent interferences.

Thus writing inscribes truth 'in a system in which it is only a function and a locus' (*WD*, 296), 'a system of figures not dominated by the value of truth, which then becomes only an included, inscribed, circumscribed function' (*M*, 18). This writing 'cannot be governed by the motif of truth whose very horizon it *frames*' (*D*, 296). Every debate about the true is governed and enframed by the play of rhetorical or syntactic structures on which the question 'true or false' has no hold. Syntax, an affair of spacing and intervals, does not lend itself to the question of truth, which concerns only fixed and stable statements. A 'horizon', the ground upon which these statements emerge, would still be subject to the question of truth, especially when it is posed in Heideggerian style. But 'enframing' cannot be mastered by that question. If truth then no longer regulates our discourse as an immovable criterion, our speech become a net thrown into the dark, responsive to that otherness of the real which eludes it, and which it can only aim at in adventurous strategy, and misses if it tries to name it directly: 'In the delineation of *différance* everything is strategic and adventurous. Strategic because no transcendent truth present outside the field of writing can govern theologically the totality of the field' (*M*, 7).

No text attains the signification it aims at. The more elaborately it develops its resources to express what it wants to say, the more the envisaged meaning becomes muddied and withdraws. Instead of referring directly to its content, the text is caught up in the play of its own elaboration, which one cannot cut short. The final relation of this play to the thing itself cannot be fully elucidated:

> The infrastructures dissolve the comprehension of the thing itself. Instead of offering themselves, they withdraw. They efface themselves, constantly disappearing as they go along. 'They cannot, in classical affirmation, be affirmed without being negated' (*D*, 157). What thus makes its entrance into philosophy is the very possibility of a disappearing of truth. (Gasché 1986, 150)

In the same way, the other, whoever or whatever it may be, resists our horizons of understanding and cannot be presented and seized in its 'truth'. A fully literary text, that is, a reflected text which has permitted the laws of the textual to work themselves out in all their complexity, will resist all efforts to bring its meaning back to a thematic unity and to subordinate its statements to the regime of judgements of truth. The more a writing is refined, the less it presents itself as true. This is not to say that it loses itself in falsehood, for the refined text is assuredly 'closer to truth' than a banal one. Thus the domain toward which writing burrows is that of the neither true nor false, that of the undecidable.

In the essay on Mallarmé, Derrida plays off the subtlety of writing against 'the *ontological*: the presumed possibility of a discourse about what is, the deciding and decidable *logos* of or about the *on* (being-present)' (*D*, 191). In writing 'there is no longer any textual difference between the image and the thing, the empty signifier and the full signified, the imitator and the imitated, etc.' (*D*, 209). Language does not state the truth of things from a position external to them, but sets in motion a to-and-fro between signifier and signified in which it becomes impossible to abstract the signified in a pure state. One must find one's way within this situation, without any possibility of jumping out of it to some 'outside-the-text'. 'What is produced is an absolute extension of the concepts of writing and reading, of text, of hymen, to the point where nothing of what *is* can lie beyond them' (223).

Mallarmé's *Mimique* describes a scene in which Pierrot mimes the murder of his wife as he has first premeditated, then accomplished it:

> The scene illustrates but the idea, not any actual action, in a hymen (out of which flows Dream), tainted with vice yet sacred, between

desire and fulfillment, perpetration and remembrance: here antici-
pating, there recalling, in the future, in the past, *under the false
appearance of a present*. That is how the mime operates, whose act
is confined to a perpetual allusion without breaking the ice or the
mirror: he thus sets up a medium, a pure medium, of fiction. (quoted
in *D*, 175)

This refined fiction exposes the infrastructural conditions of what we call
'truth'. Between the imitator and the imitated the relation is no longer
one of simple exteriority, but an undecidable 'hymen', or 'between' (*entre*)
which 'renders this alternative between internal and external inoperative'
(*D*, 221):

> In this perpetual allusion being performed in the background of the
> *entre* that has no ground, one can never know what the allusion
> alludes to, unless it is to itself in the process of alluding, weaving its
> hymen and manufacturing its text ... That this play should in the
> last instance be independent of truth does not mean that it is false,
> an error, appearance, or illusion. Mallarmé writes 'allusion', not
> 'illusion'. Allusion, or 'suggestion' as Mallarmé says elsewhere, is
> indeed that operation we are here *by analogy* calling undecidable.
> An undecidable proposition, as Gödel demonstrated in 1931, is a
> proposition which, given a system of axioms governing a multi-
> plicity, is neither an analytical nor deductive consequence of those
> axioms, nor in contradiction with them, neither true nor false with
> respect to those axioms. *Tertium datur*, without synthesis. (219)

Mallarmé's writing breaks up the Platonic economy of mimesis; it is no
longer truth which judges the mime's performance, but the performance
enframes and circumscribes truth. In Mallarmé's description:

> What is marked there is the fact that, this imitator having in the last
> instance no imitated, this signifier having in the last instance no
> signified, this sign having in the last instance no referent, their oper-
> ation is no longer comprehended within the process of truth but on
> the contrary comprehends *it*, the motif of the last instance being
> inseparable from metaphysics as the search for the *arkhē*, the *eskhaton*
> and the *telos*. (207f)

Truth is reduced to a thematic effect, subordinated to the machinery
which stages it, 'the irreducible excess of the syntactic over the semantic'
(221). The scene of writing exceeds the thematic content it presents within its framings. If we focus on this content we will talk with ease of its
meaning and truth, but if we attend to the writing as such we find that the

notion of truth has no grip on it. The reader is involved in it in an active way; every reading is part of the play of writing, whose borders are forever changing according to changing contexts.

Analysis of the excess of the text over its content brings to light the quasi-transcendental infrastructures, never the same from one text to another, which assure that one will find at bottom every time something one cannot master by a definitive identification. This undecidability is the seal of the alterity of the other, which imposes respect. The text shows itself to be caught in a double bind which is the very law of its composition and which imposes itself on the reader: one writes to state the true, but the truth of writing is that the true, the thing itself, perpetually withdraws. Similarly, another person, or God, or being, or the moral law, or the desire constitutive of the human subject make themselves known only under the species of a double bind obliging us to engage in a struggle of interpretation. Derrida insists that the impossibility of imposing a closure on *différance* and the undecidable doesn't imply any paralysing indeterminism, but an alert openness to the other and a freedom for creative interventions. But does this way of seeing things leave any place for theoretical or ethical judgements which would be other than arbitrary?

2. *How Truth Exceeds Writing.* The textual inscription of truth mirrors the way that in everyday life the utterance of truth is a performative act, limited by the situational constraints of a concrete context. Derrida admires the 'Nietzschean' (*M*, 187) daring of John L. Austin's cashing of 'truth' in terms of felicitous speech-acts:

> It is essential to realise that 'true' and 'false,' like 'free' and 'unfree,' do not stand for anything simple at all; but only for a general dimension of being a right or proper thing to say as opposed to a wrong thing, in these circumstances, to this audience, for these purposes and with these intentions. (Austin, quoted in Staten, 113)

But taken literally this, like Rorty's pragmatism, is an incomplete definition of truth. If there is an excess of the situation, or the text, over the truth-effect inscribed in it and which it makes possible, may there not also be an excess of truth over its conditioning contexts?

This way of talking of truth-effects and of subordinating them to a wider context seems to imply a naturalistic attitude reminiscent of Wittgenstein, for whom the association of 'true' and 'proposition' is no more significant than that 'l' comes after 'k' in the alphabet:

> In *that* sense 'true' and 'false' could be said to fit propositions; and a child might be taught to distinguish between propositions and

other expressions by being told 'Ask yourself if you can say "is true" after it. If these words fit, it's a proposition'. (*Philosophical Investigations* 137)

Such naturalism glosses over the distinction between meaningful concepts and true judgements. To say, with Waismann, that '"True," "agreement with reality," etc., are expressions within a calculus, not expressions connecting the calculus with reality' (Baker and Hacker, 254) is to deny this distinction, insofar as it is suggested that 'truth' is merely a further determination of a proposition in addition to the conceptual grasp of a possible state of affairs which the proposition contains. Affirmation and denial have a specific ontological import that is missed when we grasp them only as applications of a truth-value calculus.

Against Derrida's subordination of truth to its textual inscription, I would see propositional truth as the lever that raises the truth of judgement out of its subordination to the mechanisms of language. 'Is it really the case?' – the instability that this question induces is incommensurable with the reflections on the semantic conditions of enunciation, to which Derrida confines himself. Even if meaning is always vulnerable to dissemination, the application to a given statement of the question, 'true or false?' brings into play an instance which is not affected by the possible divagations of meaning. However, it is true that the text as such may elude this question; to ask whether a Mallarmean sonnet is true or false is as futile as to ask whether an apple is true or false. Derrida would argue that any statement, viewed as a textual performance, is equally impervious to the question of truth, and that it points rather to the element of archi-writing, where the notions of truth and falsehood no longer apply.

'True' textuality outstrips truth and is itself beyond the grasp of the category of truth. But the truth of true statements in its turn outstrips the textuality in which these statements are inscribed. What the 'textual inscription of truth' actually overcomes is a conception of truth as correspondence based naively on the analogy with the correspondence between a thing and the label attached to it. This notion of true statements as a mimetic mirroring of the world is the fallacy Derrida unmasks. But is it correct to say that it is essentially in this way that the whole of Western philosophy has understood judgement? Does Derrida himself confuse two senses of reference? When a word refers to a thing there is a relationship of mimesis, which indeed turns out to be more complex than Plato suspected. But when we affirm a true proposition the manner in which this proposition refers to the truth has little to do with mimesis, and thus the critique of Platonic mimesis has little reference to the truth of propositions (which is the principal sense of the word 'truth' both in philosophy and in everyday life). The textual inscription concerns the dimension of signs and meaning, but doesn't embrace what is quite other, the truth or falsity of a proposition. One might say that undecidability characterises the material basis of true utterance, but once truth is uttered the contact with the real which has occurred can no longer be recuperated by the structures examined by Derrida.

The question 'true or false?' directly applies only to assertions. In a literary fiction all the assertions are false, if one insists on the criterion of factual reality; but it is better to say that the question 'true or false?' is inapplicable. Similarly, the infrastructural domain to which Derrida wants to recall truth eludes the question 'true or false?' in virtue of the fact that no assertion can be formed there. This milieu can enframe or permit assertions but it cannot master them or triumph over them, for what transpires in an objective judgement is incommensurable with this matrix which is its condition of possibility but not its sufficient reason. Finite truths can be uttered, even if always subject to a possible redescription, and even if every utterance affects thousands of other utterances and finds itself solicited by them in an infinite textual play. Even within this 'textual labyrinth panelled with mirrors' (D, 195) one can formulate a true judgement, and this effect of truth as such escapes from the labyrinth, as an irreducible remainder not brought into the economy that presides there.

When the truth or falsity of a statement has been established, what exactly has happened? Not an encounter of *intellectus* and *res* (for how speak of such an encounter without figuring the thing known independently of the cognition by which one knows it, which is impossible; truth is not a noematic object); not the overlapping of the structure of language with the structure of facts as in Wittgenstein's *Tractatus*; not a moment in a dialectical progression to total comprehension as in Hegel; not an ontological unconcealing as in Heidegger; not the affirmation of a fiction useful for practical purposes or for the will-to-power. It seems that what takes place in a judgement of truth eludes all categorisation. Perhaps truth can be described only by referring to categories which are equally indefinable, such as being: 'a true judgement is the affirmation of what really is (or is the case)'. Such discourses indicate only in a vague way what happens when one utters a truth. We run up here against a limit of language; but it remains instructive to meditate on this indefinable and ineffable character of truth as such.

Derrida's efforts to subordinate truth to textuality often play on the imperfect accounts of truth we have examined above. Thus in the following passage he identifies truth with what presents itself in a revelation of its presence:

> The truth of *Choral Work* (Peter Eisenman) . . . is not a truth: it is
> not presentable, representable, totalisable, it never shows itself. It
> gives rise to no revelation of presence, still less to an adequation . . .
> all these layers of meaning and of forms, of visibility and invisibil-
> ity *lie in* each other, *on* or *under* each other, *in front of* or *behind* each
> other, but the truth of this relation is never established, never sta-
> bilised in any judgement. It always causes to be said, allegoricallly,
> something different from what is said. *In a word* it causes to lie. The
> truth of the work is this power of deception. (*Psyché,* 505)

An intricate writing (or play of architectural codes in the case of an
Eisenman building), which launches the reader from one layer of meaning to another without allowing any halt in a firm judgement, frustrates
the desire for truth and shows that the haste to form judgments is inadequate to the texture of reality. Such writing can stage the deceitful ideals
of the true as revelation or representation and thus show up their illusory quality. It can reinscribe these images of unveiling, adequation, full
presence, givenness, used in a loose rhetoric to point toward truth, and
show that they are fictions, which become undecidable structures when
one allows their fictive powers to be deployed. But the true as such is not
entirely mastered by this machinery any more than it had been by the
suggestive, indicative images this machinery undoes. It may frustrate the
application of the question 'true or false' but it does not put it out of play
for ever.

The fable of *The Emperor's New Clothes* is seen as another example of
the enframing of truth by writing:

> A 'literature' can thus produce, stage and put forward something
> like truth. It is thus more powerful than the truth of which it is
> capable . . . The psychoanalytical scene, as stripping off and decon-
> stitution of *Einkleidung,* is produced by *The Emperor's New
> Clothes* in a scene of writing which undresses, without appearing to,
> the master meaning, the master of meaning, the king of truth and the
> truth of the king. (*La carte postale,* 447f)

But if Andersen's story sticks in the memory, is it not as a celebration of
the power of truth to cut across the weavings of fashion and of signifiers
without a basis? Note that the greatness of this fable is shown by the fact
that everyone knows it though very few can remember having read it; it
circulates orally, in everyday allusions or in the nursery. The claim that
this eulogy of plain truth is even in its oral forms a sophisticated text aiming to relativise the true, or even crude images thereof, is implausible. Be
that as it may, the story would in any case not be an attack on truth but
merely on conceptions of truth as unveiling. The more basic point is that

efforts to state the truth bluntly and directly are betrayed once they are put into words, for words bring into play illimitable intertextual contexts and call for endless commentary to clarify their meaning. The prophet stands up to cut through webs of deceitful verbiage, but his own words are immediately woven into the web. To speak an effective word one must first calculate its relation to the web in which one would intervene, and one is already in the text before one speaks.

THE BIBLICAL INSCRIPTION OF TRUTH

Mutatis mutandis one could apply all these remarks to the biblical text. Truth seeks to inscribe itself, and is inchoate and inarticulate until it finds verbal form. It has a passion for manifestation, and that passion seeks outlet at first in prophetic speech:

> If I say, 'I will not mention him,
>   or speak any more in his name',
> there is in my heart as it were a burning fire
>   shut up in my bones,
> and I am weary with holding it in,
>   and I cannot. (Jer. 20:19)

But the spoken prophecy constitutes a text, and soon the passion for manifesting truth become 'the passion of inscription', the writer's desire to give body to truth in the adventure of composition. As the text grows more labyrinthine, its truth shifts from the initial dogmatic clarity to the register of the undecidable. It is in the total movement of the text, with its loose ends and open questions, and in its intertextual resonances that its truth finally resides. Select out one proposition as for ever and ever true, and you have hewn a sword for sectarian warfare. The abiding truth of such a proposition as 'I am the way, and the truth, and the life' (Jn 14:6) can be upheld only in constantly referring the proposition back to its entire literary and historical context; its sense and truth are carried by the entire Johannine revelation-event and its inscription.

However suggestive the prophetic word or its literary recomposition, it is always a limited and limiting precipitate of the wider, vaguer truth one sought to express in it. The moment of inscription is 'the moment at which we must *decide* whether we will engrave what we hear' (WD, 9). The biblical words are decisions about what can be said, and they carry with them a sense of the solemnity and venturesomeness of what is there decided. The calculation behind the setting down of the biblical words is usually mediated by a long process of sifting traditions, of which only the end-point is preserved in the Bible. This palimpsest quality of the Bible is a necessary feature, for the articulation of revealed truth is too solemn a matter to be left to individual inspiration. Thus though the Bible is a rich source for mystical and prophetic exploitation, for Gnostics and Kabbalists, it is also a carefully constructed fortress, with moats and trellises to keep the mystic at bay (see Scholem, 11–48). If the complexity of inscription frustrates the dogmatist, its fixity as durable mark resists mystic dissolution.

Yet there have been massive rewriting projects, that recuperate the entire scriptural text and alter its fundamental orientation. The most successful such enterprises have added a new scripture to the old – Paul, Muhammad, the Mahāyāna Sūtras. In such cases the defenders of the old scripture will denounce the new as an imposture, and the new will claim to provide the sole adequate hermeneutic of the old, understanding it better than it understands itself. From these mutual recriminations we can draw the lesson that no scripture has as firm a hold on truth as it imagines.

A historical spiritual movement that precipitates a set of scriptural traces cannot control their intertextual relation to other such traces, except by a sweeping *fiat* which tries to make history and textuality transparent and univocal in a way that they can never be. Yet religions need not be fundamentally mistaken about their own identity, even if inadequate categories force them to caricature the identity of the other. Judaism, Islam, Christianity, early and later Buddhism may all be regarded as fundamentally true on their own terms. Each opens a space of textuality, a way of writing human existence and history, which has unique validity, though much of the small print will inevitably turn out to be time-bound. The play between these truths is as complex as the play between their textual traditions, which cannot be overleapt towards some simplistic doxographical rapprochement. Truth is captured in the errances of writing. Scripture aims at the univocal, curbing the captious intellect and the superstitious imagination at every turn, yet the space of clarity it creates is finally a very limited, fragmentary one, and what marks its limits most is the indeterminacy of its fraying edges, the incursion of opacity whenever we try to pull the text into the light and examine its understitchings. Subjected to such treatment texts fall silent before our demand for their truth, unravel into mere redactional marks for which no bedrock anchor in the thing itself can be discovered. The communities that live from old scriptures use them well in allowing them to conjure up their spaces of vision; the scholar who traces the light back to its opaque source in the warp and woof of writing will emphasise the historical finitude of this particular perspective on truth.

Inscription actualises 'the excess of signifying possibilities preceding the text' (C. Johnson, 29), but it is always haunted by this excess which it has failed to master and so it constantly requires to be supplemented by other inscriptions and reinscriptions. The pain and passion that mark the passage to insciption is the pain of passing from intuitions of infinity to incarnate finitude. Each book of the Bible is marked by this pain, particularly apparent in a religion which has renounced all monist fusions or endless incantations in order to state precisely what it is that God has to say to us in the historical here and now. A spirit, an élan, pervades the biblical text, never caught completely in its letter, which always threatens to kill it; but we do not have access to this spirit independently of the letter which gives it form. The economy of the inscription of biblical truth is that of all successful writing: the 'fall to inscription', the 'fall from excess to finite totality' (58f) is *temporalised*, bearing with it the past to which it alludes and the future of its supplementations and reactualisations. One frees the letter from sterility by stepping back to the past and to the unimaginable infinite origin from which it speaks, and by stepping forward to the unimaginable 'fulfilment' of the biblical word. 'The "trace" is a diminished effect of an originary, conditioning force in which that force is preserved [*se garde*] and saved from singular annihilation' (60). The force of the Spirit traverses its traces in the letter of Scripture; the letter controls an excess of blind force but at the same time it must keep itself open to the upsurge of the Spirit.

The Bible is full of scenes of revelation and recognition. But the revelation inscribes and incarnates itself; the recognition is always tied to a particular context, and it is staged in a text which surpasses this context, re-enacting or actualising it in view of another context; the successive contexts of the text's readers then actualise the recognition in as many new ways as they read in new contexts. The text is a machine for producing effects of revelation. There is no unitary revelation-event that embraces the plurality of biblical texts and contexts, but the adventure of inscribing truth has always to begin anew in a risky act of writing or reading. What we call revelation is a series of particular events of all sorts, which we know only through literary narrations. To judge the exterior multiplicity of biblical writing in the light of a unitary and interior notion of revelation, as Origen and Augustine did, instead of trusting to the texture of the biblical world, as Irenaeus, Luther and Calvin did, is a Platonic bias that represses awareness that every effect of interior illumination is captured in advance in the web of writing (by Lacan's symbolic order, one might say, but Derrida makes this order too mobile to be dominated by any paternal authority; every instance of transcendental stability is structurally dependent on its an-archic counterpart).

The myth of interiority, which opposes the world of spirit to the exteriority of the body, is far from being overcome in our theology. We seek a spiritual truth hidden behind the plurality of the biblical gestures, not seeing that it's in these gestures themselves that truth happens. 'All is in order' (Wittgenstein) in the language that these gestures create; espousing their rhythm one is freed from the compulsion to seek their hidden foundation.

The heterogeneity of the biblical narratives is marked also in the varying degrees of their theological refinement, literary quality, and historical value. All dramatise the revelation of God, but rather than spelling out its content with univocal clarity, they mime this revelation in an allusive way. The text is neither interior nor exterior to the divine word to which it witnesses, but situates itself in the 'between'. It can be appropriated only by a play of interpretation, which itself is neither within nor outside this event of witness. If the intention of the biblical authors was to formulate a determinate content, the contradictory plurality of their witness and the obsolescence of their presuppositions make impossible for us a direct and immediately transparent reading, and oblige us to take them as an immense literary performance miming the event of revelation. Every univocal notion of this revelation is absorbed as but one in a multitude of such mimings.

Acceptance of this situation would give biblical studies a new pertinence for theology. What now seems a detour and a distraction would then be seen as the normal mediation of the divine presence or absence. If we query the logocentric habit of postulating an origin, if we sound the retarded character of every image of an initial, foundational word of revelation, if we make theology face the irreducible facticity which shows through the biblical texts, renouncing all the avatars of the *sensus plenior* – every notion of a theological centre unifying the sacred texts – then we find that religious language points to the transcendent in a new way: 'The infinite distance of the Other is *respected* only within the sands of a book within which wandering and mirages are always possible' (*WD*, 69).

If all particular truths as well as truth in general – divine revelation – are inscribed in and exceeded by the textual play which stages them, then it becomes very difficult to say in what sense the Bible communicates truth. One might see the language of Scripture more as a strategic writing aimed to free us from illusions and fixations than the direct transmission of a concrete message; as an ensemble of language games to be practised, not in the confidence of uttering truth, but in an effort to maintain the demystificatory force of this mature and subtle language without falling back into the platitudes of a less refined one. The concern with truth and falsehood remains as vital as ever, but its application to the biblical witness comes down to clear 'yes or no' statements only with great difficulty, for in the realm of religious truth any such statements demand commentary and commentary becomes an endless, unmasterable text.

THE ART OF JUDGEMENT AND
THE ABYSS OF *DIFFÉRANCE*

In a world in which meaning is never perfectly stable, to judge is more an art than a science. Judgement becomes in part a strategic choice, carried out by a more or less arbitrary cut or halt whereby the mobility of the signifiers is provisionally suspended. I stop the drift of the words, and of a sentence as a whole, to apply the words to a given context. This suspension of the drift is a creative intervention, almost a fiction, and not a simple transparent presentation of the things themselves. Does judgement then become merely an agile and inventive participation in the play of the undecidable statements, whereby one shakes the chains of ex-signifiers in a liberating fashion? Or is the work of formulating and criticising propositions in view of truth not so much abolished as integrated into this play, losing nothing of its necessity though caught in a process that exceeds it and that it cannot master?

Faced with undecidable structures, it is useless to invoke the hope of an eschatological clarification, for even the last judgement is put under erasure in a revision of the notion of apocalyse: apocalypse is no longer the bringing to light of naked truth, but the revelation of the undecidability which dominates all judgement:

> an apocalypse without apocalypse, an apocalypse without vision, without truth, without revelation, *envois* (for the 'come' is in itself plural), addresses without message and without destination, without decidable sender or addressee, without last judgement, without any other eschatology than the tone of the 'Come,' its very differance, an apocalypse beyond good and evil. (in Coward and Foshay, 66; translation modified)

The apocalyptic, in this sense, would be 'a transcendental condition of all discourse' (57). The absolute authority of the true, recognised implicitly in each of our statements, is undone when we try to state it as such. The law of every discourse turns out to be structurally untenable; the truth of truth turns out to be non-true.

What is the meaning of the following remarks?:

> in no case is it a question of a *discourse against truth* or against science. (This is impossible and absurd, as is every heated accusation on this subject.) And when one analyzes systematically the value of truth as *homoiōsis* or *adequatio*, as the certitude of the *cogito*

(Descartes, Husserl), or as a certitude opposed to truth in the horizon of absolute knowledge (*Phenomenology of the Mind*), or finally as *alētheia*, unveiling or presence (the Heideggerean repetition), it is not in order to return naively to a relativist or sceptical empiricism... I repeat, then, leaving all their disseminating powers to the proposition and the form of the verb: *we must have [il faut]* truth. For those who mystify (themselves) to have it trippingly on the tongue. Such is the law. (*Positions*, 105)

Is this a thoroughgoing fictionalism? But that is a Nietzschean thesis which Derrida explicitly criticises, opposing to it the subtler implications of Nietzsche's thought. Thus John Caputo's interpretation may be contested:

> It is *différance* which makes possible the endless linkings of signifiers in an irreducible diversity of combinatorial and associative chains and interweavings... Now, on one level, Derrida thinks that it is a matter of living with this drift, coping with it, so that what Heidegger would call our 'average everydayness' may continue its undisturbed routine. Truth, after all, is necessary – that is to say, we need our fictions. (That is why Derrida writes that he is not a sceptic, in that he recognizes the Nietzschean and pragmatic *need* for truth as a necessary fiction. 'We must have truth'. 'Il faut la vérité'.) We cannot function without taming the wildness of the play, without *imposing* normality, without a certain measure of stilling the flux. (Caputo, 144f)

In arresting the polysemic play of 'il *faut* la vérité' to make of it a pragmatist thesis, Caputo holds that truth is nothing more than a necessary fiction. This thesis cannot be stated without self-contradiction, unless one puts this 'fiction' at the service of some materialist or mystical super-truth (life, will-to-power), or enlarges the meaning of the word 'fiction' to the point of abolishing any effective contrast with its opposite, truth. The fictionalist and pragmatist dogmas belong to an anti-metaphysical way of thinking which remains the captive of the categories it combats, and which effects no 'step back' toward the ground of truth as Derrida promises to investigate it. Caputo eludes the double bind of this 'il *faut*', which says both 'truth is necessary' and that 'truth *is lacking*'. '"Il faut" does not only mean it is necessary, but, in French, etymologically, "it lacks" or "is wanting"' (Derrida, in Coward and Foshay, 315). Truth makes its exigence felt by constantly withdrawing from our grasp.

The first movement of deconstruction is to avoid judgement and to err perpetually on the level of meaning: 'the whole discourse on *différance*,

undecidability, etc. can be seen as a dispositive of reserve towards judgement under all its forms (predicative, prescriptive, always decisive)'. But
judgement imposes itself as the very law of every discourse. To speak at
all is to find oneself, like the character in Kafka, 'before the law': 'It
would be easy to show that, under this apparent reserve, a judgement has
installed itself or returned, commanding the scene from which it seems to
be absent with a denegatory tyranny all the more impossible to overcome' ('Préjugés' 95f). Here Derrida sets up a thoroughly abstract law of
judgement which seems to refuse to be cashed in any definitive way in
particular judgements (just as he espouses an eschatology without a
concrete eschaton, a messianism without a Messiah, a truth which is
non-truth). Against him, I would maintain that individual true judgements, however provisional their language, attain a core of truth which in
itself is not caught up in the movement of universal contextualisation and
relativisation, though it is impossible to isolate this core in a pure form,
independent of its relative inscription.

With Lyotard, Derrida states that:

> Judgement is neither founding nor founded. It is perhaps secondary
> but for that very reason it cannot be a question of getting rid of it . . .
> It is because it rests on nothing, and does not present itself, espe-
> cially not with its philosophical titles, its criteria and its reason, that
> is, its identity card, that judgement is paradoxically ineluctable. (97)

He adds a few twists to this conception of judgement. For Lyotard, 'there
is a law but one doesn't know what this law is saying. There is a kind of
law of laws, a meta-law which is "Be just"' (107). For Derrida, the purity
of law is always contaminated by its necessary reference to a narrative,
not only in the Bible but even in Kant. The law is always thus caught
in the net of *différance*: 'the discourse of law doesn't say "no" but "not
yet", indefinitely' (122); 'the law which *isn't there but that there is*. The
judgement, itself, doesn't happen' (123).

This paradoxical structure of ethical law is similar to that of the literary text: 'The text keeps to itself, like the law. It speaks only of itself, but
then of its non-identity with itself. It does not reach itself or allow itself
to be reached. It is the law, makes the law and leaves the reader before the
law' (128). The same structure lies at the heart of the referentiality of our
most ordinary statements: 'the play of enframing and the paradoxical
logic of limits which introduces a sort of perturbation in the "normal"
system of reference, while *revealing* an essential structure of referentiality'.
This structure of referentiality does not itself refer, 'any more than the
eventhood of an event is itself an event' (131). Once again he is not questioning the reality of reference, but he is examining its transcendental

condition. Our judgements obey a law, the '*il faut*' of truth, but this law eludes every demand for face to face vision. This instance is a kind of empty transcendence presiding over all language, but on which language never has a direct hold, like the apocalyptic 'Come!' which relativises and disqualifies every concrete apocalypse. One may ask if the experience of judgement as an affirmation of being might not allow another approach to the enigma of referentiality. If truth makes itself known as what escapes our grasp, it is an equally significant phenomenon that being is objectively given in each true judgement. Without this grasp of being, the enigma of the irreducible otherness of truth would have little interest.

Derrida's theory of truth is an elaboration of Nietzsche's remark that truth 'has not let herself be won – and today every kind of dogmatism stands sad and discouraged'. Theologians have pursued truth with what Nietzsche would see as a 'gruesome earnestness', a 'clumsy importunity', 'inept and improper means for winning a wench' (*Spurs*, 55). Can we bring the theological style of stating the true into accord with the oblique, elusive and plural mode of being of 'truth as woman'? Such truth is the complete unfolding of undecidability, which

> engulfs and distorts all vestige of essentiality, of identity, of property. And the philosophical discourse, blinded, founders on these shoals and is hurled down these depthless depths to its ruin. There is no such thing as the truth of woman, but it is because of that abyssal divergence of the truth, because that untruth is 'truth'. Woman is but one name for that untruth of truth. (51)

This realm of the undecidable and of *différance* is not simply a linguistic or logical condition of everyday 'true propositions'; *différance* is the very grain of the real; to deconstructionist 'atheologians' it even seems to bear the face of the divine in its irreducible alterity, neither transcendent nor immanent, neither absent nor present. This reduction of meaning and truth to the infrastructural conditions of their enunciation, and this reduction of divine transcendence to *différance*, are short-circuits.

Caputo's reduction of the necessity of truth to a pragmatic fictionalism is another short-circuit. Anti-dogmatism merely inverts the over-direct procedures of dogmatism. It corresponds to what Derrida calls 'anti-castration':

> 'Woman'... no more believes in castration's exact opposite, anti-castration, than she does in castration itself. Much too clever for that ... she knows that such a reversal would ... only amount to the same thing and force her just as surely as ever into the same old apparatus. (61)

In veiled polemic against Lacan on the one hand and Deleuze on the other, Derrida declares that the metaphysical notions of truth-presence function as fetishes aiming to supplement and hide the lack of phallus of truth as woman; but that if one rebels against truth, seen as castrating, one falls into the phallocentrism which inspires this denial. Reduced to a fiction truth is still something under our control. But 'castration *does not take place*' (61); the '*il faut*' of truth, as the 'law' of judgement, cannot be fixed in a stable, fetishised way. We are caught in its play without being able to master it, either by raising it to dogmatic certitude or unmasking it as illusion.

This Nietzschean vertigo replaces the Heideggerian vision of the essence of truth, the *Ereignis*, event of being. Derrida opens the *Ereignis* onto the enigmas of truth as woman, not to dissolve the truths of science, ethics, psychoanalysis or ontology, but to show the abyssal ground in which they are rooted and which they can never recuperate or reduce. The *Ereignis*, interpreted in this way, subordinates presence to a play of the simulacrum and of seduction, for the *Ereignis* reveals itself to be 'origin-heterogeneous' (*Of Spirit*, 107); instead of recollecting in itself the essence of being, it dissolves every notion of proper origin or foundation.

One might equally attempt to conceive the truth of God, pneumatic truth, as origin-heterogeneous, as the non-place of woman. The perpetual variability of religious discourse would then be the mark of its function of espousing this originary *khōra*, which like Buddhist emptiness is the kenosis of every fixed identity, a milieu in which nothing exists except in relation – but in which, however, an ultimate reality announces itself. Derrida evokes this space in an abstract way, as the place of *différance*, the spacing of archi-writing. This ultimate foyer of Derrida's thought invites comparison with the Spirit of Hegel, the Being of Heidegger, the Infinite of Levinas. Perhaps what Derrida is pointing to from afar, and in an oblique way, is the dimension that Buddhism apprehends as emptiness. At least we may attempt to give a new force and coherence to his thought by interpreting it in light of this spiritual tradition.

5

EMPTINESS AND
THE TWO TRUTHS

EMPTINESS

The reader who has kept with me up to this point may wonder if our path is not leading into a morass of uncertainty. But 'half yet remains unsung': we turn now to religious sources, in search of fresh persuasive horizons of faith. The first of these, Mādhyamika Buddhism, will expose us still more fully to the power of the negative, luring us indeed to the brink of Absolute Nothingness, yet with the assurance – if we can trust it – that by letting go all secure identities, pulverising them in what Zen Masters call the Great Doubt, or the Great Death, we will find ourselves set back in touch with ultimate gracious reality. This passing over, through the looking glass, to a Buddhist perspective is intended merely as an exercise in theological theory. But perhaps it may not be entirely irrelevant to those engaged in the practice of Buddhist wisdom amid everyday stresses and frustrations. If a bridge can be built between contemporary philosophical awareness, the attraction of the Buddha, and the claims of Christian faith – three forces which uneasily co-exist in many searching minds – then a source of intellectual and spiritual headaches can be turned into a fruitful interplay of complementary perspectives.

With increasing insight into the genealogy, the culture-bound status and the irreducible pluralism of religious languages, one senses their 'emptiness', the flimsiness and illusoriness of the web of images and concepts which they spin. From classical negative theology and doctrines of analogy, but still more from the Mādhyamika ('middle path') tradition of

Buddhism, one may however draw sustenance for a paradoxical expectation, namely, that if such straw-like fragility is embraced as the inevitable condition of religious language, this language may be restored on fresh terms as a provisional means to be used adroitly and inventively in the search to know and to communicate truth.

Despite its cultural remoteness, Mādhyamika thought has acquired resonance for contemporary theologians and philosophers of religion, for its reflection on the status of religious language seems both to outstrip the Western hermeneutics of suspicion and to provide a confident justification of religious language. The paradox is twofold. On the ontological level, the initial negative insight that all entities are dependently co-arisen (pratītya-samutpāda) leads to an embrace of emptiness (śūnyatā), and this permits a restoration of the conventional world on fresh terms. On the corresponding linguistic level, insight into the provisional and conventional character of words and concepts permits a skilful and demystified use of language, in which all the discriminations of conventional discourse can be respected within the limits of their applicability. One need not subscribe blindly to Mādhyamika doctrine, or expect from it direct answers to current questions, in order to draw inspiration from it for the construction of a similarly comprehensive and flexible theory of religious language suited to present needs.

The Mādhyamika school derives from Nāgārjuna (c. 200 CE), author of the Mūlamadhyamaka-kārikā (MMK) or Basic Middle Way Verses, which give logical support to the doctrine of emptiness set forth in the Perfection of Wisdom sūtras, fundamental scriptures of Mahāyāna Buddhism. The classic commentary of Candrakīrti (6th century), available to Western readers in a variety of partial translations (de Jong; May; Schayer; Sprung), fills in the context of debate and puts flesh and bones on Nāgārjuna's laconic verses. It lays the basis of the most influential Prāsaṅgika line of interpretation, continued in Tibet by the dGe lugs pa founded by Tsong kha pa (1357–1419). Of course the tradition has its share of internal diversity, and we need not resolve the controversies between Candrakīrti and Bhāvaviveka, between the Prāsaṅgika subordination of logic to spiritual insight and the Svātantrika stress on logic as having intrinsic validity (which may be a betrayal of Nāgārjuna's radical detachment from 'views'). It is sufficient for our purposes to acquire familiarity with these paths of thinking, to navigate on the sea of emptiness as we have navigated amid the complexities of the notion of being.

Like the idea of being in the West, the notion of emptiness varies in import according to the context and gives rise to aporias in the course of its development. An irremediable heterogeneity seems to disqualify any effort to put emptiness and being in direct relation. A critique of this or that discourse of being can draw on the diverse resources of the tradition of emptiness. But a synthesis of the two traditions, or a general triumph of Indian emptiness over Greek being, would be a too global speculative gesture. The internal problematic of each tradition is enriched by their interferences. If some great principles of mathematics or logic can be applied in every time and culture, this is not the case for great principles of philosophy or religion such as being and emptiness. They remain in dependence on the tradition of life and thought which founds them and cannot be transferred to other environments without an alteration of their meaning.

Emptiness eludes definition quite as much as being. The notion derives from the basic ontological analyses of early Buddhism, in particular the theory of dependent origination or dependent co-arising, the emergence or the becoming-manifest of things in function of an ensemble of conditions. Nothing in the world of becoming (*samsāra*) is without cause; nothing is produced *ex nihilo*; nothing has permanent existence. This is a middle way between determinism and anarchic causelessness. All phenomena are impermanent (*anitya*) and insubstantial (*anātman*), and thus painful (*duhkha*) if we cling to them, but the emergence and disappearance of these phenomena, far from being left to chance, is regulated by the law of dependent co-origination. The doctrine concerns above all the causes of existential suffering and the method of escaping from it. It is presented first as an analysis of the genesis of suffering, summarised in the twelvefold chain: 1. ignorance, 2. activities, 3. consciousness, 4. name-and-shape, 5. sense, 6. contact, 7. feeling, 8. craving, 9. grasping, 10. becoming, 11. birth, 12. decay, death, lamentation. More comprehensive is the claim that every event arises in interdependence on all others, but this too is stated in an existential and situational style: 'When that is present, this comes to be; on the arising of that, this arises. When that is absent, this does not come to be; on the cessation of that, this ceases'.

In Mahāyāna the doctrine is further radicalised. Finding antinomies in both the theses of abiding identity and of discontinuity, Nāgārjuna concludes that causation is ultimately self-contradictory; it has a merely conventional reality; the same must be said of previous representations of dependent co-arising. But in transforming causation into a transcendental principle of universal relativity, identical with emptiness, he claims to provide the only truly intelligible account of the conventional phenomenal world.

Early Buddhism taught the insubstantiality of all dharmas, but the Sarvāstivādins – against whom Nāgārjuna argues – distinguished between entities existing only in designation, such as the self, and the underlying dharmas, ultimate momentary events, to which they attributed inherent existence or own-being (*svabhāva*). The Sautrāntikas anticipated the Mādhyamika critique; they saw the cardinal Buddhist principle of insubstantiality compromised in the Sarvāstivādin attribution of inherent existence to the dharmas. For Mādhyamika every entity is empty (*sūnya*) of *svabhāva*, and exists only in designation. Since dependent co-arising entails that all things are empty, it is a co-arising that in reality gives rise to nothing, for nothing inherently existing is produced or destroyed. The logical analysis of dependent origination reveals that it is really non-dependent non-origination, the absence of inherent existence in things.

However, this is not purely negative, for the analysis also lights up the structure and order of worldly phenomena. The affirmation of dependent co-arising, implying recognition of regular causal sequence, avoids the extreme of nihilism, while the affirmation of emptiness, the insight that dependent co-arising undermines every claim to inherent existence, avoids the extreme of eternalism. The ultimacy of emptiness goes hand in hand with the provisionality of dependent co-arising. It is not mere nothingness, but a designation of the way things are. To say that all things are empty of own-being is not a denial of the existence of the world, but a clarification of its ontological status. Emptiness is not set up as a thesis, but is shown by refuting all theses that are proposed. Candrakīrti (commenting on *MMK*, 20.1–3) is taken by an opponent to be denying the existence of effects, in defiance of common sense. His reply is a characteristic vanishing act:

> We do not wish to establish their non-existence. Rather, we refute that they exist as our opponent imagines. But neither do we wish to establish their existence. Rather we refute that they do not exist as other opponents imagine. For we wish to avoid those two extreme theses and establish the middle path. (de Jong, 45f)

Blunt statements about existence and non-existence are systematically undone in this dialectic, which shows up the inadequacies of everyday thinking, its lack of grasp on the ultimate nature of things. The more this unravelling proceeds, the more we see that the 'suchness' of things attracts to itself the name 'emptiness' rather than 'inherent existence' – an illuminating and liberating discovery.

According to Guy Bugault, whereas Aristotle grounds the principle of contradiction and the excluded middle on a metaphysic of essences, which ensures that things are what they are, Nāgārjuna finds things so lacking in self-identity that they can both be and not be, and neither be nor not-be. Aristotle, like Hamlet, confines himself to the dilemma, abhorring the sophistic possibilities of the tetralemma. In contrast, Nāgārjuna embraces the tetralemma, and goes still one step further. Though he favours the fourth and most negative proposition – neither to be nor not to be – as the least false, he insists that it, too, must be abandoned, for ultimate truth lies beyond all the logical dichotomies which busy the mind (see Bugault, 246ff). However, it may be that Nāgārjuna's denial of inherent existence and inherent non-existence does not entail a real transgression of the excluded middle (see Napper, 60ff).

The natural attitude is attached to the security of well-defined concepts and essences, be they even subtle or negative ones such as non-being or *nirvāṇa*. To realise the radical relativity and the superficial, provisional character of all such logical and ontological constructions, is to know by the same token ultimate reality as emptiness. Thus, on the gnoseological side, true knowledge of the texture of our world in its lack of ontic solidity is aligned with that absence of all concrete grip which characterises the state of ultimate liberation. We should not think of *saṃsāra* as different from *nirvāṇa*, but as coextensive with it (*MMK*, 25.19f). This non-difference is not identity (the excluded middle does not apply) for there is no positive relation between the deficient existence of *saṃsāra* and *nirvāṇa* as extinction of the alternatives of being and non-being (1–18; see Bugault, 272). Yet the breakdown of all concepts that attempt to grasp the samsaric world throws us back on the realisation that ultimate reality emerges only in the dissolution of these concepts. *Saṃsāra* leaves our minds in the lurch, forcing us to let go and fall into emptiness. On the ontological side, the absence of own-being in things is not distinguishable from ultimate reality itself. As forms are seen to be empty, emptiness is seen as their veritable essence. The sheer conditionality of things reveals the unconditioned as their true nature. This is a partial explication of the famous sentence in the *Heart Sūtra*, the shortest of the *Perfection of Wisdom* sūtras: 'Form itself is emptiness, emptiness itself is form'.

THE RELATION OF THE TWO TRUTHS

Mādhyamika thought becomes particularly interesting when it faces the paradox that the concepts it has so thoroughly refuted, especially the notions of identity and causality, continue to be indispensable in everyday life and in most theoretical reflection. This situation could be met by a sweeping denial of all the differentiations of the empirical world. But instead, Mādhyamika develops a distinction between:

1. *The truth of the highest meaning.* That which exists within a nexus of cause and effect cannot be real in and for itself (that is, its individual existence cannot be grounded outside the context of everyday experience).

2. *Conventional truth*. The sole criterion for empirical reality is existence within the nexus of cause and effect which defines our shared sociolinguistic experience. (Huntington, 48)

Conceptual discriminations are condemned to the register of the conventional: ultimate, ineffable reality eludes their grasp, even when that reality is correctly conceptualised. All concepts and words belong to the level of worldly or screening truth, *saṃvṛti-satya*. Even at their most precise they can serve only as useful expedients, pointing to what they can never grasp, *paramārtha-satya*, ultimate cognition or its object, ultimate reality. On the conventional, world-ensconced level a distinction can be made between purely illusory thoughts and thoughts which correspond to the dependent condition of the samsaric world, between the conventionality of everyday beliefs (always prone to become simply false) and that of a philosophical reflection (rather like the meta-metaphysics of the *Critique of Pure Reason*) which has one foot in the worldly and the other in the ultimate.

Nāgārjuna shows, like Zeno, how none of the commonsense conceptions attached to the idea of movement hold up (*MMK*, 2): the non-existence of past and future movement entails the non-existence of present movement as well. To predicate moving of a mover is a meaningless reduplication; neither a walker nor a walking nor a walk (as trip) are found in reality.

> Does this mean that in Nāgārjuna's eyes movement is non-conceptualisable? He says nothing of the sort, nor does he ever profess irrationalism. Rather it is through applying the binary and ternary schemas of the sort we have examined that one manages, more or less, to code the phenomena. But these schemas have no other function and are bereft of any existential or ontological bearing. They are views (*dṛṣṭi*) of the mind, constructions of the imagination, operating by a sort of implicit abstraction and as if unbeknown to us. Useful and valuable at the pragmatic level of the coded truths (*saṃvṛtisatya*) which regulate everyday transactions (*vyavahāra*), they trap us when we ascribe to them the character of existing. (Bugault, 229)

Insight into the conventionality of concepts allows conversion to the existential real which concepts can never close in on. (Bugault is probably underestimating the solidity of the conventional here; see Napper, 101–11).

That is why the perfection of giving is attained when neither a giver nor a gift nor a receiver is found to exist (Lamotte, 724–50), an idea echoed in recent comments of Derrida and Jean-Luc Marion on donation

(Marion, 1994). For Derrida the condition of the possibility of giving is the condition of its impossibility; the purity of the gift is contaminated by the contractual system from which it cannot escape. Marion sees him as denying the reality of giving. But in fact Derrida's demonstration of the aporetic character and uncertain borders of concepts such as presence, truth, meaning, the proper name, the birth date, judgement, responsibility, friendship, death, 'the other as the impossible' and 'the gift as the impossible' (*Aporias*, 15f) are never to be taken to mean that the realities these concepts attempt to designate do not exist; the condition of impossibility is also the condition of possibility, or of authenticity. Marion offers instead of such dialectic a 'phenomenological reduction' of giving which successively eliminates the giver (the right hand knows not what the left does), the recipient (one gives to the 'enemy', who is thus the friend of authentic giving), and the gift itself (for the substance of what is given, the widow's mite, is indifferent). This construction has to explain away the more contractual *do ut des* texts in the Gospel. This discussion might be clarified by distinguishing between a conventional everyday language of gifthood, always entangled in contractuality, and the insight into the ultimate emptiness of giver, recipient and gift which emerges in the aporetic breakdown of the everyday language when pushed to its limit.

On the level of ultimate truth, conventional views, even those of Buddhist orthodoxy, are left behind in an immediate gnosis, in intuitive wisdom, *prajñā*. Ultimate reality is grasped only conventionally by concepts, and is fully attained in liberation from all conditioned thought, enacting the basic Buddhist movement of escape from samsaric suffering through suppression of the conditions that produce it, namely ignorance (*avidyā*) and craving (*tṛṣṇā*). Whereas even the most refined religious concepts, which concern not the empirical world but ultimate reality, are made as fragile as any other by their dependence on contingent contexts and subtle interpretations, there is a nonconceptual knowledge which escapes this condition: 'Impossible to know through another, quiescent, not differentiated into objects of discursive thought, withdrawn from this thought, without diversity of signification. These are the characteristics of reality' (*MMK*, 18.9).

But despite its eminence and its central place in their thought, this level is not what most occupies the attention of Mādhyamika thinkers. Though ultimate reality is independent of what characterises conceptual thinking, the task of elucidating the realm of concepts and of dealing with it skilfully remains capital, for in its very fragility and contingency, conceptual thinking is a convention which can facilitate or block access to the knowledge of the ultimate. The Svātantrikas are particularly vigilant here, though tending to give valid reasoning an autonomy that Nāgārjuna would refuse. For Bhāvaviveka the ultimate 'is not the object of inference, but inference has priority, because there is no other way of investigating what is true and false' (Eckel 1987, 128). Jñānagarbha sees reason (*nyāya*) as the royal road to the ultimate, though the conceptual grasp of the ultimate is still produced from the relative point of view and is inferior to a non-conceptual awareness that eliminates discursive ideas (112f, 126).

Conventional truth includes the evidence of daily life as well as the highest insights of Buddhism, and at each level it is opposed to what is false at that level. At no point does higher wisdom fly in the face of empirical evidence or logical necessity, or devalue activities of compassion and love. One should never relinquish critical reason for worldly experience, which is unguarded against inbuilt blind spots. Instead, one must 'hold out until critical wisdom experientially becomes the reliable and liberating intuition of reality' (Thurman 1991, 171).

Paul Hoornaert stresses that correct insight into ultimate truth is attained only at a stratospheric level of spiritual attainment (unpublished lecture, Tokyo, June 1995). Mādhyamika is distorted if one freely draws on this level of insight as if it were available at the lower reaches of the teaching. The dialectic of the two truths is a strategy guiding advance along a spiritual path. Its diachronic and functional character is essential to it. It is not a matter of applying a stable prefabricated doctrine.

1. At a basic level the Buddhist teaching tackles the ignorance (*avidyā*) of ordinary people, who live, think and behave as if 'I' were a self-sufficient, inherently established existence. Here the Four Noble Truths are proposed: liberation from *saṃsāra* and attainment of *nirvāṇa*, through the practice of the path. Analytic reasoning dismantles the illusions of everyday conventional existence. First, the disciples are taught to thematise their innate conception of true existence, which is identified as *svabhāva* or inherent existence. It is shown that such inherent existence can be enjoyed only by entities that own their existence independently of anything else, and own it so securely that they are not able not to exist. But all claimants to such ontological status are successfully discredited by the Mādhyamika analysis. It turns out that such inherent existence is nowhere to be found, whether in the self or in any other phenomenon. Ignorance is overcome by demonstrating the non-existence of that to which it clings.

2. But analysis equally demonstrates that the very ideas of *saṃsāra* and *nirvāṇa* lack inherent existence. The initial presentation of the teaching turns out to have been a conventional one. Now one gives up thinking of *saṃsāra* as something to be left behind and of *nirvāṇa* as something to be attained. Only emptiness, the absence of inherent existence, is the true

own-nature of things, for it alone meets the conditions of *svabhāva* as defined by Nāgārjuna. It is the non-contingent and non-dependent mode of being of all contingent and dependent entities. In the vision thus established all things are grasped as arising in dependent origination and thus as empty of own-being. All things are empty of inherent existence and inherent non-existence, and the same holds true of emptiness itself. The true own-being of entities is non-own-being (*a-svabhāva*). Paradoxically, it is only this radical emptiness which gives its logical foundation to the basic Buddhist teachings (see *MMK*, 24). If *nirvāṇa*, *saṃsāra* or *śūnyatā* itself had inherent existence, or were inherently non-existent, the entire Buddhist teaching would run aground on antinomies; but since they are empty of own-being, discourse about them can function conventionally as the most effective means of liberation, as the truest discourse there is.

3. Yet the entire realm of conceptual analysis itself remains on the level of conventional truth, although at a level of insight that lies far beyond the delusions of the everyday. All our concepts and words are mistaken projections of inherent existence, because through concepts and words we identify things by differentiating them from each other, and thus impute inherent existence to them. Even the truest conceptual understanding of emptiness ultimately obstructs the realisation of emptiness. One must root out, by the practice of mediation, the ingrained habit of apprehending things through concepts and words. Moving from non-svabhavic thought to the absolute cessation of conceptual thought, the yogin undergoes an experience like the Great Death of Zen, and no longer perceives any particular thing. This does not mean that nothing at all is experienced. Emptiness 'remains' and is experienced. At this level all conceptual discriminations, such as that between *saṃsāra* and *nirvāṇa*, fall aside. Such designations can guide people through the conventional to the ultimate, but cannot bring them across the threshold to direct realisation.

4. Advanced yogins enjoy the direct perception of emptiness in a state of meditative absorption (*samādhi*) in which the whole phenomenal world disappears from consciousness, as does consciousness itself as perceiver of phenomena. But they do not yet possess the perfect, uninterrupted vision of emptiness, for on withdrawing from *samādhi* the usual image of a world of juxtaposed and quasi-independent entities imposes itself on their perception again. Only Buddhas are capable of simultaneously seeing the world and its emptiness: 'a single gnosis can directly understand all the phenomena included within the two truths simultaneously ... It understands the conventional as it seems to be and does not understand it as it is' (Cabezón, 383). Seeing the world without seeing any inherent existence, a Buddha grasps each and every entity in

its infinite interrelationships with all other entities. Such omniscience is necessarily a nonconceptual knowledge, for if the true nature of things is their emptiness, their radical dependence on a web of infinite interrelationships, then there is nothing solid here to be pointed to and nothing for the concept to grasp. These accounts of what Buddhahood is like may seem excessively lofty, but they are grounded in the logic of emptiness and in contemplative experience.

The rejection of all svabhavic affirmations or negations produces a self-effacing thought and language which dissolves obstacles to liberation. The concepts of own-being, other-being, being, non-being if stretched beyond their conventional realm of application are each of them self-contradictory, and if we use them to name ultimate reality they make us obtuse to the Buddha's wisdom (*MMK*, 15.1–6). They are discredited less by their inbuilt antinomies than by reference to reality itself, the awareness of emptiness. It is this spiritual vision that is the starting-point of the logical argumentation; 'Nāgārjuna merely attempted to translate into philosophical terms a mystical experience, a direct and individual experience of an ineffable reality' (de Jong, xii).

Even at the conventional level, the categories of existence and non-existence have no application to *nirvāṇa* or to the nirvanic reality of the Tathāgatha, the perfectly realised Buddha. To affirm anything as inherently existing, or non-existing, or both, or neither, is to err, for none of these four theses can account for the process of salvation. There is a temptation to reduce Mādhyamika thought to a solid ontology, either substantialist (absolutist) or nihilist. It is even misleading to present it as a middle position between these extremes: 'the middle is no position; it is beyond concept or speech; it is the transcendental, being a review of all things' (Murti, 129). In Nāgārjuna the middle path is nothing other than emptiness itself as the middle between being and non-being, the substantialist and nihilist extremes: 'Those who see only the existence and non-existence of things cannot perceive the salutary quiescence of the empirical world' (*MMK*, 5.8). At the highest level, even the concept of emptiness is left behind: 'It should not be said that the Tathāgata is empty, or non-empty, or both empty and non-empty, or neither empty nor non-empty. And yet all this is said for the sake of letting the Truth be known' (22.11).

The use of any of these expressions keeps us captive to language and its proliferating differentiations. Ultimate reality has no need of these efforts to define it, yet as pointers to the nature of ultimate reality any of these terms may be used as provisional designations, 'in a special and secondary sense', 'in an everyday transactional way as it suits those who are to be guided' (Sprung, 201). Thus the term 'empty' serves to rupture habits of thought and language that are based in a clinging to existence; 'non-empty' corrects the extreme of nihilism and reminds one of the reality of Buddhahood; at a high level of attainment, 'neither empty nor non-empty' frees the mind from conceptual fixation, to let it know reality as it is, in the letting-go of every conceptual grasp.

Mūlamadhyamaka-kārikā 24.18 is a key text for the Mādhyamika doctrine of two truths. The Sanskrit reads:

> *yaḥ pratītyasamutpādaḥ śūnyatāṃ tāṃ pracakṣmahe*
> *sā prajñaptir upādāya pratipat saiva madhyamā.*

'Whatever is dependent co-arising, that we explain as emptiness. It [emptiness] is a designation having recourse [to the dependently co-arisen] and it is the middle path' (on the problems of translation, see Swanson, 3–6). The four items named here are four ways of naming the one reality. Candrakīrti comments:

> since emptiness means that all things without exception do not arise self-existently, it avoids the two extremes of existence and non-existence, and is said to be the middle way or the middle path. Thus it is that 'emptiness', 'provisional designation', and 'middle way' are the different names of one and the same production by conditions. (May, 239)

The 'designation' seems to correspond to dependent co-arising as properly grasped, in the awareness of its emptiness – or as revived from within emptiness after having first been negated. The world of dependent co-arising retains a provisional, conventional reality or truth. Even when we call that world 'empty' this, too, is only a provisional, conventional designation.

Emptiness, as named and discussed, still belongs to the level of conventional truth, while ultimate truth remains ineffable:

> *Śūnyatā* is a metaphorical designation of absolute reality (*MMK*, 24.18), or more exactly a designation of absolute reality by means of the surface reality... The emptiness of the surface reality designates, makes known absolute reality. One is here at a point of contraction of the two realities. One could also say that the absolute reality, conceptualised, appears as the empty surface reality, observing that this equivalence and the preceding one put *śūnyatā* on the side of *saṃvṛti*. *Śūnyatā* is thus not rigorously equivalent to *paramārtha*, but is still only a designation of it. Here we glimpse the 'flight of the absolute' that André Bareau sees as an important trait of the history of Buddhist speculation. (May, 238)

This flight of the absolute can become an abstract negative theology, but it can also take a practical form, as a vivid realisation of the impossibility of grasping ultimate reality by any of our words or thoughts, an impossibility which obliges us to a spiritual versatility that excludes dogmatism as well as lazy scepticism.

T. R. V. Murti's account of the two truths slants the Mādhyamika doctrine in the direction of Vedantic absolutism and phenomenalism: the worldly truth concerns only illusory appearances and the sole truth is the absolute which these obscure. The Vedantic account of the two truths in Śaṅkara (700–50) is itself marked by Mādhyamika influence, transmitted via his predecessors Gauḍapāda and Govinda; and Śaṅkara had to fend off the accusation of being a crypto-Buddhist. An Indian scholar summarises Śaṅkara's view in these terms:

> The principle of two truths is a direct consequence of the principle of superimposition [adhyāsa]; according to the latter, there is a formless and hence nameless reality that manifests itself as different worlds of phenomena under different superimpositional frameworks.

We superimpose on non-dual reality the concepts and percepts which are the stuff of all expressible and communicable knowledge. Pluralism prevails at this level, but:

> since there is but a single, non-dual, unitary reality – Brahman – there is and can only be one higher truth, which, transcending all superimpositional frameworks, is non-perceptual, non-conceptual, direct, and intuitive . . . And what remains, as the ultimate residuum after the disappearance of all objects, all contents of consciousness? Just consciousness, Atman, consciousness without objects, and this consciousness is indeed Brahman. (R. Puligandla, in Pappu, 187)

From a Buddhist point of view, this is a substantialist and foundationalist doctrine, that misses the complete freedom of nirvanic emptiness.

For Murti, the two truths are two modes whereby we apprehend one and the same Reality. 'In fact, there is only one Truth – the paramārtha satya, as there is only one real – the Absolute. The other is *truth so-called* in common parlance; it is totally false from the absolute standpoint' (Murti, 251). Murti identifies the Mādhyamika *saṃvṛti-satya* with Śaṅkara's superimposition. The two truths reduce to a contrast between non-dual intuition and the illusory phenomenal world of *māyā*, 'between the thing as it is, unrelatedly, absolutely, and how it appears in relation to the percipients who look at it through views and standpoints' (243). Murti sees conventional truth as a ladder to the absolute, but he overlooks the degree to which this entails positive, rational ontological insight, and focuses too simply on the idea that through the removal of the conventional superimpositions one unveils the absolute (253), an idea that fits better an absolute conceived as supreme being than one conceived in terms of emptiness of own-being. From the Mādhyamika point of view this contrast of appearance and reality is a short-circuit. The two truths:

> are not only and not primarily two modes of knowledge. The two truths are two levels of reality *and* two corresponding levels of knowledge. They each have an ontological *and* a gnoseological aspect and the ontological aspect is more fundamental than the gnoseological. (Hoornaert, 591)

Yet it would also be a mistake to reduce the doctrine of emptiness to a mere assertion of the relativity of beings. To know emptiness is to know the absolute, the unconditioned reality of *nirvāṇa*:

> Empty entities and Emptiness are not identical and yet they are so close to being identical that the danger of denying the reality of one or both always exists. The denial of the reality of Emptiness corresponds to the mistaken view that everything is relative and no ultimate truth exists. Conversely, the denial of the reality of empty entities corresponds to the mistaken view that emptiness exists intrinsically. (595f)

At first it looks as if Hoornaert is exaggerating the differences between Mādhyamika and Vedānta. After all, Śaṅkara's superimposition provides the fabric of the world of everyday knowledge, and writers on Vedānta often stress that the notion of *māyā* does not mean that this world is unreal. *Māyā* is not mere non-being, but a dispersion of being in a network of illusory differentiations (Lacombe, 74). Meanwhile, even in early Buddhism the dependently arisen world is seen as a bubble, a mirage or a magical trick (see Lamotte, 357–87). Nāgārjuna uses this rhetoric and Candrakīrti loves to quote such texts: 'Everything pretends to be what it is not; it is essentially a swindle; it is unreal; it is a conjuring display (*māyā*); it is the babbling of a child' (Sprung, 44); 'The true (*satya*), however, is what does not pretend to be what it is not; *nirvāṇa* is the sole instance of this' (145). Conventional reality is finally false; to the saint it is not truth but mere occlusion. Again, Tibetan Mādhyamika texts present worldly phenomena as merely products of conceptual thought. 'the snake is something that is labeled onto the rope by conceptual thought' (Cabezón, 162). Conventional reality, for Buddhism, seems to have the same ontologically ambiguous and illusion-ridden status as *māyā*.

However, the Buddhist utterances take on a new meaning when we realise that even ultimate reality is seen as a mere label of conventional thought: *nirvāṇa* itself is empty. Candrakīrti quotes *Perfection of Wisdom* texts:

> Buddha himself, venerable Subhūti, is like *māyā* or a dream; and the essential qualities of Buddha are like *māyā* and a dream... The Truth, properly understood, is devoid of an existence of its own; enlightenment, properly understood, is devoid of an existence of its own; and one who would enter the way is also devoid of self-existence ... Even *nirvāṇa* is like magic and a dream; how much more other truths. (Sprung, 200f, 205)

Bhāvaviveka, who insists so strongly on the reality of conventional objects in their proper sphere, also holds that 'the Absolute may well exist conventionally, but ultimately it is as empty as anything else' (Eckel, 1985, 40). For Jñānagarbha, 'nothing ultimately real is left after dualities have been stripped away... he is unwilling to attribute any ultimate reality to *paramārtha* or to the cognition of emptiness' (Eckel 1987, 116). For the dGe lugs pa theorists 'nothing truly or ultimately exists ... One cannot maintain that conventional phenomena are truthless while claiming that reality, the ultimate quality of conventional phenomena, truly exists' (Cabezón, 471).

Paradoxically, the Vedantic absolutism of being is forced to deny the reality of everyday being, whereas the Mādhyamika doctrine of ultimate emptiness can rejoice in the everyday world even as it undoes the illusions of own-being which prevent us from seeing that world as it is. Thus Mādhyamika, though often thought to be a nihilism, may in fact have a happier relationship to the world of everyday realities than Vedānta has. The lack of own-being of entities does not put them in disaccord with ultimate reality, but actually shows their accord with this ultimate reality as emptiness. Moreover, the empty entities do have a nominal or conventional existence:

> The way in which we label all phenomena by conceptual thought resembles the way we label a rope as a snake. Yet they are utterly different in that the former exist nominally as they are labeled whereas the latter does not. (169)

Murti does not do justice to this point, claiming that 'only Emptiness is real while empty entities simply do not exist' (Hoornaert, 586).

For Vedānta the realm of *māyā* is the realm of ignorance (*avidyā*) masquerading as knowledge (see Lacombe, 122); saving knowledge means release from it, its dissolution as a sheer illusion. Vedānta too speedily dissolves the worldly conventional distinctions; against Vaiśeṣika realism some Vedāntins 'argue against the very possibility of defining entities, of establishing them in their individual identity, and of defining and establishing being itself in its distinction from nonbeing' (Halbfass, 232). In contrast, the mirages denounced in Mādhyamika are only the ascription to the worldly existence of an own-being that it does not have. One can enjoy conventional knowledge, and there is a sober and responsible intellectual reflection within the domain of conventional reality. Saving knowledge does not annul the conventional, but establishes a discerning and liberated relation to it. The world of nominal existence or relative reality marshals all the resources of language and logic; the attempt to understand it is already a step towards ultimate reality. The alternative, which Mādhyamika rejects, would be a mystic leap cutting short such attention to the conventional and leading in all likelihood to an absolutist or nihilist fixation. Religion, in the Mādhyamika understanding, does not release us from intellectual responsibility, but rather restores to the mind its full freedom, including the freedom to recognise in the end that reality transcends all its constructions. The subordination of mind to anything less than ultimate reality – to views, emotions, imagination, authorities, texts – is a bondage from which it seeks to release us. But the mind is shown the path to its own release.

In Chinese versions of the two truths doctrine:

> Co-arising, emptiness, conventional existence, and the Middle are not four realities, four separate existences or four independent doctrines, but four ways to express the same one reality, the Buddha-dharma, which is *saṃsāra* to us common ignorant mortals and *nirvāṇa* to a Buddha ... *Saṃvṛtisatya* is the mistaken perception of the world as existing substantially, not the actual existence of substantial Being itself. (Swanson, 5f, 53)

The positive aspect of conventional truth as appropriate to the relatively real character of conditioned existence is recognised, and the bodhisattva works with it from the perspective of insight.

Swanson corrects a misunderstanding generated by early Chinese translations of Mādhyamika terminology: 'the misleading identification of the real truth with "non-existence" (*wu*) and the mundane truth with "existence" (*yu*), rather than a clarification of the true meaning of existence as conventional *pratītyasamutpāda* existence which is empty of substantial Being' (64). The dialectical cast given to the two truth theory is perhaps a result of tensions induced by this initial misprision. Emptiness, conceived as non-being (*wu*), is the negation of dependent co-arising (*yu*); emptiness in turn is surpassed in the provisional designation which reinstates being; finally, the middle path emerges as the synthesis which avoids the extremes of emptiness and being. Emptiness, the provisional, and the middle become the three truths of the T'ien-t'ai school of which Chih-i (538–97) perfected the theory.

THE STATUS OF LANGUAGE

One misses the force of Mādhyamika if one takes it to present all language and thought as a tissue of misunderstandings with no objective value, to be abandoned as soon as possible. If language were no more than that, the elaborate critical efforts of Nāgārjuna would be disproportionate. His teaching is concerned less with the escape from language than with managing it in such a way as to bring it into accord with the awareness of emptiness as ultimate truth. How are we to think the samsaric world and move in it in such a way as to open it to the nirvanic dimension which appeases all differentiations in the intuition of emptiness? Not by denying the reality of this world, but by espousing its texture and its inner coherence in an appropriate language and conceptuality. In the last analysis this texture is revealed to be nothing other than emptiness, which does not then work against language and the logical but is the condition of their correct functioning. The encyclopaedic reprise of abhidharmic lore in the vast Mādhyamika treatise *Mahā-prajñāpāramitā-śāstra* (Lamotte) is proof enough that the apprehension of emptiness does not paralyse discriminating thought, but rather frees it.

The thought of emptiness is a refined strategy for putting worldly language at the service of an ultimate intuition. Only a modest language, aware of its purely functional status, can serve to light up the texture of the real. Any concept, however lucid and useful, is but a provisional designation, depending for its validity on a particular context. Some concepts attain a high degree of invariability and universality due to the stability of their context; but the hold they give on the world is not a grasp of reality in itself. The ultimate reality of emptiness is known on a plane beyond language and concepts, but our everyday world is formed by language and concepts and shares their fragility. Language and world are produced in dependence on one another, nor does the samsaric world exist independently of its linguistic construction. As we learn to deal with language without 'attachment to words as having self-nature', we simultaneously begin to overcome 'attachment to objects as having self-nature' (Suzuki, 87).

Analogously, to use dogmatic language without illusions as to its permanence or substantiality, yet without sceptical lassitude either, is an apprenticeship in understanding God as Spirit. Theological language should deconstruct the fixity and reification of conventional religious language while also constantly effacing itself, aware of its own provisionality. To do this it must work at a critical retrieval of the traditional conventional language while at the same time rupturing it, opening it to ultimate reality, through the invention of concepts comparable to 'emptiness', which reinscribe (re-mark) on the language its finitude and inadequacy in face of what it designates.

The enlightened person can handle language in an intelligent and salutary way, aware of the emptiness of each of its terms. When one returns from the intuition of ultimate reality to worldly formulas, for example those of prayer, one finds that these formulas are charged with renewed meaning. One frequents alternately the world of dependent co-arising and the reality of emptiness, or the world of conventional designations and the world of ultimate meaning: in both cases the move to the ultimate is a liberating leap or break and the return to the dependently co-arisen or the conventional is a restoration of things in their modest non-substantial there-being. The emptying out of conventional existence and language gives a new rigour and vibrancy to our dealings with them. Conventional existence provides the support for the quest of ultimate reality. One may return from the ultimate to the relative, now grasping it – not *sub specie aeternitatis* in a rationally grounding Spinozan sense – but in view of the thusness, emptiness, nirvanic freedom which is its ultimate truth.

This middle path, which allows continued engagement with the language, thought and action of the empirical world, in the awareness of its radical inadequacy, escapes the nihilism which sees language as a futile game and the substantialism which would attach each word to a stable and determinate referent. Derrida and Wittgenstein are not so well guarded against nihilism. For remedy they offer the assurance that once freed of logocentric fixations, we shall find that all is in order, and the ghostly perils of scepticism and nihilism will have disappeared. In contrast, the Buddhist tradition keeps up a steady resistance to nihilism, which it fears no less than substantialism, stressing that misapplied negativity is as fatal as deluded affirmations of being. The overcoming of nihilist fixations is one aspect of the 'emptiness of emptiness'; the other is the refusal to give emptiness itself the status of an essence or substrate:

> One who, not seeing the due distinction between the two truths in this way, grasps at the lack of self-existence in all composite things and dwells on it, eager for liberation, either he imagines that all composite things do not truly exist or that the absence of self-existence in them itself exists like a thing, in which case he imagines a self-existent reality of the nature of devoidness. In either case the

doctrine of devoidness, wrongly understood, would inevitably destroy such a one. (Sprung, 232f)

The last rejection of reification, namely the refusal to reify emptiness itself, is paradoxically what preserves this negative way from nihilism. An enlightened language, which has broken with the everyday conventional attribution of an abiding identity to concepts or entities, serves to orient us in the samsaric world, sharpening awareness of its provisional character, and thus by the same token it orients us to the ultimate. In Zen dialogues, an oscillation between down-to-earth banalities and inconceivable paradoxes enacts this conjunction of the worldly and the ultimate.

The emptiness of emptiness means that the ultimate reality is not a self-existent thing but simply the denial of every ultimately real element in existence:

> As Bhāvaviveka demonstrates so vividly, the very structure of the Mādhyamaka argument leads away from the ultimately real and back to the conventional. It is only from the conventional perspective that the reality of the path can be guaranteed . . . If the reality of the path were based on a covert assumption of the reality of the Absolute, conventional reality would be decidedly unimportant. But in Bhāvaviveka's system, the conventional is the locus of whatever reality there is. (Eckel 1985, 42)

Perhaps in Christianity too the ultimate reality of the divine remains unsayable and ungraspable, and it is only in the realm of historical, incarnational conventions that we remain in touch with reality. The discretion of God, the flight of the absolute, may summon brave spirits to mystic transcendence, but it normally consigns the believer to the world of mediations.

Some see Nāgārjuna's critique of language, and 'the quiescence of fabrications' he aimed at (*MMK*, opening verse), as a radical destruction of the capacity to make meaningful or true statements, leading to an intuitive leap beyond concepts and words. More helpful for contemporary reflection on religious language is the Wittgensteinian interpretation that sees him as a linguistic therapist, working with critical, conceptual vigilance to safeguard a correct understanding of ultimate reality by refuting efforts to grasp it in inappropriate concepts. The dexterity of this logic is subordinate to the actual experience of that reality. By the same token a correct understanding of conventional reality is secured:

> The non-egocentrist outlook is essentially critical of all givens, not by taking as 'given' the essential unreliability of everything, as does

the absolutistic skeptic, but by never being satisfied with any supposedly analysis-proof element, and by sustaining the critical process itself as a valid mode of thought, cultivating a high tolerance of less than absolute security. The non-egocentrist's attitude toward the empirical is thoroughly relativistic and conventionalistic. Having found that life goes on even without any irreducible element, he works flexibly with what is consensually established, and yet does not abdicate the task of refining the consensus. He considers philosophy itself a therapeutic process, rather than a constructive metascience. (Thurman 1991, 95f)

The limits of language and concepts appear starkly when they try to grasp the ultimate reality, but even their everyday functioning is shown to be metaphorical and approximative as the ultimate untenability of the distinctions with which it works comes into view. Ultimately, even the concept of emptiness must be abandoned in a move to non-conceptual apprehension: 'Emptiness is taught to bring to quiescence every differentiation without exception. Thus the goal of emptiness is the quiescence of the differentiated world as a whole' (May, 223). But short of this ultimate realisation, linguistic inventions are 'appeased' not by destroying them but by bringing them into perspective. The destruction of 'views' is directed more against an insufficiently critical way of thinking than against any particular concept. Far from destroying the conventional world-ensconced truths – such as the Four Holy Truths – it is emptiness which gives them their only logical basis. It is their lack of inherent existence which renders the phenomena of suffering and liberation possible:

> Only what is produced by conditions is pain, not what is not so produced; but what is produced by conditions is empty, because bereft of own-being. If pain exists, the origin of pain, the cessation of pain, the way that leads to the cessation of pain are logically based. (235)

The interpretations which recognise that Nāgārjuna restores language in a demystified consciousness of its fragility risk, however, falling back into a mere pragmatism, which admits no meaning in words outside their opportunistic use. Huntington advances such a reductive interpretation:

> His concept of 'dependent designation' (prajñaptir upādāya) recognizes that the meaning of words derives exclusively from their usage or application in everyday affairs. Accordingly the significance of the words and concepts used within the Mādhyamika system derives not from their supposed association with any objectively privileged

vocabulary supporting a particular view of truth or reality, but from their special efficacy as instruments which may be applied in daily life to the sole purpose of eradicating the suffering caused by clinging, antipathy, and the delusion of reified thought. (Huntington, xii)

Interpretations that make conventional language merely a matter of pragmatic adroitness, with no concern with conceptual definition and logical consequence, are refuted in the Mādhyamika orthodoxy of the dGe lugs pa (Cabezón). Thinkers of great conceptual refinement, the Mādhyamika philosophers could see every formulation as provisional and superficial without thereby excusing themselves from the conceptual labour required to assess and regulate the use of language. Their analysis of conventionally existing things amounts to a demonstration or at least confirmation of emptiness, each line of analysis leading to contradictions, which oblige one to abandon the illusion of self-existence and recognise that emptiness sovereignly imposes itself as the higher reality. This logic undoes delusive cognitive claims while advancing none of its own:

> If a Mādhyamika does not, in any sense at all, advance cognitive claims, how is your assertion 'things do not arise spontaneously or because of another, or because of both or from no cause at all' to be understood? It has the form of a cognitive claim.
>
> Our reply is that this pronouncement is an assertion for the ordinary man because it is argued solely on a basis which he accepts. But it is not a cognitive assertion for those wise in the Buddhist way... The higher truth, for the wise, is a matter of silence. How then would everyday language, reasoned or unreasoned, be possible in that realm? (Sprung, 50)

Such detachment from views is not a mere conventionalism, but springs from the conviction that no view can do justice to the absolutely real. What is involved is not merely a renunciation of emptiness as philosophical view in favour of a practice of emptiness as a mode of existing free from attachments (the root of substantialism) and aversions (the root of nihilism). The process also brings a cognitive advance, allowing thought to rejoin the true nature of reality.

Ultimate reality is not given as a referent; reference functions only at the level of conventional truth. As R. M. Gimello writes:

> As there are really no determinate entities to be referred to, so words do not actually refer. Their indexical function is illusory, indeed it is one of the major fabricators of illusion. What is, and the emptiness thereof, will simply not submit to the language of determinateness.

This no doubt accounts for the intractable character of the emptiness teaching and for its frequent misinterpretation. (quoted, Huntington, 31)

However, Mādhyamika does recognise the referentiality of language at the conventional level, though querying the status and upshot of this reference. The register of conventional truth is so firmly structured that it permits words to keep their referential function and it lends itself to probing philosophical analyses. It might be instructive to compare the screening conventional truth, which is both gnoseological and ontological, with the occultation of being by beings in Heidegger. Conventional truth is in perfect accord with the world of being and of everyday activity, but even when it correctly names the ultimate as emptiness it is still occluding it.

MĀDHYAMIKA AND WESTERN THOUGHT

We have seen that a dialogue with the past – and this is doubly true when it is a question of the Asian past – cannot be reduced to a conceptual discussion, for each past concept is inserted in a context we can scarcely reconstruct and which even if we succeeded would be more foreign than ever. The controversies of Buddhist philosophy are a stimulus for our thought, but we cannot adopt as it stands any system or even any concept. Our confidence in the adequacy of Western categories is shaken, but the non-Western ones are of no direct help. The insecurity caused by conceptual pluralism prompts us to move to a higher level of reflection, where the status of conceptuality itself is put in question.

Finding its bearings in relation to Buddhism, Christian thought can neither assume a position of mastery nor suppress the attraction and challenge of the foreign tradition. Unlike its negotiations with philosophers such as Wittgenstein, Heidegger, and Derrida, this debate goes to the heart of theology, for the dialogue-partner is not merely a thinker, from whom one may learn some rules for a reform of theological thought, but carries the weight of a religious authority, which imposes respect the more one frequents it. One can leave the philosophers behind once they have made their critical corrections of theological language, but contact with a great Buddhist thinker is of more than temporary interest; for that thinker's religious witness to ultimate truth, even if we understand it poorly, enters the horizon of Christian thought as an essential reference.

Sensing the relevance of the old debates for current philosophical and religious questioning, we are tempted to overlook the incommensurability between our preoccupations and arguments and those of ancient India and China. The resulting misunderstandings may be very fertile. But if our interaction with Mādhyamika is not to dissolve into harmonising speculation, we need to keep up the search for a precise understanding, in increasing awareness of the finite, particular, historical character of the two languages which meet here. Scholarly research has a key role in keeping before us the challenging otherness of the tradition, which may reserve many lessons and insights beyond what we currently need or can absorb.

The sequence from Mādhyamika, a critical philosophy establishing conventional knowledge on new, more modest bases, to Yogācāra, a philosophy of mind which both resists and absorbs its critical precursor, has recalled to Western scholars the sequence from Kant to Hegel. This is one of those local affinities that have some heuristic value in expounding Indian thought, if accompanied by the necessary differentiations. Scholars are currently using Derrida and Wittgenstein as heuristic keys to Mahāyāna philosophy. There is evidently ample room for hermeneutical naivety in parallels between the Mādhyamika critique of Abhidharma and Wittgenstein's post-positivist or Derrida's post-structuralist problematic. Such rapprochements are inevitable, not only in speculation, but especially when thinking seeks its bearings in regard to ultimate questions, refusing confinement by the details of a system or of a particular historical debate. Felt affinities seek to articulate themselves, even if the only language available is irremediably imprecise and even if one cannot develop a hermeneutics powerful enough to master objectively the relation of the two traditions. Such collage is harmless if it recognises its poverty and does not take itself for a magisterial synthesis.

David Loy creates too close a parallel with contemporary problematics when he states that 'Buddhism includes a strong ontotheological element' which Nāgārjuna seeks to deconstruct. Heidegger's analysis of onto-theology is properly applicable only to the Western thinking of being. Buddhism fights against the temptation to make of the absolute or of irreducible elements (*dharmas*) a transcendental signified, a fixed anchor to which thought can cling; but to call this a debate about 'ontotheology' is to miss all that separates the historical horizons of Nāgārjuna and Heidegger or Derrida. Loy explains the Mādhyamika distinction between conventional and absolute truth in Derridian terms. First, 'language must be used to expose the traps of language' (in Coward and Foshay, 227, 241), then a more disruptive strategy invokes 'a "higher" or "surpassing truth" that points beyond language and therefore beyond truth, raising the question of "the truth of truth" and the very possibility of truth in philosophy' (241) – 'the "higher truth"... is that there is no truth' (244). This gives ultimate reality a too uniquely negative function. Derrida interrogates a philosophical rhetoric of truth in the light of the written condition of every presentation of the true, to show that truth is exceeded by the undecidable, but Nāgārjuna contests the conventional truth in the name of what is truer than every worldly truth and more real than every thinkable reality. Such an aspiration has only tangential relations with deconstruction or any other form of Western dialectics (Platonic, sceptical, Kantian, Hegelian, Wittgensteinian). A soteriological goal orients Nāgārjuna's procedures and keeps them irreducible to any philosophical schema.

Loy quotes *MMK*, 25.24: 'Ultimate serenity is the coming to rest of all ways of taking things, the repose of named things; no Truth (*dharma*) has been taught by a Buddha for anyone, anywhere'. But this beyond of named or conceptual teaching at the highest stage of enlightened perception does not entail that precise doctrines are not taught on the way to this goal. The final, full realisation of the truth of these doctrines reveals the conventionality of their formulation, but by no means equates them with mere delusion. Merely to drop all truth-claims as delusive, on the grounds that 'all truth is error on the Buddhist path' (Loy, in a lecture in Tokyo, June 1995), would be to fall into a quasi-Nietzschean annihilationism. Loy claims that this is the Zen way, and indeed it was precisely such a drastic leap to freedom from all views that was rejected by the Mādhyamika side in the famous Lhasa debate (792–4 CE). But ultimately, it is not truth or truths that are rejected, either in Zen or in Mādhyamika, but a fixated clinging to truths or to Truth. The overcoming of such fixation is not a destruction of truths but a liberation of them through their reinsertion in a functional context, as Loy himself acknowledges when he speaks of Buddhist truths as 'a roadmap showing us where to go'. Underlying these epistemological quibbles lies a more basic issue: is Buddhism radically opposed to the Christian belief in eternal life, which it shows up as a comforting delusion, blind to the truth of impermanence? I think it equally plausible to maintain that the Buddhist language of *nirvāṇa*, in its delicate strategic positioning, could allow the Gospel promise to be rehearsed in new, more credible terms.

Robert Magliola errs in the opposite direction (substantialism) when he speaks of a to-and-fro between logocentric and differential language: 'The logocentric and the differential (own-being and emptiness) become, then, two "frequentings". And the two frequentings are at the command of the "enlightened person"' (Magliola, 123). 'Logocentric formulations, while not having absolute propriety, retain *internal* propriety as long as the operations within the logical frame are themselves "logical"' (217). But it is rather misleading to refer to the truth of everyday conventional existence as logocentrism. Logocentrism is better identified as uncritical imprisonment within conventional discourse, and as such it is not to be frequented at all. Critical frequenting of worldly reality can respect everyday logic while also remaining conscious of the inbuilt antinomies that mark it as non-ultimate. Even the sophisticated differential logic which thus undoes logocentric mystification, remains itself a mere *upāya*, and one 'frequents' it freely in the awareness of its provisional status. The to-and-fro between logical conventions and their critique is overshadowed by a more fundamental to-and-fro between the ultimate and the conventional, between emptiness grasped in silent contemplation and the entire world of language and form.

One might apply to religious language, and in a specific way to Christian language, what David Loy says of philosophical language:

> Philosophy cannot grasp what it seeks in any of its categories, but, as language becoming self-conscious of its function, it can learn to 'undo' itself and cease to be an obstruction, in that way allowing what we have long sought to manifest itself [in] a nondual way of experiencing language and thought. (Loy, 251)

The contemplative experience language aims at is not, however, an identical experience across all times, the same for Nāgārjuna as for Pseudo-Dionysius; it takes diverse hues according to the ways in which particular languages undo themselves in view of it.

Nāgārjuna warns against every tendency to reify the real through some privileged definition which would arrest the critical dynamics of emptiness. Yet he invokes an ineffable experience of the ultimate reality as the goal of religious practice. Is not this a foundationalism, a metaphysics of presence and pure origin? Is not this pure experience a transcendental signified in Derrida's sense?

Let us note first that this ultimate reality is not approached along the paths of Western rationalism or irrationalism. The founding instances of Western rational philosophies do not imply such a leap beyond the conceptual register and its reduction to a provisional means. To be sure, the sixth-century Neo-Platonist philosopher Damascius unmasks the incapacity of language to name the ultimate except 'by way of allusion (*kata endeixin*)', and is sufficiently anti-foundationalist to suspect even a notion as subtle as that of a being 'beyond every opposition' as serving the construction of a metaphysical 'superlativism' (Combès 254, 212). Does he thereby escape from the 'ontological high bidding of hyperessentiality' which Derrida unmasks in Pseudo-Dionysius and Eckhart? No, for he fails to question the ontological structuring of the world which provides the starting-point of every Platonic quest of the absolute, and he still moves within the onto-theological logic and grammar which appropriate deconstruction for negative theology by claiming: 'hyperessentiality is precisely that, a supreme being which remains incommensurate to the being of all that is, which *is* nothing, neither present nor absent' (in Coward and Foshay, 78f; translation modified).

This approach to the absolute via a return to the eminently simple One, beyond every essence, or to the pure origin, before every essence – even if it loses itself more and more in the ineffable, in a nothingness beyond every affirmation and every negation, as when Damascius describes the all-embracing ineffable One as 'so ineffable that it is not at all unique, or all-embracing, or ineffable' (quoted, Combès, 219) – cannot escape the onto-theological structure of its point of departure, under pain of losing itself in empty abstraction.

In contrast, Nāgārjuna's point of departure, dependent co-arising, opens onto emptiness without recourse to the aporetic and dialectical process of an ever more radical apophasis. The dependently co-arisen world has nothing to do with the Platonic world deriving from an absolute. One does not transcend the world of dependent co-arising towards its absolute origin, but rather perceives its lack of ontological anchorage and how, in its very texture, emptiness shows through. Emptiness is demonstrated not by an aporetic bearing on ever more refined expressions, but in the dissolution of the illusory substantiality projected in all statements. This emptiness is not a nothingness beyond being, and it does not emerge under the auspices of the notion of unity. For all these reasons it cannot be seen as a foundation in the sense of Western metaphysics even in its most apophatic form.

The leap that Nāgārjuna takes from the world-ensconced truth to ultimate truth presents only superficial analogies with a Kantian leap from the empirical to the transcendental or from phenomenon to noumenon (the unknowable thing in itself):

> To interpret the Two Truths in this way is to overlook the all-knowability on which Buddhism insists; and to interpret them as appearance and reality, the one delusive and the other true, is to fail to take into account the Buddhist conception of the unconditional realness of what there is. (Guenther, 19)

Buddhist all-knowability is not a phenomenalism, for in tasting the thusness of things one is in contact with their very reality. One might propose an analogy with Bergson, in that the conventional level entails a certain alienation from this thusness, to be overcome by a leap from conceptual construction to immediate givenness. As Guenther remarks, 'it is the aesthetic, intuitive factor that is declared to be ultimately real, while the theoretically designated factor in our experience is only relatively so'.

But in the last analysis the alternation of samsaric and nirvanic perspectives, of conventional and ultimate truth, does not fit into any system of Western philosophy, for it lies beyond dualisms of appearance and reality and the ontotheological concern with grounds. Ultimate reality is the basis of conventional phenomena, but not their cause or sufficient reason. It does not found discourse, but slips its grasp. By showing up its own projections, its lack of basis, a self-critical discourse becomes an enactment of emptiness. Emptiness works in such a discourse not as its foundation but as a critical resistance against objectification. One form of objectification is to represent emptiness as a foundation. If one grasps the ultimate, one grasps it as foundation; to accede to it one must renounce all grasping, and the entire regime of determinations and reference.

RELIGIONS AS *UPĀYA*

Some hold that Mahāyāna Buddhism breaks with the basis of Western thought by a purely irrational rejection of the principle of contradiction. This view derives from an incorrect interpretation of the paradoxical expressions in the sūtras. Sentences such as 'The mountain is not the mountain, and for this very reason the mountain is the mountain', characteristic of the *Diamond Sūtra* (*Vajracchedikā*), later prized by Zen Buddhists, entail a logical contradiction only if one supposes that the word 'mountain' means exactly the same thing in its four occurrences. The sentence can be read as saying: 'The mountain, the thing in itself, in its "suchness" (*tathatā*), is not the "mountain" of our habitual language, thought and perception; its ultimate reality is other than what is grasped in these worldly designations and representations. It is empty of the self-existence that our language projects on it. The reality of the mountain is its emptiness; its own-being is its lack of own-being. One grasps the reality of the mountain by a leap beyond illusory representations, in an intuitive grasp of the phenomenon; and if one still calls this phenomenon "mountain" it is only in a play with the conventions of language, for its ultimate reality is ineffable. It is only now that one can use the expression "mountain" appropriately, in a provisional and pragmatic way'. The word 'mountain' is correctly used only when we realise that it is merely a skilful means (*upāya*) for designating that which is ultimately ineffable.

There is no contradiction here, but ideas remotely akin to what Kant and Heidegger suggest about the capacity of human language to occlude that to which it refers, so that it has to be recalled to a sense of its limits (Kant) or opened out into a poetic saying (Heidegger). All our language about things (and *a fortiori* about God) is a tissue which depends on our historically situated subjectivity; the noumenenon attests its reality in escaping the grasp of this language, which finds itself constitutively inadequate and a prey to the illusions of worldly existence. But this noumenon is not a pure unknown; it is given as phenomenon in the spiritual awakening that is the aim of Buddhist meditation. This relation between the fragility of all language and thought and the assurance of touching ultimate reality is what makes necessary recourse to the topic of the two truths, which provides homeopathic therapy for the modern suspicion that religious representations are intrinsically illusory.

If a quantity of illusion has inevitably entered the alloy of our religious conceptions, and if we subject this mass of illusions to an analysis of its genealogy and its social or psychological functions, what will remain of faith? A Buddhist answer might go as follows: recognising the provisional and conventional character of all religious language, one is freed from reifications which impede spiritual freedom, and one can use the classical language adroitly in function of particular contexts and situations as a means of pointing to that which it cannot claim to grasp. The great texts of the past can be retrieved as pointers to transcendence, despite – or because of – our insight into the fictive texture of their narrations and into the presiding rhetorical machinery.

Nāgārjuna shows language to be a fragile convention, yet capable of functioning as a provisional designation of the reality apprehended in intuitive *prajñā*. We inflect this teaching by adding that every designation is also provisional too by reason of its historical and cultural determination. The dependently co-arisen character of things is mediated by their historical and cultural constitution as they give themselves to be known and perceived. After Wittgenstein and Derrida a convincing account of dependent co-arising has to take on board these hermeneutic or historicist inflections. That is why we do not apply Nāgārjuna's theses in a direct way, but only by reshaping them in function of the pressure of the contemporary Western questioning of religious language. This recontextualisation of Buddhist thought about the ultimate brings it near to the middle path of Derrida, the path of the 'between' which avoids freezing truth as presence, without thereby declaring it abolished.

Thus extended, Madhyāmika thought becomes more useful for dealing with religious pluralism. The sense of historicity exposes the religions as bereft of own-being, for they emerge only in relation to the other spiritual forces of history and they change constantly in reponse to the solicitations of the latter. Each defines itself by contrast with the others, thus in dependence on them. To say, then, that 'God' is the correct name for the ultimate is but one move within the web of conventional language, and when the term 'God' has become a fixed, habitual one, reinforcing a clinging to security, its use become unskilful and new terms are needed to point to the ultimate. To say that other namings of ultimate reality, produced in other histories, such as 'Brahman' or 'emptiness', are insufficient is to assume the position of the ultimate reality itself, forgetting that in fact one's discourse has a finite place in the play of conventional languages. Even an encyclopaedic mastery of the interplay of religious traditions would be a poor warrant for such a judgement, for each tradition can be known only from the inside, and the more one enters into the interiority of the other tradition the more the possibility of final judgement recedes. The complex event of biblical revelation eludes an objective, comprehensive judgement, though its appropriation includes an ongoing process of critical sifting. Much more does the truth-event constituted by one of the other great traditions elude our mastery.

We can distinguish between a conventional religious language which is unaware of its limits and constantly projects illusory reifications of that to which it refers; and, secondly, a theological language which has taken cognisance of the problematic character of this conventional language as well as of its own provisional status. These languages correspond to *two levels of conventional truth*. Does the second surpass and enclose the first, which henceforth can be dispensed with? Does it tolerate the first only as a second best for those incapable of theological penetration, or as a simplification for those who are still children in the faith? The early Christian Fathers felt the attraction of such a view, but finally rejected it. Theology does not surpass the first-order language of faith, but serves to clarify it, to measure its status and limits, and to preserve it from distorting interpretations. A theology of Buddhist inspiration could preserve religious language from seeking foundations which merely double and weigh down its referential force. Exposing the emptiness of these alleged foundations, it would leave the first-order language to itself, helping it to deploy its resources more freely and creatively, as provisional expedients allowing the reality of God and salvation to be evoked.

The recognition of the conventionality of religious language and of the underlying emptiness gives that language a space in which it can function in a freer, saner, more functional style, becoming an *upāya*, a skilful means *Upāya* in Indian usage suggests an efficacious remedy, for a snakebite for example. As *upāya*, a religious language is the raft built hastily by someone who wants to cross a river – however impressive its utility for that purpose, it does not mean he need carry it on his back henceforth! The word *upāya* also has the sense of 'approach' or 'drawing near'. If we see religious constructions as skilfully fashioned approaches whereby we are drawn near to enlightened insight, to a grasp of ultimate reality, then our relation to them is transformed

Michael Pye connects the notion of *upāya* with the modern insight that 'religious language is always inadequate to its subject and yet that some kind of inadequate language is always necessary' and 'religious language is essentially indirect, allusive, based in cultural circumstance, and subject to qualification and to criticism' (Pye 1990, 20). Mobile, flexible, provisional: these features of religious language heal the immobility, inflexibility and absolutism that have been so damagingly endemic to religion, or at least they give another upshot to this deliberate immobility. Even if one insists on the stability of confessional forms, the attached interpretations are constantly changing, and this desire for stability is itself a skilful strategy for coping with the instability of religious existence in time. The permanence of formulas reflects a certitude of transcendent and ineffable reality. But this does not mean that the formulas are a connatural expression of this certitude. Their inalterability is a fictive, metaphorical performance which alludes to this depth-dimension.

The sage who has perceived the emptiness of things knows how to manipulate worldly language (including actions and gestures) so as to lead all suffering beings to liberation:

> 'Mañjuśrī, a bodhisattva should regard all living beings as a wise man regards the reflection of the moon in water or as magicians regard men created by magic. He should regard them as being like a face in a mirror; like the water of a mirage; like the sound of an echo; like a mass of clouds in the sky; like the previous moment of a ball of foam; like the appearance and disappearance of a bubble of water; like the core of a plantain tree; like a flash of lightning...'
>
> 'Noble sir, if a bodhisattva considers all living beings in such a way, how does he generate the great love toward them?'
>
> 'Mañjuśrī, when a bodhisattva considers all living beings in this way, he thinks: "Just as I have realised the Dharma, so should I teach it to living beings". Thereby, he generates the love that is truly a refuge for all living beings; the love that is peaceful because free of grasping; the love that is not feverish, because free of passions; the love that accords with reality because it is equanimous in all three times...; the Buddha's love that causes living beings to awaken from their sleep'. (Thurman 1975, 56f)

Some accuse Indian ascesis of being insensible of the reality of persons, as it aspires to an ocean of emptiness from which all love and all human relationships are absent. But the text we have just read suggests that the Christian emphasis on 'person' and 'love' needs to be subjected to the ordeal of emptiness in order to be a more skilful means for opening up the experience of spiritual freedom – an experience on which none of our categories, not even 'person' or 'love' has a definitive hold. In turn, the sense of emptiness can be enriched by being opened to the traditions of love (if not to their corrupt language); there is no obstacle to this in principle.

The virtuous bodhisattvas deploy skilful means in complete freedom, with a wisdom and compassion that only the consciousness of emptiness allows:

> In order to help the living beings,
>> They volontarily descend into
> The hells which are attached
>> To all the inconceivable buddha-fields ...
>
> They intentionally become courtesans
>> In order to win men over,
> And, having caught them with the hook of desire,
>> They establish them in the buddha-gnosis ...
> Well trained in liberative technique,
>> They demonstrate all activities,
> Whichever possibly may be a means
>> To make beings delight in the Dharma. (70f).

In the second chapter of the *Lotus Sūtra*, a *locus classicus* for the notion of skilful means, the Buddha emphasises the gentle tact of this style of teaching: 'Ever since I became Buddha, with various reasonings and various parables I have widely discoursed and taught, and by countless tactful methods have led living beings, causing them to leave all attachments' (Kato et al., 51). This salutary tact is rooted in the Buddha's unfathomable knowledge of the real, which cannot be communicated directly, for the dharma resists verbalisation: 'It "cannot be indicated" and "the terms for it are characterised by nirvana"' (Pye 1978, 21). Deliverance is inexpressible. Hence the Buddha's hesitation at the moment of commencing his teaching. What can be said? Silence can be the most effective way to speak of it. Still, the ultimately ineffable can be shown through a judicious use of world-ensconced language. An amusing passage in the *Nirvāṇa Sūtra* (Taisho edition, vol. 12, col. 688c) compares this task of communication with that of explaining the word 'white' to one born blind: 'It's like snow' – 'So it's cold?' – 'It's like rice powder' – 'So it's soft?' etc.

That religious discourse and the religions themselves are *upāya* is an idea which is difficult and dangerous to handle. It seems to have caused misgivings in ancient India comparable to those felt by Christians today. The polemical and probably caricatural account given in the *Lotus Sūtra* relates that some, believing themselves to be in possession of a clear teaching which showed the way to *nirvāṇa*, were scandalised at the suggestion that religious teaching was now to take an indirect and flexible form, adapted to circumstances. As the Scribes and Pharisees are portrayed as baffled at the parables of Jesus, so these *śrāvaka* and *pratyekabuddha* (representing earlier Buddhism) can make nothing of skilful means and leave in a huff. The old teaching centred on *nirvāṇa* appears as but one of the forms truth can take, a provisional means which is surpassed in the larger vision now emerging. This invites comparison with the attitude of the first Christians to the Hebrew scriptures. If we emphasise in the New Testament and the *Lotus Sūtra* the spiritual opening they bring about, rather than such pejorative recuperation of prior tradition, we learn dialectical flexibility in our use of religious ideas and are freed from dogmatic mental habits that resist this opening.

Each religion, then, will take stock of the provisional character of its language in the way that suits it. The results will be a new freedom in the enunciation of religious truths within each tradition and a climate of modesty in interreligious thought. One discerns the appropriate means in function of their *telos*, spiritual emancipation. If spiritual emancipation – understood in the broadest sense – is the heart both of Christ's and the Buddha's teachings, appeal to it as supreme criterion cannot be in conflict with the basic truth of the traditions they founded, however subversive its first impact. 'All provisional vehicles must give way to the final intention of the teaching or they lose their value altogether. It is only by being dismantled that they come to fruition' (Pye 1978, 26f). To treat dogma as a provisional vehicle fits its historical and epistemological status as clarified by the hermeneutical labours of the last two centuries.

The fortunes of the idea of skilful means beyond India are rich in instruction for theology. The Mādhyamika demonstration of the provisional character of language was grafted onto Chinese pragmatism, as it is reflected in Daoism:

> As the universe is seen as eminently changeable, what is good at a given moment is not at another, a place which is auspicious at one moment is not at another. Thus, an event, fact, or individual, acquires its meaning in a given context, constructed according to a system of interrelations of which one must know the morphology. (Robinet, 51)

This is why the quite orthodox reply of a Zen disciple may be met with a shout or a blow, as not stemming from the disciple's actual existence. In China, the notion of skilful means helped Buddhism to work out its relations with other religions and folk religiosity. It is a key to the Japanese economy of religious investment, which combines a serene agnosticism and scepticism about all dogmatic claims with a pervasive religious sensibility that can enter freely into the spirit of religious places and ceremonies, and that cherishes the sacredness of ordinary things in everyday life. Self is not insisted on, for self too is a doubtful dogma, but harmony is cherished, and what serves harmony is cherished as a skilful means. This attitude muddies the borders between belief and unbelief, religion and irreligion, and shows up the Western insistence on such borders as a source of destructive tensions.

'As the ignorant grasp the finger-tip and not the moon, so those who cling to the letter, know not my truth' (Suzuki, 193). In proverbial terms: 'The sage points to the moon with his finger, but the fool gazes at the finger'. The finger cannot touch the moon, which exists in sovereign independence, an independence not to be conceived in substantialist terms. Buddhist talk of pure experience, ineffability, or the true Self, all too easily falls prey to a substantialist pre-comprehension which blocks experience of the 'suchness' of things. An antidote to this potential for illusion ingrained in language may be found in the dialectical vigilance of Zen dialogues, which recover or preserve on the experiential plane the critical agility shown by Nāgārjuna at the conceptual level.

Zen is torn between this dialectics of emptiness (Ch *kung*; Japanese *kū*) and the monism of the *tathāgatagarbha* (matrix of the Buddha), which stresses the immanence of the Buddha-nature in sentient beings, with a tendency to reify emptiness itself into 'absolute nothingness' (Chinese *wu*; Japanese *mu*), forgetting Nāgārjuna's insistence on the emptiness of emptiness itself. However, when the 'critical Buddhism' movement of Shiro Matsumoto and Noriaki Hakamaya declares *tathāgatagarbha* thinking and all traditions influenced by it, including Zen, not to be Buddhism at all, one is inescapably reminded of the summary executions of metaphysics perpetrated by some Western theologians. The objection is as old as the *Laṅkāvatāra Sūtra*: 'Is not this Tathāgata-garbha taught by the Blessed One the same as the ego-substance taught by the philosophers ... an eternal creator, unqualified, omnipresent, and imperishable?' To which the Buddha replies that the *tathāgatagarbha* is nothing other than 'emptiness, reality-limit, Nirvana, being unborn, unqualified, and devoid of will-effort', and that it is taught 'to make the ignorant cast aside their fear when they listen to the teaching of egolessness and to have them realise the state of non-discrimination and imagelessness' (Suzuki, 69). Such a skilful means may be treacherous if taken in the wrong way. But it is not only this terminology, but any terminology at all that can threaten spiritual sclerosis. Perhaps the best way to overcome the actual or potential distortions in *tathāgatagarbha* thought is by a step back to its roots in the emptiness-tradition, treating it as 'a development from within this tradition, rather than an antagonist standing without' (King, 16).

Buddhist critical agility is entirely at the service of a conviction about ultimate reality and its accessibility to a privileged knowledge of a non-conceptual kind. To reify this reality may be a deplorable perversion, but to deny it altogether is to eliminate Buddhism.

Even so slight a sketch as we have attempted here should suffice to indicate that the concerns of ancient Buddhist thinkers are in uncanny proximity to those of questioning Christians today. Remote from us in time, culture and language, these sages have insinuated themselves into our world with no other recommendation than the apparent radicality of their thought. Meanwhile, the great philosophers and Doctors of the Church who used to provide the familiar framework of our world seem to drift away from us, estranged from us by the questions they did not ask. What divides us from them, and unites us with strangers we may not even understand, is a watershed event best marked by the prophetic career of Nietzsche: the end of the self-sufficiency of Western thought. The word 'God' bolstered that self-sufficiency, but now undermines it, for that word now seems opaque, highly problematic, crumbling in obsolescence. A critical stock-taking of what that word has meant in history is afoot, and on this basis strategies for its possible future use can be devised. Dialogue with Buddhism gives this effort at critical retrieval a larger space in which to manoeuvre. Can it also restore a healthy complexion to our language about God and Christ? In the remaining chapters, I shall work towards an interpretation of these fundamental Christian doctrines in terms of emptiness, beginning in each case with critical hunches emerging within theology and showing how they are best developed when opened out onto an embrace of Buddhist radicality.

6

'GOD DECONSTRUCTS'

It is time to substantiate the various suggestions we have gleaned from deconstruction and from Buddhism about how language, and especially religious language, functions. We can do so by homing in on two central topics in Christian discourse: the first and second articles of the Creed. In assessing the status of language about God and Christ, we begin to move from the realm of fundamental theology into that of dogmatic theology, for a shift in our sense of how language functions will imply a subtle reshaping of the doctrinal landscape itself. This transposition of the Creed into a different key is required by the constraints of the contemporary epistemological context, which has rendered some forms of faith and religious knowledge obsolete, while opening up new possibilities. Many major theologians have resisted this change, unable to break out of a fixated or restorationist position; many others have reacted to the pressures of the situation by courting a dissolution of faith in God and Christ. We shall attempt to show that when the credal language is allowed to undergo its metamorphosis, orthodoxy reemerges in a new form as the secure middle path between these tempting extremes.

THE NAME OF GOD

In general, the use of a proper name does not demand a very rich context; minimal information suffices to identify the one who is being spoken of. A proper name is a convenient and pragmatic substitute for a precise description, permitting us to refer to objects without worrying about the problems of such a description (see J. Searle in Strawson, 89–96). In the case of 'God', however, the proper name does not function quite so smoothly. As soon as we attempt to describe, even minimally, what the name refers to, we find ourselves entangled in philosophical, mythological or biblical presuppositions, and whichever of these we decide to take aboard, as part of the minimal description encapsulated in the name, will turn out to be fundamentally questionable, and to have already in fact attracted a long tradition of questioning. If I say 'Cicero', in a normal context, I have effectively referred to Cicero, even if I imagine him to be someone other than Tully; but it is not so clear that to say 'God', even in a theologically orthodox statement, guarantees effective reference to God.

Reference can fail for ontological reasons. For example, since nothing in God is accidental, if I attribute an accident to God it is no longer evident that it is of God that I speak: '*Nihil in eo secundum accidens dicitur quia nihil ei accidit*' (Augustine, *De Trinitate* v.6), just as I would not be speaking of Cicero if I attributed to him a quality which contradicts his essence: e.g. 'Cicero is triangular'. However, if one presupposes reference as given from the start, even the most nonsensical sentence will have a meaning read into it; accidental predications of God will be read as substantial, or as metaphor or paradox.

Reference can also fail for contextual reasons: if I say 'I saw Cicero on the Champs-Elysées', only the hypotheses of mendacity or hallucination can assure the hearer that the reference is indeed to Cicero. Likewise, if I say that 'God is he who sustains kings', the unrelatedness of the utterance to the present cultural context makes it doubtful if I am referring to God. Language about God has to be rightly directed if it is to refer to its object; and right direction involves the way of life and the long tradition which lies behind the religious use of 'God'. This use is not effected by mere cogitation or piety, but is a creative accomplishment within a given culture, implying a critical appropriation of the history of its previous uses. The individual who speaks well of God does so in virtue of the efforts of the believing community over generations. What the Bible presents as divine self-naming is also, through and through, a human construction, determined by political and cultural factors that invite analysis.

The event of calling someone by their proper name is menaced by reabsorption in the linguistic network which makes it possible, as are the events of communication, judgement, perception, presence. Yet these events nonetheless take place. To call God by God's proper name is a bold extension of a performance already fragile and problematic on the everyday human level. Yet though we scarcely know what we are doing in this case, the act as it is carried through is felt to make sense, and we find meaning, too, in the biblical representation of God as calling us by our names. At least provisionally, for the time being, our naming of God or God's naming of us establishes an identity, with serviceable bounds. But no divine name can fix the identity of God for ever. The naming is always a context-bound and culture-bound performance. The role of proper names in the mechanism of singularising reference is assured only if the names in turn can be identified by their insertion in a narrative; the event of naming is a narrative event. To name 'God' without such narrative context is a helplessly vague gesture at some unthinkable ultimate. Only stories, explicit or implied, taking the form 'the God who...' give the proper name its bearings.

The utterance of a proper name always takes place under a double bind, for the mark exists only by its difference from all other marks. Hence 'the constitutive erasure of the proper name' in archi-writing:

> proper names are already no longer proper names ... their production is their obliteration ... the proper name has never been, as the unique appellation reserved for the presence of a unique being, anything but the original myth of a transparent legibility present under the obliteration ... the proper name was never possible except through its functioning within a classification and therefore within a system of differences. (G, 109)

A proper name cannot be absolutely singular, because then it would have no place in language; on the other hand, every linguistic utterance is a singular event, so that in a loose sense it may be said that there are only proper names:

> The problematic status of the proper name (its double condition of *interminable term*, at once indicative and descriptive, singular and indefinite) reveals that the singular lacks identity with itself, so that it is necessary always to renew its nomination, although this is always insufficiently defining. (A. Campillo, in Mallet, 375)

'God' is both indicative and descriptive, singular and indefinite; it is an unsettled expression, opening up many contending narratives which would fix its sense, and which never fix it with a more than relative adequacy. Such a venture of naming has no chance of success if God does not enter into the game and allow himself to be named by us, just as we assume before society, albeit uneasily, our name and the responsibility it entails: 'So speak and act that each word and action can carry your name and that your name can carry them all with it' (376). Not to take in vain the name by which God allows himself to be called implies a double task: on the one hand the name of God must not be divorced from the concrete promises which it carries, to float in philosophical detachment; on the other hand it must not be used as a means of holding God hostage in some reductive classification.

In Jewish thought the name of God is the seal of his irreducibility to the dimensions of human understanding. When God is named outside a context of authentic faith, this supreme proper name becomes a talisman against the collapse of the identity of a nation, or the possible failure of its armies (*Gott mit uns*), or its money (*In God we trust*). This is a perversion of the biblical function of the proper names of God: *El, Eloha, Elohim, Ehyeh asher ehyeh* ('I am who I am', Ex. 3:14), the Tetragrammaton, *El Shaddai, Adonai Tsebaoth*, to which one can add *Adonai* 'which became as it were the name of the Name: a name which personalises the Name once for all for one who invokes it and at the same time definitively conceals the Name', and *Ha-Shem* 'the Name' (B. Dupuy, in Kearney and O'Leary, 106):

> The attempts to harmonise the revelation of Sinai with Greek ontology have long obscured the sense of the disclosure of the divine name. It entails the rejection of all anthropomorphism, the relativisation of all the figures used to apprehend Him who is beyond being and non-being and thus 'without analogy'. (119)

The materiality of this name as a 'mark' keeps it free of the grasp of any system of thought seeking to reduce it to transparent meaning.

The Name is distinguished from the epithets attributed by humans – such as the Great, the Strong, the Terrible – which are 'subject to the variations of meaning that the period gives them' (120). But does not every attempt to declare this independence of the name carry the imprint of its period? For example, the expression 'beyond being and non-being', though purely negative, suggests a Greek way of indicating from afar the mystery of the Name, and the very institution of the Name undoubtedly depends on concrete conditions in Hebrew language and culture. According to Levinas 'the presence of God in his Name remains free in regard to every historical context. A Word for ever disincarnating itself, even of the flesh it seems to wear in discourse'. However the name which serves to guard this divine freedom depends on a concrete function: the divine name, in the Talmud, 'receives a sense from the human situations in which it is invoked'. 'To utter the Name is not a knowing. But the human situation in which the Name is uttered gives a positive sense to the negativity of this non-knowing' (Castelli 1969b, 56, 65).

Apart from its use as proper name the word 'God' has a larger use in which it serves as a designation ('There is a God') or as a predicate

('Yahweh is the true God', 'What is created cannot be God'), something that is impossible for an ordinary proper name. Since, in Christian theology, and also in the most natural use of this expression, 'God' is not only the one who possesses deity but is identical with that deity, the slippage from 'God', proper name, to 'God' as designating the divine essence is quite justified (see Aquinas, *ST* I. 39.4). Is the biblical use of 'God' as proper name (of a person) a semantic deviation, or is it rather the philosophical and impersonal use of 'God' as predicate or designation (of an essence) which deviates from the use of 'God' as proper name, offending against its sublime inviolability? Aquinas himself seems to hesitate on this point, as noted by Ockham (*In I Sent.*, d.4).

Biblical language says first: 'God, your God, is one; there is no other' and only in second place 'there is only one God'. The movement goes from the proper name to the predicate. The latter sentence fits comfortably in biblical diction when it is taken as a statement about the personal God who has made himself known. 'God' here is a proper name and the effective subject, though not the grammatical subject. One hears the sentence with a different ear when 'God', while remaining a proper name, becomes the object of a neutral constatation without any confessional investment. Then it belongs to the discourse of philosophising apologetics, and has a distancing and objectifying effect which makes it comparable to the sentence, 'there is only one Waldschmidt in the phone book'. Eventually the sentence refers to God no longer as a being known by his proper name but as an entity of a certain metaphysical rank. God is no longer the subject. The statement now resembles a sentence like, 'there is only one legitimate Queen of England', a statement bearing on a legal status rather than a personal subject. Each of these three ways of understanding the sentence locates us in a different space of thought, or rather it is a different 'we' which is engaged on each occasion, and it is also a different 'God'. The first version of the sentence is the closest to the biblical sense of God's irreducible mystery. It might be objected that the biblical personal language is naive, and that to insist on it spells resistance to a prior and more originary (or posterior and more legitimate) discourse in which 'God' figures rather as designation of the divine. But the biblical usage of the divine Name, and the personal pronouns 'Thou' and 'He', is less a facile personalisation than a method for guarding the revelation of the Holy One from all too readily available conceptualisations of the divine. Far from being naive, such locutions are marked by a tense awareness that the Name signals that God is one who acts in entire freedom and forbids the reduction of God to an impersonal deity, a pure absolute like the Plotinian One.

David Strauss spoke of God as having a 'housing problem' in a demythologised universe, but there are subtler reasons why the place of 'God' in our language is no longer assured. We can no longer securely define God in relation to a universally shared understanding of the onto-theological structure of reality, or as the goal of the transcendent sweep of the human mind, or even as the necessary correlate of 'religious experience'. All metaphysical locations of God turn out to be culturally idiosyncratic. Only the history of its usage gives the word 'God' any concrete sense now, and as we take up the word anew we intervene in that history, to judge and reshape it, on a premise of basic trust but in the light of new perspectives that disqualify much of what we used to say. To say 'God' is to set in motion all the strategies of the monotheistic tradition for addressing the ultimate. It is to associate oneself with the essential movement of this tradition, in awareness of its finitude as one human way of organising the space of religious perception. Both the proper name of God and the metaphysical conceptions of God turn out to be only provisional means, culturally inscribed.

Is the abundance of historical notions of God finally reducible to some standard notion which is revealed as the true form to which they clumsily aspired? Certainly, in the course of history there emerge notions of God which impose themselves by their clarity, replacing a whole series of confused representations. Thus the Thomist *ipsum esse subsistens* renders useless the rival construals of the being of God in medieval scholasticism. But the claim to furnish a strict concept of God shows itself to be illusory, at least once the metaphysical system in which this concept is inserted begins to show its wrinkles. If we try to determine the status of God in terms of a discourse on being, we have to assume the burden of defending the context this presupposes, namely a metaphysical discourse on being in general or on being in itself – a highly dubious enterprise epistemologically and 'grammatically'. To speak of God as supreme being in some vague sense is to lapse into metaphor, abandoning the attempt to define God. The breakdown of a metaphysics of supreme being is repeated for every other attempt to formulate a metaphysical definition of God: each of them projects an idea of the absolute in function of the knowledge of an epoch, and from the sequence of these ideas it is scarcely possible to extract a common core, a minimal, general definition.

On a less purely intellectual plane, key texts such as Deuteronomy or the Johannine corpus open a perspective on God which surpasses and abolishes, in principle at least, the previous more primitive languages. But these great clarifications take place within a circumscribed cultural space. These local triumphs of an idea of God do not produce a universally valid notion, for one cannot transfer them to another cultural space without altering them. The biblical namings of God breathe in a contemporary horizon only in virtue of retouchings and misunderstandings which mask their foreignness. To evoke the transcendent holiness of God by a Name that ruptures the envelopments of contemporary language may require a new style and tactic of naming.

The unification accomplished by a classical naming of God crumbles again at another turn of history, and one rediscovers the plurality of notions which it had covered over during the period of its ascendancy. The strong synthesis of an epoch becomes a notion among others, and one seeks elsewhere a central formulation carrying conviction. When, for instance, the name 'Father' is discovered to enshrine patriarchal bias, it can no longer claim to fix the sense of 'God' definitively; so one turns instead to other representations of God within and outside the Bible and Christian tradition which the ascendancy of the name 'Father' had thrown in the shade. Again, the existential contrast between the God of Abraham and the God of the philosophers may have served at one time to disengage the concrete contours of the biblical God; but it no longer has this role in a pluralistic culture, where it appears rather as a simplification, for the 'God of Abraham' already refers to a plural tradition, and the 'God of the philosophers' does not figure as his principal or only rival except in quite narrow historical contexts, and even then under a great variety of forms.

The irreversibility of this double crisis of the historical effort to give a sense to the word 'God' is all the clearer when we see that the problem also affects non-biblical religious discourse. The history of religions introduces a levelling perspective, showing that the Western crisis is a variant of a problem experienced whenever human beings seek to construe the meaning of life and the universe. They begin from the conviction that a supreme reality has been manifested to them. Progressively, the language which aims to refer directly to this experience is reinforced – or replaced – by quasi-philosophical ratiocination. Then comes a third stage, the relativisation of these two languages, the realisation that they are constructions: here Buddhism is far ahead of us, encouraging us to pursue to the end the revision of the status of religious language which has been afoot since Kant. In the course of their long history, the monotheistic traditions have beaten a track of discourse which permits without doubt a penetration of the real, but which does not necessarily enjoy such a privileged relation to the real that all other paths are to be judged inferior.

USING 'GOD' SKILFULLY

The entire labour of religious discourse proceeds under the double bind inscribed in the very name of God, which obliges us to recognise God's irreducible otherness. For one must speak of God – *vae tacentibus de te, quia loquaces muti sunt* ('Woe to those who are silent about you, for though loquacious they are mute', Augustine, *Confessions*, 1.4) – but whatever one says falls flat. Augustine eludes this aporia by a renewal of the obedience of faith, his labour in the aporetic domain serving as a launching-pad for adoration, as a Zen kōan issues in a leap to the actual, beyond or before conceptuality.

There is a Derridean aspect to this double bind: it is necessary to 'translate' the old language about God if it is to make sense today, but a faithful translation is impossible. A living translation demands the creative participation of the translator, who inevitably brings into play the horizons of his time and thus creates new meanings. Nor can one fix a firm frontier between the original scene of writing and the scene of translation conceived as enframing it from outside. Fidelity to the old is possible only as infidelity, the creation of the new. 'God' is a construction, and the more we labour on this construction, the more it wobbles. This law, figured in the tower of Babel, is that of 'the impossibility of completing, totalising, saturating, achieving something which would be of the order of edification, architectural construction, system and architectonics' (*Psyché*, 203). It is not by totalisation but by discovering the impossibility of totalisation that we move toward an apprehension of the divine, at the heart of the emptiness of all our constructions.

Like every other signifier, 'God' cannot be isolated from the totality of language: 'language is a system of which all the terms are solidary' (Saussure, 159):

> Without the assistance of signs, we should be incapable of distinguishing two ideas in a clear and constant way. Taken in itself, thought is like a nebula in which nothing is necessarily delimited. There are no pre-established ideas, and nothing is distinct before the apparition of language. (155)

This is particularly true of religious language. No 'idea of God' pre-exists the play of signs by which we try to speak of God. 'God' makes sense in our languages only by a labour which sets this word in relation to the totality of signifiers furnished by the culture.

Another remark of Saussure is suggestive: 'The French *mouton* can have the same significance as the English *sheep*, but not the same value, and this for several reasons, in particular because in speaking of a piece of meat prepared and served on the table, the English say *mutton* and not *sheep*' (160). In Japanese the word *kami* serves only awkwardly to indicate the monotheistic God, even when one associates with it the other terms (creation, salvation, divine attributes) which fix the identity of God in Christian discourse. In each language, 'God' is located in function of a situational space, a space that the religious imagination tries to master and restructure by a reading of the signs of the times. If 'the value of any term whatever is determined by that which surrounds it' (ibid.), the term 'God' acquires present significance through its interconnection with other terms chosen to sketch a contemporary religious interpretation of the world. Thus, the word 'God', in a certain Christian rhetoric today, tends to be very close to the word 'liberation', a rapprochement entailing an extensive rearrangement of the semantic site in which 'God' is placed.

Today the synchronic aspect of a language or a religious system seems to prevail less and less over the diachronic awareness of change. We are more aware that each of our representations is subject to alteration and that the sense of words is not stable; in language as in religion, individual inventiveness – whether on a journalistic or an erudite level – is seen not as a marginal activity, but as an intervention in an ongoing evolution. 'A language will change hardly at all during a long interval, and subsequently undergo considerable transformations in a few years' (142). Saussure wrote at the end of an epoch of relative linguistic stability, and just before the Joycean explosion. A sharper sense of pluralism and historicity is changing the texture of our religious language, destabilising its terms just as the words of the English language were set tottering by Joyce.

Our efforts to differentiate clearly the use of 'God' as proper name and 'God' as predicate, the living God and the Absolute, first sense and derived senses of 'God', are undermined by the growing awareness that none of these terms are fixed. They are alternative ways of constructing a language about 'God', and the conflict between them, their mutual cont-amination, affects the status of each. They are attempts to speak rather than entirely coherent and self-sufficient discourses. The tug-o'-war between these different uses reveals that the tensions inscribed in the word 'God' expose it permanently to self-deconstruction. The proper name par excellence has become the improper name par excellence. We wish it to refer directly to a Thou, but it seems to refer centrifugally to all the divergent paths opened by its past uses. Perhaps we can use it today only in a detour through the troubled memories it stirs, only in the awareness that 'God' is a citation from a vanishing past. 'God' is not a self-explanatory expression. To cash its meaning we may have to translate it as denoting 'that which was aimed at by the old discourses on God, in their impasses as much as in their lucid breakthroughs'.

To be sure God is not a mere cipher of the unknown; God is known as the God of grace, proclaimed in the Gospel. Yet we find it much easier to talk of the Gospel event of grace, though it, too, eludes our conceptual grasp, than to talk about God. Even the prayerful address 'O God' creates a sense of subtle disarray, not simply the disarray of the creature or the sinner in face of the divine other, but the disarray of our own history of talking about God, the gnawing question: 'What after all do I finally mean when I say "God"?' It is as if the image of God becomes still more blurred in the abundance of the concrete revelation of God as gracious. 'Dark with excessive bright thy skirts appear.' This suggests that when God is a self-evident reality what we are dealing with is an idol, and that the withdrawal of God is the other side of his drawing near in grace. The word 'God', then, does not easily come to rest in its referent; it is a word that searches, that burrows at the old obscure question pervading the long history of its usage.

When one acquires a reflexive awareness of the sequence of citations that is the language of monotheism, a language that humanity has built up over time and that has no natural necessity, the use of the word 'God' takes on a new allure. In each case it is a matter of exploiting an ancient *topos* for creative ends. As the modern poet uses the word 'rose' or 'love' with an ironic awareness of drawing on a tradition of worn rhetoric, the contemporary believer cannot utter the word 'God' without a similar feeling of moving in the realm of citation. This irony need not lead to a suspension of language, but to its more flexible rhetorical deployment, in a parallactic interplay of conflicting perspectives.

The reference effected when one names God thus resembles the reference of a poetic expression or a fiction, relating to the real in a new way each time, and at the risk of lacking any link with reality, either by platitude or incoherence. The metaphoric character of a divine name, as oblique trace of an ineffable mystery, its synecdochic character as standing for a vast tradition of religious discourse, its metonymic function as pointing away from itself to the saving message or prophetic challenge that gives it its concrete profile in a given situation, its ironic character as an impossible name – all these rhetorical complexities prescribe a certain poetic freedom, sustained by a tradition, for the skilful use of divine names, and they imply that apparently contradictory statements about God can each have their truth. The adventures of quantum physics make this aspect of theological speech less implausible. The pluralism which thus troubles discourse on God can even put in question the use of the word 'God' itself: a-theology may be a useful if dangerous rhetoric, as long as it does not collapse into flat substitutions of some finite reality for God.

Should we recognise in this very instability the contemporary signature of God? In a pluralist world, the presence of God is no longer associated with a single metaphysical or symbolic economy, or even with a single community, but is dispersed in fragmentary indications of all sorts – in the religious traditions which have been burst open, in the arts and literature, in social movements, in certain scientific projections. Even if the Bible and the liturgy remain privileged sites of the presence of God, they, too, are intrinsically disunited languages.

'God' evokes the entire cortège of the ancient images of God which no longer accord with our disenchanted consciousness and our criteria of intellectual maturity, but which nonetheless continue to haunt the imagination. To chase away these shades, we try to name God in an original way, or to give an original accent to the inherited words, above all the biblical names 'Yahweh' and 'the Father'. We play with these names to ensure that the liberative associations triumph over the oppressive ones when the name of God evokes the Almighty, the good God, the Eternal, the Judge. The failure of language before God is not a fixed ontological situation but a history of diverse impasses and collapses, having poetic and political dimensions.

Instead of being at the mercy of the insoluble controversies it raises, theology can deploy this improper name, 'God', in a liberating way if it takes cognisance of its impropriety as an essential feature. To name God is to enunciate on each occasion only a local and contingent religious truth, drawing on a tradition of linguistic invention whose makeshift character is betrayed in a thousand flaws. The reality of God is felt across the play of these designations as a process of dynamic expropriation. If one uses the name of God in a consciously subversive way, leaving it none of the solidity of a great master-name, if one assumes it as an excentric name which no longer furnishes a stable centre to the self that invokes it, but rather dislodges the self from its habitual ruts, then the meaning of this God cannot be known in advance. 'God' functions not only in a dialectical way, in Barth's sense, but in a differential way. It lacks self-identity. Its significance is always situational. Hence, a successful naming of 'God' carries an element of surprise. It is not the divine nature in itself but an entire situation that the name lights up. This mobility of language about God is not based in any intra-divine process; it is merely the mark of God's transcendence. We cannot rest in any finite representation, but are summoned both to affirm and deny each of them, in an ineluctable double bind which seals our experience of the divine otherness.

It might be claimed that all divine names are formed with polemic intent. Hence to speak of 'God' is to stir up a historical hornet's nest of warring significations, a strife the homonym is powerless to quell. Jesus used the name 'Abba' not from anthropomorphic or sentimental piety but in resistance to other names that blocked the path to a liberated relationship to the God who is close. 'To love God' meant to hate all oppressive images of God; the surprise at the end of a parable often consists in the revelation that God is freedom and not servitude. When John declares that 'God is light' (1 Jn 1:5), he is not putting forward a Hellenistic banality but is opposing the idea of a malicious or equivocal God. Generalising from these examples, a first rule of theological rhetoric might be stated: the word 'God' should never be employed except in such a function of opposition. Every invocation of God signifies the refusal of some false God. From this would follow a first rule of a theological hermeneutics prescribing that the entire history of religious language be reread in function of this principle. 'God' is never a neutral term; it entails a choice, a polemic judgement. If I want to avoid such a choice, limiting myself to seemingly harmless expressions such as 'God is the Father Almighty' or 'Pure Being', it turns out that these expressions are less anodyne than they seem, if only because of what they bury in silence.

The discourse of monotheism is traversed by a tension between two styles of naming God: the philosophical and the prophetic. The first has to do with God's absoluteness and the second with the concrete face of God. To name God is to invoke the absolute, denouncing other gods as non-absolute, as idols failing to attain the status of God due to a misplaced concreteness. This insistence on the divine purity has been codified in religious metaphysics, from Philo to Spinoza, as well as in the counter-tradition of negative theology which attempts to leap beyond metaphysics. Against this stress on purity, the prophetic naming of God marks the fact that God is known as the living God only in local, concrete, revealed forms. His proper name abolishes every abstract projection of divinity or the absolute. To think God as the absolute is to miss God as effective existence, and to fall into an idolatry of the abstract. A sentence such as 'God is great' expresses in a context of faith a personal knowledge, and 'God' figures as proper name. But in philosophy the sentence might be no more than a rule of speculative grammar, 'God' standing for the notion which completes the theoretical edifice and prevents it from collapsing. This ambiguity ensures a constant supply of tensions and confusions. Lofty philosophical discourses will be taken for the language of faith while, conversely, the language of faith will be misheard in a philosophical key. Moreover, religious authenticity is not entirely on one side or the other, and the frontiers between philosophical questioning and believing affirmation are not impermeable. If 'to speak of God as a *He*' can be more religious than 'the invasion of the *Thou*' (M. Nédoncelle, in Castelli 1969a, 349), in the same way the cool thinking of a Plotinus or Spinoza may establish a truer relationship to God than pious invocations which do not engage the intellect.

If the opposition of faith and philosophy marks the primary field of tensions in the language of monotheism, each of these discourses on its own harbours a constant strife between the absolute and the concrete vectors of the name 'God'. Among the ancient quarrels inscribed in our language about God, we find on the Hebrew side the battle between the local cults of Palestine and emergent henotheism and monotheism, and on the Greek side the tension between personal and impersonal divinity: 'The wise is one alone, unwilling and willing to be spoken of by the name of Zeus' (Heraclitus, fr.32, trans. C. H. Kahn). These controversies in turn rest on an immense pre-history. In the epoch of metaphysical theology, it seemed that they had been definitively settled. But today the metaphysical concept of God is recalled to the historical field of forces of which it is the product.

When Judaism and Hellenism came together, God was defined as the One, foundation and origin of all things. The war of Yahweh against false gods was sublimated into a war within the One, insofar as the unique God of Abraham remained in tension with the God of philosophy. This war of the Unique against the One (to which corresponds in Hegel, for example, a war of the One against the Unique) was muted in the Fathers who, taking their cue from the Areopagus discourse (Acts 17), held to a convenient accord with the Platonists on the nature of the highest God. To swing in the other direction, with Luther, Pascal and Kierkegaard, could produce a Pyrrhic victory of the Unique over the One, for without the critical rigour of the thought of the One, the cult of the Unique degenerates into violence. Thus the notion of divine unity, far from being the monument of a debate forever closed, carries within it all the tensions of its history, now unfolded according to the contemporary economy of a reflection aware of its historicity.

The concern of philosophy is not with the saving power of the name 'God' but with its rational meaning. Against anthropomorphic and polytheistic tendencies it conceives God as guardian of unity, summit of intelligibility and intelligence. Even if it sees God as exceeding the level of the intelligible, as in Plotinus or Kant, it is in order to anchor reason in the contact with the absolute that only a leap of philosophical faith can attain. The God of philosophy is foundation rather than saviour. But this absolute foundation withdraws; it becomes less and less possible to appeal to an immediate contact with it. The philosopher becomes more and more the thinker of distances, more and more incapable of disengaging himself from the mediate. This withdrawal becomes the very mode of the presence of the absolute.

The philosopher who seeks to forge for 'God' a transparent reference cannot do justice to the historical efficacy of this name, and to the semantic polyvalence which enables it to deconstruct not only idolatrous substitutes but also its own meanings. The philosopher will agree that any name attributed to an absolute (whether it be God, the One, the Good, truth, beauty, reason, or love) secretes war: not only war with its rivals, but one that inwardly tears it apart. This dynamics of self-surpassing inscribed in the name of the absolute takes the philosopher onto the path of negative theology, in which God is invoked as that which delivers us from God. Yet this dialectic reproduces the objectifying effect of metaphysics in an inverted form.

God transcends his names less effectively by such abstract withdrawal than by the shocks of history, which generate new ways of naming God and by the same token light up the functional and situational status of all such creations of religious language. The absolute of negative theology is inadequate because ahistorical; only the exodic breakthroughs of history can reveal transcendence as freedom, as the Spirit which blows where it wills. Eckhart's dictum, 'to leave God for God' (*Gott durch Gott lassen*) can thus take a prophetic sense: 'to leave the abstract for the incarnate God'. The name of the incarnate God escapes from the spiral of negative theology, which is always seeking a purer intuition of the absolute. When believers say 'God', they affirm a reality which surpasses all that can be said of it, but they know this reality by and in the events they narrate.

The theologian, situated half-way between philosopher and prophet, seeks to assure the functioning of the prophetic naming of God, preserving it from the philosophical insistence on intelligibility, universality and absoluteness. Insisting that God can be thought of in a concrete way only as incarnate, the theologian subordinates the philosophical critique to the prophetic task, while at the same time seeking to make the prophet aware of the pressure and gravity of the philosophical concern.

GOD AND DECONSTRUCTION

Derrida's polemic against phonocentrism has a particular piquancy for theologians in that he cites as the supreme instance and ground of phonocentrism the self-presence of God in his eternal Logos:

> This absolute logos was an infinite creative subjectivity in medieval theology: the intelligible face of the sign remains turned toward the word and the face of God ... The sign and divinity have the same place and time of birth. The age of the sign is essentially theological. (G, 13f)

If the entire medieval discourse on God is a product of logocentrism, this leaves little room for the recognition of an objective foundation or referent for it. Yet Derrida denies that he is rejecting this discourse; he is merely pointing out that its closure has come into view. The value of the discourse for theology can be retrieved only by an oblique strategy. If we differentiate authentic use of the word 'God' from its logocentric sense, then we can reread medieval discourse with an eye to those aspects that are not simply reducible to the logocentric economy. 'God is the name and the element of that which makes possible an absolutely pure and absolutely self-present self-knowledge ... God's infinite understanding is the other name for the logos as self-presence' (98). But it may be that the name of God, even in medieval theology, does not always have this obscuring function.

For Rodolphe Gasché, the myth of God must be dissolved into the reality of *différance*:

> As a full presence, an immobile and unfading substance, God neutralizes all anteriority and exteriority by making the trace derivative to Himself ... What is the trace but the minimal reference to an Other without which no God can come into His own, and which, on this account, always makes God differ from Himself? In this sense God is necessarily the effect of the trace ... God *as* God is dependent on a structure of referral that, *as such*, ceaselessly refers to an Other, away from itself, so as to have itself no as such. (Gasché 1994, 159–62)

This is an orchestration of Derrida's own doctrine:

> If the idea of divine presence (life, existence, parousia, etc.), if the name of God was but the movement of erasure of the trace in presence? Here it is a question of knowing whether the trace permits us to think presence in its system, or whether the reverse order is the true one. It is doubtless the *true order*. But it is indeed the *order of truth* which is in question. (WD, 108)

But there is a qualifier: 'The name of God, at least as it is pronounced within classical rationalism, is the name of indifference itself' (G, 71). Beyond classical rationalism, and within the rifts that any theological discourse is bound to create in this rationalism, Derrida sights another way of naming God in which difference is freed for its play.

In metaphysics the name of God signifies the erasure of difference, but there is another way of speaking that name, in which it is linked with the unnameability of death rather than with a logocentric repression of death, and associated with the differential movement of the trace, with the inevitable risks, leaps, discontinuities, loss of mastery that writing entails. As soon as God is named at all, that naming becomes idolatrous, and the only thinking of God that is worthy is one that is constantly coming to be and passing away, having espoused the fragility of language and its trace-structure. Unless finitude, mortality, difference become intrinsic to the naming of God, no concrete identity of God can be determined. God is always other, yet when conceived as the one absolute Other, or as the pure inconceivable and ineffable One, the idea of God serves as an obscurantist defence against the trace-structure in its plurality and differences.

Can there be theology beyond the age of the sign? In an ardent commentary on Edmond Jabès, Derrida entertains the notion of a God revealed in the open dissemination of writing. The writing of Jabès espouses the exile of finitude, refusing to surpass the Hegelian 'unhappy consciousness' towards a realised eschaton. To put it in the terms of Boehme, Schelling or the Kabbala, this writing is born of a rift in God, which allows the errance of history to arise. The 'God beyond God' postulated by writing shows up the God of classical philosophers as an idol blocking the play of *différance*. When God writes himself he sacrifices his pure self-presence and infinite self-possession. Instead of presenting himself as a stable foundation, God makes himself felt only by withdrawing as a great question. 'If God opens the question of God, if he is the very opening of the question, there can be no *simplicity* of God. And, thus, that which was unthinkable for the classical rationalists here becomes the obvious itself' (WD, 68). 'God himself is, and appears as what he is, within difference, that is to say, as difference and within dissimulation' (74). God needs writing to make himself known, and cannot be thought of as purely separate from the language and history in which he is made known.

It may be that 'God' in this context is merely a literary or philosophical cipher. Our reflections on the multivocity and contextuality of religious expressions, on the writerly character of revelation, and on the *upāya*-status of religious language, suggest that such a contaminated discourse on God can be most richly developed within theology proper. Derrida's play of difference between the Rabbi and the Poet, and their two interpretations of interpretation, is not the preserve of writers and philosophers alone. Within theology, too, the Rabbi's quest for definition and univocity is shadowed by the writerly instability of the language he works on, so that even to be a good Rabbi he has constantly to take this irreducible mobility into account.

When he speaks of 'the closure of the book' and 'the opening of the text' as 'a fabric of traces marking the disappearance of an exceeded God or of an erased man' (294), Derrida is not proclaiming an anti-human atheism or nihilism. It is rather a question of resituating the signifier 'God' in the play which determines its meaning according to given contexts. Derrida provides us with categories for rethinking the phenomenality of

God, not as a *numen* beyond language, but as troubling our language from within. Containing in itself the entire history of the tensions from which it is born, a divine name unfolds its significance only in opening up to the new tensions its use generates today. The tensions may become so intense as to render its use impossible, yet if there is no tension the name can hardly serve as an indicator of transcendence. 'God' has been used to suppress the tensions of pluralism, but now the name which betokened the ultimate reponse to all our questions, the alpha and the omega of creation and salvation, is becoming the cipher of an unfathomable question, a question that takes a multiplicity of conflicting forms as it comes to awareness in different local perspectives.

If conflict about God is inherent in the very name of God, it offers no escape from conflict but engages us therein more deeply: 'The war he declares has first raged within his name: divided, double-edged, ambivalent, polysemic: *God deconstructs*' (*Psyché*, 207). The God of which Derrida here speaks (even if only a philosophical metaphor) has the traits of the biblical God, the one who cannot be neatly disengaged from the times or the places in which we have access to him. The biblical God 'deconstructs' not as the pure absolute showing up the weakness and complexity of our languages, but insofar as he names himself. It is not by a pure silence that this God unsettles us, but by a finite, broken speech, punctuated by a varying silence that invites our spoken response. It may be that in Jabès's poetic world God no longer speaks, but even if one believes that God still speaks, that speech never saturates our minds with full self-present meaning; rather it opens a space of questioning – we are questioned by God and question God in return.

God's speech is in the register of the undecidable, in a stronger sense than that which Derrida explored in *Dissemination*:

> *this particular* undecidable opens the field of decision or of decidability. It calls for decision in the order of ethical-political responsibility. It is even its necessary condition. A decision can only come into being in a space that exceeds the calculable program that would destroy all responsibility by transforming it into a programmable effect of determinate causes. There can be no moral or political responsibility without this trial and this passage by way of the undecidable. (*Limited Inc*, 116)

God's justice lies elsewhere than in the precise details of the Law; a certain shattering of the tablets may even be the condition of its emergence. Nor can it be cast into the mould of the Kantian categorical imperative, as a rational principle. For it matches time and finitude, wherein law and reason always come a little late and falter behind the complexity of concrete decision. The exigence of justice builds up systems of law and reason, yet its teleology always reaches beyond them, disqualifying radically their totalising ambition. Thus justice undermines what it builds up, in a variant of the Babelian double bind that runs through Derrida's writing.

The law of Babel remains for Derrida a gracious *Ereignis*, a gift which withdraws itself, a quasi-feminine *khōra*, which will already have preceded all the constructions of language and thought. If one tries to think of God according to the rhythm of *différance*, associating the divine with the elusive *khōra* of truth-as-woman, this may bring a dissolution of metaphysical fixations and patriarchal images of the divine, which have so often given rise to violence and fanaticism. It may also release a thinking of the divine originarity, long covered over by too rigid divine names or by metaphysical projections of a God-foundation. If God is the mystery at the heart of the universe, should he not be as supple as the laws of nature, the rhythms of time, the waves of the sea? The Mahāyāna bodhisattvas, who descend from *nirvāṇa* to aid suffering beings, incarnate emptiness as compassion. The approach to God via *différance* and the trace may allow similar resonances to be heard between these three notions: divine emptiness, divine compassion, divine femininity.

But Derrida constantly warns against an onto-theological reappropriation of this dimension:

> Radically nonhuman and atheological, one cannot even say that it *gives* place or that *there is* the *khōra*. The *es gibt*, thus translated, too vividly announces or recalls the dispensation of God, of man, of even that of the Being of which certain texts by Heidegger speak. (Coward and Foshay, 106)

Nevertheless, 'the barren, radically nonhuman, and atheological character of this "place" obliges us to speak and to refer it in a certain and unique manner, as to the wholly-other who is neither transcendent, absolutely distanced, nor immanent and close' (108). 'Atheological' does not imply atheism, but a rejection of the use of God as a totalising instance or transcendental signified (see Hart, 26–34). One acknowledges this elusive anteriority by a 'yes', a *Zusage*, whereby one surrenders rationalistic control over it.

Derrida's thought is best understood as a questioning openness to otherness, even divine otherness; but this openness is emptied of concrete theological content. His eschatology renounces any concrete Messiah, any concrete eschaton. He sees the biblical story as offering a set of images for a universal structure of experience, for that expectant hospitality towards the future which is the atheological legacy of messianism, 'the arid soil on which have sprung up, and passed away, the living figures of all the messiahs'. This desertified, 'despairing messianism' has 'a curious taste, sometimes a taste of death' (*Spectres de Marx*, 267f). The shadow of the Holocaust lies across such pages. Deconstruction stumbles on a bedrock reality which is no longer deconstructible, and which is identified as 'a structural messianism, a messianism without religion, a messianic, even, without messianism, an idea of justice' (102).

Derrida tends to reduce the biblical language too easily to this transcendental structure. Linking God with the aporetic indeterminacy of the Platonic *khōra*, he dilutes the determinate contours of the biblical theophanies. When he speaks of God as writing himself in the empirical text of history, he is making a merely philosophical point: the origin is always already inscribed. What the Bible presents as a revelation of God in history, the philosopher deciphers as an allegory of a general law. Divine transcendence is absorbed in the movement of *différance*: 'Language has started without us, in us and before us. This is what theology calls God' (in Coward and Foshay, 99). Instead of God's transcendence being indicated by the mobility of our language about God, here the transcendence is reduced to being nothing more than that mobility.

No longer having a clear identity as transcendent Lord, God becomes as elusive and unthinkable as death:

> Less than for any other noun, save 'God' – and for good reason, since their association here is probably not fortuitous – is it possible to attribute to the noun 'death', and above all to the expression 'my death', a concept or a reality that would constitute the object of an indisputably determining experience. (*Aporias*, 22)

Yet the entire point of the biblical story is to replace such an uneasy vagueness about the ultimate with a clear and strong recognition of divine holiness and power. If such a recognition is no longer accessible, because of the obsolescence of the biblical world, then theology must close shop. Derrida's reductive statements betray a short-circuit in his relationship to theology, which has to be corrected if his insights are to be put to theological use. He projects this short-circuit onto theologians, when he imagines them apostrophising Heidegger in the following terms:

> But what you call the archi-originary spirit, which you claim to be foreign to Christianity, is indeed what is most essential in Christianity. Like you, it's what we would like to revive under the theologemes, philosophemes, or common representations . . . When you say all that, we who would like to be authentic Christians think

that you are going to the essence of what we want to think, revive, restore, in our faith, even if we have to do it against those common representations with which you wish at all costs to confuse Christianity ... You say the most radical things that can be said by a Christian today. (*Of Spirit*, 110f)

Real theologians are unlikely to subscribe blindly to the parallelisms between Heidegger and Christianity in which Derrida's caricatural theologians revel. When theologians invoke Heidegger for a critical retrieval of the tradition, they do so in full awareness that their goal – the specific radicality and authenticity (terms Derrida treats with excessive irony) of the biblical message – is quite other than what Heidegger is listening for.

Derrida's Heidegger eludes the theologians by a retreat or step back to a yet more originary thinking, in which the origin itself is problematised: 'I'm simply trying, modestly, discreetly, to think that *on the basis of which* all this is possible ... I follow the path of a repetition which crosses the path of the entirely other', but the theologians are eager to recuperate his thought here as well: 'That's the truth of what we have always said, heard, tried to make heard ... The misunderstanding is that you hear us better than you think or pretend to think' (111, 113). If theology is tempted, perhaps obliged, to see a reflection of itself in any philosophical reflection on ultimate origins, the irreducible otherness of the biblical God keeps it from converting the analogies it glimpses into the massive identification imagined in Derrida's foreshortened conception of theology. Theology may draw from Heidegger, Derrida or Buddhism a grasp of the texture of the real which brings the biblical message into new perspective; but if it undermines the autonomous revelatory power of the message, then theology has died, and might as well recast itself as a *Geistesphilosophie*.

GOD AS SERENDIPITY: GORDON KAUFMAN

If the situation we have described allows considerable freedom and inventiveness in talk of God, this does not mean that such talk is free from all responsibility to the biblical sources and the doctrinal tradition. The Bible is a touchstone for the phenomenality of God, the sense of divine transcendence and of God's saving involvement in history; the tradition offers seasoned rational reflection, clarifying and defending the biblical experience. Thus standard metaphysical and phenomenological criticism of new constructions of the meaning of 'God', backed by straightforward appeals to biblical and dogmatic tradition, remains a legitimate proceeding.

However, the ultimate status of religious language as *upāya* is not subordinate to such metaphysical and phenomenological argumentation, but embraces it. For the tradition itself within which this argumentation is developed and in which its constraints hold sway is nothing more than a skilful means, serving to point to what surpasses it. The language of faith, and the coherent logic of doctrinal reflection, have only an oblique and opaque relation to the noumenal thing-in-itself. On the level of conventional truth, we must uphold vigilantly the correct forms of this language, trusting in them and believing that our use of them refers objectively to the real. We give this language the form that sober reason prescribes, but we cannot ultimately control the modality of its connection with the mystery to which it points.

The phenomenological apprehension of the biblical God witnesses to what has been actually lived by believers of all times. But the status of this experience itself is not absolute. For this experience has the particularity of the historical culture that has shaped it and can be evoked only by using a style or rhetoric whose Greek and Jewish components can be identified. If today we graft Buddhist elements onto these, this must be done with tact and discretion, without the least suspicion of arbitrariness. Thus the Babelian instability of religious language remains a regulated process, guided by the tact which the Spirit can teach.

A language that seeks to express anew the biblical revelation of a gracious God cannot rely on speculative shortcuts. Before drafting ambitious theories about a kenotic God, a suffering God or a process God, one should linger long with the biblical witness to a loving creator and redeemer. The metaphysician who claims privileged insight into the nature of God is likely to condemn the elementary and easily mastered data of Scripture. Even a speculation that modestly professes to offer useful constructions of thought rather than direct insight into the way things are, is likely to be more infatuated with these models than with the reality that eludes them. To overcome the unreality of such thinking, a conversion of mind is required, that can reroot our thinking in the things themselves. Auxiliaries to such a conversion include logical demonstration of the antinomies on which such speculation runs aground, historical siting of each of the terms it employs, phenomenological querying of its concrete content and the richer apprehensions it misses, grammatical and stylistic critique showing its impracticability or inappropriateness as an account of religious insights.

Conversely, however, the epistemological and ontological questions surrounding religious belief cannot be resolved by the shortcut of a simple leap of faith back to the biblical data. The place of rational, conceptual thought cannot be defined externally, in a way that does not attend to and allay the claims of reason on their own terms. To resist the absorption of religion by reason, while at the same time respecting the necessity of reason, a rational theory of the limits of reason is required. Reason situates itself as referred to the phenomena and as ultimately constituting a conventional discourse which cannot close in on the thing itself. Reason is transcended by a pre-conceptual point of departure and a trans-conceptual point of arrival, but it has to argue itself into opening up to both of these. Revisionist theories of doctrine distract from this task of opening up because they seek a solution to theological malaise merely in rearranging of rational cogitations. To a theological reason that has put itself in context such ongoing revisionist speculation has only a secondary importance. Much of the impatience of the revisionists with classical positions such as the doctrines of divine immutability and impassibility, is in reality an impatience with the limits of reason and of conventional truth. Their breezy confidence that if we correct a naive metaphysics, and get our thinking right, then theological reason will come into its own, overlooks the abyss that separates correct conceptualisations of ultimate reality from that reality itself. At the rational level one can clarify the legitimate and illegitimate uses of a given cluster of culture-bound categories, yet the legitimacy one establishes is always provisional, dependent on changing conditions.

The more theological reason learns its situatedness and conventionality, the firmer and stronger should its grasp become. Critical self-clarification within the realm of conventional truth is a discipline that draws on all the resources of logic and that fully respects their necessity. Some theologians, such as Gordon Kaufman, have gone too far in the direction of modesty, treating theological ratiocination as a trade in projections and suppositions. Others, such as Jean-Luc Marion, attempt to arrest the pluralistic mobility of theological imagination and reason by elevating a set of key phenomena to a supreme speculative status. Their effort, pursued in radically different styles, to attune themselves to the primary experiences at the origin of theology leads in Kaufman's case to a dissolution of theological discourse into philosophic generalities and in Marion's case to a freezing of that discourse in a posture of attestation to a single theophanic form.

For a way of talking about God that is firmer ontologically, subtler phenomenologically, and more flexible in its categories, we shall turn finally to a group of thinkers who seek to relate the biblical God and Buddhist emptiness. Here again there will be much to criticise, but the upshot will be a heartening sense of new possibilities of speaking of God, at a time when even the most brilliant exploitation of Western resources seems incapable of attaining the required breakthough.

In a patient apologetic, Gordon Kaufman assembles the 'small steps of faith' whereby humans, struggling to find a meaning for their existence, gradually build up the idea of God. The idea is made persuasive by the way it chimes with and encourages the best aspirations of the race: 'the mythic objectification of liberative activity in the symbol "Yahweh" made possible a growing consciousness of the universality of the demands of morality' (Kaufman, 247). The symbol 'God', through which 'our western languages and cultures most fully and profoundly represent to us that which is ultimately Real, True, Good' (237), functions only within the general framework of representations in which it has this privileged role, a world-view produced by culture and history, and which there is no possibility of comparing with some world-in-itself independently ascertained. Of course this categorial structure varies greatly from epoch to epoch, as does its ultimate point of reference, the idea of God.

Yet this culture-dependent character of 'God' need not entail that the construction of God is merely a product of human ingenuity. Ultimate reality may be making itself known in and across this process of construction. Religious conceptual frames are not only bulwarks raised by human imagination against the void, but may also convey insight into how things really are. It may be true that the God of Augustine is not that of Aquinas, nor is either of them ours, and that there are only 'family resemblances' between these constructions; but we also want to say that it is to the one living God that these various discourses witness, and that a new construction of God today has to proceed in fidelity to this tradition. Kaufman continues to refer to 'the real God who is in fact our creator, sustainer, and redeemer, and thus the God whom we today can and should worship and serve with unqualified devotion, respect, and love' (249), and he finds the concrete specification of the nature of God in 'Jesus and the new order of human relationships surrounding him' (388). But the weak cognitive grip he attributes to God-language does not allow him to give a full-blooded content to these traditional expressions.

He insists that theological concepts are fundamentally imaginative constructions rather than abstractions or deductions based on empirical data. Thus the evaluation of these constructions is no longer a matter of comparing them with the objects they are supposed to represent, but poses a more basic question for the intellectually responsible believer, namely: What justifies us in embarking on such construction in the first place? The time has come to take critical stock of the long history in which our religious imagination has sketched its elaborate pictures of ultimate reality. Retrieving the entire process from the ground up, we can find a demystified and rational way of handling the term 'God' to name 'that reality which grounds, makes possible, and calls forth all that exists' (245).

This approach leaves to religious proclamations a greatly reduced epistemological status. Religions affirm that there is ultimate meaning, and that it is concretely known. Kaufman places an agnostic proviso over all such 'constructions': 'We really do not know, and we can see no way in which we will ever be able to plumb, the ultimate meaning of life – or whether there is such a thing as "ultimate" meaning' (6).

This agnosticism is linked with a reception of Kant that is prone to rely on a simplistic opposition of the world as represented and the world as it is in itself: 'Even such a familiar reality as the sun is not known directly and immediately in experience for what it is; what we take it to be is constructed imaginatively on the basis of experienced patterns of light and heat here on earth' (255). Kaufman's Kantianism comes close to the 'as if' epistemology of Vaihinger, who tendentiously states that 'the object of the world of ideas as a whole is not the portrayal of reality', an impossible task, but rather 'to provide us with an instrument for finding our way about more easily in the world' (236). The first step in criticising Kaufman's theology would be to ask whether his philosophical presuppositions do justice to the fact (demonstrated by Kant himself in the *Critique of Pure Reason*) that the subjective texture of human knowledge does not undermine its objectivity.

Even if we accept Kaufman's genealogy of religion, it should be added that religious constructions are confirmed not only by their usefulness for the evolutionary advance of humanity, but by the fact that they function as vehicles for the felt presence of a gracious other. The sun may be an imaginative representation, but we do not doubt its reality as it dazzles and scorches us. Similarly, religious constructions are traversed by an electric current of faith from the believer to the ultimate in response to an electric current of revelation in the other direction. It is this living encounter rather than theoretical projections of ultimate meaning that makes faith-language tick. If this experience is not delusive, it must entail some objective referentiality for the terms faith uses. How can they bring us into vivid touch with the ultimate, unless they are bearers of truth not only about God but from God?

When Kaufman spells out more concretely his rational reconstruction of faith, his refusal to 'reify' the reference of biblical metaphors such as 'creator' in fact licenses a cashing of these metaphors to produce a quite unbiblical definition of God as 'the evolutionary and historical processes which produced us' (330); 'the cosmic serendipitous creativity active in the evolutionary-historical trajectory toward humanization' (352). This erases the biblical differentiation of God from metaphysical principles and cosmic forces as something richer, more living and personal. Kaufman's caricature of biblical 'reifications' of God as 'an arbitrary, imperial potentate, a solitary eminence existing "somewhere" in glorious transcendence of all else' (332) closes the door to a subtler phenomenology of transcendence derived from lived encounter with the divine presence and call. To pray to God is more than to focus on the unity of cosmic forces making for good; it is distinctly, phenomenologically, a step beyond such a conception of the divine. The personal language may be inadequate, no more than a skilful means; but if Kaufman is right it begins to look more like an unskilful means.

Kaufman is not stepping back to the truth of biblical tradition, but away from that tradition to another one, which Christian theology has constantly rejected. Hume's Epicurus puts negatively what Kaufman advances as a positive vision, in limiting the concept of God to the dimensions of the cosmos. This imperfect cosmos does not testify to a Creator of 'superlative intelligence and benevolence': 'you have no ground to ascribe to him any qualities, but what you see he has actually exerted and displayed in his productions. Let your gods, therefore, O philosophers, be suited to the present appearances of nature' (Hume, 137f).

Newman's strictures against Humean immanentism might apply to Kaufman as well:

> God is an Individual, Self-dependent, All-perfect, Unchangeable Being; intelligent, living, personal, and present; almighty, all-seeing, all-remembering; ... who will judge every one of us, sooner or later, according to that Law of right and wrong which He has written on our hearts ... Nothing is easier than to use the word, and mean nothing by it ... The Almighty is something infinitely different from a principle, or a centre of action, or a quality, or a generalisation of phenomena. If, then, by the word, you do but mean a Being who keeps the world in order ..., who acts towards us but only through what are called laws of Nature, who is more certain not to act at all than to act independent of those laws ...; such a God it is not difficult for any one to conceive, not difficult for any one to endure. (Newman, 46f)

Certainly this language has to be scrutinised in its mythical and metaphysical implications, which may be largely obsolete; yet the tension of biblical faith, the sense of God's otherness, has to be articulated with equal strength today if the word 'God' is not to be jettisoned altogether. Kaufman identifies his God as the object of Christian worship, who remains transcendent in the sense that 'everything (else) must be understood in relation to the (imagined) ultimate point of reference' (Kaufman, 327). But this is a limited transcendence: 'we refrain from postulating an "other side" or "other world" at all. There seems no good reason for such a postulate – except that that is the way these ancient myths, regarded as authoritative in our religious traditions, spoke' (325). Yet the alternative of an immanentist cosmic religious language was available to the fashioners of those myths. Had they no good reason for refusing it? Religious thinkers stress the immanence of the transcendent in the world, of *nirvāṇa* in *saṃsāra*, but they have intellectual and experiential grounds for refusing to doubt the absolute status of the former.

Kant, in response to Hume's demonstration of the limited reach of arguments for God based on cosmic teleology, turned to ethical reason for a worthier projection of God, as moral creator. Kaufman is closer to Kant than to Hume in that his version of evolutionary teleology is instinct with ethical passion, yet the God it projects still seems to enjoy only a limited, conditional transcendence. Moreover, it is hard to see, even if the thought of God may induce repentence (369), how one could meet this God as the God of gracious forgiveness. No doubt 'the idea of a divine super-Self outside of or beyond the universe (which is hundreds of millions of light years across) boggles the mind' (305); yet our cosmos is now understood to be temporally and spatially finite, which was not always the case. Meanwhile there are experiences of love and grace which have little to do with space and time and which point to a dimension, or respond to a presence, so independent of materiality and change that it can only be called eternal. Thus evolutionary process is too narrow a basis for the contemporary revision of God-language, for despite its cosmic sweep it does not do justice to these phenomena of love and grace. The universe can be reinterpreted in the light of the 'order of charity' (Pascal), even as cosmic context brings out new features of God's gracious presence. Again, the dominance of the evolutionary model might be qualified by drawing on Buddhist ontology as an alternative model for the revision of God-language. In a universe of empty dependently co-arising entities it might turn out that the invocation of a personal God, freed of substantialist projections, can arise more naturally than within the constraints of an evolutionist horizon given absolute status.

Perhaps it is no longer possible to differentiate cleanly in our religious thinking between what belongs to 'unaided human reason' and what belongs to the revealing activity of God, what is projection or illusion and what is emergence of unmistakable truth. Even when, in Kaufman's writing, the concept of God shimmers between transcendent world ruler and immanent evolutionary force, clear demarcations between adequate and inadequate language, between rational reductionism and irresponsible mythmaking, do not impose themselves, and one may enjoy considerable freedom to veer in one direction or the other, with reference to what is salutary in a given conjuncture.

Even if Kaufman underplays the claim of the biblical tradition to a unique dignity or efficacy, he is right not to exempt it from the common laws of religious construction. The universality or primacy claimed for biblical revelation is not something given once for all; it is concretely realised only as the Bible is put in relation to comparable formations in other religions. This relation will in many cases be a critical one: the thoroughgoing radicality of the biblical God will overcome the mythical softness of other conceptions of a God or gods. But in other cases the biblical message has itself to undergo a critical overhaul. Buddhism shows up a precipitation, a naivety, an arbitrary violence in the premises of monotheism; primitive religions recall what monotheism has repressed – the earth, the body, human vitality in its labyrinthine texture; scientific cosmology prescribes a larger, subtler thinking about the divine. The biblical God remains the living God only by such a constant sacrifice of limiting determinations. Yet the Bible is not to be jettisoned, for across the revisions the biblical text continues to speak of God, nor does any one line of revision establish itself as having an authority simply superior to that of the Bible.

INVIOLATE DISTANCE: JEAN-LUC MARION

Phenomenological hermeneutics is the royal road of a theological thinking which seeks to reground Christian thought in its founding events. By opening up a domain of thought – prior to concept and logical argument – where previously there seemed to be only a fuzziness which eluded thought, the return to the phenomena reins in rationalist imperialism and provides faith with a style of thinking more suited to its content. To be sure, a purely non-conceptual or preconceptual apprehension of the phenomenality of revelation is impossible; but one can move in the direction of originariness by thinking against the concepts that too speedily enframe the event of revelation. The labour of the concept cannot be relinquished; but the event of revelation calls for other modes of apprehension and of thought, which come nearer to its inner texture, and which are practised in an overcoming of rational hegemony, a prising open of conceptual idolatry.

However, to be useful to theology, phenomenology has to be transformed into a properly theological mode of perceiving and thinking the phenomena, a believing mode: 'Faith is the assurance of things hoped for, the conviction of things not seen' (Heb. 11:1) – and a pneumatic one: 'they are spiritually discerned' (1 Cor. 2:14). The phenomenon faith discerns is a situation of encounter and engagement; it is in part created by our participation in it, our way of hearing and responding to the divine summons. Thinking participates dynamically in the movement of the essence, *das Walten des Wesens*. Likewise, to think the Christ-event is to reactualise it in a present *kairos*. Awareness of the finite historicity of Christian tradition facilitates this contemplative step back, preventing the contingent conceptions and formulations of the tradition from becoming a screen against the eventhood of revelation. The step back can itself be seen as a contingent strategy, responding to particular historical circumstances.

The phenomena have to be freed from the metaphysical regime which allows them to appear only conditionally, as licensed by Leibniz's principle of sufficient reason or Kant's strict conditions for the possibility of experience (see Marion, 1992). The phenomenon is that which shows itself from itself and is not answerable to the conditions of its emergence. But perhaps the Christ-event has to be freed also from the unitary stylisation implied by describing it as a phenomenon. The effort to concentrate the sprawling processes of biblical revelation in something so pure as a phenomenon reflects a philosopher's desire to clarify a single founding essence.

Though sharing Marion's desire to retrieve the sense of the divine names in a phenomenological key and his fascination with the phenomena of divine transcendence, the crucified Christ, the Holy Spirit, the biblical word, love and being, one might feel that his enterprise needs to be revised so as to do more justice to the differentiations between philosophical and theological thinking as well as to the intrinsic pluralism of both. Marion presents divine transcendence as the phenomenon of the 'paternal distance', 'the coming to us of a withdrawal', in which 'the intimacy of the divine coincides strictly with the withdrawal' (Marion 1977, 183f). This coming is manifested in the granting of certain divine names, above all 'the name which is above every name' (Phil. 2:9) conferred on Christ. This schema could be modified in a pluralistic sense by replacing the divine names in their historical context. The divine distance is indeed a 'saturated phenomenon', inspiring endless avenues of thought which can never exhaust it. But is this phenomenon simply one? God is revealed not in a single definitive name, but across an entire Babel of religious discourse. Marion's theology of revelation is dramatically concentrated in the moment, the *Augenblick*, in which God gives his name (as love, in the figure of Christ crucified), but this history cannot be distilled into a pure lightning-flash. God is the one who names God, 'it is for the distance itself to enunciate itself' (186), but this happens only via human discourses which God inspires.

'Human language should receive the Name, as Christ received the Name from the Father. This reception imposes self-emptying and obedience unto death' (189). I should like to translate this into pluralistic terms as follows: 'Human languages in their plurality bend themselves to a naming of the divine, and it is above all in recognising their emptiness and finitude that they measure up to this responsibility, as Christ incarnates the divine Word only in assuming fully the plural and relative condition of historical existence'.

God preserves himself from an idolatrous grasp, says Marion, by his 'unthinkable' character, which is:

> the *aura* of his advent, the glory of his insistence, the brilliance of his withdrawal. The unthinkable determines God as the seal of his definitive indetermination for a created and finite thought. The unthinkable masks the gap, a fault that is never closed, between God and the idol. (Marion 1991, 72)

We are always obliged to conceive God in some way, but every thought of God betrays a constitutive inadequation and a lability due to its historical and cultural character. Marion's emphasis on the unthinkable obscures this historical fragility, and permits him to put forward a stable divine name, withdrawn from the perils of historicity: the name 'love'. But if God remains unthinkable, nevertheless God prompts an effort of thinking which marshals all the resources of the available language. Far from limiting the thought of God to one privileged term, the seal of his unthinkability, one could consider this thought, with Kant, as a last horizon of the whole labour of language. This horizon – the withdrawal of God – is manifest in a different way in every developed religious language. Does the language of the New Testament replace this plurality of paths by the finally adequate naming of the divine nearness and distance? Even within the New Testament the terminology of love is only one among others, and in the wider context of previous and subsequent tradition this linguistic pluralism is still more evident. Each vivid apprehension of the divine generates an original way of speaking thereof.

The historical character of the construction of God in our language is not in contradiction with the enigma of God's self-donation and self-withdrawal in this language. At the core of each set of religious representations is found a blind spot, a bright darkness, expressed linguistically as the proper name of God. For the Christian, it is in Christ and the cross that this effect is most fully concretised. 'The distance of God is experienced firstly in the figure of Christ: there, it finds its unsurpassable foundation and its definitive authority' (Marion 1977, 203). A static representation of the figure of Christ risks missing the concrete bond between divine revelation and human history. We should rather think of the figure of Christ as permanently surpassing itself and as witnessing to divine transcendence only through its refusal to be fixed in a definitive version. The figure of Christ cannot be thought or even discerned without all the thickness of his past and future; and it is consequently impossible to totalise the meaning of this figure – and of the God it reveals – since it is impossible to totalise the meaning of history.

The biblical text, for Marion, is another saturated phenomenon, giving rise to pluralistic horizons of interpretation. But he insists that this pluralism cannot undermine the univocity of the original founding event, whose richness inspires the plurality of literary genres in Scripture as various attempts to bear witness to it. Here again a certain phenomenological stylisation threatens to occlude the historical texture of the process of revelation. The phenomenon of divine distance transcends the pluralism of its interpretative horizons and holds them together; yet there is a sense in which the phenomenon itself is pluralised. The same tension between centering unity and horizontal pluralism affects Heidegger's *Ereignis* (event of being), which some exegetes (Reiner Schürmann) have attempted to portray as a principle of anarchy, alive with pluralistic possibilities, while others (Jean Greisch) see it as naming the essence of being, and as gathering beings into unity. I would maintain that historical traditions have an identity rooted in a central realm of grounding phenomena, but that this identity is open-ended and prone to alteration under the impact of other traditions (see O'Leary, 1992).

Marion wants to free the idea of God from the hold of the notion of *being*, either in its medieval or its Heideggerian senses, in order to interpret God exclusively as *love*. This is a classical response to the crisis of God-as-being, but it seems that contemporary religious thought is already in the process of outgrowing this stage of reflection. Despite the subtlety with which he unfolds the notion of love, Marion remains immersed in the quest for the supreme category, the finally suitable name that expresses the essence of God. To free the thought of God from the idolatrous grasp of being we must 'work conceptually on love (and in turn work on the concept through love), to the point where its full speculative power can deploy itself' (Marion 1991, 73). But is this speculative critical power of love to be grasped as that of a name, a concept or a sign? Should we not enlarge the horizon to see in it rather the movement of the Spirit across the diverse languages of history? The freedom and truth of faith are not preserved in the speculative development of a single theme. The life of the Spirit requires not correct categories but a style of thought that shares its mobility.

If God 'is not, but loves', then 'no condition can restrain his initiative, amplitude and ecstasy' (74). The Johannine 'God is love' could be interpreted more modestly – not as defining God, but as naming the lived situation of the early community and the mode in which they were acquainted with the divine presence. There is nothing speculative in this naming, or in the similar declarations that 'God is light' (1 Jn 1:5) and 'God is Spirit' (Jn 4:24). In each case an event is named: the triumph of light over darkness, love over hate and fear, spirit over carnal blockages. To these events corresponds each time a precise communal behaviour. Light, love, Spirit cannot be thought outside these concrete processes. To speak of being or love in general, as unitary instances, is to miss the indirect and complex mode in which such words can acquire meaning today. This subjection of great words to concrete conditions prevents them from spreading their giant wings in an abstract, ahistorical space. To speak of God as love is not to fix God's identity in a definitive way, but is rather an intervention in the tangled web of theological language so as to introduce an opening to transcendence.

One situates God badly in identifying God as love-in-itself. Such a hypostasis is dissolved by the transitive uses of the verb 'to love'. The word 'love' has no univocal sense but refers to a variety of heterogeneous ideals and practices. Situating the rhetoric of Marion in relation to New Testament *agapē*, Platonic *eros* and Augustinian *caritas*, its status as a new intervention in the tradition of love-languages becomes apparent. He does not discuss the historical and theological tensions between the classic languages, and perhaps assumes that a synthesis of them has been achieved. In reality he has created a new language which on a local and strategic plane designates the divine mystery; but he misconstrues the force of his own discourse, and its limit, in elaborating what appears to be a metaphysics of love. One would have to convert this metaphysics into a rhetorical strategy presenting itself as an alternative to the rhetoric of being, in the awareness that in both cases what is in question is a cultural and historical formation among others equally possible.

The mobility of the historical languages betrays the weakness of all our contingent and provisional categories, love not less than being. These categories have played the role of provisional expedients in the course of the historical construction and deconstruction of monotheism, a role too central for either to be excluded henceforth as radically unworthy. The ancient language of God as being is indeed impossible for us, but this obsolescence can be seen as a historical metamorphosis rather than the sudden overturning of an idol.

To deny that ontological language has been a skilful means for point-ing to the reality of God would be to brand as idolatrous the Septuagint translation of Exodus 3:14, the Johannine prologue, and all the Fathers. Aquinas states that the name 'He who is' most properly names God for, according to John Damascene, 'God is being containing all in itself as a sort of ocean of substance, infinite and without limits' (*ST* I. 13.11). This language of being is a strategy for freeing the idea of God from all circumscription by finite categories, in the awareness that every discourse, however refined or apophatic, remains far from the possibility of naming the mode of being of God-in-himself.

'He who is' has no longer the supreme radiance which it had before the metaphysical framework became problematic. The language of being has the reduced status of one among many constructions of transcendence, all of which are but provisional means for indicating the divine eminence. To invest in only one of these language games to the exclusion of the others would be an idolatrous fixation of the theological aim. Even the names 'God' and the Tetragrammaton must be reinserted in the flux of the history which produced them. Aquinas himself suggests that the Tetragrammaton acquires its unique status (as the name that most properly signifies the incommunicability and 'singularity' of the divine essence) only in a precise setting, for he associates its use with the Hebrews (*ST* I. 13.9). Names such as 'God' or 'Lord' may no longer carry the aura of transcendence, serving only as stopgaps while we wait for the emergence of a more concrete face of the divine.

When Marion names God in a rigid and ahistorical way, his account of human being becomes similarly stilted. In his terminology, the believer is the one claimed, the summoned, the one called par excellence – who comes to be in responding to the pure call by a 'Here I am!' 'The claim calls *me*; even before I am able to say *I*, it has already caught and comprehended me, summoned and named me as a *me*' (Marion 1989, 297).

Transposing this into a historical key, one could say that the subject does not come to itself except as inscribed in an intersubjective history and exposed to many calls mediated by this history. To define the subject abstractly as an 'I outside of being' corresponding to 'God without being' is to capture only the shadow of this concrete history. Just as the concrete sense of 'God' is constituted in narrations of God's acts, so the human subject is first grasped as a history, and it is only by the diciest abstraction that one can isolate in him/her an underlying 'call-and-response stucture'.

For Marion the structure of the call is the foundation of the phenomenality of all phenomena, more radical than Heidegger's listening to the call of being. But is there really any such founding originary datum? Are not the phenomena from the start too mobile and plural to be mastered by any universal naming of the being of what is or the granting of what is given? Marion's account of Heidegger's thinking of being forces it into a doxographic straitjacket, and even reduces Heidegger's ontological utterances to what seem merely ontic terms. He similarly reduces the plural and diverse terminology of 'givenness' in Husserl and others to a single somewhat grandiose notion of 'donation'. All of this facilitates the entry of the biblical God into phenomenology, as the one who grants being.

The notion of 'call' is given the same implausible univocity. Marion distinguishes between a Christian and a Jewish call, and grounds both in the pure call which he finds enunciated in Deuteronomy 6:4. But how decide that only one of the numerous calls that punctuate the biblical tradition corresponds to this pure form of the call? Indeed, the Bible itself seems to suppress the metaphysical phantasm of an absolute call coming from a sovereign distance in favour of a series of particular calls, each of which corresponds to a historical engagement. These calls never constitute their recipient as an abstract 'me', but confer on him or her – and here one is still dealing in fictive stylisations – a concrete task, a vocation (Samuel, Isaiah, Jeremiah, Peter, Paul).

GOD AND EMPTINESS

The serenity of Buddhist non-theism throws an unflattering light on the rhetoric of monotheism, which is seen as pervaded by illusion. But this does not condemn us to agnostic fumblings, for Buddhism offers a spiritual horizon in which we may be able to convert our language of God into one more adequate to the phenomenality of transcendence. The illusion most criticised in Buddhism is the projection of a stable ego as a refuge against the precariousness of existence:

> Even as those not suffering from eye disease do not see the hairs and mosquitoes and such things which are perceived by those with eye disease, so the Buddhas in no way whatsoever see self and non-self as self-existing realities in the way ordinary people imagine them. (Sprung, 177)

To realise the emptiness of the ego and of every conditioned entity is to open oneself to the calm and freedom of *nirvāṇa*. Clifford Geertz writes:

> The Western conception of the person as a bounded, unique, more or less integrated motivational and cognitive universe; a dynamic centre of awareness, emotion, judgment, and action organized into a distinctive whole and set contrastively both against other such wholes and against a social and natural background is, however incorrigible it may seem to us, a rather peculiar idea within the context of the world's cultures. (quoted in Collins, 2)

The Western notion of a self-sufficient God, independent of his creatures, can likewise seem an abstract and rarefied extreme in relation to the multiplicity of religious representations.

For Buddhism, the two notions are substantialist illusions, and the divine omnipotence in which the believer trusts appears as a projection of weakness. In denying the 'eternalist' thesis of an immortal soul, one must not fall into its 'nihilist' contrary, the idea that the soul is destroyed at death: the middle path between these extremes consists in accepting the non-existence of the soul as a substantial entity and the texture of existence as a perpetually self-transforming energy. Analogously, the idea of God has to avoid eternalism and nihilism. God as Spirit can espouse the texture of existence without imposing on it the violence of a substantialist interpretation. This reduction of reified conceptions of God and soul is not a speculative exercise, but a way of living and of being aware.

The defensive reaction of a worried church to the popularity of Yoga and Zen is understandable, for these practices relativise the personalised conception of God that has been claimed to mark the superiority of Christianity and in which there has been a great affective investment. The mutual embrace of Buddhists and Christians can become the occasion of a dissolution of God, creator and judge, in favour of 'absolute nothingness'. The latter expression is associated with the Kyoto philosophers Kitarō Nishida (1870–1945), Hajime Tanabe (1885–1962) and Keiji Nishitani (1900–90). Its best-known source in Zen is the first kōan in the *Mumonkan* collection:

> A monk asked Jōshū, 'Has a dog the Buddha Nature or not?' Jōshū answered, 'Mu' (No).

The nothingness to which the answer points is not a speculative construction but an immediate, non-differentiating perception of the real, at a level beyond the dualistic thinking that informs the unnamed monk's yes-or-no question. Such a 'step back' seems to relativise or abolish as well the dualisms that structure Christian tradition: Creator and creature, grace and sin, good and evil, self and other. But perhaps it offers access rather to a dimension of less cluttered perception, from whence the Christian categories can be used in a more discerning way, as conventional means of teaching that must not be allowed to congeal into rigid definitions.

Nishida's speculative exploitation of the idea of nothingness is a rather murky affair, and the nuts and bolts of his argumentation do not bear close scrutiny. He mapped the 'place' or milieu of beings (the term is modelled on Plato's *khōra*) as absolute nothingness. This absolute differs from Hegel's in that it is more 'infinity' than 'totality' and in that it is 'otherwise than being' (to use Levinas's terms). Tanabe, developing this vision more rigorously, claims to radicalise the Kantian critique to an 'absolute critique', in which all beings are shown to be empty of own-being and to exist only as mediations of absolute nothingness. A comprehensive two-way movement between absolute nothingness and relative beings can alone avoid the antinomies in which reason becomes trapped when confined to the relative. Nishitani reanchors the thought of his two predecessors in its Buddhist origins, preferring the original Mahāyāna term 'emptiness' (śūnyatā) to the later Taoist-influenced 'nothingness'. A student of Heidegger, he expounds his 'standpoint of emptiness' in phenomenological style rather than in fearsome dialectical jargon, and holds it out as a homeopathic antidote to the nihilism diagnosed by Nietzsche.

For these philosophers, all things find their true being only in letting go of being and embracing absolute nothingness as the place to which beings belong. They like to quote Philippians 2:7 ('he emptied himself') and Galatians 2:20 ('it is no longer I who live'), not in order to recommend an existence sustained by faith in Christ, but in order to urge an intellectual or spiritual conversion to absolute nothingness through insight into the non-substantiality of God and of self.

Tanabe comes closest to Christianity in that, drawing freely on the Pure Land preaching of Shinran (1173–1262), he grasps absolute nothingness as a gracious event, as saving Other-power, to which we open up by relinquishing our reliance on self-power. Absolute nothingness is Great Compassion; it needs the sphere of relative existences in order to work itself out. Amida Buddha is only a metaphorical personification of it:

> To refuse this sort of philosophical interpretation and insist on the unmediated absoluteness of his being and on his solitary activity of saving sentient beings without the aid of their mediatory function is inevitably to fall into the error of converting Pure Land Buddhism into a kind of theism akin to Christianity, and thus to get trapped in the mythological scheme. (Tanabe, 213)

Absolute nothingness is a transformative power and it uses beings as skilful means (upāya) in its gracious work of salvation. Tanabe was happy to call it 'love' and 'God', but its non-existence, apart from the relative beings that mediate it, leaves no place for a transcendent personal God.

Tanabe, rather like Kierkegaard, writes a philosophy to end all philosophy, urging us to get back in touch with the misery of our existence and to cast ourselves on Other-power through 'the passive negativity of humility and obedience' (195). Detached thought is inimical to salvific action:

When the highly esteemed ideals of truth, goodness, and beauty lose the significance of serving to mediate salvation and become absolutely independent ideals, they tend in the opposite direction of hypocrisy, sin, and ugliness. In truth they are only relatively independent and function as mediators of absolute nothingness. (199)

Tanabe's existential radicality is in tension with his speculative ardour, as if he were miming a leap outside philosophy from within philosophy. He has also been accused of not allowing the absolute to be truly absolute. Yoshifumi Ueda asks:

Can an absolute that requires the working of the relative be called truly an absolute in the full sense of the word? The absolute in Shinran embraces the relative completely and functions in the world by itself, permitting no room for the activity of the relative. There is no way to obscure the radical difference in understanding of the absolute between Shinran and Tanabe. (Unno and Heisig, 137)

Jean Higgins claims that Shinran lived with a paradox: 'the abyss of karmic evil and the abyss of Amida's compassion irrevocably conjoined. Relative and Absolute become one while remaining two in an illogical yet real identification' (153). Tanabe's Hegelian mediations smooth out this illogicality, erasing the scandal *of simul iustus et peccator*.

What more fundamentally diminishes the value of the Kyoto philosophers for Christian-Buddhist dialogue is a certain massiveness in their theorising about nothingness and emptiness. As Jamie Hubbard insists:

If we try to understand how 'the Absolute is mediated by the relative' in the context of Nāgārjuna, for example, it would mean simply that there are no emptinesses apart from the things empty, emptinesses are dependently established in relation to the conventional existences, and when those conventional existences pass away so does the emptiness dependent upon them – there is no infinite, functioning emptiness swooshing around the universe, relating to dependent beings and thereby validating its own existence. (371)

To make emptiness a principle of speculative construction is to miss its value as a mobile strategy, to be differently applied from case to case, as in the Zen kōans. Emptiness overcomes rigid dualities and reifications, to free us for an apprehension of life in its thusness. But when raised to the status of a metaphysical name for the essence of reality it has quite the opposite effect, no matter how many dialectical inflections one surrounds it with.

On the Christian side, it is easy to fall into a similar heavy-handedness in dealing with the phenomena of love and grace. These too are events, ever-new, and efforts to define them in terms of being, or as 'beyond being' or 'without being', transform them into metaphysical principles in a way that cannot avoid the danger of reification. When we translate grace into ontological terms, when we explain it as utter dependence on God in our very being, or even when we compare the justification of the sinner with creation out of non-being (see Rom. 4:17), the event is subsumed in the ontological framework and no longer allowed to unfold in its lived temporality. When Paul says, 'by the grace of God I am what I am' (1 Cor. 15:10), he is speaking of his career of apostleship, and is writing out of the ongoing experience of being sustained in his weakness by the gracious presence of Christ. Translate his statement into an ontological analysis: 'Paul's being is granted as a free gift of God and has no intrinsic substantiality', and you have lost the cutting edge of the Apostle's existential utterance. Even if his utterance has general overtones, these apply to human existence as a temporal event and as a lived relationship of dependence, rather than to creaturely being as a metaphysical quantity in search of its foundation.

Grace, like emptiness, is a word used to indicate the nature of reality and to shatter false characterisations of it. The word is used particularly of the saving events of justification, sanctification, and the divine self-communication to creatures; these terms are no more than convenient shorthand for processes that resist summary and definition. But the revelation of gratuity and dependence in these events is inevitably extended from the order of redemption to the order of creation, and becomes a clue to reading all things, a clue whose application is as flexible as the realities to which it applies are diverse. The reality of grace does not allow itself to be cast in the mould of a single circumscribed concept or phenomenon, as Augustine, Melanchthon, Baius, Jansenius, and countless other theoreticians of grace have discovered to their cost.

If this is the way that the words 'grace' and 'emptiness' function, namely as powerful principles of religious thought which show their power above all in the way they elude systematic formulation, then their encounter cannot be choreographed as a dialectical interplay of metaphysical axioms. Rather two styles, two sensibilities, brush against one another, exciting innumerable vibrations, and bringing a stereophonic richness to our apprehension both of religious and of everyday realities, for now we have two languages in which to speak of them, and can blend the rhetoric of grace with that of emptiness as occasion prompts.

If such is the status of the key-terms in both religions, then the enthusiastic speculative exploitation of absolute nothingness in the American Christian-Buddhist dialogue of recent years has to be seen as a false trail.

John B. Cobb, whose work represents a speculative springtime of dialogue, proposes that the Western identification of God as pure and perfect being, the ground of being and the Supreme Being, is 'conceptually confusing' (Cobb, 111). If we recognise that the ultimate reality is emptiness, and dissolve the Western concept of being into emptiness, then we can think of God as the complete manifestation and actualisation of emptiness, in a way that implies no subordination of God to that which he actualises. This theory again hypostatises emptiness as ultimate reality. But 'emptiness' is a functional word. Its meaning resides in its application. When all has been shown to be empty of self-nature, one cannot then confidently go on to define the ultimate as empty, as if 'emptiness' denoted a positive quality.

Building on Nāgārjuna's identification of dependent co-arising and emptiness, Cobb adds:

> God must be the complete, unqualified, everlasting actualization of *pratitya-samutpada*, dependent origination ... That is, God must be totally open to all that is and constituted by its reception. (113)

This use of Buddhism to prop up a process theory that God is constituted by his relations to all that is introduces a speculative distortion that impedes reception of Nāgārjuna's freeing critical wisdom One might have expected Cobb to turn to the unconditioned, *nirvāṇa*, rather than dependent co-arising, as the more promising Buddhist analogue for God But he has read Nāgārjuna as licensing a massive two-way identification of dependent co-arising and emptiness, *saṃsāra* and *nirvāṇa*. Yet, though Mādhyamika authorities say that *nirvāṇa* is empty, I do not think they would say that it is dependently co-arisen or that it is simply identical with insight into dependent co-arising. To a Buddha dependent co-arising may be seen directly as emptiness and *saṃsāra* seen directly as *nirvāṇa*; but this means that dependent co-arising is now seen as essentially a non-dependent non-arising, for one no longer perceives separate things, and that illusion-ridden perceptions of *saṃsāra* have disappeared in a grasp of its nirvanic essence. Cobb reverses this by dissolving the supreme simplicity of *nirvāṇa*, which is utterly empty, back into the endless complexity of the world of relative entities, on the pretext that these, too, are essentially empty.

But if Buddhism refrains from thinking of *nirvāṇa* as a rigid absolute, by stressing its emptiness, it is not in order to think of it as a switchboard of relations between the empty entities of the samsaric world, but rather to let it be itself, beyond all conceptions of absolute and relative. If theology similarly itches to free God from the straitjacket of the Absolute, it is not in order to redefine God in function of the cosmos, but in order to let God be God. Letting *nirvāṇa* be itself opens a space for the free engagement of the enlightened being in the samsaric world, just as letting God be God opens a space for the covenantal engagement of God with creatures. But this does not justify accounts of the ultimate that make it subject to conditions and relations as finite beings are.

Cobb's way of talking about 'God' also takes a lot for granted. Metaphysical manipulation of this concept lends it a stability which is undone when we consult the historical plurality of Christian languages. Even if we did agree on one metaphysical account, whether seeing God as supreme actualisation of emptiness or as supreme actualisation of being, we would have to define being and emptiness in an impoverished way to make them fit the schema. Phenomenologically, neither being nor emptiness is given in such a way that it can be gathered up in some supreme instance. In a stilted metaphysical perspective, God can be seen as the actualisation of being, *ipsum esse subsistens*, but a comparable metaphysical account of emptiness would err by substantialism (reified emptiness) or by nihilism (emptiness as simple non-existence). The alternative to a metaphysics of being seems to be not a metaphysics of emptiness, but a thinking that is aware of the limits of metaphysics, and that deploys such words as 'being' and 'emptiness' adroitly as fragile products of a historical labour of thought, having only a provisional usefulness in certain contexts.

Cobb's Buddhist dialogue partner, Masao Abe, attempts to rethink the Christian faith in terms of a speculative dissolution of God in Absolute Nothingness. To assess his theory of the emptying God, we should begin by differentiating between its speculative and its phenomenological dimensions. The notion of emptiness serves at the phenomenological level as a therapy against metaphysical delusions. But in Abe's hands it becomes itself a metaphysical absolute. This leads to a speculative engagement between this absolutised emptiness and metaphysical versions of Christian theology, which themselves need to be overcome by being recalled to their biblical roots.

If Christianity and Buddhism get back in touch with their own phenomenality – that is, with the world lit up by the Gospel and with the world lit up by Buddhist meditation – the need to produce speculative theories about emptiness or the Trinity will die away. Such theories may turn out to be rendered impossible by the very texture of the religious life-worlds revealed in the fundamental Buddhist and Christian insights.

In his essay, 'Kenotic God and Dynamic Sunyata', Abe comments as follows on the biblical text which is most important to him, Philippians 2:5–8:

> In Paul's understanding the Son of God abandoned his divine substance and took on human substance to the extreme point of

becoming a servant crucified on the cross ... Christ as the Son of God is *essentially* and *fundamentally* self-emptying or self-negating ... Consequently, we may reformulate the doctrine of Christ's kenosis as follows: The Son of God is not the Son of God (for he is essentially and fundamentally self-emptying): precisely because he *is not* the Son of God he *is* truly the Son of God (for he originally and always works as Christ, the Messiah, in his salvational function of self-emptying). (Cobb and Ives, 10f)

One reading of these remarks could take Abe to be distancing himself from metaphysical kenotic speculation and seeing Christ, both divine and human, in a phenomenological way, as intrinsically 'empty'. Phenomenologically, there is merit in the proposal that the union of divine and human in Christ can be grasped in terms of 'a "nondual function" of self-emptying or self-negation'.

Johannine non-duality – 'I and the Father are one' (Jn 10:30) – which lies at the root of the Nicene and Chalcedonian doctrines, can be given phenomenological perspicuity in terms of emptiness. The mutual indwelling of the Father, the Son and the believers is a relation arising on the ground of emptiness, and actualised in self-emptying love. The insistence that Jesus's self-emptying is more than a temporary abnegation, and represents the essence of divine love, and of divinity itself, indicates a basic phenomenological reality, even if Abe understresses the particular historical eventhood of the incarnation and the cross, and the fact that in Philippians 2 it is not God who empties himself, but the human Jesus, who by emptying himself makes his existence 'empty' and thus fully open to the divine. Jesus reveals the essence of *agapē* in a human way, under the conditions of temporal existence. This limits the phenomenological viability of a transference of the language of kenosis to the divine nature. The pre-existence language in the hymn can be contextualised and demythologised in a phenomenological approach, whereas the speculative approach falls prey to mythic objectification reinforced by an unconvincing metaphysical dialectic.

This speculative element muddies Abe's existential message, that kenosis overcomes nihilism. A self-emptying God dissolves the rigidity of theocentrism, which is really a projection of human egocentrism, and thus provides the antidote to the Nietzschean nihilism which would 'sacrifice God for nothing'. 'The kenotic God sacrifices Godself not for relative nothingness but for *absolute* nothingness, which is at one and the same time absolute Being' (16). In contrast, Nishitani's conversion of nihilistic nihility (*kyomu*) into Buddhist emptiness (*mu*) remains closer to the phenomena, as does his reading of the Philippians hymn: 'With Christ we speak of a deed that has been accomplished; with God, of an original nature. What is *ekkenōsis* for the Son is *kenōsis* for the Father In the East this would be called *anātman*, or non-ego' (Nishitani, 59). This avoids the ascription of an active self-emptying to God; kenosis here is a passive quality of non-ego, not the activity of self-emptying, now called ekkenosis.

In Abe's view: 'only through this total kenosis and his self-sacrificial identification with everything in the world is God truly God ... God is God because he himself is suffering God, self-sacrificial God through his total kenosis' (quoted in Unno, 93). He quotes Karl Rahner on 'the self-emptying of God, his becoming, the kenosis and genesis of God himself' (Cobb and Ives, 14) – a piece of Hegelianism which Rahner cautiously qualifies with a tortuous quasi-scholastic distinction: 'He who is not subject to change in *himself*, can himself be subject to change *in something else*' (15). Remaining on the same speculative plane as Rahner, Abe rejects what he sees as Rahner's residual 'dualism': 'It must not be that God *becomes something else* by partial self-giving, but that in and through his total self-emptying God *is* something – or more precisely, God *is* each and every thing' (16). This pantheism is a correlate of his monophysite account of the Incarnation: 'If this total identity of God with the cruci-fied Christ on the cross is a necessary premise for Christian faith, why is this total identity of God with Christ through Christ's kenosis not applicable to everything in the universe beyond Christ?' (18).

In Mādhyamika, the emptiness of emptiness does not mean that emptiness turns itself into the whole of what exists by a dialectical trans-formation. Rather, it means that having realised that all things are empty of self-nature, we refrain from clinging to the notion of emptiness itself as if it somehow had a self-nature. It is but a provisional designation, a skilful means, to be cast aside as soon as it has fulfilled its purpose. Thomas Kasulis reifies emptiness when he speaks of it as follows: 'Why is emptiness a fullness? Because emptiness is a self-emptying (kenosis) of itself into the world, or more precisely, a self-emptying of itself as the world' (Unno, 289). This imposes on the phenomenology of emptiness metaphysical constructions of a Western type, perhaps inspired by classical or Hegelian presentations of the Incarnation.

For Abe, 'God as a subject who meets one and whom one can address as Thou is incompatible with the autonomous reason peculiar to modern humanity' (Cobb and Ives, 26); instead we must move within the absolute interior of God as non-objectifiable encompassing nothingness. Eugene Borowitz wryly remarks:

> Christian theologians like Jürgen Moltmann find it congruent with their trinitarian faith to speak of what transpires in God's interior. Masao Abe suggests that from his Buddhist perspective they ought to move on to 'the still greater interior of the interior'. On this

score, the central tradition of the Jewish people has been resolutely agnostic. It does not know much about God's essence because, as a religion of revelation, God did not say much about it. (86)

Talk of the 'interior of the interior', like similar language in Eckhart, may have some recuperable phenomenological upshot. But if it is the only authentic approach to God, then the entire religious practice of Judaism, Christianity and Islam is invalid. As Altizer puts it, 'the Christian faith in God ... can only appear as bad faith in the light of the Buddhist perspective' (69). Buddhism would then claim a higher access to God, refusing to the language of the Psalms even the status of an *upāya*. Yet phenomenologically, rather than being a barrier to insight into emptiness, that personal language can open the contemplative mind to the suchness of things, the boundless openness of reality, and a sense of God as that in which 'we live, and move, and have our being' (Acts 17:28). It is phenomenologically false to dismiss this as 'nothing but a reification and substantialization of something ultimate as the only entity that has its own being ... a special form of attachment' (49).

Does the realisation of emptiness bring the Christian discourse of salvation tumbling down like a house of cards? Altizer says that 'Abe has unveiled the contradiction between established Christian doctrines of God and Christian faith in Christ, between the glory and transcendence of God and the humiliation and servanthood of Christ, between the eternal life of God and the eternal death of Christ' (69). The complexity of a historical formation such as Christian dogma leaves it vulnerable to deconstruction, but at the same time protects it against a deconstruction proceeding by such massive oppositions. Beyond ghostly speculations wherein 'the Christian God empties itself in a once-and-for-all act, even as a Buddhist Emptiness continually or eternally empties itself' (Altizer, in Unno, 77), the salvific power of self-emptying love can be spoken of in the language of emptiness, in attunement to the Spirit that called forth the old languages of resurrection and exaltation. Such a language overcomes the monstrous images of God emptying himself on Calvary and of Buddhist Emptiness as a hypostasis involved in eternal self-emptying, as it restores the phenomenological and historical contexts within which alone the expressions 'God' and 'emptiness' have their sense. It turns out that the encounter between the God who is Spirit and Buddhist emptiness has a gentler and more open-ended character, as an encounter of styles of spiritual insight rather than of speculative visions.

One Jewish theologian, despairing of the traditional image of God as providential Lord of history, prefers to see God as 'the Holy Nothingness ..., the plenum out of which the totality of all that has existed, does exist, and will exist is derived' (Rubenstein, 144f). This finds an echo in John Keenan's Mahāyāna theology:

> The very arising of all things in inter-dependency is itself directly and immediately the presence of Abba ... Abba does not come to the rescue of bodily or mental anguish ... The Old Testament skeptics were right: Yahweh does not save his people. He allowed them to be consumed in the fires of the holocaust. (Keenan, 244)

Here the traditional notion of salvation is dissolved into consciousness of emptiness, which if not completely identical with the divine presence, seems the exclusive key to a valid apprehension of that presence. The emergence in Western thought of Nothingness as an appropriate name for God resonates richly with the Buddhist use of 'emptiness' to name the true texture of reality. But the resonance must not seduce us into rapid speculative amalgamations, or sweeping dissolutions that can easily become nihilism.

Keenan locates the heart of Christian truth in a conversion of consciousness:

> The basic structure of consciousness is already directed toward ultimate meaning and rejects God-conceptions because of their failure to ground themselves in that structure ... In awareness of the original structuring of consciousness oriented toward ultimate meaning one becomes aware of God as prevenient and encompassing. (248)

If this consciousness of God prescribes the rejection of all concepts of God, these concepts are retained on the plane of conventional truth, where they are used with critical vigilance. One passes freely between a differential language – the dialectic of God-conceptions which bears in itself the awareness that God surpasses them all while allowing himself to be indicated across them – and the silence of a contemplation which leaves aside all language. Keenan risks raising enlightened consciousness above language to the point that it is no longer clear how Christian language can preserve any objectivity. Would it not be better to say that, guided by contemplation and subordinate to it, Christian language retains, at least in an oblique way, mediated by its entire historical and strategic context, a referential power which is the criterion of its efficacy?

> Mahāyāna theology argues that all theological models (even a Mahāyāna model) are valid only within their contextuality in terms of the particular conditions in virtue of which they arise. In the words of Maximus Confessor, 'the doctrines of the Church are transcended by their own content'. (225)

But that transcendence does not leave the analogical language of faith behind as a mere 'model' having no objective connection with that to which it points.

There is at first sight a tension between the idea of religion as skilful means and the proper texture of the Gospel message. Its eschatological character sets it apart from the conceptions of transcendence advanced in negative theology and is the most powerful factor of relativisation in Christian life and discourse. The 'ever greater' God is the 'God who comes', and the inadequate language which seeks to name him is that of a faith on the way to the eschatological future; each statement of faith is an anticipation, in hope, of the light of an eschatological vision 'face to face' (1 Cor. 13:12). To speak of Jesus's 'experience of Abba (direct awareness of ultimate meaning) and his preaching of the rule of God in the world (the urgency of conventional reality)' (226) may imply a division with little warrant in the Gospels, where Abba is eschatological through and through, and where conversely the eschatological is nothing less than the transcendent. Of course we should avoid giving eschatological language an absolute status; it is only a provisional expedient; the eschatological in itself remains ineffable. The readiness with which the word 'eschatological' comes to hand in theological discussions indicates a weak spot, challenging us to think out what it is that this word is pointing to.

We cannot assess the status and function of such biblical language by measuring it from the outside according to Buddhist criteria. It is from within that language itself that its finite, dependently co-arisen character comes to light. What we have gleaned from Buddhism and deconstruction may allow us to let the biblical meaning of 'God' and 'Christ' unfold in a fresh style. As finite names of ultimate, transcendent reality, it may confidently be expected that they will effect their own deconstruction, opening our minds to a reality which we can point to but not clutch, name but not comprehend.

God and emptiness can be thought together only along the paths of a dialogue between traditions which is animated, like the encounter between Jesus and the Buddha (historical revealers of God and of emptiness respectively), by an instinctive attraction, a mutual recognition that resists translation into conceptual terms. These two ways of approaching ultimate reality cannot be reduced to unity in a speculative confrontation. These two languages have been constructed as pointers to that reality for thousands of years, and it may be that henceforth a more adequate pointer than either is the play between them, and that either without the other falls short of being a 'skilful means'.

Within every religion there are central utterances, at the pinnacle of the 'hierarchy of truths' (Vatican II), whereby that religion points beyond itself, relativises itself in view of the *paramārtha-satya*. One may take refuge in these utterances when what is lower in the hierarchy comes to seem uncertain, or, as in the case of miracles, embarrassing if certain. We iron and press our dogmas and historical claims, but sense a flimsiness to them which the Bible itself takes little pains to conceal. They are precious skilful means, but their ultimate value consists in the efficacy with which they point to what lies beyond them. In biblical Judaism all the tales of God's actions are surpassed and relativised by the simplicity of such an utterance as the *Shema*: 'The Lord our God is one Lord; and you shall love the Lord your God with all your heart, and with all your soul, and with all your might' (Deut. 6:4). In Christianity the same utterance has the same function (Mk 12:29f). Jesus points not to his own uniqueness but to the supreme reality which makes his message indistinguishable from that of the Hebrew Scriptures. And the finger points beyond the limits of the biblical horizon altogether: for what is God? The word can embrace the biblical creator or the Quranic Allah, the Augustinian *internum eternum* or the Vedantic *tat tvam asi*, yet this dizzying universality is focused by the stricture of a proper name, for God is the one we name as 'God', 'our Father', and the intimacy of this naming seems profoundly right, and no betrayal of the absoluteness and intangibility of what it names.

One cannot surpass the monotheistic language in favour of alternative constructions of a purely theoretical order. A religious language is not built in a day. The only alternatives to this language are those assembled over millenia in the other great religions. If one names the object of the religious quest 'God', one will feel the need of a larger space or horizon as the background against which this invocation of God will take place. For Heidegger this would be the horizon of being, but there the biblical God is subjected to the laws which govern the epiphanies of Greek divinities. If we say instead that it is the larger horizon freed by Buddhist emptiness, we must beware of similar drastic subjection of God to laws of discourse tailored for quite other purposes.

But facile manipulation of the notion of God is impeded by the fact that it carries with it the whole tradition which has formed it. Leaving monotheistic space for Buddhist space, one is not leaving the true to enter the false. Some would say it is like moving from everyday space into subatomic space, or from the spectrum of colours to the radiological spectrum. Limits of monotheistic language come to light, which however do not disqualify this language; God is absolute, but 'God' is not. This way of seeing things is suggestive, but schematic. The notion of God cannot be abstracted from its tradition to be set in relation to Buddhist emptiness in a space of speculation. The contact between these two notions demands that one rethink the entire rapport between the tradition of God and the tradition of emptiness, and that one let the traditions play together, in the awareness of their provisional and fragile status.

The monotheistic language and the language of emptiness: two fingers pointing to the moon. Human reason is not installed at the centre of reality as Hegel thought, but bears on it from a particular angle. 'The parallax effect resulting from this excentric situation of our mind is represented in Thomism by the theory of analogical and symbolic cognition of the absolute realities' (Maréchal, 174). All the more precious then is the complement of Buddhist discourse, with its quite different techniques of sighting the ultimate from the angle of the conventional. The mutual correction of the two linguistic apparatuses assures to both the required mobility. Just as the value of a pointing finger varies with the movement of the moon across the sky, so the efficacy of both these languages is variable. In some historical conjunctures it will be the monotheistic affirmations that strike more in the direction of truth, while in others the subtle language of emptiness will be a more appropriate vehicle. If the economy of the discourse of monotheism is in league with truth, so is that of the Buddhist discourse. No discourse of the true-in-itself can be established. In the interplay of the two traditions, truth is not on one side or the other in a stable proportion. If the victory of truth results from their 'loving strife', it will not come from the direction one expects – for the finger cannot dictate the position of the moon.

7

THE EMPTY CHRIST

In the case of statements about God or about ultimate reality, it is not insuperably difficult to square their historical relativity with their claim to objective truth, since they concern what relativises from the start all efforts to conceive or express it. Even claims that associate the transcendent with particular historical events can be softened and relativised by the thought that the transcendent is revealed more generally in all events. But when a single event is designated as the supreme and definitive locus of revelation, a painful logical alternative seems inescapable: we are forced either to de-absolutise this event, or to insist that all other historical vehicles of revelation are subordinate to it a priori. If the 'Christ-event' is the site of full revelation and salvation, then non-Christian traditions may serve as providential avenues of approach to it, or may provide some perspectives for its interpretation, or may even be supplementary channels of its grace, but ultimately their significance is decided asymmetrically by this unique event. Thus Christianity seems to claim to understand the other religions, beginning with Judaism, better than they can understand themselves.

This asymmetry is deeply unsatisfactory. It defines the status of other traditions and the meaning of history prior to any acquaintance and concrete study. It contradicts the other traditions' sense of their own significance. The more we listen to those others on their own terms, the more the claim that God is fully and definitively revealed only in Christ seems in need of revision. Each religion cuts its distinctive path of truth, creates a distinctive style of approach to ultimate gracious reality. Empirically, the revelation in Christ neither absorbs nor discredits the truth-events centred on the Torah, the Quran, the Vedas or the bodhisattva path. Moreover, the frontiers of Christ's identity are uncertain. The Word of God – the transcendent revelation-event in its undisposability (Barth's *Unverfügbarkeit*) – has indeed elected to be named Jesus Christ. But the sense of that name emerges only as we relate Jesus to the other worlds of truth.

THE ONE SAVIOUR

'He came to them, walking on the sea' (Mk 6:48). The encounter with a saviour, who brings the answer to our most unsettling questions – the pardon of sins, the remedy for suffering and mortality – is at the heart of most religious experience. But the saviour's identity differs from one culture to another, as does the nature of the salvation promised. Krishna's claims are as universal as those of the Johannine Christ:

> Thou art the Imperishable, the supreme Object of Knowledge;
>> Thou art the ultimate resting-place of this universe;
> Thou art the immortal guardian of the eternal right,
>> Thou art the everlasting Spirit, I hold
>>> (*Bhagavad-Gītā* 11.18, trans. Edgerton)

And the accents are as intimate and as persuasive:

> Further, the highest secret of all,
>> My supreme message, hear.
> Because thou art greatly loved of Me,
>> Therefore I shall tell thee what is good for thee.
> Be Me-minded, devoted to Me;
>> Worshiping Me, revere Me;
> And to Me alone shalt thou go; truly to thee
>> I promise it – (because) thou art dear to Me. (18.64f)

The promises of Amida Buddha or the other saviour figures of Mahāyāna Buddhism, or those of the gods and goddesses of devotional Hinduism, are equally touching. Nor can one confidently claim that the faith, love, devotion these figures inspire is existentially less real or authentic than that of Christians.

Yet objectively, it might be argued, these saviour-figures are only imaginary personifications, projections in which religious longing fills out the lineaments of its dream, whereas Jesus is a historical human being. They remain docetic amalgams of finite and infinite, whereas he marks the point where finite and infinite meet in their distinctness, not in myth but in mystery. In the higher reaches of religion personal saviours tend to be identified with or dissolved into broader impersonal platforms of salvation: Brahman, Dharma, Buddha-nature, Torah. The apologist will see these as dim participations in the Johannine Logos, which is definitively made known, and decisively related to human, historical reality, only in Jesus Christ.

Some such critique of the claims of other saviours may be an essential component of Christian apologetics. Yet the credibility of the Christian claim depends in turn on honest assessment of what these troubling parallels to it imply. Their continued vigour undermines the self-evidence of the confession of Christ as saviour, making the figure of Jesus enigmatic in an unexpected way. He who is the answer to our existential questions has himself become a question. We go to meet the other religions with the assurance of having a saviour, but also with questions about his place in the interreligious horizon. Moreover, the very notion of salvation has become problematic. Doctrines of salvation seem to reduce the variety of human ills under a single essentialist rubric such as *duḥkha* or sin, in order to provide an equally monolithic antidote to them. In all this we cannot presume to subordinate divine revelation to a more global horizon; rather we must follow the concrete openings towards the other which are inscribed in the revelation itself, both in its transcendent aspect – the illimitable reach of the notion of Logos – and in its empirical aspect – the open-ended, incomplete historical texture of the Christ-event.

The inclusivist claim that whatever salvation seems to come from other traditions in reality comes from Jesus in a hidden or anonymous fashion, or at least converges on him as its fullest embodiment, so that he is the privileged focus of human progress toward divinisation, is suspiciously convenient. Yet it is equally facile to speak of a plurality of saving instances having equal status, or to suppose that the universality of Christianity will emerge in the course of interreligious encounters by a progressive dechristianisation, just as the universality of Western reason is realised as its progressive dewesternisation. We do not know what the slow mutation of Christian identity, in the course of many complex interactions, may bring forth; but the function of Christ, endlessly reinterpreted, must remain central to this identity. As we think more largely of God and of human history, our understanding of Christ is concomitantly released from anachronistic thought-forms, while it remains coterminous with our grasp, or non-grasp, of transcendent reality on the one hand and of historical humanity on the other, as what mediates between them.

It may be objected that this is a wishful predetermination of the outcome, and that it is more likely that Christ will appear in the interreligious horizon as simply one agent of salvation among others, over whom he enjoys no special primacy. Or agnosticism may seem the most honest attitude: we simply do not know whether or not Christ has a primacy as saviour, for we do not understand well enough the upshot of his saving work and its relation to the other kinds of salvation there may be, so that in practice all we can do is to follow the path opened up by the Gospel without worrying about its relation to other paths.

Yet it is not possible to follow Christ without making, explicitly or implicitly, some strong dogmatic claims for him, though one may emphasise these claims more modestly and discreetly than before. Dogma need not be rigid. It develops as an attempt at critical clarification of what faith affirms spontaneously, singling out points which come increasingly to seem crucial while toning down other aspects which had been too naively and massively asserted. No matter what one chooses to believe, agnosticism coexists with the instinct of faith, and assails it with questions to which the answers are never all given together. Yet in regard to the basic conviction of Christ's status as saviour, the Spirit enables a leap of faith beyond the circle of pressing doubts, and the New Testament witness, however tempered and demythologised in subsequent reflection, firmly sustains these promptings of the Spirit.

Within this conviction, we may seek to distinguish between what faith, led by the Spirit, apprehends as the soteriological primacy of Christ on the one hand, and on the other what is merely a matter of dogged dogmatic assertion or bondage to traditional habit. However, it is hard to mark a clear boundary here. Faith cannot be cleanly differentiated from respect for tradition, or even from an element of indoctrination. Hence any claim to hold something by faith carries a margin of fragility, requiring to be compensated for by the ongoing effort to reground faith-claims in a more existential apprehension of the Christ-event.

Those who respond to the call, 'Come unto Me', whether it come from Christ or Krishna or Amida, do indeed find rest unto their souls, grace, peace and joy. If to be devoted is to be duped, to hold back sceptically is a formula for sterility: *les non-dupes errent* in their refusal of commitment (Lacan). The devotee gravitates to an exclusivist position; the logic of love justifies this investment of absolute trust in a limited human form, this identification of the ultimate in the singularity of a sacred name. But a pluralist theology, while respecting such commitment, seeks to open devotion to a wider disinterested questioning which learns from all traditions. Devotion remains an essential strand in the fabric of religion, but blind devotion must be outgrown. And devotion must not idolise itself, but should be constantly interrogated, with a view to clarifying the encounter which is at its core.

An apologetic defence of Christ's unique status should begin not from the full-blown doctrine of the Incarnation but from a more basic premise:

namely that God was at work in Christ, that the ultimate reality and nothing less or other is encountered across the words and deeds of Jesus and their ongoing interpretation. Here is a bedrock certitude, which has a plausible phenomenological foundation and which involves no immediate tension with the claims of other religions. The foundation in question is not provided by any single experience, however privileged, but by immersion in the entire spectrum of the teachings of Jesus and the Gospel stories, as they are interpreted and lived by Christians today.

At a second stage, one attends to the distinctiveness, in comparative perspective, of this manifestation of the ultimate in the life of Christ. If we recognise comparable encounters with ultimate reality at the core of other religions, then the distinctiveness of Christ may reside less in what he incarnates than in the 'how' of that incarnation, less in his divinity than in the mode of the conjunction of that divinity with humanity.

A generous view will see each saving path as a local enactment of a universal process. 'Salvation' as an unimaginable, transcendental movement, shading into other such inconceivables as the Good or the True, is not to be read off automatically from the concrete heterogeneous modes of local salvation-traditions, nor resumed in Christ as 'concrete universal'. The Buddhist and Christian doctrines of salvation attain a very high degree of universality, yet each is limited by its distinctive realm of application. Buddhism is as universal as its spiritual analysis is valid for all humans, but the analysis is incomplete, culture-bound, and can be improved on. Christian universality is associated with the decisiveness of the prophetic tradition in its dealing with history, the proclamation of God's saving will at work in history. But this proclamation remains very general and enigmatic. It is given maximum concreteness in the crucified Jesus; yet even the cross is a sign to be interpreted, and its interpreting community, the Christian faithful, cannot declare its universal applicability in an automatic way but must seek first to understand empirically its power to save in their own historical struggle.

How does Christ save? Our answer to that question even for ourselves is always shifting, and can be communicated to humanity only to the degree that it acquires concrete lineaments that have a universal power of persuasion. It never in practice acquires an entirely universal form, all that can be done is to present the currently most vital images of Christ as Saviour; and these images too will differ from culture to culture – one that speaks eloquently to Latin America may fall flat in Australia or Japan. Universality thus takes the form of a pluralistic proliferation of Christ-stories.

At a third, more esoteric level of inquiry, we attempt to retrieve the truth of the dogmatic claims about the divinity and humanity of Christ.

These came first in the past; but this may have been a short-circuit, generating intolerance and violence. Now, rather than a first datum, the divinity of Christ becomes a delicate naming of what the story of Jesus ultimately means. Our traditional language has been massive and overwhelming, like similar language about the Buddha in the Mahāyāna sūtras. When such language is recalled to its basis, it is seen as attesting the transcendent scope of the founding events, the impossibility of confining them within the categories of finite existence, an impossibility perhaps better indicated today by the use of negative language.

In what does the distinctness, or the primacy, of Christ's saving role consist? Five possible answers are: his *ontological* constitution; the fulness of the *revelation* he brings; his role as the one who *reconciles* us with God; the event of his *resurrection*; his *eschatological* role. Classically, one would say that his ontological status as true God and true man is what grounds all other aspects of his primacy. But one could try to invert these relations. One could found ontology on revelation: Jesus is identified with the Logos insofar as his life bears the imprint of the reality of God and opens a space within human history for the encounter with that reality. Soteriology too could be reduced to revelational terms: it is by revealing the inner nature of death that Christ's death frees us from it, and his resurrection is the pneumatic revelation of the sense of his existence as opening human life to divine transcendence; we share in this risen life less by a physical causality than by the opening up of vision. Again, Christ's eschatological role lies in his revealing the meaning which human history has before God. Such a revelational reduction can easily go too far, undermining any objective primacy of Christ. Thus Gordon Kaufman sees Christ as:

> that figure from human history who is believed by Christians to reveal or define, on the one hand, who or what God really is, and, on the other hand, what true humanity consists in. The historical figure of Jesus Christ thus gives concreteness and specificity to the understanding of both God and humanity. (in D'Costa, 11)

But a richer concept of revelation could retain the full weight of the ontological claims. If the being of God is light, the revelation of God is conversely a divine event; thus the claim that 'Jesus is God' could be rephrased in revelational terms without loss: 'Jesus is the event of God's self-revelation'.

Again, one might try to focus the distinctiveness of the Christ-event on the basis of its eschatological character. If one sees the divinity of Christ as residing in the revelational impact of his life, this is turn could be located in the way his life brings into view the eschatological upshot of history: that is, in the historical significance of his life as carrying the Jewish prophetic tradition to its supreme pitch. To speak of his divinity would then be a shorthand for the integral grasp of the conjunction of divine truth and human hope effected through his life. From beginning to end of the Bible God is one who comes to save, who enters history to bring all things to fulfilment. In Christ this process attains a universal sweep, and there is no going back on this; henceforth, God's eschatological promise is explicitly extended to all humanity, the Messianic invitation has gone forth to the ends to the earth.

Such a reduction of the 'divinity of Christ' to its phenomenal base would not necessarily imply a dissolution of classical doctrine. From the basic phenomenon, the Christ-event, there emanate successive layers of christological language, as ever more elusive overtones, up to the loftiest reaches of the Logos-theology. We validate these languages by regrounding them in the event, and invalidate them to the degree that they obscure it. John 1:14, 'The Word became flesh', is a hinge text, representing the high-point of New Testament Christology and the foundation of later dogma. The movement of validation and critique can be roughly divided into two phases: the testing of dogma against the Johannine vision, and the testing of John's understanding of Christ against the entire New Testament experience which it attempts to encapsulate.

It is only within the context of such ongoing critical sifting that the doctrinal claims can be persuasively enunciated. Since dogma in any case plays the indispensable initial role of pointing back to the phenomenon it defends, and since the phenomenon can never be completely extracted from the dogmatic pre-understanding which brings it into view, the effort to think the Christ-event should never simply undercut the claims of orthodoxy. These claims are best satisfied by identifying those aspects of the meaning of Christ which originally gave rise to them. The doctrinal claims will never succeed in entirely silencing their critics, but imaginative rehearsal of the pre-dogmatic significance of Christ, like a superb performance of some contested piece of music or theatre, is the best strategy for making those claims seem worth defending. But before going any farther, we need to query the fragile and contingent status of any language we use, attending first to the term 'Logos' and then to the term 'flesh'.

THE STATUS OF 'LOGOS'

The question of the ontological status of Christ should not emerge prematurely in interreligious dialogue, where the first concern is to focus the significance of Jesus (or of the Buddha or Muhammad) phenomenologically and historically. This lesser emphasis on dogma comes from the fact that the religions present themselves as vital forces, whose impact is a concrete, empirical matter, whereas their dogmatic claims concern invisible realities, scarcely verifiable. Perhaps the concrete aspects that come to the fore on the interreligious plane will react on the internal debate of each religion, reducing their insistence on what they take to be their pillars and allowing them to become more aware of the problematic character of these ancient claims. The question of the ultimate identity of Christ, and matters of comparable import in other religions, will be interpreted more flexibly as attention is concentrated on the task of understanding the phenomenon of Christ's saving action as more immediately grasped in the language of faith. Dogmatic claims and questions are implicit even in this first-level language, but their explicit discussion must come after a full exploration of what is nearest to hand phenomenologically and historically. One proceeds to the level of doctrinal reflection only with great hesitation and with a sense of the delicate and problematic nature of the language one is now forced to employ.

At this second level of reflection, one may reach the conclusion that only the Johannine vision of the Logos made flesh can provide a firm basis for the conviction of Christ's primacy. A Christology that falls short of it makes Christ the merely human agent of divine purposes. But the dogmatic claim here is credible only if we can trace its emergence from its phenomenological context. Such regrounding of the Logos-Christology in the Christ-event is favoured by John himself, for more than a metaphysical theory of Christ's origins, the Johannine doctrine is a quasi-phenomenological lighting up of the full significance of that event. For John, the meaning of Christ cannot be circumscribed by the categories of ordinary human understanding, or even by any of the titles previously conferred on Jesus and which are assigned their place in the Johannine spectrum. Only the notion of the divine Wisdom or Word, also received from a rich anterior tradition, is commensurate with the significance of Jesus' life. His presence was that of a living, penetrating word of judgement and grace, which came from God and imprinted itself in the hearts of its hearers with a pneumatic immediacy. The scope of this word is unlimitably universal, for it is spoken from the unmasterable divine dimension. It is an epiphany of the divine glory, particularly in the hour of the cross. Its authority is not lessened by the limitations of its historical form, for these are overcome by the interpreting Spirit (Jn 14:26; 16:7–14).

It might be claimed that this pneumatic phenomenology no less than later church doctrine is a violent occlusion of 'Jesus the Jew' (Geza Vermes). To bridge the gap between 'Jesus' and 'Christ' the Johannine vision of Jesus as God's Word needs to be regrounded in the word Jesus actually spoke, the message of the Kingdom. The portraits of Jesus in Matthew and Luke reveal that the Christ of faith can be read into the historical Jesus without scandalous distortion; the light of the resurrection seems rather to bring out new depth and universality in the words of Jesus and to give them a permanent resonance.

In John's vision, the Word is at work in the world from the beginning. Its enfleshment in the life of Jesus is a *novum* that classical Christology has hastened to express in ontological terms; but these can be cashed phenomenologically as meaning an unprecedentedly concrete articulation of the divine Word. The truth of God and the truth of humanity are here brought into conjunction across the total reality of a spiritual event, a finite but open-ended and ongoing history, centred on the figure of Jesus; to assert the ontological claim in abstraction from this history is to set up a rival dogmatic event, an idolatrous distraction from the event of revelation. A demythologised retrieval of Johannine contemplation shows up the clumsiness of metaphysical slogans such as 'Jesus is God' or 'God became man', and replaces such expressions as 'My Lord and my God' (Jn 20:28) within an open-ended revelational situation. We should leave the notion of Logos as indeterminate as possible, hewing closely to what this language suggests in John, and seeing it as an *upāya* to be deployed skilfully in order to do justice first to the phenomenality of the Christ-event. This means that the formulation of some necessary logical consequences – such as the need to mark a distinction between God and God's Logos without prejudice to the divine status of the Logos or to the unity of God – will not attain the inflated self-sufficient status of trinitarian speculation, but will present no more than a set of modest rules for the usage of a language each of whose terms eludes our grasp.

A definition of this Logos can never be established as an abstract truth outside of time, as has been attempted since the Fathers. That attempt runs aground on the historicity of theological language and the impossibility of constructing a stable account of divine reality (even if with the Fathers one calls it 'unknowable' or 'incomprehensible'). The makeshift nature of mythical and metaphysical languages has become evident. If we translate them into a more existential or subtle language, this too is a clumsy expedient unless it integrates a reflexive awareness of its own historicity and of the fact that religious language has never more than a relative fittingness, in relation to some precise context, as a more or less skilful intervention in the field of the sayable in order to witness to the unsayable. 'The Son of man has nowhere to lay his head' (Lk. 9:58): the truth of Christ is mismatched to all historical frameworks – be they Jewish apocalytic or Greek metaphysics, contemporary existentialism or evolutionism – and it is this very inadequation which witnesses to the non-masterable character of the Logos. The Logos is not captured in our language, nor does it present itself as an objective existence independent of it. It makes itself felt as the yawning gap on which all human speech founders. It is less the total fulness of our speech than that which makes such totality impossible.

To bring Jesus Christ into perspective, or rather to shatter the narrowing perspectives in which he has been imprisoned, one should cultivate insight into the finitude and provisionality of all historical constructions of his significance. As we leave a world in which the horizon of religious truth was determined exclusively by Christianity, we flounder blindly in interreligious space as long as we are content to repeat the christological formulas shaped in the ancient debate with Judaism and Hellenism, and finalised within a narrowly Christian context. The new space imposes an unprecedented awareness of the limits of received historical language. It shows up the idiosyncratic and contingent status of Johannine christology and its Nicene and Chalcedonian elaboration. The truth expressed thereby in the past has become archaic and awaits a redescription which will be its dynamic equivalent under present epistemological conditions.

The Logos cannot be spoken of as an object independent of every 'subjective' perspective. First, because Christology originates not in the search for intemporal truths but in the conviction of the universal significance of what has taken place in the concrete figure of Jesus; it can never lose sight of its reference to this historical event. If the level of timeless truth is reached, the statements about this level are few in number and of an abstraction that limits their scope. Every construction of God-in-himself is rooted in the phenomenality of God-for-us; in fact it is only the deep structure of God-for-us that we isolate in formulating a description of the Trinity. Father, Logos, Spirit; silence, speech, breath; revealer, revealed, revelation (Barth); divine emptiness, form of this emptiness, immediacy of the two – these efforts to construct a trinitarian topology of the Christ-event have no coherence independent of their rootedness in this event. A Christology from above cannot begin from the Logos-in-itself, but only follow the phenomenological routes from an apprehension of the Logos as fulness of Christ.

Commenting on R. C. Moberly's question of 1889 – 'Is it true that he was very God? It is either true or false ... If it is not absolutely true, it is absolutely false' (Morgan, 85) – Rowan Williams remarks:

> I take it that part of the force of the doctrine of the hypostatic union is precisely to deny that 'Incarnation' is an isolable event in or prior to the biography of Jesus, and that 'divinity' is some *element* in that life ... A phrase like 'The Incarnation as the Basis of Dogma' begs a fundamental question by assuming that the fact of God's taking

human flesh is the fundamental theological datum, intelligible (at some level) in abstraction from the realities of truthfulness and finality, encounter and judgement, in the presence of the entirety of Jesus' story, which I have been trying to characterise as the source of the pressure towards dogmatic utterance. That the language of God's taking flesh remains a crucial part of the exposition of the judgement of Jesus' history needs to be argued, and argued with conscious attention to the particularity of the 'flesh' involved... Moberly is right to see dogma as representing the Christian concern with truth; but this concern is less to do with rationality or comprehensive elucidation, more involved with the need to preserve the possibility of the kind of encounter with the truthtelling Christ that stands at the source of the Church's identity... (88)

Christian truths are the formulation of a personal encounter, and depend for their utterance on a constant reference to this encounter and an existential correspondence to the one who has thus made himself known (Emil Brunner). As the expression of these truths grows away from this context, it loses its precise meaning and its referential efficacity.

It is this non-objectifiability which dooms every theoretical explication of the meaning of Christ – as of that of the Buddha – to a certain frustration. If it could be fully adequate, such an explication would make superfluous the witness of the Christian life, which gives the Gospel its force and intelligibility. Theoretical explication serves to highlight this witness and the figure of Christ himself in overcoming the interpretative frames of a mythology or piety which have become sources of blindness. Like the Buddha, Jesus represents a perfect (but not exclusive or exhaustive) realisation of a spiritual tradition, whence flows at once a great richness and a great simplicity. When theology loses sight of this central clarity, the witness of the saints brings it back to it, demanding of theology a luminous clarification of the meaning of Christ. Today, such a clarification is being sought at the crossing of three paths of thought: the exegetical quest for the biblical Christ, reflection on the liberative social implications of the Gospel, and interreligious questioning. The image of Christ which emerges at this crossroads is no longer a stable presence set before us as an object of adoration, but rather a dynamic process inscribed in the very texture of our life. This process destroys every rigid form, making itself felt on each occasion as a new departure. Every form taken by Christianity in history is relativised, but not the process of creative transformation by which Christianity lives and which it knows as the Christ (see J. B. Cobb, in Rouner, 176). Christ is not this or that figure that we project, but the entire process of transformation his name evokes. The meaning of Christ consists entirely in his identity with this universal process, and in the exemplarity with which he realises it and carries it to its perfect form.

The impossibility of objectifying the Logos is also apparent when one considers the texture of christological language, of which the basic terms – Son, Logos, Wisdom – are poetic metaphors, drawn from a certain tradition, and cannot be taken as a conceptually transparent description of that to which they obliquely refer. The use of these provisional designations obeys the art of deploying language as a skilful means in the environment of a given culture; as circumstances change, so must this language. Thus it is a mistake to multiply trinitarian statements in the belief that they give a grip on concrete and substantial entities. However refined the procedure by which one sets about stating truths at this level, even in the Johannine prologue or the Nicene Creed, they are expressed in a culture-bound language of which the metaphorical character shows the provisional status. Awareness of this situation may rob the great christological conflicts of much of their drama.

The objectivity of the trinitarian statements of the Patristic era depends on the topology of revelation of the Hellenistic world; that world having disappeared, this objectivity is itself menaced. To repeat is to betray. To suppose that one can master the biblical and the contemporary horizons starting from a dogmatic structure set up in Patristic times is a double obscurantism. This structure, like all historical constructs, is caught in a movement of perpetual alteration. Certain negative constraints remain in force – the prohibition against denying the divine unity or any distinction between Father, Son and Spirit; these rules are necessary to preserve the integrity of the New Testament revelation. But expressions such as *hypostasis* and *ousia* have meaning only in an obsolete framework. Representations of the Trinity-in-itself, such as the 'eternal generation' of Origen, the 'procession of the Word' and the 'spiration of the Spirit' as analysed in medieval theology, and above all the currently popular notion of a 'community of persons' are illegitimate projections from the biblical experience of the divine as Father, Logos and Spirit. In a different cultural context, if the Gospel had emerged in China for example, this experience might have been expressed by other names which would provide no basis for such representations.

The distinction between Father, Son and Spirit belongs in the first place to the phenomenality of revelation; it emerges within the 'divine milieu' opened by the New Testament as a basic law which assures the meaning of the propositions there enunciated. The quest to formulate the ontological basis for this law, the transcendental conditions of its possibility, moving from the revealed God to an independent discourse on God-in-himself, is not feasible, and even if it were, it would involve a distortion of the phenomenality of God as revealed. Certainly, one must maintain that this God really is, and that the trinitarian distinctions have an objective basis in God's being; but this is less a question of giving metaphysical foundations to the first-order language of faith than of defending the integrity of that language against scepticism. To elaborate a speculative metaphysics is a poor defence of the objectivity of first-order trinitarian language; a more effective one would retain only the essential, and the best formulation of this would be negative: 'it is false to deny that God exists and that he is one, it is false to say that the distinction between the three aspects of the phenomenality of God disappear at a deeper level of divine being'.

To keep open the perspectives of the New Testament a trinitarian theory is required, but it should be confined to a minimum and kept in the background. Some theologians see the mission of Jesus Christ as being primarily to disclose the mystery of the Trinity. This creates a distorted perspective on the event of salvation, of which the trinitarian doctrine is only a kind of syntax. 'When the Spirit of truth comes, he will guide you into all the truth'. The truth referred to is the full eschatological manifestation of Christ, 'the things that are to come' (Jn 16:13), and not the immanent Trinity, 'the eminent historicity of God himself', as Emilio Brito suggests. To talk of a '"hermeneutical circle" between the experience of faith and Trinitology as interpreter of revelation' (Brito, 167) invites a speculative idolatry of the immanent Trinity. Trinitology should be no more than logical and linguistic clarification of the structure of the revealed:

> The rules of language (one essence, two processions, three persons, four relations), perfectly justified as rules of language, have degenerated into the arithmetics of a transcendent ontology... If one wants to preserve the only intelligible and authentic significance of trinitarian doctrine, that which it has from revelation, one must remember again that 'significance cannot be separated from the access that leads to it' (Levinas), that 'the access is part of the significance itself'. (Bouillard, in Castelli 1969a, 338)

Even so refreshing a perpective as David Nicholl's invites similar caution:

> Paul wrote of the risen Christ as 'interceding for us' in heaven (Rom. 8:34). In the Epistle to the Hebrews Christ is the eternal high priest, representing the redeemed, and 'ever lives to make intercession for them' (Heb. 7:25). For the Johannine writer, 'we have an advocate with the Father, Jesus Christ the righteous' (1 John 2:1).

What sense can these images make unless they assume that there is within the life of the Godhead a conflict between Father and Son, a conflict of principles and interest whose resolution is only possible in the concrete case? (Nicholls, 6)

The role of the human Christ before the Father certainly gives access to the immanent Trinity, but that access also limits what can be thought or said about the Trinity. Conflict in the Bible is always between humanity and God, never between God and God. The idea that the risen Christ intercedes with the Father simply means that his atoning death reconciles humanity with God. To imagine the divine Logos as such interceding with God is incompatible with the biblical way of imagining God. The saving role of the human Jesus is an incarnation of this Logos, and such activities as pleading and interceding characterise this human incarnation rather than the Logos in its divine nature. A conflictual model of the relation between Jesus and the Father may be valuable, but its transference to the Trinity-in-itself is a needless doubling of the economy. Ascent from the work of the Trinity in the economy to the immanent Trinity should proceed negatively, shedding all models and conceptions based on human relationships, for the Trinity-in-itself is not human.

In the phenomenality of the Christ-event one recognises the God and the Spirit of the Hebrew scriptures, now associated with the one whom God has sent (the 'Son') and who gives the Spirit. The life, death, and post-Easter presence of Jesus Christ are an enfleshment in history of the Logos of God. This Logos, like the Spirit, has a long pre-Christian history, and does not entail, any more than the Spirit does, a breach in the divine unity. Once we surmount the tendency to speculate on the Trinity-in-itself, we see that the New Testament adds little to the Jewish understanding of the nature of God; it is but another chapter in what was always a very dynamic history. Its claims have chiefly to do with the divine action in history and with the dimensions of God's universal saving will. In the figure of Jesus Christ, the God of Israel reveals himself fully, as his saving will towards all humanity is declared and as he communicates the fulness of his Spirit. But this does not necessarily mean that God hid or only partially revealed his nature in the Old Testament, or that the Trinity is to be thought of as a secret now at last disclosed.

THE STATUS OF 'FLESH'

'The Word became flesh' is a statement of the same order as 'God is Spirit' or 'God is light'. As a résumé of the entire Christian vision and experience, it conveys a contemplative insight which one can appropriate only by a continual opening of the mind. Rigid, wooden conceptions of the personal identity between Jesus Christ and the eternal Logos have turned the nondual wisdom of the incarnational vision into a paradox that repels the mind and invites a dangerous investment of blind faith. The 'true God and true man' of Chalcedon is a piece of shorthand that risks freezing in a rigid ontological amalgam (Origen's *syntheton ti chrēma* or 'God-man') something that should rather be conceived as a process with delicate and subtle contours. To say that 'Jesus Christ is God' is an unskilful expression, unless one understands that 'is' in a special sense, integrating layers of reflective mediation. Such reflection will note that 'God' here means not the Father but the Logos. Against the proposals of Arianism, it has to be maintained that the Logos which is manifested in the Christ-event, and which is the inmost truth of that event, is nothing less than God; but it is God in a certain aspect, not as turned to Godself in absolute aseity but as turned to the other as creative Wisdom or Form or Word or Self-Revelation.

Introducing reflective mediations at the level of the 'flesh', one might say that the human historical reality centered on the figure of Jesus chimes so well with divine truth that it brings a definitive concretisation of this self-revealing aspect of God for humanity. This could be taken to mean that Jesus marks an evolutionary breakthrough of human reality to the level of Logos; such a breakthrough would be effected not by divine fiat, intervening arbitrarily in history, but as the result of contingent circumstances, a convergence of various factors permitting a quantum leap forward, as in the case of the evolution of the human brain itself. One advantage of thinking in this way is that it envisions the creative power of God as working in the same way in Christ as in all other events of evolution and of history.

If no human being is an island, the Son of man less that any other can be separated from his fellows, as is especially stressed in the Epistle to the Hebrews. Christ emerges from the humanity that we are, and if he is called an incarnation of the divine Logos, this means that the Logos has become incarnate in all human history. The Incarnation cannot be confined to the (non-existent) limits of a single human life. As Rowan Williams puts it:

> That movement of manifold change, the endless variety of imitations of Christ, is where we recognise the divine action as *spirit* – the same divine action as establishes the form of the incarnate logos, but working now to realise that form in a diversity as wide as the diversity of the human race itself. Thus, in theological terms, human history is the story of the discovery or realization of Jesus Christ in the faces of all women and men. The fulness of Christ is always *to be* discovered, never there already in a conceptual pattern that explains and predicts everything. (D'Costa, 8)

Rather than a concord of the human and divine natures at the moment of Jesus's conception, the Incarnation can be conceived as the dwelling of the Word among us across the entire historical career of Jesus, one of us. His 'divinity', like his 'resurrection', are better thought of as events or as emergences of meaning than as ontological attributes. Divinity does not attach itself to another thing; it is not a transferable quantity. The claim that Jesus Christ is 'true God' has no clear meaning on its own. Its meaning resides in the entire history in which the figure of Jesus is set.

The 'flesh' of John 1:14 is not the physical flesh of a single human being but the entire historical world in which the Logos pitches its tent. This Logos is at work in all history, but lodges there in a definitive way through the life, death and resurrection of Christ. The Logos is incarnate in Jesus in the totality of his relationships. Here the distinction between Jesus of Nazareth and the paschal Christ is of crucial import, for it appears that Jesus grows into his role of incarnate Logos and fully assumes it only after Easter (see Rom 1:3–4; Acts 2:36; John 7:39; Heb 5:8–9):

> The exaltation of the Son of Man, which happens to him because he has glorified God in his own death, is just this: to differ from the Logos no longer but to be the same as the Logos. For if 'he who is united to the Lord becomes one spirit with him' (I Cor. 6:17), so that it can no longer be said of him and the Spirit, 'They are two', how much more must we say that what of Jesus is human has become one with the Logos. (Origen, *Commentary on John* 32.325f)

The paschal Christ is, even less than the pre-paschal Jesus, an isolated individual. He is 'a life-giving spirit' (1 Cor. 15:45), the opening up of a pneumatic mode of existence, which is realised as a communal phenomenon: 'and dwelt *among us* ... from his fulness have *we all* received' (Jn 1:14, 16); 'that which we have seen and heard we proclaim also to you, so that you may have fellowship with us' (1 Jn. 1:3). The Word is incarnate in a communal movement which extends along historical paths to all humanity, and which has already engaged all humanity in principle, by reason of the interdependence of all. All aspects of human life can be ciphers of the divine; Christ emerges at the heart of this universal field of revelation and incarnation, from which he cannot be extracted. This universal revelation is cashed as a patchwork of local and particular revelations, and relates to the Christ-event not by being unilaterally subsumed into it, according to an a priori ontological necessity, but in historical negotiations which are mutually enlightening. Hegel's effort to link all history, and especially the history of religions, to Christ can be retrieved in more open style as the mapping of connecting-lines in a dialogical network. To 'take every thought captive to obey Christ' (2 Cor.

10:5) is then not an imperialistic aim, but the opening up of avenues of communication and communion.

Chalcedon teaches that:

> One and the same Christ, Son, Lord, Only begotten, made known in two natures (which exist) without confusion, without change, without division, without separation; the difference of the natures having been in no wise taken way by reason of the union, but rather the properties of each being preserved, and (both) concurring into one Person (*prosopon*) and one *hypostasis* – not parted or divided into two persons. (Grillmeier, 544)

To respect the unity and distinction of the natures, it should be stressed that Jesus is called God not in direct identification but in virtue of the *communicatio idiomatum*. The fact that the divine Logos is revealed across his human life implies an identification between the Logos and that life, which allows the attributes of the Logos to be conferred on him; a principle which has been abused in Catholic and Lutheran theology. As a human being, Jesus is one of us, in no way sheltered from the contingencies of historical existence. But insofar as his life becomes a vehicle of revelation in some definitive, unsurpassable way, it is seen as the Logos made flesh, and its ultimate meaning, the ultimate identity of Jesus, are henceforth to be sought in that dimension.

The Virgin Birth has functioned as a myth of pure origin enframing retrospectively the figure of Jesus. In Luke, by contrast, it can be seen as placing the figure of Jesus in the historical context of the promises made to Israel. To suppose that Jesus had a purer origin, a more autonomous identity than any other human being is to miss the reality of incarnation as a manifestation of the divine in the very element of the contingent, and the non-originary. We can begin to close the abyss between the idealisations of theological history and the contingencies of real history by recalling the notion of Christ's ontological divinity from his conception to a subtler apprehension of divinity manifested across the entire event of his life. Just as in the Eucharist, the meal-event is 'transubstantiated' into a communion in the paschal mystery, so that its basic reality or 'substance' now has no independent existence alongside what it has become, so in the case of Christ, his entire historical life in all its extensions is the Logos incarnate, and it has no independent meaning or significance not absorbed in this. A craving for reassurance prompts us to fix precisely the moment at which occur transitions involving the frontiers of our identity: the moment at which God infuses the human soul in evolution or in the foetus, the moment of death. Analogically, the moment of Christ's conception or of the eucharistic consecration have acquired a fetishistic status in theology. But the element of undecidability attending the attempt to define such moments forces us to a letting-go of identity and an acceptance of open-ended process as the very medium of our existence.

If Jesus could not become the Christ except in a precise cultural context, can he have been Christ, and Word incarnate, from his very conception, as classical christology teaches? Would this not entail that every contingency that might have cut short his activity – e.g. death in childhood – was a priori impossible? Such predestination of an individual's life cuts into the flow of history and denatures it. The historical life of Jesus would be protected, as no other human life is, from unforeseeable accidents and the common laws of existence. Instead of fulfilling the Messianic hopes and prophecies by a free creative act, he would obey a destiny fixed in advance and of which no circumstance could disturb the unfolding. With the loss of credibility of a such a myth of destiny, the docetic character of such conceptions becomes clear. A special providence may have presided over the life of Jesus, shaping even his death (another contingent event that might have been otherwise) into part of his messianic vocation. But if we say that the success of his mission was inevitable, due to the fact that he was from the start on a different ontological plane from other human beings, are we not in the realm of myth?

It is not easy to square the pursuit of such reflections with the claims of orthodoxy. Theology, indeed, seems condemned to this uneasiness, for orthodoxy is never something automatically guaranteed, but a balance to be kept in view as an ideal aim. To strike, or to sustain, the Chalcedonian note means resisting the attractions of adoptionism and Nestorianism while trying to do justice to their reminders of the contingency of the personal development of Jesus. In negotiating a path between opposed distortions we might do well to recall the traditional insistence that the modality of the union between the divine and the human in Jesus Christ is utterly ineffable (see Aquinas, *In 3 Sent.*, d.1, q.1). This apophatic note is not a bar to thinking the incarnation, but it qualifies our constructions of the meaning of Christ as merely provisional clarifications, which adjust currently usable concepts so that doubts and objections are pacified and the presence of Christ in Scripture and Church can communicate itself freely not only to the simple faithful but to questioning intellects.

Joseph Moingt, rejecting the adoptionist temptation, writes: 'the person of Jesus, at its foundation, acquires its "subsistence" in the word of love whereby God bestows on this person the gift of existing for God alone and whereby God consents to exist in Jesus in communion of Spirit' (Moingt, 628). The person of Jesus is thus from the start brought into being by the divine word, 'the word which pre-forms his person from the

moment of his coming into the world' (636) – a word which Moingt conceives as a 'pro-existent project' directed from eternity to the figure of
Jesus.

Insofar as all these constructions remain speculative and metaphysical
they are extremely fragile, and one seeks to ground them securely in a
phenomenological comprehension of the Christ-event. The reduction of
the eternal logos to a time-directed project, a possibility waiting to be
realised, is an unsatisfactory way of going behind the scenes of this event,
and entails a phenomenologically unconvincing reconstruction of the
life of Jesus. The notion that Jesus's identity is radically determined by
the divine Word which calls him into being could be deployed in the
following way: all human beings are called into existence by the Word;
and are oriented to an ultimate *reditio in Deum* mediated by the same
Word. Jesus corresponds to that divine call into existence, and call to
return to God, in so perfect a way that his human life becomes a definitive expression of the Word in human and historical terms, its enfleshment;
his identity as a human being is thus in its inner core identical with the
presence of the Word in the world; he is the man of the Word (*homo
assumptus*). Thus, with Origen (*Contra Celsum* 6.47f) and Karl Rahner
we might interpret the hypostatic union as the perfect realisation of the
reality of grace, on the model of the moral union described in 1
Corinthians 6:17: 'he who is united to the Lord becomes one spirit with
him'. Though Jesus grows in grace, growing into his role, there is no
duality of subjects: the Word is his ultimate identity and the human
subject is perfectly at one with the Word.

This may recall Piet Schoonenberg's theory that the Logos is first
'personalised' in Jesus; but there is no need to deny a distinct hypostatic
identity of the Logos independent of the incarnation; such an identity has
little to do with personhood in the human sense and is not a rival to Jesus'
human personality. Thus the union between Jesus's personhood and the
hypostasis of the Logos could be described as enhypostatic (Cyril of
Alexandria), and we can even adopt the Neo-Chalcedonian *anhypostasia*,
since Jesus has no ultimate identity independent of the Logos. It is
important in any case to develop such hunches phenomenologically, not
as abstract metaphysical patterns; and the phenomena are not accessible
independently of the communal praxis in which they emerge.

One could compare the manifestation of the eternal Word in the life of
Jesus with the attainment of a supreme illumination in the life of the
Buddha. An absolute truth breaks through in these lives, in function of
cultural conditions. Starting from this breakthrough, narratives are constructed which aim to do justice to the incomparable event which has
taken place in these lives, but which risk falsifying everything by a docetic

short-circuit: mythologies of the birth of the child Jesus or the child Gautama; an ontology of the pre-existence of Jesus (first as pre-designated eschatological Messiah; then as eternal Logos); fables of the anterior lives of the Buddha, also issuing in ontological theories of a fundamental pre-existent Buddha-essence (*adhibuddha, dharmakāya*).

Jesus is the man who, carrying to perfection the insights of his tradition, discovered the true relation between God and humanity; this quite contingent evolution obeys the pressure of the divine Logos which seeks to make itself known, and which does so with divine power in the teaching of Jesus. The ontological explanations which were constructed beginning from this event must be recalled to it in order to keep their credibility and avoid distorting what they serve to interpret.

THE ESCHATOLOGICAL PRIMACY OF CHRIST

If the Logos is not incarnate in the sharply-delimited individual figure of Jesus, but in human history as brought into focus by this figure, does this mean that every particular form Christ takes is dissolved in a universal transformative flux? No, for even if the dimensions of the meaning of Christ exceed our grasp, the encounter with the Crucified anchors our thought about him in a concrete event. Christ is not an abstract emblem or symbol of the salvation afoot everywhere, but rather gives it the concrete and historical character it lacked. Salvation enters history not by an arrest of the movement of history, its enclosure within a salvation-history centred on the life of Jesus, but rather through events in which the cause of God is revealed as one with the historical struggle of humanity. The uniqueness of the death of Christ lies in the way in which it manifests the radical identity of these two instances. Every effort to live history religiously and religion historically is henceforth summoned and guided by the figure of the Crucified. Christ's universality as Word made flesh, or as focus of a universal striving of divine truth towards incarnation, is inseparable from this singularity of the cross.

The crucifixion is also a merely contingent event. It is the way that Jesus's prophetic insight into the identity of divine will and human liberation was acted out under particular circumstances. Yet, just as in Heidegger care, being-unto-death, and resoluteness concentrate and project forward the authentic essence of human existence, so this uniquely eloquent event concentrates the essence of the human struggle and propels it forward to its final goal. Thus we overcome mythical structures that are no longer credible by founding claims about Christ's uniqueness and his divinity in his eschatological role, and by founding this in turn in the exemplarity of his living-out of the prophetic insight into the nature of history, a living-out that itself is a distinctive historical event – the only event within history that can take the measure of history itself.

What happened on Calvary derives this unique authority not from its historical and cultural particularity – the tenebrous imbroglio of a vanished world – but from the forces it joins together: divine transcendence and the human struggle against oppression. 'His bodiliness and his passion are the will of God and the salvation of the world' (Hilary of Poitiers, *Commentary on Matthew* 4.14). Christianity consists in nothing other than the maintenance of this conjunction. This is less a stupefying paradox than the reconciliation of two realities destined to meet: divine holiness and human freedom. Note the specific modality of this conjunction: Christ is presented as an executed criminal, not as an enlightened prince. The cutting edge of the Incarnation is seen here, at a point where the logic of prophetic monotheism is taken to its extreme. In the Buddha's peaceful life every phenomenon is ordered in view of the eternal, but in Christ's prophetic career God is at grips with the particular injustices of historical existence. Buddhist doctrine has no fundamental need of individual Buddhas; the basic structure of bondage and liberation would remain the same even without them. But Christian doctrine cannot be disentangled from the concrete, historical role assumed by Jesus. The prophetic tradition culminates in a single man, chosen by God, while the Buddhas are ultimately numerous, all discreetly retiring behind their teaching. The style of interpretation that the memory of Jesus requires is prophetic and engaged, and always concerns concrete cases, whereas Buddhist wisdom focuses on the essential structures of existence, often unmasking the element of illusion in the apparent urgencies of history.

Paul van Buren, limiting the boundless universality automatically claimed for Christ as saviour, centers his significance in a specific historical event: Jesus opens a new chapter in history by prophetically discerning God's purpose for the Gentiles. This event is 'God's radical new expression of his eternal faithfulness to his creation, whereby he has added to his beloved Israel also his beloved Church in the service of his redemptive purpose' (van Buren, 252). The divine Logos is identified as God's 'covenantal outgoingness' revealed in the figure of Jesus:

> He who has looked into the face of this suffering Jew... has seen the Father (John 14:9), not a being of one substance with the Father (Nicea), not a divine creature (Arius), but God the Father of Israel and of Jesus Christ. That is how God makes himself present to and known by his Church – he addresses them in just this way: they are

addressed by that Jew. Consequently their fully appropriate confession, made while looking directly into the face of this crucified Jew, is, 'My Lord and my God' (John 20:28)... The move that the Fourth Gospel dares the Church to make is that of risking and trusting the judgement that this man is precisely the way in which the suffering Father of Israel and all creation has chosen to open a radically new chapter in the continuing history of his involvement in human affairs. (224)

Associating the human Jesus immediately with the eternal God of Israel, van Buren is impatient with the language of the classical trinitarian and christological doctrines. Of the expression 'the divinity of Christ' he writes:

That phrase sounds as if the Church knew something reliable about divinity and so felt it was justified in predicating this of Christ. The fact of the matter, of course, is just the opposite: the Church has learned whatever little it may know about divine matters from the things concerning Jesus of Nazareth. It might well speak of the Christ-likeness of divinity, or, more boldly, the Jesusness of God. It has no grounds whatsoever for speaking of the divinity of Christ... The highest possible Christology will be one that sees in the lowly crucified one the very heart of God the Father... The lowliness of this crucified Jesus is his 'divinity', his Godliness, and just this is what is confessed by the Church when it says of this Jew, 'God of God, Light of Light, true God of true God'. (293–5)

The primary phenomenon of the revelation of God in Jesus need not exclude the background implication of the divinity of the Logos, as providing the space in which that primary phenomenon can emerge fully. Instead of telescoping the language of Nicaea onto the figure of the historical Jesus, it is better to respect the distance between the two levels of language, seeing Nicaea as a set of rules for speaking of the Logos. Dogma is not intended as a direct transcription of the New Testament revelation of God in Christ; when it has usurped that role the result has been a forgetfulness not only of the Jewish humanity of Jesus but of the dynamic of revelation in its New Testament forms. That God is from all eternity not only Father, but 'covenantal outgoingness' in Word and Spirit, and that this outgoingness of God finds its fullest historical actualisation in the life, death and resurrection of Jesus Christ is a version of the classical doctrines that could embrace the language of Nicaea and Chalcedon, with suitable hermeneutical adjustments.

Van Buren never lingers on this eternal Word in any other form than that of its historical manifestations, among which he gives pride of place to the Torah:

> A Church that means to affirm the eternal convenant between God and the Jewish people will have to put the Torah first ... The consequence for the Church's Christology is that the term 'the Word of God' will need to be thought through primarily from the perspective of Sinai. (247)

This reinsertion of Jesus in the Jewish context heals the violent divorce with Judaism created when Jesus is made the absolute and only vehicle of God's saving presence. Jesus is the occasion of the extension of the covenantal grace at work in Judaism, and it is by this extension that he incarnates God's outgoingness with a measure of 'grace and truth' (Jn 1:17) that is unlimited in principle – 'it is not by measure that he gives the Spirit' (Jn 3:34) – though its full realisation remains a matter of eschatological hope. The violent divorce between the Torah-event and the Christ-event is one of the tragic obstacles to the unfolding of grace and truth; another is the violent exclusivism or inclusivism practised by Christians towards the non-Christian religions.

Fuller dimensions of the Incarnation come into view as the calling of the Gentiles is seen to include an opening of the Gospel to the human quest for truth and salvation in its entire reach. As Christians learn from the religious vision of others and from their social and political struggle to create a better world, the Kingdom message of the prophets and of Jesus grows towards the universality that is intrinsic to it. The Kingdom ceases to be a sectarian claim and is seen to be coterminous with the divine Torah or with the divine Logos. Van Buren does expect 'theological discoveries through interfaith dialogue' and that 'the Church will learn better to understand and accept the Lordship of Christ through discovering what Christ's Spirit has been accomplishing outside the Church' (271). But the privileged place of covenantal language in his diction might impede the emergence of alternative languages in this dialogue. The 'Jewish-Christian reality' may be demystified as it comes into perspective in relation to the other religious paths. Its redescription in an interreligious perspective will not abolish the covenantal character of God (for God cannot contradict himself), but may show the biblical covenant to be but one form of the working of the divine in history – a form that can however claim a certain primacy in virtue of its unsurpassed historical concreteness and eschatological reach. The eschatological dimension of God's revelation in Torah and Christ cannot be confined to the Jewish or Christian communities, for the revelation is intrinsically destined to all humanity. One might toy with a Joachimite triad: the Jews are the ones through whom God was first made known in history; the Christian community of Jews and Gentiles is based on the fuller explicitation of that knowledge in the life and teaching of Christ; and now the Spirit is leading us to the ultimate all-inclusiveness of the Kingdom community, as we reach out to the entire human family with its traditions, renouncing the sectarian enclosures that have prevailed until now.

Sociologists sometimes caricature Christianity as a religion of pure interiority divorced from political and social reality:

> For his God is so detached from the bonds of this world that it would have no meaning to confront in his name the earthly thrones and dominations. It is in the secret places of the heart that he gives himself, at an infinite distance from what Caesar demands, and which must be rendered to him in the quiet assurance that the true Kingdom is elsewhere. God's universal omnipotence is not to take shape in a future worldly empire, but is attested here and now in its radical foreignness to the affairs of this world, a foreignness such that it knows no people but only interior beings who have been elevated to a capacity to understand him by their own detachment from the things of the world. (Gauchet, 160)

This deformation of the Christian message may correspond to a spiritualistic or gnostic temptation which has accompanied Christianity throughout its history, but it does not match the reality of evangelical charity either in its biblical charter or as effectively practised. Reading the sayings of Jesus against the background of the prophetic tradition, we see that the coming of the Kingdom has nothing to do with individualistic withdrawal; it explodes at the heart of history as a communitarian, political and social event. To think this out fully requires a practical context in which it is enacted. It may well be that even the New Testament praxis is only a primitive or experimental enactment of Christianity, and that its deficiencies leave a residue of abstraction or vagueness in the accounts of what the Kingdom entails; or its may be that the praxis and the accounts were perfectly adapted to that time but have to be elaborated anew for ours.

If rather than reducing the Incarnation to an invisible event of a spiritual and ontological order and treating its concrete historical effects as inessential, we focus instead on these effects, seeking to interpret them as indicative of an eschatological conjunction of the human struggle and God's saving purpose, then the distinctiveness of Jesus is seen as residing in the new orientation he brings to human history. The cross desacralises salvation by bringing it into accord with fleshly realities – not only individual suffering and death, but also communal challenges of injustice and violence. In the contemporary economy of meaning and value, which refuses to be governed by great doctrinal principles, the christological faith survives as an empirical apprehension (in a broad sense) of the meaning of Christ. As a figure of justice and solidarity at the human level and of God's eschatological will, Christ crucified reveals to every generation, in varying presentations, the basic truth about God and humanity – a truth which exists only in relationships between God and humanity, as a dynamic interchange from which a pure definition of God or of the creature made in God's image can never be extracted.

Replaced in this context, 'justification by faith' signifies that if we are associated with Christ crucified, we are headed for the future willed by God. So we are free in principle from past bondage and put in contact with the deeper vital movement of history, made flesh in the life and death of Jesus; this gives meaning (justification) to our activities and ends the futility of an aimless existence. This event of justification takes place between God and humanity and cannot be formulated in an objectified way; hence the immense confusion of the debate on this topic, in which one appreciates the great voices, those of a Luther or a Newman, which speak from the heart of that 'between' – 'everything . . . is played out in the entre' (D, 222) – even though when they go on to cast their convictions in metaphysical form they become entangled in antinomies (see O'Leary, 1991).

The primacy of Christ, then, is less a matter of ontological superiority than a precise and irreplaceable function. It is true that the message of the coming of the Kingdom remains quite indeterminate as far as its content goes. It is the messenger himself who gives it a concrete face, enacting in his life and death the principles of the future prepared by his Father and creating a community which is to live in view of the promised end. All the visible historical acts of Christ and of his community are but an inadequate anticipation of the fulness of the eschatological Christ. Nevertheless, the coherence of the witness they constitute renders credible their claim to light up the orientation of history as God has willed it. The eschatological future is proclaimed in universalist terms, as the accomplishment of the hopes of all humanity and as surpassing all particular forms of historical Christianity – which is itself but a prophetic sign serving to keep open the promise of this future; yet there is nevertheless an indissoluble bond between that promised fulfilment and the historical figure of Jesus Christ.

The figure of the Crucified points toward an unknown future, but it indicates the path of life which is most appropriate to the expectation of this future. Dazzlingly simple, but at the same time unfathomably enigmatic, the gap between this historical figure and the eschatological one that exceeds the resources of the imagination leads to a great variety of interpretations. The foundational event of the Gospel withdraws from our grasp, and its eschatological clarification remains of course utterly unimaginable. So we spell out our series of gospels, using well the interval. We settle down in each of these gospels in turn, only to be dislodged each time by the untamed residue of the Gospel's prophetic thrust.

The Gospel is a wound which the tradition wants to heal. Christianity can be seen as a system which 'trans-codes its initial conditions by transforming them into inherent moments of its self-development', repressing 'the real of a violence *founding* the system and none the less *disavowed* once the system reaches the level of its self-reproduction' (Žižek, 214f). When the authentic figure of Christ emerges anew in history, the original wound is reopened, and the historical Jesus is rediscovered under a surprising aspect. At the same time the eschatological hope revives, and one realises afresh that the Christ to come is always greater than what we have thought we understood about him up to now. When the Gospel inspiration is most alive, its judgement on the past is most severe: the prophets, Paul, and Luther are unjust to tradition, for they judge it by eschatological standards or in the name of an impossible step back to 'the beginning'. This injustice is of the essence of prophetic religion, for it lives by a future opened up in divine promise (the promise inscribed in the heart of the Torah or in the teachings of Jesus), and any received formulation or enactment – even the letter of Scripture itself – will seem an alienation and a betrayal of the original opening.

A historical figure can acquire all his significance from his dedication to an absolute. Thus the meaning of the Buddha is *nirvāṇa*; he is its contingent, fragile, historical vehicle. Such a life discloses the meaning of every human life, as it enacts our deepest and least acknowledged aspirations. The significance of Jesus Christ is resumed in his mission of announcing the coming of the Kingdom; only this gives the contingencies of his life and death their universal, post-paschal, pneumatic meaning. The Gospel texts exhibit a well-focused grasp of the significance of Jesus in their eschewal of biographical curiosity and subordination of every narrative to the essential theme of the Kingdom. One may detect a similar economy in the Buddhist canon, despite its prolixity. The founder of a religion has only one reason for his existence, which the witnesses seek to extract in its purity. Having rediscovered the eschatological meaning of the life of Christ, we can attempt to rethink all the ontological categories of incarnation and redemption in eschatological terms. We could say that Jesus Christ incarnates the divine Word in living a human life entirely open to the Kingdom, and in sharing this mode of life with others and inviting them to live it. The human may be rendered as transparent to the divine in the Buddha as in Christ, but the eschatological character of Jesus' message and the paschal mystery gives them an extra dimension, making them the incarnation of the Logos specifically in history.

To be sure, this eschatological language is still a Jewish and Christian construction, a contingent and fragile myth permitting a grasp of what is happening in the Christ-process, and whose function is to go much further than its direct content suggests. When we set the figure of Jesus in a cosmos which is not thousands but thousands of millions of years old, and which is headed not towards an imminent end, as Jesus expected, but towards further billions of years of evolution, what becomes of his eschatological claim? In a million years will a vastly transformed human species be able to make anything of the historical figure of Jesus?

The enlargement and transformation of the memory of Christ and of the eschatological horizon he opened up is a project that will leave much of the biblical matrix behind. Yet the New Testament itself, in its basic thrust, calls for this enlargement, in the course of which its central words are renewed again and again, even if the letter of the text shrivels into ever greater obscurity. The presence of Christ as a life-giving spirit outstrips the limits of first-century Palestine or any given stage in humanity's evolution, for it is a dynamic orientation to the divine fulfilment of the human project and is coterminous with the illimitable openness of the human future. 'My words will not pass away' (Mk 13:31) because their ultimate source is not human but divine; because their content – love, truth, justice – is of permanent bearing, however primitive its expression; because they are only a beginning, straining proleptically toward the eschatological goal which fulfils them; and because the Spirit continually reinterprets them in the Christian community, so that they bear new fruit from year to year.

There is a pluralism of eschatologies even within the New Testament, and the eschatological focus has wavered throughout history in tandem with the shifting fashions of human hope and desire. The ancient eschatological and apocalyptic schemas will have to be rethought when more light comes from interreligious encounters. Every religious message has to 'pay the price of its existence' (W. E. Hocking), and cannot surpass the conditions of its historical contingency. To demythologise eschatology, we could try to redefine it in almost tautological terms: it is that toward which the Christ-event points, the full truth of that which has taken place in Christ. This would allow the notion of eschatology to mean that toward which the whole spiritual quest of humanity points, the full truth of the religions, and all else.

To see Christ as the eschatological prophet, however, risks reducing the Incarnation to a genial intuition of Jesus identifying the divine will with human liberation. The titles conferred on him would then be only a retrospective confirmation of the value of his insights and his fidelity in living them out. As the focusing genius of his religious tradition, who himself drew out its deepest consequences, he might well be acclaimed in mythical language as its Messiah. The danger of such a reductive account need not, however, prevent us from saying that all that we designate by the term 'the Incarnation' is mediated by the privileged historical role of Jesus Christ as the one who reveals the concrete significance of Jewish monotheism for human history beyond the frontiers of Israel.

One might risk the following proposition: 'it is because Jesus was such a man at such a moment in history that he became Son of God'. The inverted form of this proposition – 'it is because he is Son of God that Jesus became man at that moment in history to reveal this truth' – can have a certain value on the level of hymnic evocation, but it should not blind us to what is afoot on the scene of history, before our eyes, namely, that a man shows forth in his teaching and in his life the unity of divine truth and the truth of human existence, and that from the enactment of this unity flows a charge of pneumatic power, the resurrection. The resurrection-event resides less in the phenomena of the appearances or the empty tomb, which witness to it, than in the pneumatic unfolding of the full meaning of Jesus, now known as Christ, in the hearts and in the lives of the first witnesses to him. This spiritualising interpretation is suggested by the one eye-witness account we have (Gal. 1:16; 1 Cor. 15:8), for we may take it that Paul's experience was of the same order as that of the other apostles a few years earlier. If the appearance to more than five hundred brethren (1 Cor. 15.6) corresponds to Pentecost, then the nature of the resurrection experience may be less inaccessible than is usually thought. The encounter with the risen one is in continuity with the normal pneumatic life of the Church with its bounty of charisms and spiritual insight.

Are these events intrinsically more mysterious than those of the life of the Buddha, who realised, taught, and lived the path to a universal liberation from suffering? Jesus opens history to the power of a God who saves. The Buddha opens human existence to the dissolution of its illusions, and to the vision of reality as it is, in the enjoyment of *nirvāṇa*. Both established modes of religious life which remain viable and verifiable. Both were human beings, who became the instruments and revealers of a transcendent reality.

It may be that as one draws near to Jesus, Jesus himself disappears and one is with the God of Jesus, just as when one draws near the Buddha, the

Buddha himself disappears and one is on the path to *nirvāṇa*. The Christ cult and Christ myth of the early Church are then a penetration of the essence of Jesus, as openness to the Father, not the erection of Christ as a screen against his message. But in the case of Christ one must recognise a non-duality between the instrument and the divine action which takes place by its means: 'I and the Father are one' (Jn 10:30); 'He who has seen me has seen the Father' (Jn 14:9). A unique status: the one who reveals the action of God in human history is also the one through whom God inserts himself in an exemplary way into human history. But need we oppose so rigidly revelation and insertion: is there not also a non-duality between making known the convergence of God and humanity, and bringing about this very convergence? The nirvanic transparency of the life of the Buddha has made him a 'refuge'. Perhaps it is in a similar fashion that the utter obedience to God's saving will expressed in the life of Jesus makes him saviour and Lord?

It will be objected that the primacy we claim for Christ is merely relative, and the stress on eschatology reflects the bias of a history-oriented culture. The eschatological vision did emerge within such a culture, and it may have to be enlarged greatly for its kernel of universal appeal to become manifest. The enfleshment of the Word is not an abstract lesson in philosophy of history, but enactment in human relationships of divine love – the Christmas story with its family comings and goings and its political schemings already shows the Incarnation as steeped in a social and relational web. This fleshly milieu is what we call history, but our present schemes for interpreting the human adventure are as flimsy and provisional as those of any other age or culture. Salvation comes along other paths than this engagement within human historical relationships. If it is measured solely in terms of spiritual liberation, for example, or of upright living or pure worship of God, then one would have to say that there is no reason to claim a primacy of Christian salvation over Buddhist, Jewish or Islamic salvation. But if history can be redeemed, then Christ alone emerges as the historical saviour.

Burton Mack denounces such claims as mythological, pointing out that the myth of pure Christian origins has in reality added to the burden of tragedy in human history: 'The holocaust was also a gospel event' (Mack, 375). Yet his sociological explanation of the myth seems implausible: we are asked to see Jesus as a Cynic philosopher, his personality in the passion narrative as a product of martyrological narrative convention, the Eucharist as a Hellenistic symposium, Paul as 'an unstable, authoritarian person' and his gospel as the production of 'a brilliant mind' (98). The Christ of faith was created as a reference for authorising unconventional practice and adjudicating internal conflicts over authority, and his stature ('the very stupendous claims made for Jesus') grew through 'a feedback mechanism whereby, once accountability had been transferred to the champion, the champion was there to assume ever greater burden for the new' (353).

A similar account could be given of Buddhist projections back onto the historical Buddha, and it would accord with the constructive, imaginary character of religious conceptions. Yet the founding event in each case has deeper roots than this theory can explain, and it opens up a way of life and a vision of existence which demythologisation of the sources may enhance rather than discredit. The pluralistic texture of the Christ-event, if we can recover it, undermines the destructive myth of innocence, plunging us into a labour of interpretation in which the Jews are our indispensable partners. Even if the figure of Jesus was constructed as a pure logocentric origin, its deconstruction may reveal that in a subtler way something new and powerful did originate within the matrix of the time, in indissoluble connection with the person of Jesus of Nazareth.

It might be objected that eschatology is too murky a topic to allow any firm self-positioning of Christian existence or language. It has always been a field of controversy, full of polarisations – between Church and Kingdom, the hieratic and the prophetic, ideology and utopia, world-affirmation and world-denial, prophetic realism and apocalyptic fantasy, realised and futuristic eschatology, imminent and delayed parousia. All these old polarisations continue in new forms today. But they also indicate the middle way which overcomes them, the incarnate balance between a positive naming of God's purposes in the present and a sceptical review of this naming in order to prevent any absolutising of human language and insight (see P. D. Hanson, 210). The unresolved controversies of the eschatological tradition have at least the merit of keeping us from resting easily in any vision of the meaning of historical existence. Faith in God's saving will goes hand in hand with questioning of the signs of the times in an ongoing effort to discern that will.

To speak of God's will and purposes is clumsy anthropomorphism, yet it names what faith senses as the centre and foundation of reality, a truth which attests itself powerfully in Scripture and in conscience as well as in the thrust of cosmic evolution. As opposed to Kaufman's 'cosmic serendipity', such primitive expressions as 'the will of God' point to that which transcends any order we can grasp. 'Thy will be done' is a prayer that leaps beyond cosmic process and consigns all things to the sovereign disposal of the ultimate good. Eschatology reduces to the belief in such ultimate sovereign goodness, beyond all identifiable worldly orders.

This transcendence may make eschatology a vacuous discourse. The content of eschatological hope is not spelled out in Jewish or New Testament apocalyptic. They fade into dream as if deliberately to frustrate the quest for a concrete vision. Yet on the other hand the core of biblical eschatology is the fact that salvation is indissociably tied to the real history of humanity and takes the form of a promise bearing on its future. Even the most unworldly forms of biblical apocalypse retain this preoccupation with the meaning and goal of history, a theme which has secure theological status. Today the entire scaffolding of the biblical eschatologies – including the ideas of election, Messiah, and salvation-history – has to be restructured in the light of the alternative viewpoints of Eastern traditions, which compensate for their reticence about history by a keener insight into the depth-stucture of temporal existence. Furthermore, a revision of all religious traditions in the light of current cosmology and sociobiology could broaden the eschatological problematic to fit the dimensions of the known universe.

Yet none of this restructuring is likely to give the eschatological dimension the well-defined contours characteristic of ideological predictions such as those of Marxism. Its biblical emblem is the cloud: 'they will see the Son of man coming in clouds' (Mk 13:26). It muddies our coordinates, arising as a disturbing question in the midst of our life and our history in an always unpredictable way. We are tempted to repress this dimension or to put it in its place so that it can no longer upset us. Even in theology it can be felt to be an irritating topic, a distraction from the task of constructing the system of our thoughts or of reconstructing the historical past. But if we permit our language to show its flaws, the law of Babel inscribed in it, then eschatology, far from seeming foreign to the task of theology, appears as the very milieu in which this task is to be pursued. The task of theology is to maintain the eschatological tension of the language of faith, so as to keep it open to the ever-greater God. The labour of construction or reconstruction is entirely subordinate to this task. Forgetting this, theology loses touch with the basic conditions of its existence.

The eschatological future, in which faith will yield to a vision face to face, is ineffable; when we try to speak of it we fall into flat mythologies of full presence. Yet it may be spoken of obliquely, for it is inscribed *en creux* in a Christian discourse aware of its imperfection and finitude. Such a discourse remarks its own provisoriness and fragmentariness, measuring the extent of its lack so that it is all the more galvanised by eschatological longing. Its emptiness of substantial attainments points to a God who eludes the grasp of every concept and is revealed as dwelling at the very heart of this emptiness. Indeed, we may suppose that the face to face vision will not fill in this empty space, but free us for a more radical experience of emptiness.

Visionaries may imagine apocalyptic glory, but the normal life of faith knows the eschatological only by the gaps in its own performance and language. Love lived under the limitations of time, in daily fidelity, is a fragile sowing in view of an inconceivable harvest. To limit its scope to its visible fruits is a formula for despair; hope keeps open a space of promise always exceeding the provisional closure brought by a temporal achievement. Similarly, the language of faith is never more than a temporary figure of a truth which it can never definitively fix. All is passage, and becomes a cul-de-sac if one tries to fix one's dwelling there.

Beyond myths of inevitable progress or decline, theological realism takes as base the poverty and the possibilities of the present, as the biblical tradition permits them to be grasped. A language steeped in this present and tempered by a long historical experience can confront the tragic aspects of history while keeping open the horizons of hope. It cultivates a discreet and judicious tone, seeking the words called for by the pressure of the *kairos*, neither in flights of Utopian imagination (Moltmann) nor in totalising speculations on the meaning of history (Pannenberg). Renouncing the ambition of mastering the past and predicting the future, it rediscovers a freedom that this ambition inhibited. Instead of trying to complete historical and sociological insight with a theological hyper-insight, or to the contrary losing itself in a cloud of unknowing, eschatological faith is content with knowing what it can and ought to know, namely the Christian meaning of our present.

What secures this eschatological middle path is above all the person of Jesus Christ. The cross gives a sharp historical edge that stems the drift into utopia, while at the same time disrupting all ideological recuperation. The constant refocusing of the figure of Christ, in the light both of the tension-ridden Old Testament background and the equally chequered history of the Christian community, provides a graphic correlative for the shifting emphases of eschatological vision. Confidence in the Saviour takes us a step beyond the investment we may have made in any given style of eschatological hope, and even where there is a radical divergence among Christians about the goal to which they strive, they are at least united in naming it Jesus Christ.

THE PROBLEM OF PRE-EXISTENCE

The position we have arrived at is close to Bultmann's view that all claims for Christ derive their truth from the fact that he is the Eschatological Event. Bultmann saw pre-existence as a mythical projection from the authority of the kerygma, 'an idea of which we no longer have any need' (quoted in Kuschel, 167). He 'degnosticises' Paul's pre-existence language to reveal its existential core: 'the person and destiny of Christ do not derive their origin and meaning from the network of innerworldly events but only from the fact that therein God has been at work' (178). John's pre-existence statements mean that 'the real legitimisation of Jesus is precisely his earthly unlegitimisability' (188).

Yet faced with a doctrinal tradition which has not hesitated to step 'behind' the Christ-event to its ontological foundations, we can refrain from the traditional ontology of Trinity and Incarnation only at the cost of implicitly affirming some form of unitarianism. Karl-Josef Kuschel proposes a rather full-blooded ontology of the pre-existent Christ, but one that is problematic both in what it affirms (a pre-existence of the humanity of Jesus) and in what it denies (a pre-existent eternal Logos). One can defend the Logos-doctrine as providing the space within which the Christ-event can deploy its significance, while rejecting myths of a pre-existence of the human Jesus. These doctrinal points have a phenomenological function, and are subordinate to the event of revelation, from which they cannot be abstracted. They belong to a secondary level of reflection, as spelling out a negative logic that our statements about Christ should not transgress. Doctrine may shed light on the Christ-event, but since that event is its only source and warrant we are moving within a strict hermeneutical circle which leaves little room for a theology from above.

Kuschel loses something of the specificity of Christian revelation from the moment that he sets the christological problematic in the context of an alleged perpetual human quest for 'the beginning of all beginnings, the ground of all grounds, the origin of all origins of time, history and cosmos' (20). He conflates under the rubric of pre-existence such heterogeneous phenomena as Barth's sense of the sovereignty of God and Hofmannsthal's poetic vision of an originary state of 'pure magic' in which self and world are one, 'a unity before all temporal and spatial differentiation' (87). Modern painters and dialectical theologians are seen as sharing a quest for 'the basic structure of being, the depths of creation, the originary ground of the real, which is God' (96). This language elides what is specific about the world of Barth and Bultmann, falling back into just the religiose rhetoric that they sought to overcome. Barth at his best focused on a biblical and existential paradox: not a pre-existent eternal invading time, but a divine word confronting us in judgement and grace.

Kuschel, like van Buren, is inspired by the later Barth's notion of God's 'self-determination' in the covenant. Not content with the pre-existent Logos, Barth projected the flesh-and-blood figure of Jesus back into the realm of pre-existence: 'In free self-determination, God has from eternity chosen to be the bearer of this name (Jesus)' (124); 'Since this Jesus Christ – including his earthly fate – already "exists from eternity in the divine decree," it was not only fitting and worthy, but even *"necessary"* for God to be the Creator' (132). This *hysteron proteron* undercuts the reality of historical contingency and human freedom. It would be enough to say that God is by nature covenantal; any further effort to predetermine how that covenantal love works itself out in creation and salvation history is a metaphysical construction doubling real history with a shadowy transcendental history that undermines its reality.

The metaphysical obsession with pre-existence which would project the human Jesus back into eternity distracts from the concrete phenomenality of what is revealed in Christ. If instead we confine pre-existence language to the Logos, God's covenenantal outgoingness, to be conceived above all in negative terms as resisting our totalising grasp, then we leave Christ free to give this Logos its historical face. The ungraspable, empty Logos is incarnate in a succession of singular forms and in the dialectical tensions between them, and the figure of Jesus Christ focuses this incarnational process distinctively, eschatologically. When theology gives a face to the pre-existent Logos above and beyond these forms, it creates a rival to them, which by its claim to be their metaphysical ground risks eclipsing them.

Kuschel's reduction of the pre-existent Logos to a pre-existence of Jesus proceeds from the post-paschal insight that 'the person of Jesus Christ belongs fully to the definition of the essence of God' (643). He develops this idea in strained metaphysical argumentation on the notions of eternity and time: 'Jesus Christ is – as Spirit and in the Spirit – present to all times, contemporary with all times, free in regard to all times. Nothing else is meant when we talk of the pre-existence of Christ' (644). This language needs to be recalled to its phenomenological basis. The classic Logos-doctrine leaves to Jesus all his historical contingency, furnishing a space in which his revelatory significance can unfold, without any need to inflate his humanity so as to have it share divine eternity 'from always', ripping it out of the realm of space, time and contingency. Chalcedon's teaching that the divine and human natures are 'unmixed', prevents mythic conflations between God's eternal nature and God's self-manifestation in time. That Jesus gives a human historical face to God's eternal self-determination does not entail that God determines himself further in becoming incarnate. The incarnation is the Logos of God unfolded in our human world, but it does not require any mythic humanisation of God.

For Kuschel, the notion of pre-existence comes from the reflection that 'If the risen one has such significance for God, must he not always already have been in God's thoughts?' (601). The divinity of Christ means simply that '*God himself* has revealed himself in Jesus and that Jesus himself can be understood at the deepest level only from God' (604). Somewhere along the trajectory of this approach one might retrieve the contemporary sense of Chalcedon, but as it stands it is reductive. Kuschel is happy with Schillebeeckx's interpretation of the divinity of Christ:

> According to Christian faith Jesus is (a) the decisive and definitive revelation of God, and (b) he shows us therein at the same time what and who we humans can ultimately be and ought actually to be . . . We cannot separate God's nature and his revelation. Therefore the determination of that which the human Jesus is involves in fact the nature of God. (quoted, 616)

He deplores the complex trinitarian language with which Schillebeeckx elsewhere feels compelled to underpin this biblical vision. It may be that both theologians need to undertake the same critical work on the language of classical doctrine as they have consecrated to Scripture, under pain of falling into abstract and implausible constructions whether metaphysical (Schillebeeckx) or mythical (Kuschel).

According to Kuschel, the resurrection is not, as Pannenberg claims, 'the revelation of a metaphysical duality of Father and Son "always already" given from all eternity', but rather means that '*the entire Jesus-event*, the preaching, the passion, the cross and the resurrection of Jesus, is to be understood *as a revelation of God* for the salvation of humankind' (527). There is a certain 'identity of nature between Jesus and God', in the sense that 'in the event "Jesus Christ" God has manifested historically not just one "aspect" of himself but his entire being and nature' (528). If God has revealed himself fully in this way there is no call to go behind this phenomenon into the ineffable inner life of the divinity: 'No speculation about an eternal divine Son independent of the human Jesus!' (586). Here the words 'speculation' and 'independent' imply a hasty dismissal of the Logos-doctrine. To call the eternal Logos 'Son' is misleading theological shorthand, for it projects the human personality of Jesus onto the divine, suggesting either a monophysite conflation, or a Nestorian doubling of the Son's personhood. 'Born of the Father before time began' is then a mythological expression, licensed only by the *communicatio idiomatum*. Kuschel thinks it must mean that the human Jesus was in some sense born of the Father before time began. If instead we stress the temporality of Jesus and the eternity of the Logos – using the words 'temporality' and 'eternity' as counters indicating rules of speech – then we see Jesus as the one through whom the Logos acquires a human, personal, temporal, historical face, or as the incarnation of God's covenantal outgoingness.

The Logos-in-itself is eternal divine wisdom; it is manifested in all things and nothing is independent of it; what is unique about Jesus is the concreteness with which his life, death and resurrection sets humanity in relation to God, becoming the central Logos-event in human history.

Again the objection will be raised: how can we reconcile our insistence on the Logos-doctrine with what we have said about the contextuality and provisoriness of all dogmatic language, its status as human interpretation and construction, as strategic *upāya*? We recognise a double constraint at work in the mobility of the tradition: on the one hand the constraint of fidelity to the phenomena of revelation and to the full vital significance of the Christ-event; on the other the constraint of reason, even if its classical, metaphysical form no longer seems suited to designate the identity of God and of Christ. Those who reject the doctrine of the Councils without submitting it to a probing historical and philosophical examination have not negotiated these constraints and have thus not correctly identified and linked up with the currents of change in the present transmission of the doctrinal heritage.

Yet in the end the status of this entire tradition, with all its logical and phenomenological constraints, remains contingent. It is an interpretation whose relation to the truth of things in themselves eludes us, even if we say that in revelation the truth is no longer noumenal but is given as a phenomenon to be lived, that life takes a variety of forms, and is enacted as a series of finite occasions. Conceptual and doctrinal constructions come second to this lived reality, a secondarity keenly sensed in Heidegger, Zen, and Christian mysticism. Thus the doctrinal tradition is worthy of credence, but it points only obscurely to the experience of the real, and this experience itself is different for each epoch so that even poetic or mystical language has but a limited range of evocation.

In both Buddhism and Christianity a powerful rational interpretation has won out over less convincing and coherent ones, while remaining itself full of inconsistencies and awkwardnesses and subject to possible revolutions in light of new ways of understanding. The labour of logic and the concept produces genuine and necessary clarification and effectively validates the claims of the tradition. Yet logic and concept serve to discern also their own limitations and the ways in which the truth they envisage ultimately slips their grasp. Or again, in both traditions certain canonical experiences have been set on a pedestal, and certain styles of apprehending ultimate reality have been inculcated. But these incursions into the real remain particular cultural attainments, and while they may discipline and guide, they cannot forestall the invention of new modes of life that open to the ultimate in unforeseen ways.

THE UNKNOWN CHRIST

Traditional theology applied the high ontology of Nicaea – 'God from God, light from light, true God from true God' – directly to the human Jesus, helped by a short-circuit in the interpretation of Johannine texts such as 'I and the Father are one' (Jn 10:30). This may indeed have involved a form of idolatry: 'from the beginning Jews, and later Moslems, held that Christians, in their extravagant christological claims, were guilty of idolatry; that is, that in their talk about Christ they seriously confused and compromised the most fundamental of the monotheistic categories, *God*' (Kaufman, 84). Indeed, even if indefectible in orthodoxy at some deep level, the Christian community seems to have been spared no form of idolatry: idolatry of narrow conceptions of God, idolatry of Christ, of the Bible, of the Church, of church structures, of sacramental rituals – each of these has distracted faith from its supreme concern and become an end rather than a means.

In response to crisis, theology has always sought a return to the sources: from the prophets' recall to covenant obedience, to the Pauline centering of the Gospel on Christ crucified and risen, to Augustine's *redi in te*, to Luther's recovery of the Word and Schleiermacher's regrounding of religion in communal experience. Dialectical theology met the crisis of metaphysics with an equivalent of the phenomenologists' slogan, *Zu den Sachen selbst*, and the present crisis of pluralism also sends us back to the basic phenomena or founding-events of Christianity. But this time it may be counter-productive to insist on the 'essence' of Christianity. It may be that the urgency of such insistence is just what is blocking our path to a demystified apprehension of the meaning of Christ, and a 'quiescence of fabrications'. Perhaps we need instead to let go a little more: to draw sustenance from the readily available sources of spiritual insight our world presents in the sciences, in literature, in the modern experience of human solidarity, in a catholic appreciation of all cultural and religious traditions – and leave the Christian claims to look after themselves. A theology which models its tone and tempo on the discretion of Jesus, who emptied himself and did not cling to his own identity, can allow the figure of Jesus to emerge on the new pluralistic landscape in its quiet power – the 'quiet power of the possible'. Such releasement best allows the meaning of Christ to emerge beyond the accumulation of doctrinal debate and historical investigation. Presuppositionless Buddhist *prajñā*, penetrating discernment, should come before the investment of faith, clearing the ground for a demystified apprehension of the phenomenon of Jesus so that this phenomenon in its 'thusness' can draw forth the appropriate response of faith, which may no longer be that of biblical or classical Christian times, but something quieter, subtler, more open-ended.

A non-Christian religion may constitute an autonomous wisdom sufficient to make sense of life and to deal with tragedy. The Christian might call it a share in Logos. Nevertheless the preaching of the Gospel will not necessarily communicate immediately with this non-Christian wisdom. The meaning of Christ can be conveyed only by telling the entire story of a covenant between God and humanity, of how it was broken by sin, and how atonement was required. Even with a complete explanation this story will fall idly on the ears of those to whom its basic presuppositions are foreign. Though the biblical way of constructing the human dilemma is equal in consistency to the Buddhist construction, it is not immediately translatable into a horizon in which the notions of God and sin are far less determinate, if they exist at all. Rather, it is perhaps the governing secular horizon of our world that provides the lingua franca in terms of which both the Gospel and the Buddha's teaching can be reformulated, with their respective challenges to the self-sufficiency of that secularity. Thus it would be by the detour of an opening to the world that the two ancient religious traditions become able to meet one another.

Here a gap has become apparent between the ideal universality of the Logos incarnate and the historical particularity of how the meaning of Christ has unfolded amid the contingencies of Israel's history, Jesus's own life, and the Christian enactment of his message. The Christ-event touches the deepest realities of life and death, humanity and God, and these realities are met everywhere, but this universality in principle is slow to become fully manifest. Historical Christianity cannot claim to have mastered the revelation to which it witnesses, and it leaves ample margins for the work of other religious traditions. It finds itself outstripped on every side, but by that very reality which is at the heart of its preaching and which it clumsily calls the Logos incarnate. Its quest, then, is not only for the unknown God – the *Deus semper maior* – to which every religion points in a fragile and provisional way, but also for the unknown Christ who awaits us in every religion, and indeed in every human being.

If the life of Jesus is throughout a revelation of ultimate reality, this reality manifests itself always and everywhere (Jn 1:4f). The revelation in Christ unfolds its sense freely only in relation to the countless other fragmentary breakthroughs of divine truth in history, all contingent, limited and to be transcended. By his body Jesus is rooted in the history of the people of Israel and of the Christian community, his 'mystical body'; but this particular historical enfleshment is not dissociable from history as a whole. Thus the contingency of incarnation rejoins the universalism, and the necessity, of the manifestation of ultimate reality. The Logos incarnate is in search of itself in all history; evangelisation or dialogue consist in this encounter of the Logos incarnate in a contingent history with the universal Logos sown in every human heart.

When the Gospel encounters a foreign religious or philosophic horizon, it recognises there things belonging to its own essence, which provokes a partial jettisoning of its previous forms and a restructuring of its content in the perspective thus opened. In these encounters, the kerygma of the cross is freed from the double danger that haunts it: the danger of being reduced to an abstract schematism whose effective meaning slips through our fingers (justification before God, to die in order to be reborn, redemptive suffering); and the danger of its petrification in an empirical history which is both inaccessible in its archaic aspects (the Messiah, the Kingdom) and disturbing in its present resonances (antisemitism). The kerygma of the cross needs the encounter with other religions to be set in a healing perspective.

The ground is everywhere prepared for the Gospel kerygma, though on both sides rigidity of thought-forms and spiritual inertia limit what is possible in the way of creative transformations. This potential universality of the Gospel furnishes the medium in function of which one can speak of a cosmic Christ. Where the terrain is already occupied by another religious vision, it is natural to seek possible correlations between this vision and the Christian one. For instance, in an encounter with Plotinus, one might find a functional equivalent of the Johannine Logos in the domain of the *nous*. Similarly, one will note how Krishna identifies himself as a manifestation of the Logos:

> By Me is pervaded all this
> Universe, by Me in the form of the unmanifest.
> All beings rest Me,
> And I do not rest in them. (*Bhagavad-Gītā* 9.4)

Again, the Buddhist equivalent of the Logos would be the 'Dharma body', which is both a manifestation of the absolute and the ultimate truth of the figure of the Buddha (or Buddhas). Yet one cannot make a synthesis of these different constructions, putting them alongside one another in some speculative space, for they belong to complex traditions from which they are inseparable.

Doctrines about the mediation between the absolute and the world cannot be formulated without a permanent concrete reference to this world. In the case of Christology, this reference has a firm historical rooting: Wisdom chooses to dwell among a particular people; then the Incarnation of the Logos takes place in the life of the one who crystallises and raises to a new level the religious wisdom of this people. Confronting this language with analogous constructions in another religion, one notices affinities which suggest progress toward the same univeral fulness of meaning. One may even admit that the universality claimed on both sides is at bottom the same, and that in some ultimate clarification, surpassing what we can at present conceive, the Logos will embrace the whole truth of Buddhism and the universality of the Buddhist message will find its full realisation in the Logos. This regulative idea can inspire speculative anticipations. However, these remain desperately abstract, and are to be seen as incidental fabrications, insignificant side-products of the concrete play of traditions, each carrying the density of its historical flesh.

On the ontological plane, it is interesting to note a partial homology between the doctrine of the triple body of the Buddha and the three states of Christ. First, the eternal Logos corresponds to the 'Dharma body' of the Buddha; then the 'body of fruition', the form in which the Buddha is manifest to bodhisattvas in the Buddha-lands, invites comparison with the spiritual body of the risen Christ; lastly, the 'transformation body' which differs for every historical Buddha could be seen as corresponding to the Jesus of history. Christ and the historical Buddha, entirely distinct at the level of the transformation-body, begin to draw near at the spiritual level of the body of fruition (the risen Christ, the heavenly Buddha-figures), and are basically one at the level of the dharma-body. God, in that case, would be one with the ultimate reality, or emptiness, which Wisdom contemplates. Or should one put God, too, on the side of wisdom and see him as transcended in turn by the absolute of 'the nothingness beyond God?' But to pursue such questions is to be lost in baseless speculation. The notion of emptiness, like that of Being in Heidegger, has its field of application only in the phenomenality of our world and cannot be applied to God except to the degree that he reveals himself in beings or their emptiness. To project these categories onto the plane of absolute reality is to fall into onto-theology and logocentrism.

Whatever the ontological background of the primacy of Jesus, this primacy unfolds only in historical encounters, that is, in the element of contingency and of the possible. The encounter of the Christ-event with other great events of history – Socrates, the Buddha, Muhammad – unfolds according to the laws of historical existence. Such encounters do not generate an artificial and arbitrary syncretism, but set off a long-term negotiation of which the tension is broken only in breakthroughs of the true. Jesus Christ is not a revelation of God all on his own, but only in relation with a concrete historical interlocutor on every occasion. The relation is asymmetrical in the case, for example, of the encounter between Christ and philosophy, for the result of this encounter is not a contribution to Western philosophy but a new figure of Christ as saviour.

In the relation between Christ and the Buddha, in contrast, this asymmetry yields to a parity of the two figures.

All religious discourses and the play between them, indeed all the forms of the created world, can be seen as manifesting Logos, in that they serve to give form and expression to the absolute and ineffable truth. Within the whole universe of forms, explicitly religious expressions aim to reproduce the Logos directly under the conditions of a human, mortal word. They are 'incarnations' of it, but not in the sense of grasping it substantially. Rather as provisional designations they attest Logos in imitation of the poverty of the cross. This vulnerable enterprise succeeds only as sustained by the revealing grace of that Logos itself. Most religious language dies when the moment of grace has passed. Yet sometimes when a cathedral in stone or writing seems to have outlived its time and to be no longer capable of housing the divine glory, or even an illusory, idolatrous counterfeit of it, there may occur a surprise of the Spirit: the water may run in dried canals and a dusty terminology become eloquent anew.

The notion of Logos is a poor abstraction, a makeshift designation of what we glimpse across the entire series of expressions and forms in which meaning or intelligibility is manifest in cosmos and history. If all meaning is dependently co-arisen and in consequence empty of self-identity, the Logos underlying this process does not end the intertextual drift, but makes itself known as this intertextuality itself, as the space in which all particular discourses can breathe and deploy a meaning. The figure of Christ and the discourses created in memory of him are a specific incarnation of this universal Logos, giving it a more concrete and personal face. However, we must beware of naive amalgamations between the Logos incarnate in Christ and the Logos as glimpsed in Greek or in Buddhist philosophy. John speaks of the Logos in personal terms in order to ward off such identifications which reduce the divine to an abstract cosmic principle.

If in general Logos, meaning, shows itself to be empty of own-being, dissolving back to ultimate emptiness, in the Christ-event this movement from form to emptiness is concretised as the personal return of the Son to the Father, while the converse movement from emptiness to form becomes the sending of the Son from the Father into the world. The Johannine truth-event resonates with the deepest philosophical insights, both Greek and Indian, into how meaning and truth emerge, yet it transcends these by its distinctive personal naming of the God revealed in Christ. The dialogue, begun by John, between the Christ-event and the versions of Logos apprehended elsewhere, is always marked by that excess of the named, personal God over more general approaches to the absolute. This excess prevents the Christ-event from being reabsorbed into a phenomenological or speculative interpretation of the world.

The non-duality of form and emptiness is exhibited in the way Christ's lack of self-nature, his being as dependently co-arisen, opens on a gap, an emptiness, which is no longer an abstract Logos but the Word of a personal God: 'He who has seen me has seen the Father' (Jn. 14:9). The Logos, always condemned to the limitations of its temporal presentations, assumes these limitations fully in the mortal flesh of Jesus. At this depth of finitude the human Jesus is one with the Logos, not by inflating himself, but by an obedience that removes all barriers of human self-assertion that prevent the emergence of Logos in human life. Sacrifice, which lives finite existence as a free gift, confers on mortal existence its meaning and intelligibility, impressing on history and its contingencies the mark of their origin and end. It is because finite existence thus attests to the greatness of God, that its contingencies are transformed into a revealing Logos without ceasing to be contingent. In consigning himself to the risks and the opacity of history Jesus is the paradoxical sign of divine transcendence, his entire life 'a finger pointing to the moon' in virtue of its accomplishment of a fundamental accord between the reality of God and human reality.

We have tried to show the mobility of the forms the Logos takes, both on the interreligious level and within the Christian tradition. This mobility may suggest Hegelian dialectic, but we do not see the history of religious language as culminating in a finally adequate conceptual grasp; rather its dialectic remains radically open to and incarnate in finitude and contingency. The incarnate finitude of the language of faith is not compensated for by an infinite which integrates the finite in itself, but by the dynamics according to which all Christic forms tend beyond themselves. This eschatological openness is the counterpart of the incarnate condition of Christian language.

Deconstruction shows that mortality is inscribed in our very language. In metaphysics, a projection of transcendental forms guaranteeing the identity and continuity of the self brought about a repression of differences, of yawning gaps. Those who protect Christian language against such gaps, seeing it as controlled by the *eidos* of Christ, might well recall that this *forma Christi* is that of the Crucified, a cipher of human finitude and mortality. The language of faith speaks well of this when it reproduces the fragmentedness and tornness of Christ. God, writing straight with crooked lines, manifests himself in the Bible through human beings who show their mortality and sinfulness; the regime of allegorisation long masked this carnality of revelation. Christian language, similarly, is always exposed to obsolescence and an 'errance' of which its numerous errors are a painful reminder. It is perpetually embarrassed, though it hide its poverty through flattering associations with philosophical and political systems equally over-assured of their own stability. To repeat dogmas valid for all time no longer immunises against the anxiety of temporal existence, for we know that the language of dogmas also belongs to time, carrying the hue of the age which fashioned it and traces of decay where more recent time has done its work.

However, Christians cannot wallow in the postmodernist masochism which pushes to its last conclusions the idea that 'God is dead'. One such conclusion is that the laws of logic being merely human constructions, any security to which our thought or language pretend is but a projection of narcissistic desire. To be sure, the laws of logic in their formulation owe much to human culture and invention. Yet how deny the presence in them of a transcendental rational force? Even if logic is not as inexorable as is usually thought, and even if its constraints do not operate in a single uniform way, still the traditions of reason, however elastic they turn out to be, retain a compelling force.

Theology is more vulnerable than logic to the charge of being a human projection, but it has its own coherence. The Christ-event survives the inevitable obsolescence of every local or epochal account of it. Is it a narcissistic defence to insist on this permanence? It would be, if Christ himself did not again and again attest his pneumatic presence to believers in a way that is always surprising. If one persuades oneself that logic is only a subjective projection, one will hardly credit the objectivity of Christ. But, conversely, if Christ resists our narcissism, somewhat as logic resists it, then it may be that the perpetual play of our discourses tends not to abolish faith in him, but to keep us in touch with his mystery by an adroit tact in the deployment of our *upāya*.

To be sure, religious language contains so large a contribution from the human imagination that wish-fulfilment must play a large part in its composition, and we cannot securely sift out this element. Historical criticism and logical vigilance whittle it down, but when that process goes too far it is resisted by an upsurge of spiritual awareness and the irrepressible instincts of faith and hope. Authentic religious thinking makes its home in this perpetual systole and diastole between too lofty affirmation and too sweeping negation. It is a practice of assessment and querying, fundamentally sustained by faith, but attended at all its margins by an open-ended agnosticism.

The fact that we have kept the notion of 'tradition' as what links together the various narrations of Jesus Christ invites the suspicion of logocentrism, despite our insistence that the only Logos we know is incarnate. The very fact of linking the diverse Christian cultures in a single history centred on Christ is an interpretation dictated by faith and therefore suspect to historians. All our characterisations of Christian tradition and the meaning of Christ are in fact methods for handling history and finding a sense in it, which cannot be justified by historical reason alone and which are subject to revision. For some, the continuity of tradition is a narcissistic projection, masking the epistemological breaks and the bricolages which make all tradition a hotchpotch of opportunistic arrangements. Is there a real transmission of an identical faith from the time of the apostles to the present? To deny all continuity is to destroy the meaning of the tradition. But that the tradition stays alive only through perpetual invention, that it disseminates itself in formations too heterogeneous to have any unity other that that of the history which has produced them, and that only this creativity testifies to the permanence of the presence of Christ in it, is a thesis which can resist the hermeneutics of suspicion and discontinuity on one side, and break with myths of continuity on the other.

The incarnate condition of Christian discourse puts it on a footing with the other religious languages of humanity, equally incarnated in the cultures and practices of historical peoples. If God is revealed in our tradition, no firm frontier cuts revelation off from what is afoot in neighbouring traditions, which have often mixed their riches with ours in the course of time. Christian language, however pure it wishes to be, belongs to the family of religious languages and shares in the immense travail of imagination and articulation by which humanity seeks to reproduce in its idioms the voice of the absolute. To be sure, Christian language, by its excellence, judges many others as unworthy and inferior; but in turn it is often judged by other languages, such as that of Buddhism or even those of Western modernity. The Barthian claim that such mutual critique belongs to mere religion and leaves unaffected the sovereignty of revelation has to suppose that the vast open-ended world of Scripture, so permeable to dialogue with other traditions, enshrines a revelation which has clear and distinct frontiers against any other emergence of transcendent truth. But is this compatible with the logic of incarnation? A logos which incarnates itself sacrifices its immunity against dialogical contamination; it is incarnate not in one tradition only but in the network of relations onto which this tradition opens.

If the universality of Christ is worked out thus in a series of situations of encounter, then it is no longer an arbitrary or imperialist claim. It is not Christianity as it now exists that is universal, but rather the ongoing deployment of the meaning of its founding event. This event is in search of its interpretation, a search that is as long as history itself. The role of other religions is not to furnish the Gospel with cultural orchestration or a supplement of contemplative Wisdom. How they will interact with it cannot be determined in avance. From every encounter will emerge the uniqueness of the cross, but always in an unforeseeable way, in which the kerygma is bound to undergo modification and reinterpretation.

The kerygma of the cross is presented as the last word on life and death; to refuse it this status is to denature it. But does it follow that every other religious and cultural expression can claim only the status, at most, of penultimate word? In that case one would say that these second-last words open the perspectives of human hope, and that only the last word brings divine salvation. Humans are powerless to free themselves from sin and death; but no religion has contented itself with making this powerlessness evident. Every religion lives from the conviction that a saving process is underway in it. May one not then say that salvation comes not from the bare kerygma of the cross but from the encounter between this kerygma and its interpretative context, a context in which God is already at work? The version of the good news which is born of an interreligious encounter is the fruit of two religions. In the New Testament itself the cross is an event of encounter between the Jewish and Gentile worlds. This paradigm can be carried over to every other encounter under the sign of the cross.

The intrinsically dialogical character of the cross undoes any imperialism by exclusion or inclusion. Its universality subsists as does that of a great poem, in the echo that it encounters in the diverse experiences of humanity. There is no question of a sudden arrest of the pluralistic opening; the cross rather carries this to a deeper and more concrete level, undoing the fixated self-identity of the believer and enabling a radical opening to integral pluralism, somewhat as confidence in Western reason frees the thinker to appreciate the intelligibility of every other tradition.

A theory according to which the cross, beyond the forms of its explicit annunciation, is present wherever human beings assume their finitude in hope and love, might block the free emergence of the unpredictable effects produced by the meeting of the cross with a concrete tradition touching on life and death. The cross is an open question, to which every situation gives a new and provisional answer. Jean Ansaldi's way of underlining the particularity of the cross seems to limit the universal scope of this question:

> a theology of the cross founded on the *sola fide* has no hypothesis to offer about the relation of its God with the non-Christian religions ... There is no other site of christological knowledge than the Incarnation. The dimension of the eternal Logos should certainly be

postulated, but (against the recourse to a universal *Logos sper-matikos*) it has no other function than to articulate the Incarnation, the advent of Emmanuel ... Faced with the problem of the non-Christian religions, theology must affirm the fulness of the manifestation of God in Christ, and also the *undecidability* of the question as to how this God is related to the various claims to know another revelation. (Ansaldi, 83f)

This point of view underestimates the imperative of universality inscribed in the cross. For if 'there is no other name under heaven given among men by which we must be saved' (Acts 4:2), this name itself demands translation. It is not the *logos spermatikos*, but the name of Jesus itself which unfolds its universal meaning in the course of its encounters with particular historical contexts. And like the name of God the name of Jesus seals its transcendent irreducibility to the categories of any given context in a double bind whereby it both must and cannot be fully translated. The universal meaning of his name is of a concrete historical kind: it is the eschatological future of all humanity. As Donald Dawe puts it:

The 'name of Jesus' is the disclosure of the structure of new being. It is the pattern of salvation. So the universality of Christianity is grounded in the translatability of the 'name of Jesus', not in the imposition of particular formularies on others. This power of new being operates throughout the world under the names of many religious traditions. It is recognized and celebrated by Christians because they know its pattern or meaning through Jesus of Nazareth. (Dawe and Carman, 30)

Christian theology does not offer precise hypotheses a priori about the role of other religions, but it does expect to find in them elements that accord with its own understanding of salvation and that can enrich it. Far from being content with an abstract 'undecidability' which consigns its dealings with the religious other to superficiality, it goes to meet the other on the basis of a set of insights summarised in the name of Jesus; as these resonate with comparable insights in other traditions, each such interchange gives a new accentuation to the name of Jesus, whose universality unfolds as this capacity for encounter and reciprocal illumination.

The eschatological temporality that shapes Christian language and doctrine is reinforced by the interreligious encounter and in turn lends new meaning to this encounter. The eschatological figure of Christ lights up the dynamism whereby religions tend beyond themselves toward the goal in function of which they have been constructed. The eschatological vision bears not only on Christian existence, but on the entire cosmos: 'the creation waits with eager longing' (Rom. 8:19). The figure of Christ addresses the other traditions with the assurance that they have a special role in the universal travail of the creation of meaning, which is constantly corroded by the nihilating power of time and contingency. To extend a fraternal hand to struggling humanity while ignoring the immense investment of hope and passion of which the religions are the monument, would be an impoverished and unimaginative way of translating the message of the Kingdom.

By viewing other religions in the perspective of its own eschatological hope, Christianity puts pressure on them, bringing to bear the biblical vision of history, a vision confirmed by the unique role of Jesus Christ. But in return Christianity expects the other religions to throw light on its eschatological vision and to give it a more determinate shape. The obscurities of Christian eschatology refer us to the broken lights of the other religions, and the plurality of eschatologies deepens our sense of how enigmatic and opaque is the future envisaged in religious hope. This obliges us to recall eschatology to its ground in the processes of salvation that are afoot in the present and that can be phenomenologically discerned. The path of enlightenment, the path of the Kingdom, the path of Torah-fidelity, each contain their future in their present enactment; the true outline of the promise, stripped of all imaginary projections, lies inscribed in what it nearest to hand. The eschatological primacy of Christ unfolds in dialogue with all other forms of hope and expectation, and can emerge convincingly only as the message of the Kingdom is enacted in present circumstances.

FOR AN EMPTY CHRISTOLOGY

In determining how traditional Christology, whether 'mythic' or dogmatic, can still function as a 'skilful means' for bringing into view the truth revealed in the Christ-event, we must find a middle way between substantialist attachment to traditional conceptions and nihilistic critique which robs them of all authority. This can be done by reflecting on the intrinsically 'empty' and provisional character of these conceptions, as makeshift historical constructs marked by all the inadequacies of human language and thought in face of the transcendent. Accepting this emptiness, one may retrieve the traditional language in a modified form, and use it more lightly and adroitly. It is by its lack of a definitive and substantial hold on its object that it witnesses best to the 'emptiness' of that object; for Christ is not a substance to be defined, but an event to be interpreted, and the process of interpretation – as the Gospels already show – advances by letting go of definitive understanding in order to open up to a reality which eludes our conceptual clutches.

We have seen that Christology is always a culturally determined construction, which can never yield a final understanding of the meaning of Christ, for this meaning is constantly renewed according to the responses of the cultures which receive and interpret it. The Incarnation implies an accommodation without reserve to the heterogeneous possibilities of history and culture. This mystery cannot, and does not want to, be expressed in terminology other than inadequate, and at the same time it pushes us to surpass the inadequacy of each of the successive interpretations. The meaning of Christ, as a breakthrough of divine freedom in human life, carries all the marks of the places and times in which this breakthrough happens. If one seeks to resume in a general ontological structure the sequence of events in which Christ is known, the resultant statements will themselves bear the marks of a particular cultural site; an archaic metaphysical language will have been imposed on the vital unfolding of the Christ-event across our history.

In the interreligious horizon the figure of Jesus can emerge anew in its attractive force. No longer as the Christ-king of Christendom, nor as the remote depersonalised figure which the language of dogma unwittingly projects, but as a concentration of enlightened, compassionate wisdom, as one who is saviour not by acting on the world from the outside in some inconceivable mythical or metaphysical process, but by the prophetic truth of the cross which transforms the world according to the laws of its own inmost aspirations.

Neither Buddha nor Christ are conceivable without the culture which permits their discourse and its continuing interpretation. The luminous innovation they bring makes sense only by reference to a prior religious tradition which it transcends. It is only under the limiting conditions entailed by this inevitable historicity that they are bearers of a revelation of the absolute. Moreover, the absolute element at the heart of the narratives and discourses through which their message comes can scarcely be sifted out; it is a perfume which pervades the entire Christian or Buddhist tradition, an intangible melody suggested everywhere. The basic inspiration which underlies all the variations of the melody can never entirely lose its original Indian or Hellenistic Jewish character, but it communicates itself along the paths of history by creative interactions with the cultures it successively meets. When philosophies meet, the aim is to 'open the concept without destroying it' (Merleau-Ponty). In the same way, Christology is opened up, through listening to its distant resonances in other traditions, and there is no need to destroy it as a myth that allegedly obstructs dialogical listening. Its structural resistance to closure positively favours this opening to the other.

It is clear that such a point of view implies a fundamental criticism of the Johannine schemas of pre-existence and of the ontology of Nicaea. Unless they are reinterpreted in depth, transferred from the direct to the oblique, these pillars of traditional Christology are in contradiction with the contingency of history. One cannot erect a historical figure, carrying the mark of all the contingencies of human existence, and subject to the play of interpretations to which everything historical lends itself, into a transcendental signifier, pure sign of the ultimate transcendental signified, God. Such an autonomous and fully adequate revelation never takes place; the meaning of Jesus Christ, as of any historical event, is always on the way to being defined. Against the Derridian critique of the status of transcendental signifier accorded the phallus by Lacan, it has been claimed that for Lacan this signifier signifies only 'difference' (B. Johnson). Christ, too, can be seen as a mobile signifier, marking the difference and forming a link between the divine and the human in a great variety of ways, and having himself no fixed form outside this function. If the name of Jesus functions as transcendental signifier, it is as marking the site of a whole process of signification which has no end, other than an eschatological one. This signifier, like the divine names, serves to protect the signified from any definitive grasp.

Two expressions have emerged as central to our reflections in this book: 'emptiness', an abstract philosophical word, the key theme of the Perfection of Wisdom *sūtras*, which sums up centuries of Buddhist analysis, and 'Jesus Christ', a concrete proper name, the centre of the New Testament, which is the most pregnant cipher of the actualisation of God's Word in human history. Each of these words provides a field of application for the modern philosophical insights rehearsed in our opening chapters: the pluralism and relativity of historical meaning, its Quinean indeterminacy or Derridean dissemination, and the resulting situatedness and provisionality of any statement of truth. From Buddhism we learned that the fragility and conventionality of thought and language does not exclude, but rather enables, their use as a soteriological 'skilful means', and does not render otiose a concern with rationality and truth. We saw that the biblical naming of God assumes this fragility and conventionality into a dynamics of incarnation, whereby God is manifested across the tangled historical dialectic of our efforts to name him, a process marked at every step by the kind of constricting double binds that delight Derrida.

Is a final synthesis possible between these two paths? Can we make 'emptiness' rhyme with 'Jesus Christ'? 'Rhyme' is the right word here, with its suggestion of creative artifice, for it would be a mistake to expect that the two traditions can neatly dovetail. Rather we have to construct a bitonal counterpoint in which powerful affinities continue to co-exist with pungent clashes in a give and take that is likely to nourish religious thought for a long time.

The most powerful effort to rethink Christ in terms of emptiness is John Keenan's. His groundbreaking intuitions can be consolidated by close study of particular Christian texts, wherein one may identify places at which substantialist ontological presuppositions can profitably be wedged open to the Buddhist sense of emptiness. His account of Christ as 'empty of any essence and engaged in the dependently co-arisen world in all its radical contingency' (Keenan, 225) tries to do justice to the teaching of Chalcedon, while contesting the use of rigid metaphysical categories:

> Jesus as empty of any essence whatsoever is an ineffable outflow from the ultimate realm. But as emptiness is identical with dependent co-arising, so Jesus is enmeshed in the web of the constantly flowing and changing events of his time. He is ultimate and absolute inasmuch as he is totally empty, and human and relative inasmuch as he is totally interrelated with the world. (237)

As empty, Jesus exists as openness to God, in direct awareness of ultimate meaning; as dependently co-arising he is engaged in this world in the preaching of the Kingdom. Perhaps Keenan associates these two indissociable aspects of Jesus's humanity too quickly with his divinity and his humanity respectively: 'Whereas the pair of terms, divine and human, function as opposites in the traditional account, emptiness and dependent co-arising are convertible, complementary, each fully interpenetrating the other' (238). The ultimacy of Jesus is not merely his transparency to the Father in the Abba experience; it is the constitution of his entire human life as the enfleshment of the eternal Word. On the ontological level, the divinity and humanity of Jesus are certainly not convertible, however far the 'communication of idioms' is pushed.

Yet though the Word infinitely transcends its fleshly vehicle, it is concretely known and felt only through this enfleshment, so that on the gnoseological level there is a convertibility between the limited contingent figure of Jesus Christ crucified and the infinite divine Word (see 1 Cor. 1:23f). Though we may say that the divine Word is above and beyond the realm of dependent co-arising, we have no access to that Word independently of the incarnational unfolding which occurs in the most salient and concentrated way in the story of Jesus. Just as one cannot set *saṃsāra* and *nirvāṇa* in opposition (Nāgārjuna, *MMK*, 25.19f). so one cannot set the being of Christ in his dependent co-arising over against his being as Logos. To know him in his dependently co-arisen humanity is to know him as

Logos; nor can one be known without the other; they are in this sense coterminous. Though we can imagine the Word as eternal and unchanging, this becomes a barren projection if we do not at the same time seek to hear that Word in the mobile variations of its historical unfolding. The attempt to think the Word apart from its incarnation results in an image of God modelled on the human mind, as in the Augustinian and Thomist presentations of the Trinity. Such projections exist only to be shattered by the concrete manifestation of the Word in history, which has to be sought again and again.

Keenan correlates the two truths with 'the transcendent dimension of Jesus, expressed through his experience of Abba' and 'the incarnational dimension . . . expressible in a host of languages and cultural philosophies'. But the incarnational dimension is itself the happening of transcendence, just as dependent co-arising is itself emptiness. Should not the two truths correspond rather to two ways of apprehending this total event, a conceptual way and a transconceptual one? Keenan suggests as much when he writes: 'The resurrection was presented by these early communities as a doctrinally empty, vertical experience of ultimate meaning in Jesus alive as Christ and enunciated horizontally in the kerygma' (234). Thus there is no privileged a-historical discourse of Jesus's Abba-experience as opposed to the preaching of the Kingdom, but there can be a contemplative apprehension of the entire event in both its protological and eschatological reach, through a union with the risen Christ which is qualitatively other than the conventional representations of the kerygma. However, since faith in the Word of God is more central in the Christian economy than contemplative insight into the divine presence, a conventional discourse which closely engages with historical contingencies can have a higher profile there than in Buddhism. For the Christian to understand Christ as 'the worldly and conventional speaking of God' is not something less than to understand 'the naked Logos' as Origen imagined, nor need one itch to transcend this conventional level to attain the ultimacy of immediate gnosis.

In any case it seems clear that from the point of view of Buddhist ontology there can be no fixed substance of the humanity, divinity, person, or nature of Jesus Christ. Chalcedon can be brought into accord with this, for it is not part of the intent of the dogma to attribute either to the human Jesus or to the divine Word a substantial self-contained self; their hypostatic union can be interpreted rather as the mutual openness of two dynamic processes. In Jesus the Word is incarnate in history, in a world textured as universal co-referentiality. To say that 'Jesus is God' or that 'Jesus is the Saviour' makes sense in this context only as a twitch in this universal web, a pointer to the place where divinity or salvation emerge.

This place is not a fixed point: it is the network of relations in which Christ unfolds his being.

Jesus is empty of own-being in virtue of his interdependence with all other humans, fully assumed and expressed in his cross. In principle, then, to return to that human, historical Jesus, or to find Christ in one's concrete historical neighbour, is not to leave the Christ of faith but to pass freely from the emptiness-dimension to the form-dimension of the one Christ. The emptiness of the risen Christ is one with the emptiness of the eternal Logos, the emptiness of God himself. Yet this does not abolish the ontological gulf between the human and the divine. Since Buddhist emptiness does not transcend dependently co-arising forms in anything like as clear a way as God transcends creatures, the application of the Mahāyāna language here stumbles on discords and resistances which must be carefully negotiated and which cannot be brushed away.

We have sought a middle path between abstraction and particularity, between dissolution of Christ in a process of general revelation and sectarian fixation on limited images of Christ. This chimes with the central intuition of Mahāyāna Buddhism: 'form is itself emptiness, emptiness is itself form' (*Heart Sūtra*). The relation is the same as the one in Christian teaching between divine 'emptiness' and the particular form of Christ crucified, or between the 'emptiness' of Christ as universal, pneumatic Lord, and the particular forms that he takes in the practical reinventions of the Gospel, that is, in every local community which is able to give body to the commandment of love. There is no simple identity here: the relation is kenotic in both directions. God is emptied of his abstraction when recognised in Christ; Christ is emptied of his particularity when acknowledged as divine. Again, Christ is emptied of his abstraction when Christians make him incarnate in particular styles of life, born of the encounters between Gospel and culture; but in referring all established embodiments of Christ to the eschatological 'Lord', always other, always greater, which is 'Spirit' (2 Cor. 3:17), they prevent these formations from becoming rigid. The form of Jesus in its relation of interdependence with all other human beings is fully opened to the divine emptiness, and this is what legitimates the identification of the life of Jesus – in its widest, historical, pneumatic and cosmic extensions – with the Logos of God.

Jesus crucified assumes fully the *manque-à-être* (want of being) which is constitutive of human existence, just as the Buddha unflinchingly gazed on the texture of existence as suffering, impermanence and non-self. The obverse of this recognition is the discovery of the eternal life or *nirvāṇa*, human existence broken open to ultimate reality.

But the dynamic equivalence between these two versions of ultimate bliss cannot elide the heterogeneity between the different ways of focusing the ultimate in each religion. One is constructed on the basis of the biblical separation of finite and infinite, the other ignores this distinction and bases its economy of meaning on the perception of reality as such. One crystallises in a personal language which places the creature before a Thou, the other dissolves such personal language by its fidelity to the ultimate real which no category can express. One is a harmonious movement back and forth between two registers, which become one to the Buddha-eye; the other is a constant discovery of an infinite Other, to be rejoined across the uneven, chequered Calvary-path of history.

Thus, even as the Buddhist analogies crowd in on us, we must retain a sense of the irreducibility to Buddhist categories of the incarnational covenant between a transcendent God and human finitude. While admitting that the ontological vision of the world as dependently co-arisen opens existence onto the nirvanic dimension underlying it, which is that of the Logos and divine transcendence, one must avoid saying that this structure of finitude, even as lit up by the cross, is itself the presence of the infinite, just as dependent co-arising is itself emptiness according to Nāgārjuna. To escape monism, it is better to say that the finite world is broken open to the divine emptiness which infinitely surpasses it. As an event of grace, this breakthrough cannot be reduced to a perception of the true ontological texture of the world. Similarly, one should not simply identify the revelation of God in Jesus Christ with the discovery of emptiness in Buddhist meditation. God is incarnate in Jesus not in any arbitrarily chosen form or in a general fashion in all forms as such, but in a very particular narration addressed, through precise historical mediations, to the problems of sin, death and ultimate human liberation. Buddhist thought opens new paths to the understanding of this narration, but at a certain point it sends us back to the perpetual task of theology, that of thinking the meaning of Christ in the terms suggested by Christ himself. The Christian narrations are not a conventional language indicating an absolute reality better grasped by a leap beyond them. If God allows himself to be 'entangled in stories' (in the sense of Wilhelm Schapp's narrative phenomenology), it is because the concrete meaning of our finite lives cannot be fully revealed in more abstract languages and because God himself is known only abstractly as long as he has not introduced himself into our stories and our history.

Thus from the Christian vantage point the Buddhist to-and-fro between form and emptiness is to be regrounded in the more concrete coming and going between God and human stories. Buddhist thought stops us from conceiving this in a naive or anthropomorphic way, but conversely the powerful Christian story makes impossible any forgetting of the suffering flesh of real humanity. It is here that the biblical God writes his revelation, in forms not destined to effacement in some mystical subtilisation, and which can rejoin 'emptiness' only via a real transformation of their being, or what we call the resurrection of the body.

Thus the breaking-open of the dependently co-arisen world to ultimate divine reality which is effected in Christ is mediated by the eschatological aspect of Christ's existence, as always transcending itself towards the future of the Kingdom. The step back from Christ to God is less a mystical quest for the beginning than a prophetic anticipation of the end (1 Cor. 15:24–8). Economy opens onto theology not by a blurring of its historical contours but through pursuing to the end the consequences of this historical enfleshment. The event of salvation, historical and fleshly, in which we are caught up, according to the Gospel, cannot be reabsorbed into any general philosophical vision, even that of Buddhism. Every philosophical or religious encounter throws new light on it, but does not muddy or replace its essential references to the God of Israel and the figure of Jesus.

The continuation of this adventure, in fuller awareness of its historical particularity and with greater freedom towards the languages in which it has sought to grasp itself, is assured by no general philosophical or religious ideal, but only by the vivid memory of Jesus Christ. This would be a fragile foundation if this memory belonged only to the past, but the Christian trust is that this Jesus 'is going before us' (Mt. 28:7), and is always ahead of us 'to the close of the age' (Mt. 28:20).

WORKS QUOTED

WORKS BY JACQUES DERRIDA

D: *Dissemination*, trans. Barbara Johnson. University of Chicago Press, 1981.
G: *Of Grammatology*, trans. G. C. Spivak. Baltimore: Johns Hopkins University Press, 1976.
M: *Margins of Philosophy*, trans. Alan Bass. University of Chicago Press, 1982.
WD: *Writing and Difference*, trans. Alan Bass. University of Chicago Press, 1978.
Spurs: Nietzsche's Styles, trans. Barbara Harlow. University of Chicago Press, 1978.
'Living On'. In: *Deconstruction and Criticism*. New York: Seabury Press, 1979.
La carte postale de Socrate à Freud et au-delà. Paris: Flammarion, 1980.
Positions, trans. Alan Bass. University of Chicago Press, 1981.
'Préjugés – devant la loi'. In: *La faculté de juger*. Paris: Éditions de Minuit, 1985.
Ulysse gramophone. Paris: Éditions Galilée, 1987.
Psyché: inventions de l'autre. Paris: Éditions Galilée, 1987.
Limited Inc. Northwestern University Press, 1988.
Of Spirit: Heidegger and the Question, Trans. Geoffrey Bennington and Rachel Bowlby. University of Chicago Press, 1989.
Spectres de Marx. Paris: Éditions Galilée, 1994.
Aporias, trans. Thomas Dutoit. Stanford University Press, 1993.

GENERAL

Ansaldi, Jean (1991). *L'Articulation de la foi, de la théologie et des Écritures*. Paris: Éditions du Cerf.
Baghramian, Maria (1990). *Logic, Language and Relativism*. Ph. Diss., Trinity College, Dublin.
Baker, G. P., and P. M. S. Hacker. *An Analytical Commentary on Wittgenstein's Philosophical Investigations*, I. Oxford: Blackwell.

WORKS QUOTED

Banner, Michael C. (1990). *The Justification of Science and the Rationality of Religious Belief*. Oxford: Clarendon.

Barth, Karl (1934). *Weihnacht*. Munich: Kaiser.

Barth, Karl (1934–70). *Kirchliche Dogmatik*. Zürich: Evangelischer Verlag.

Bergson, Henri (1984). *Oeuvres*. Paris: Presses Universitaires de France.

Bernstein, Richard J. (1985). *Beyond Objectivism and Relativism: Science, Hermeneutics, and Praxis*. University of Pennsylvania Press.

Bloom, Harold (1975). *Kabbalah and Criticism*. New York: Continuum.

Brito, Emilio (1992). 'Schleiermacher et la doctrine de la Trinité'. *Ephemerides Theologicae Lovanienses* 23, pp. 145–71.

Bugault, Guy (1994). *L'Inde pense-t-elle?*. Paris: Presses Universitaires de France.

Bunge, Mario (1974). *Treatise on Basic Philosophy*, II. Dordrecht: Reidel.

Byrne, James M., ed. (1993). *The Christian Understanding of God Today*. Dublin: Columba Press.

Cabezón, José Ignacio (1992). *A Dose of Emptiness: An Annotated Translation of the sTong thun chen mo of mKhas grub dGe legs dpal bzang*. State University of New York Press.

Caputo, John (1987). *Radical Hermeneutics: Repetition, Deconstruction, and the Hermeneutic Project*. Indiana University Press.

Castelli, Enrico, ed. (1969a). *L'Analyse du langage théologique: le nom de Dieu*. Paris: Aubier.

Castelli, Enrico, ed. (1969b). *Débats sur le langage théologique*. Paris: Aubier.

Clooney, Francis X. (1991). 'The Study of Non-Christian Religions in the Post-Vatican II Roman Catholic Church'. *Journal of Ecumenical Studies* 28, pp. 482–94.

Cobb, John B. (1982). *Beyond Dialogue: Toward a Mutual Transformation of Christianity and Buddhism*. Philadelphia: Fortress.

Cobb, John B., and Christopher Ives, eds (1990). *The Emptying God*. Maryknoll: Orbis.

Collins, Steven (1982). *Selfless Persons: Imagery and thought in Theravāda Buddhism*. Cambridge University Press.

Combès, Joseph (1989). *Études néoplatoniciennes*. Grenoble: Millon.

Coward, Harold, and Toby Foshay, eds (1992). *Derrida and Negative Theology*. State University of New York Press.

Critchley, Simon (1989). 'Within the Reasonable Limits of the Tradition'. *New Formations* 9, pp. 149–56.

Currie, Gregory (1982). *Frege: An Introduction to his Philosophy*. Sussex: Harvester Press.

Davenstock, Reed Way, ed. (1993). *Literary Theory after Davidson*. Pennsylvania State University Press.

Davidson, Donald (1984). *Inquiries into Truth and Interpretation*. Oxford: Clarendon.

Dawe, Donald G., and John B. Carman, eds (1978). *Christian Faith in a Religiously Plural World*. Maryknoll: Orbis.

D'Costa, Gavin, ed. (1990). *Christian Uniqueness Reconsidered*. Maryknoll: Orbis.

Dean, Thomas, ed. (1995). *Religious Pluralism and Truth: Essays on Cross-Cultural Philosophy of Religion*. State University of New York Press.

de Certeau, Michel (1987a). *Histoire et psychanalyse entre science et fiction.* Paris: Gallimard, 'Folio'.

de Certeau, Michel (1987b). *La Faiblesse de croire.* Paris: Éditions du Seuil.

de Jong, J. W. (1949). *Cinq chapitres de la Prasannapadā.* Paris: Geuthner.

Dummett, Michael (1981a). *Frege: Philosophy of Language.* Harvard University Press.

Dummett, Michael (1981b). *The Interpretation of Frege's Philosophy.* Harvard University Press.

Eckel, M. David (1985). 'Bhāvaviveka's Critique of Yogācāra Philosophy in Chapter XXV of the *Prajñāpradīpa*'. In: *Miscellanea Buddhica*, ed. Chr. Lindtner. Copenhagen: Akademisk Forlag, pp. 25–75.

Eckel, Malcolm David, trans. (1987). *Jñānagarbha's Commentary on the Distinction between the Two Truths.* State University of New York Press.

Eisler, R. (1979). *Kant-Lexikon.* Hildesheim: Olms.

Feuerbach, Ludwig (1903). *Das Wesen des Christentums (Sämtliche Werke VI).* Stuttgart: Frommanns.

Foucault, Michel (1971). *L'Ordre du discours.* Paris: Gallimard.

Foucault, Michel (1976). *La Volonté de savoir.* Paris: Gallimard.

Gasché, Rodolphe (1986). *The Tain of the Mirror: Derrida and the Philosophy of Reflection.* Harvard University Press.

Gasché, Rodolphe (1989). 'In-Difference to Philosophy: de Man on Kant, Hegel, and Nietzsche'. In: *Reading de Man Reading*, ed. Lindsay Waters and Wlad Godzich. University of Minnesota Press, pp. 259–94.

Gasché, Rodolphe (1994). *Inventions of Difference: On Jacques Derrida.* Harvard University Press.

Gauchet, Marcel (1985). *Le Désenchantement du monde.* Paris: Gallimard.

Geffré, Claude, ed. (1989). *Michel de Certeau ou la différence chrétienne.* Paris: Éditions du Cerf.

Greisch, Jean (1977). *Herméneutique et grammatologie.* Paris: CNRS.

Griffiths, Paul J. (1991). *An Apology for Apologetics: A Study in the Logic of Interreligious Dialogue.* Maryknoll: Orbis.

Grillmeier, Aloys (1975). *Christ in Christian Tradition*, I. London: Mowbrays.

Guenther, Herbert V. (1972). *Buddhist Philosophy in Theory and Practice.* Harmondsworth: Penguin.

Halbfass, Wilhelm (1992). *On Being and What There Is: Classical Vaiśeṣika and the History of Indian Ontology.* State University of New York Press.

Hanson, Paul D. (1975). *The Dawn of Apocalyptic.* Philadelphia: Fortress.

Hart, Kevin (1989). *The Trespass of the Sign: Deconstruction, Philosophy and Theology.* Cambridge University Press.

Hick, John (1985). *Problems of Religious Pluralism.* London: Macmillan.

Hick, John, and Paul Knitter, eds (1987). *The Myth of Christian Uniqueness.* Maryknoll: Orbis.

Hoornaert, Paul (1991). *A Study in Mahāyāna Thought: The Controversy between the Madhyamaka and the Yogācāra.* Diss., Sendai: Tohoku University.

Hume, David (1975). *Enquiries concerning Human Understanding*, ed. L. A. Selby-Bigge. Oxford: Clarendon.

Huntington, C. W. (1989). *The Emptiness of Emptiness: An Introduction to Early Indian Mādhyamika.* Honolulu: University of Hawaii Press.

WORKS QUOTED

Johnson, Barbara (1982). 'The Frame of Reference: Poe, Lacan, Derrida'. In: *Literature and Psychoanalysis*, ed. Shoshana Felman. Baltimore: Johns Hopkins University Press.

Johnson, Christopher (1993). *System and Writing in the Philosophy of Jacques Derrida*. Cambridge University Press.

Kato, Bruno, et al. (1975). *The Threefold Lotus Sutra*. New York: Weatherhill.

Kaufman, Gordon D. (1993). *In Face of Mystery: A Constructive Theology*. Harvard University Press.

Kearney, Richard, and J. S. O'Leary, eds (1980). *Heidegger et la question de Dieu*. Paris: Grasset.

Kearney, Richard (1984). *Dialogues with contemporary Continental thinkers*. Manchester University Press.

Keenan, John P. (1989). *The Meaning of Christ: A Mahāyāna Theology*. Maryknoll: Orbis.

King, Sallie B. (1991). *Buddha Nature*. State University of New York Press.

Klein, Anne C. (1992). 'Mental Concentration and the Unconditioned: A Buddhist Case for Unmediated Experience'. In: *Paths to Liberation: The Mārga and its Transformations in Buddhist Thought*, ed. Robert E. Buswell and Robert M. Gimello. University of Hawaii Press, pp. 269–308.

Kuschel, Karl-Josef (1991). *Geboren vor aller Zeit? Der Streit um Christi Ursprung*. Munich: Piper.

Lacombe, Olivier (1937). *L'absolu selon le Védānta*. Paris: Geuthner

Lamotte, Étienne, trans. (1944–80). *Le traité de la grande vertu de sagesse*. Louvain-la-Neuve: Institut Orientaliste.

Lee, Peter K. H. (1994). 'Pathways to Faith and Interreligious Dialogue'. *Inter-Religio* 25 (Summer 1994), pp. 2–13.

Levine, James (1993). 'Putnam, Davidson and the Seventeenth-Century Picture of Mind and World'. *International Journal of Philosophical Studies* 1, pp. 193–230.

Lindbeck, George (1984). *The Nature of Doctrine: Religion and Theology in a Postliberal Age*. Philadelphia: Westminster Press.

Loy, David (1988). *Non-Duality: A Study in Comparative Philosophy*. Yale University Press.

Mack, Burton L. (1988). *A Myth of Innocence: Mark and Christian Origins*. Philadelphia: Fortress.

Magliola, Robert (1984). *Derrida on the Mend*. Purdue University Press.

Mallarmé, Stéphane (1945). *Oeuvres complètes*. Paris: Gallimard, 'Bibl. de la Pléiade'.

Mallet, Marie-Louise, ed. (1994). *Le Passage des Frontières: Autour du Travail de Jacques Derrida*. Paris: Éditions Galilée.

Maréchal, Joseph (1926). *Le point de départ de la métaphysique. Cahier V: Le Thomisme devant la Philosophie critique*. Louvain: Museum Lessianum; Paris: Alcan.

Marion, Jean-Luc (1977). *L'Idole et la Distance*. Paris: Grasset.

Marion, Jean-Luc (1989). *Réduction et donation*. Paris: Presses Universitaires de France.

Marion, Jean-Luc (1991). *Dieu sans l'être*. Paris: Presses Universitaires de France, 'Quadriges'.

Marion, Jean-Luc (1992). 'Le Phénomène saturé'. In: *Phénoménologie et théologie*. Paris: Criterion, pp. 79–118.

Marion, Jean-Luc (1994). 'Esquisse d'un concept phénoménologique du don'. *Archivio di Filosofia* 62, pp. 75–94.

May, Jacques, trans. (1959). *Candrakīrti Prasannapadā Madhyamakavṛtti*. Paris: Maisonneuve.

McGinn, Colin (1984). *Wittgenstein on Meaning*. Oxford: Blackwell.

Moingt, Joseph (1993). *L'homme qui venait de Dieu*. Paris: Éditions du Cerf.

Moore, A. W., ed. (1993). *Meaning and Reference*. Oxford University Press.

Morgan, Robert, ed. (1989). *The Religion of the Incarnation*. Bristol Classical Press.

Murti, T. R. V. (1955). *The Central Philosophy of Buddhism*. London: Allen & Unwin.

Napper, Elizabeth (1989). *Dependent-Arising and Emptiness: A Tibetan Buddhist Interpretation of Mādhyamika Philosophy Emphasizing the Compatibility of Emptiness and Conventional Phenomena*. Boston: Wisdom Publications.

Netland, Harold A. (1991). *Dissonant Voices: Religious Pluralism and the Question of Truth*. Grand Rapids, Michigan: Eerdmans.

Newman, John Henry (1976). *The Idea of a University*, ed. Ian T. Ker. Oxford: Clarendon.

Nicholls, David (1993). 'Trinity and Conflict'. *Theology*, pp. 19–27.

Nishitani, Keiji (1982). *Religion and Nothingness*. Trans. Jan Van Bragt. Berkeley: University of California Press.

Osculati, Roberto (1990). *Vero cristianesimo: Teologia e società moderna nel pietismo luterano*. Rome, Bari: Laterza.

O'Leary, J. S. (1985). *Questioning Back: The Overcoming of Metaphysics in Christian Tradition*. San Francisco: Harper and Row.

O'Leary, J. S. (1991). 'Impeded Witness: Newman against Luther on Justification'. In: *John Henry Newman: Reason, Rhetoric and Romanticism*, ed. David Nicholls and Fergus Kerr. Bristol Press, pp. 153–93.

O'Leary, J. S. (1992). 'Theological Resonances of *Der Satz vom Grund*'. In: *Critical Assessments: Martin Heidegger* I, ed. Christopher Macann. London: Routledge, pp. 213–56.

O'Leary, J. S. (1994). *La Vérité chrétienne à l'âge du pluralisme religieux*. Paris: Éditions du Cerf.

Pappu, S. S. Rama Rao, ed. (1988). *Perspectives on Vedānta*. Leiden: Brill.

Phillips, D. Z. (1988). 'Lindbeck's Audience'. *Modern Theology* 4 (1987–8), pp. 133–54.

Pye, Michael (1978). *Skilful Means*. London: Duckworth.

Pye, Michael (1990). 'Skillful Means and the Interpretation of Christianity'. *Buddhist-Christian Studies* 10, pp. 17–22.

Quine, W. V. (1992). *Pursuit of Truth*, 2nd ed. Harvard University Press.

Robinet, Isabelle (1991). *Histoire du Taoïsme*. Paris: Éditions du Cerf.

Rötzer, Florian (1987). *Französische Philosophen im Gespräch*. Munich: Boer.

Rorty, Richard (1979). *Philosophy and the Mirror of Nature*. Princeton University Press.

Rouner, Leroy S., ed. (1984). *Religious Pluralism*. University of Notre Dame Press.

WORKS QUOTED

Rousseau, Jean-Jacques (1966). *Émile*. Paris: Garnier-Flammarion.

Rubenstein, Richard L. (1985). *The Religious Imagination: A Study in Psychoanalysis and Jewish Theology*. University Press of America.

Saussure, Ferdinand de (1972). *Cours de linguistique générale*. Paris: Payot.

Schayer, Stanislaw (1931). *Ausgewählte Kapitel aus der Prasannapadā*. Cracow.

Schleiermacher, Friedrich (1980). *Ueber die Religion*. Stuttgart: Reclam.

Scholem, Gershom (1977). *Zur Kabbala und ihrer Symbolik*. Frankfurt: Suhrkamp.

Schwab, Raymond (1950). *La renaissance orientale*. Paris: Payot.

Searle, John (1994). 'Literary Theory and Its Discontents'. *New Literary History* 25, pp. 637–67.

Sprung, Mervyn (1979). *Lucid Exposition of the Middle Way: The Essential Chapters from the Prasannapadā of Candrakīrti*. Boulder: Prajna Press; London: Routledge and Kegan Paul.

Staten, Henry (1984). *Wittgenstein and Derrida*. Lincoln: University of Nebraska Press.

Strawson P. F., ed. (1967). *Philosophical Logic*. Oxford University Press.

Suzuki, D. T. trans. (1968). *The Lankavatara Sutra*. London: Routledge and Kegan Paul.

Swanson, Paul (1989). *Foundations of T'ien-t'ai Philosophy: The Flowering of the Two Truths Theory in Chinese Buddhism*. Berkeley: Asian Humanities Press.

Swinburne, Richard (1992). *Revelation: From Metaphor to Analogy*. Oxford: Clarendon Press.

Tanabe, Hajime (1986). *Philosophy as Metanoetics*. Trans. Y. Takeuchi. Berkeley: University of California Press.

Thurman, Robert A. F., trans. (1975). *The Holy Teaching of Vimalakīrti*. Pennsylvania State University Press.

Thurman, Robert A. F. (1991). *The Central Philosophy of Tibet*. Princeton University Press.

Troeltsch, Ernst (1929). *Die Absolutheit des Christentums und die Religionsgeschichte*. Tübingen: Mohr.

Unno, Taitetsu, ed. (1989). *The Religious Philosophy of Nishitani Keiji*. Berkeley: Asian Humanities Press.

Unno, Taitetsu and James W. Heisig, eds (1990). *The Religious Philosophy of Tanabe Hajime*. Berkeley: Asian Humanities Press.

van Buren, Paul M. (1988). *A Theology of the Jewish-Christian Reality, Part III – Christ in Context*. San Francisco: Harper and Row.

Žižek, Slavoj (1991). *For they know not what they do*. London: Verso.

INDEX

INDEX

INDEX

Jabès, Edmond, 174, 175
James, William, 31
Jansenius, Cornelius, 195
Japan, 156–7
Jñānagarbha, 133, 139
John, 80, 89, 117, 170, 188–9, 198, 211–14, 216, 220, 237, 241, 245, 253
John Damascene, 189
Joyce, James, 40, 41, 68, 167
Judaism, 13, 17, 26, 37, 80, 118, 156, 171, 191, 204, 212, 218, 225–8, 241
Judgement, 53, 76, 83, 98, 100–4, 106, 108, 111, 114–15, 121–5, 132, 153, 160
Justification, 195, 229, 243
Justin Martyr, 80

Kant, Immanuel, 9, 31, 32, 66, 74, 84, 103–4, 108, 123, 131, 147, 150, 151, 165, 171, 175, 182, 184, 186, 187, 193
Kasulis, Thomas, 199
Kaufman, Gordon, 180–4, 210, 234
Keenan, John P., 31–2, 76, 201–2, 254–5
Kenosis, 33, 193, 197–200, 256
Khōra, 99, 101, 125, 176, 177, 192
Kierkegaard, Søren, 171, 193
Kingdom of God, 28, 81, 84, 202, 213, 227, 228, 230–1, 243, 258
Klein, Anne C., 32–3
Krishna, 206, 208, 243
Kuhn, Thomas, 57, 75
Küng, Hans, 29
Kuschel, Karl-Josef, 237–40

Lacan, Jacques, 11, 14, 99, 119, 125, 208, 253
Language, 9, 41, 50, 60, 76, 127, 136, 141–6, 149, 151, 153–6, 160–1, 177, 179, 186–7, 189, 202, 213–14
Laṅkāvatāra Sūtra, 157
Leibniz, 186
Levinas, Emmanuel, 39, 40, 125, 162, 193
Lindbeck, George, 85–9
Logic, 22–3, 24, 29, 87, 96, 129–30, 148–9, 151, 193, 240, 247
Logocentrism, 107–8, 148–9, 172–3, 244, 247
Logos, 19–20, 23, 26, 172–4, 207, 210, 211–18, 223, 224, 226, 237–40, 242–3, 244–6, 254–5; see also Christ, Incarnation
Lotus Sūtra, 155–6
Love, 11, 30, 58, 63, 154–5, 184, 186–9, 193, 194–5, 198, 200, 228, 231, 236
Loy, David, 147–8, 149
Luther, Martin, 9, 27, 30, 56, 57, 58, 119, 171, 229, 230, 241
Lyotard, Jean-François, 123

Mack, Burton, 233–4

Mackey, James P., 16
Mādhyamika (Madhyamaka), 32–3, 126–58, 199
Magliola, Robert, 148–9
Mallarmé, Stéphane, 40, 105, 111–13, 114
Maréchal, Joseph, 104
Marion, Jean-Luc, 32, 131–2, 180, 185–91
Marks, 38, 51, 43, 46, 59, 68, 110, 118, 161–2
Māyā, 137, 138–9
Meaning, 3, 6, 37–45, 51, 62, 78, 98, 102, 107–8, 111, 114, 132, 143, 167
Melanchthon, Philip, 195
Merleau-Ponty, Maurice, 34, 252
Messiah, messianism, 123, 176–7, 211, 222, 232, 235, 243
Metaphor, 44, 45, 67, 168, 182, 216
Metaphysics, 29, 37, 51, 57, 77, 84, 89, 127–8, 157, 162, 164, 165, 170–2, 173, 178, 179, 186, 188–91, 194–5, 197, 199, 213, 223, 238, 240, 246; see also Onto-theology
Metaphysics of presence, 33, 52, 100–2, 107–8, 125, 132, 160, 172–3
Moingt, Joseph, 29, 222–3
Moltmann, Jürgen, 29, 199, 236
Monophysitism, 199, 239
Muhammad, 118, 211, 244–5
Mumonkan, 192
Murti, T. R. V., 137–8, 139

Nāgārjuna, 1, 27, 35, 127–33, 135, 138, 141, 143, 147–8, 149, 150, 152, 194, 196
Names, naming, 132, 159–65, 171–4, 175, 186–7, 190, 202, 250, 253
Narrative, 78, 161, 190, 209–10, 242, 247, 257
Negative theology, 5, 66, 126, 149–50, 172, 190, 202, 210, 222
Nestorianism, 222, 239
Netland, Harold, 94–5
Newman, John Henry, 183, 229
Nicaea, 4, 198, 214, 216, 226, 241, 253
Nicholls, David, 217–18
Nietzsche, Friedrich, 7, 122, 124–5, 158, 193, 198
Nihilism, 1, 7, 142–3, 193, 198, 201
Nirvāṇa, 94, 130, 133–4, 135, 138–9, 148, 191, 196–7, 230, 232–3, 254, 256
Nirvāṇa Sūtra, 155
Nishida, Kitarō, 192
Nishitani, Keiji, 192–3, 198–9
Non-duality, 198, 233, 246
Non-self (anātman), 7, 34, 92–3, 128, 191–2, 193, 199
Nothingness, 126, 150, 192–4, 195, 197–9, 200–1, 244; see also Emptiness

Ockham, 163

267

INDEX

Onto-theology, 95, 147, 149–50, 244
Origen, 37, 79, 119, 216, 219, 220, 223, 255
Orthodoxy, 16–17, 159, 160, 222

Panikkar, Raimundo, 28
Pannenberg, Wolfhart, 236, 239
Pascal, Blaise, 171, 184
Paul, 57, 58, 80, 85, 89, 94, 195, 230, 232, 237, 241
Peirce, Charles Sanders, 49
Perfection of Wisdom Sūtras, 127, 139
Personality of God, 13, 20–1, 163, 167, 170, 182–4, 192, 199–200, 234, 245
Perspectivism, 12, 14, 35, 77–8, 94, 96, 126
Phallocentrism, 124–5, 253
Phenomenology, phenomenality, 15, 21, 52, 84, 100–2, 178–9, 180, 183, 185–91, 193, 197, 198, 199, 200, 211–12, 213, 214, 216–17, 223, 226, 237, 238, 240, 241, 244, 257
Phonocentrism, 106–7, 172
Phillips, D. Z., 86
Plato, 1, 105, 177, 192
Plotinus, 5, 84, 163, 170, 171, 243
Pluralism, 3–6, 21–2, 23, 24, 37, 146, 152–3, 165, 168–9, 186–91
Polemic, 4, 61, 89–90, 169–72, 175
Power, 73–4, 80
Praxis, 79, 81, 86, 228–9
Pre-existence, 198, 224, 236–40
Primitive religions, 16, 17, 185
Prophetic tradition, 16, 170, 172, 209, 211, 224–5, 228, 230, 232, 241
Propositions, 3, 10, 24, 49, 76–89, 92–3, 94, 100–3, 114–15, 121
Pseudo-Dionysius, 30, 40, 149
Pye, Michael, 153

Quantum physics, 168
Quine, W. V. O., 95, 253

Rahner, Karl, 19, 30, 199, 223
Rāmānuja, 23
Ramsey, Frank P., 109
Reading, 38, 40, 52–3, 62, 111, 112–13
Reason, 62, 63–9, 75, 86, 91, 151, 171, 178–80, 204, 240
Reference, 3, 10, 12, 28, 45–6, 48–9, 58, 76–89, 95, 105–6, 111, 123–4, 145–6, 160, 168, 171, 182, 201, 215
Relativity, Relativism, 2–6, 12, 70–6, 77–8, 95, 96–7, 128, 205
Resurrection, 33, 85, 200, 213, 220, 232, 238, 239, 244, 255
Revelation, 4, 18–20, 27, 84–5, 91, 119–20, 168, 178, 182, 184–5, 186, 187, 200, 207, 210, 221, 226, 233, 239, 242, 244, 248
Rorty, Richard, 73–6

Rousseau, Jean-Jacques, 26

Sacrifice, 65, 246
Salvation, 60, 62, 200–1, 206, 209
Samādhi, 134
Śaṅkara, 27, 137–8
Sartre, Jean-Paul, 35
Saussure, Ferdinand de, 60, 166–7
Schelling, F. W. J., 63, 174
Schillebeeckx, Edward, 239
Schleiermacher, F. D. E., 26, 83, 241
Schoonenberg, Piet, 223
Schürmann, Reiner, 188
Science, 17, 50, 68–9, 75, 77–8, 185
Scripture, 18–20, 50–6, 60, 85, 89–90, 117–21, 182, 185, 188, 191
Secularism, 1, 8, 11, 29
Self-nature (*svabhāva*, self-existence, own-being), 4, 128–9, 134, 139, 140, 141, 142, 151, 193, 245, 256
Sense, 45–9, 102–4, 106
Shinran, 193, 194
Signifier/signified, 38, 42–3, 58, 59, 107, 112, 121, 122, 172–4, 253
Skilful means (*upāya*), 4, 5, 77, 149, 151–8, 165–72, 178–9, 183, 189, 197, 199, 193, 200, 202, 213, 216, 240, 247, 251, 253
Smith, Wilfred Cantwell, 26
Sociology, 6, 8, 228
Spinoza, Baruch de, 80, 142, 170
Spirit, 5, 19, 20, 33–6, 51, 63, 70, 119, 177–8, 179, 185–9, 192, 200, 208, 212, 218, 231
Strauss, David, 164
Style, 23, 24, 26, 27, 88, 179, 195, 200, 205, 240
Surin, Kenneth, 22
Svātantrika, 127, 132–3
Swinburne, Richard, 83–5

Tanabe, Hajime, 192, 193–4
Tarski, Alfred, 109
Tathāgatha-garbha, 157
Teresa of Avila, 92–3
Textuality, 3, 38, 42, 51–3, 58–60, 66, 67, 81, 90, 98–100, 109–21, 123, 174–5, 177
Thusness (*tathatā*), 142, 150, 151, 157, 192, 194, 241
Trace, 5, 32, 52, 109, 119, 168, 173–4
Tradition, 3–4, 6, 10, 25, 56–63, 153, 203–4, 230, 240, 247–8
Transcendence, 165, 177, 178, 183–4, 186–7, 190, 202, 205, 207
Transcendental signified, 147, 149, 176, 253
Translation, 49–50, 166, 167, 250
Transubstantiation, 221–2
Trinity, 5, 89, 197, 199, 213, 214, 216–18, 237, 239, 255

INDEX

Triple body of the Buddha, 244
Troeltsch, Ernst, 16–17
Two-Truth theory, 4, 130–41, 142, 147–9,
    153, 201–3, 255

Undecidability, 2, 46, 48, 98–100, 196, 115,
    117, 121–4, 174, 222

Vaihinger, Hans, 182
van Buren, Paul M., 225–7, 237
Vatican II, 5, 19, 30, 203
Vedānta, 137–8, 139–40, 203
Vietnam War 74,
Vimalakīrti Sūtra, 154–5
Virgin Birth, 221

Weil, Simone, 9
Whitehead, Alfred North, 63
Williams, Rowan, 214–15, 219
Wisdom (*prajñā*), 12–13, 30, 34, 35, 76, 91,
    132, 152, 196, 241
Wittgenstein, Ludwig, 21, 40, 42, 47,
    49–50, 57–8, 64, 86, 109, 113–14, 115,
    120, 142, 146, 147, 152

Yoga, 192
Yogācāra, 147

Zen, 11, 30, 61, 92–3, 96, 126, 134, 143,
    148, 156, 157, 192, 194, 240